Oracle Business Intelligence Enterprise Edition 11*g*: A Hands-On Tutorial

Leverage the latest Fusion Middleware Business Intelligence offering with this action-packed implementation guide

Haroun Khan

Christian Screen

Adrian Ward

[PACKT] enterprise
PUBLISHING
professional expertise distilled

BIRMINGHAM - MUMBAI

Oracle Business Intelligence Enterprise Edition 11*g*: A Hands-On Tutorial

First published: July 2012

Production Reference: 1090712

Published by Packt Publishing Ltd.
Livery Place
35 Livery Street
Birmingham B3 2PB, UK.

ISBN 978-1-84968-566-5

www.packtpub.com

Cover Image by Sandeep Babu (sandyjb@gmail.com)

Credits

Authors
Haroun Khan
Christian Screen
Adrian Ward

Reviewers
Daan Bakboord
Kevin McGinley
Ramke Ramakrishnan

Acquisition Editor
Stephanie Moss

Lead Technical Editors
Arun Nadar
Azharuddin Sheikh

Technical Editors
Vrinda Amberkar
Prasad Dalvi

Project Coordinator
Yashodhan Dere

Proofreader
Linda Morris

Indexer
Monica Ajmera Mehta

Graphics
Manu Joseph

Production Coordinator
Aparna Bhagat

Cover Work
Aparna Bhagat

About the Authors

Haroun Khan is one of Europe's leading OBIEE consultants. Being a Computer Science graduate from Imperial College, London, he has been involved with OBIEE from its early days as an acquisition from nQuire by Siebel, and subsequently as part of the Oracle family. Haroun has worked as a consultant on projects worldwide for Siebel and as a Principal Consultant for Oracle over a period of 10 years. He has specialized in BI and data warehousing over a longer period including time working at MicroStrategy. Haroun now freelances in leading and designing projects in the BI and data warehousing space, combining this with entrepreneurial activities, such as his own e-commerce business JRPass.com. In his downtime, Haroun likes to spend as much time as possible climbing in the mountains, away from a computer screen and avoiding numerous requests to write a blog or get on another plane!

Haroun works through his own company Awaan and can be contacted at his company address `haroun@awaan.eu`.

It goes without saying, but I would like to thank my parents, Zainab and Ayub for their support, encouragement and for everything, really. Also I have to include my sisters Sophia and Soraya so that they can have their name in print and I can avoid admonishments! Last, but not least, thanks to my toddler niece Sharifa for providing me with boundless distractions and opportunities to procrastinate.

Thanks goes to all those people (too many to mention) who I've worked with on great projects during my time at Oracle and MicroStrategy. Thanks also go out to Packt and their editors for their work. Finally, I would also like to extend my appreciation to my co-authors for their commitment and energy. It's been tiring but fun!

Christian Screen is a Business Intelligence evangelist with over 15 years of experience in technology ranging from low-level programming, E-Commerce, Data Warehousing, Enterprise Performance Management and, of course, Business Intelligence. In his spare time, he enjoys writing technical articles, learning new technologies, developing products, writing software, spending time with his family, trying to change the world, and running his blog and podcast at ArtOfBi.com. He is an Oracle ACE, an Oracle Deputy CTO, and holds several technology and project management certifications.

I would like to thank my family (wife Kirsten and three super children—Riley, Jaxon, and Dylan) seems so cliché but indeed their patience and support has been essential to the process of writing my first book. I'd also like to thank all of my colleagues who have provided continual intellectual ferment for our work with Business Intelligence and Enterprise Performance Management solutions. Thanks to Greg, Jason, and Tom at Analytic Vision for giving me a chance with my first consulting gig. Thanks to Amy Mayer of BI Consulting Group and Capgemini for my second consulting gig and having an unbelievable culture that I'll take with me wherever I may go. There are a few people at Oracle to thank as well, such as Mike Hallett in the UK who handles the BI/EPM partner community for EMEA and does an amazing job at building the community and keeping even us in the USA informed, the Oracle ACE Program leaders Justin Kestelyn and Lillian Buziak (Brian Stover, of course, many thanks!) for the Oracle ACE moniker, and the Oracle BI development team Matt Bedin and Phillipe Lions for their SampleApp and other assistance. I'd like to generally thank other authors of technical books that I may have referred to over the years and the many bloggers that find it their duty to share the tidbits, prose, or other knowledge that make finding an answer to daily issues merely a Google search away—thanks for sharing. A big thanks goes to the very keen reviewers of this book—Kevin McGinley, Daan Bakboord, and Ramke Ramakrishnan. We truly appreciate the time, effort, and suggestions you've provided to make this book better. Lastly, thanks to you for reading our first book—hopefully you purchased it legally—I trust you will find it useful.

Adrian Ward started working in Siebel Analytics back in 2001 and quickly realized the potential in the technology. He formed the UK's first independent consultancy focusing purely on OBIEE (née Siebel Analytics) and Oracle BI Applications. He has led many large successful OBIEE implementations in a wide range of business sectors, from Investment Banking to Military operations. His deep technical OBIEE and BI Applications knowledge has been applied on dozens of projects throughout the globe including HR, Sales, Service, Pharma, and Custom Analytics.

He was also one of the first bloggers on Oracle BIEE and today runs the Addidici OBIEE consultancy which has operations in the UK, Europe, and South Africa.

Adrian runs one of the largest Oracle BI networking groups on LinkedIn — "Oracle Business Intelligence", and helps others to network and learn about the product and its application, including organizing networking social events in London.

In his spare time he loves sailing, skiing, enjoying life with his family, and learning new technologies.

Firstly, I would like to thank my wife Sarah for her enormous love and support over the years, and in particular whilst I was writing my part of this book. Thanks too, must go to my cool children, Hugh and Hatty, for their help in keeping the house quiet and delivering endless cups of tea, and also to my Mum and Dad for being the best parents you could ask for — always there when you need.

I will be eternally grateful to Narmada for her selfless support and to Chet Justice for his great sense of humor. Special thanks go to James Robinson for my first decent job, to my great clients for employing me, and the great people I have worked with over the last 20 years (including Steve Lomax, Robert Patterson, Trev Harvey, Eric Gravil, Adrian Ball, Haider Tirmizi, Luis, Piere, Andi Schloegl, Neil Ashton, Daniel and many more).

I am also indebted to Graeme Hampshire for inspiring me to get writing, and for helping to keep sailing fun, John Dunnet and the crew of The Beefeater for putting up with my captaincy, and Jon Spencer for being a great PRO.

Finally thanks to my special friends Daniel, Andy & Jenny, and Jamie & Jackie for putting up with me over the years!

About the Reviewers

Daan Bakboord is a full Oracle BI (Applications) Consultant with extensive experience in the deployment of Oracle BI Tools (Oracle BI EE, Oracle BI Publisher, Oracle BI Applications, and so on) in general and its application in an Oracle EBS environment in particular.

Daan is employed by Ebicus—an ICT service provider in the field of Oracle/Siebel CRM and Oracle BI (Applications). Within Ebicus, Daan is responsible for the development of knowledge and the dissemination of this knowledge to the market. One of the manifestations of this is the blog (*Oracle BI By Bakboord*—`http://obibb.wordpress.com`), which is maintained by Daan. In addition, Daan is active in several (online) forums, making him a part of the major Oracle BI community.

Besides his work, Daan is a proud father of a son and a daughter. He is also active in amateur football.

Kevin McGinley has worked in BI/Data Warehousing in both IT and consulting since 1997. He has helped both large and small companies define and execute BI/DW roadmaps and implementations, focusing exclusively on Oracle BI since 2005. Kevin is a recognized expert on Oracle BI through speaking at many conferences, publishing articles, giving master classes, leading user group conferences, the co-host of the YouTube podcast *Real-Time BI with Kevin & Stewart*, and is the co-author of *Oracle BI Enterprise Edition Dashboard & Report Best Practices*.

> I'd like to thank the authors for the opportunity to review their fantastic book. There are so few books on Oracle BI out in the market and it's refreshing to see a nice, straightforward, end-to-end book on OBIEE 11*g* available for readers new to Oracle BI.

Ramke Ramakrishnan has performed the Lead Architect and Technical Leadership roles for over 15 years on Business Intelligence, by effectively managing the project team and the business customer expectations.

He delivers hands-on capabilities in the configuration of robust Oracle database and BI architectures, Oracle's Essbase infrastructure and large scale Business Intelligence Reporting, OBI Applications and EPM implementations. He is the key contributor for Business Analytics and Enterprise Reporting by integrating various applications systems into analytics to empower business customers, executives and end users.

He deployed several Enterprise Information Integration (Ei2) architectures, the core framework for Data Warehousing, Data Marts, OLAP, Business Analytics and Enterprise Reporting.

Ramke is Oracle Implementation Certified on Business Intelligence and EPM technologies. He is an active member and designated Deputy CTO (DCTO) on the Oracle Business Intelligence Investment Partner Community (IPC). He has featured in several Oracle speaking events and Oracle Press Releases on BI topics.

Currently, he is employed as Practice Director – BI and EPM with MarketSphere. MarketSphere is a strategic advisory and technology consulting firm with a strong focus on Oracle that helps our clients to deliver integrated ERP, BI and EPM solutions to optimize business performance. For more information, visit www.marketsphere.com.

I want to thank my wife Lavanya and my children Ritvik, Rasya, Rishik, and Raeya for their support and cooperation.

www.PacktPub.com

Support files, eBooks, discount offers and more

You might want to visit www.PacktPub.com for support files and downloads related to your book.

Did you know that Packt offers eBook versions of every book published, with PDF and ePub files available? You can upgrade to the eBook version at www.PacktPub.com and as a print book customer, you are entitled to a discount on the eBook copy. Get in touch with us at service@packtpub.com for more details.

At www.PacktPub.com, you can also read a collection of free technical articles, sign up for a range of free newsletters and receive exclusive discounts and offers on Packt books and eBooks.

http://PacktLib.PacktPub.com

Do you need instant solutions to your IT questions? PacktLib is Packt's online digital book library. Here, you can access, read and search across Packt's entire library of books.

Why Subscribe?

- Fully searchable across every book published by Packt
- Copy and paste, print and bookmark content
- On demand and accessible via web browser

Free Access for Packt account holders

If you have an account with Packt at www.PacktPub.com, you can use this to access PacktLib today and view nine entirely free books. Simply use your login credentials for immediate access.

Instant Updates on New Packt Books

Get notified! Find out when new books are published by following @PacktEnterprise on Twitter, or the Packt Enterprise Facebook page.

Table of Contents

users → groups (handwritten)

good theories

Preface

Oracle Business Intelligence Enterprise Edition (OBIEE) 11*g* is packed full of features and has a fresh approach to information presentation, system management and security. This book will introduce the reader to those features, providing a step-by-step guide to building a complete system from scratch. The aim of the book is to equip a developer or analyst with a good basic understanding of what the product contains, how to install and configure it, and how to create effective business intelligence.

What this book covers

Chapter 1, Understanding the Oracle BI 11g Architecture, helps you in understanding the 11*g* architecture. As with any good software suite, a solid architectural foundation is required. In today's marketplace the ability for software to scale well, meet the growing needs of an enterprise, and integrate with an organization's existing Information Technology (IT) investments is expected. Having the software be transparent enough for the average IT professional to implement it is definitely a plus. Being simple enough for an end-user to use or consume the product is a must. Oracle Business Intelligence (Oracle BI) 11*g* fits within all of these paradigms.

Chapter 2, Installing the Metadata Repository, covers how to install the required database components for your Oracle BI system to use them. Before installing an OBIEE 11*g* system, you will need to prepare a database, not for end user reporting but for the OBIEE system itself. You will also learn how to customize the installation to change the options available, and how to use the silent installation. You cannot afford to skip this chapter if you're installing your own development system! It's crucial to understand what is possible so that you can advise the database administrators, who will be managing your production environments.

Chapter 3, Installing on Windows Server 2008, provides step-by-step instructions for installing Oracle BI 11*g* on Windows Server 2008. This installation will walk you through the Enterprise installation of Oracle BI 11*g*, which is one of the three possible installation options, and will give you the best of all worlds for an Oracle BI 11*g* platform implementation. It will allow you to work/play with all of the features seen in a production Oracle BI 11*g* environment.

Chapter 4, Installation Options, covers additional installation options. The installation conducted in *Chapter 3, Installing on Windows Server 2008*, is perfect for a sandbox or a development environment. There is one more installation option, Software Only Install, which is an advanced way to conduct the Enterprise installation option. Several advanced configuration options and many production environment considerations may be made using the Software Only Install option. Additional installation and environment configuration options are what we will cover in this chapter.

Chapter 5, Understanding the Systems Management Tools, goes into greater detail on the administration interfaces, explaining what these components are, what they do, and how they work together. We will dive into the navigation of these tools so that you will become more familiar with the interfaces. Finally, this chapter is crucial to the remainder of the book as it contains the security exercises for creating the users and groups that will be used to access the Tennis Repository's dashboards and reports, which you will develop in subsequent chapters.

Chapter 6, Upgrading the RPD and Web Catalog to 11g, looks at the upgrade process for the most fundamental parts of the system from a version 10*g* implementation to 11*g*. The upgrade process for this is extremely straightforward, as Oracle has provided an easy-to-use upgrade tool that we will step through in this chapter. If you are upgrading a current live implementation, then we must consider the wider implications of the upgrade, especially the possible effects on current functionality. Therefore, in this chapter we will also touch upon the thinking and planning that is needed prior to a full upgrade for a current live implementation.

Chapter 7, Reporting Databases, introduces the main concepts of a reporting database. The process of creating an efficient database is the subject of dozens of books and blogs, and therefore the details in this chapter should provide enough information to get you started in creating a database that is fit for using in an Oracle Business Intelligence system.

Chapter 8, Developing a BI Repository, covers the development of a simple RPD from tables in a database through to how those objects are presented to us when we move on to create an actual request. This will be carried out via the Oracle BI Administration tool, which is the primary method of accessing and modifying an RPD file. This tool provides an inviting graphical interface for developing and administering an RPD file. By the end of this chapter, you will be able to complete the major tasks associated with RPD development. We will also describe the more advanced options that are available.

Chapter 9, Features of the Presentation Catalog, introduces the new interface of the web catalog and the tools that are integrated into the Presentation Services. It also explores aspects of search, catalog administration, privileges, object security, and more.

Chapter 10, Creating Dashboards and Analysis, teaches you how to create reports and group them in dashboards. In this chapter, we will also look at the various ways of representing and formatting data that are available, along with advice on best practices gained from implementation experience. This is one of the more robust chapters in the book and provides an insightful look at dashboard and report development.

Chapter 11, Agents and the Action Framework, covers the new functionality that Oracle has introduced in 11*g* for more integration with business processes, and the actions that result from producing the analytical reports. In previous versions, we had the Delivers portion of OBIEE where you could invoke basic actions, such as the delivery of reports or dashboard alerts. 11*g* has drastically enhanced this capability through the **Action Framework**, through which we are now able to initiate a multitude of additional noncore actions. During this chapter, we will look at examples of the new actions that Oracle has provided in attempting to succeed in this goal.

Chapter 12, Developing Reports Using BI Publisher, covers some of the new features of BI Publisher 11*g* as well as the general functionality of BI Publisher in order to get you up-to-speed on using the tool. It is aimed at providing a crash-course that should give any reader enough hands-on exercises to get their feet wet and enough food for thought for further research.

Chapter 13, Customizing the Style of Dashboards, provides a step-by-step how-to guide for branding OBIEE dashboards to match your corporate look and feel. It also provides several other insights for continued development and research.

Chapter 14, Improving the Performance, explores some common techniques to reduce the bottlenecks that can exist in the process of delivering dashboards and reports to the users. We will look across the whole system, defining poor performance and where required, take steps to improve the performance.

Chapter 15, Using the BI Admin Change Management Utilities, builds on the fundamental techniques of OBIEE development learned in previous chapters explores other capabilities in the Administration tool. In larger projects we may have a group of developers accessing and modifying the same RPD. The OBIEE Administration tool provides the ability to merge multiple versions of an RPD as well as functionality for groups to manage development on a sole repository (multiuser development). In this chapter, we will go over various methods of dealing with multiuser development.

Chapter 16, Usage Tracking, will demonstrate how to activate the "usage tracking" feature, and create useful reports from it. One of the great features of Oracle BI is that you can use the system—Dashboards and Analysis—to monitor the system itself, which means to say that you can use an OBIEE Analysis that tells you how OBIEE is performing for your users!

Chapter 17, Oracle Essbase and OLAP Integration, shows how OLAP technologies integrate into Oracle BI. After exploring the options, we will then focus on Oracle Essbase as the preferred OLAP technology. This chapter will show you how to integrate Oracle Essbase as a data source in Oracle BI and define several best practices for the integration. At the end of the chapter, you should have a well-balanced sense of how Essbase integrates with Oracle BI and the added value that it can bring to an organization.

Appendix A, Programs and Definitions, describes the main OBIEE command utilities and provides some reusable examples. One of the powerful features of OBIEE 11*g* administration is its ability to be controlled by User Interfaces (web browsers and Admin tools) as well as by command-line utilities. Many of the manual tasks that you undertake each day can be scripted and therefore automated. In this chapter you will learn about those automations.

Appendix B, Useful Resources: Join the Oracle BI Movement, lists some of the best books, events, groups, blogs for further reading and further practice on OBIEE 11*g*. Over the last decade, the number of resources focusing on Oracle Business Intelligence has skyrocketed. Oracle's documentation of the software has become increasingly more useful and user-friendly. Blogs all over the globe have popped-up in large numbers (though some better maintained and better written than others). Use this chapter to find where to learn more about OBIEE.

What you need for this book

The book assumes that you have no prior knowledge of Oracle Business Intelligence 11*g*. A general IT understanding will assist but is not a pre-requisite. To follow along with the most technical material in this book, you will need a workstation or server running Microsoft Windows 7, Microsoft Windows Server 2003, or Microsoft Windows Server 2008 along with the ability to download the Oracle BI and Oracle Database installation files over the internet. If you currently have a working Oracle BI 11*g* system to which you have access you will also be equipped for the material in this book.

To get the most out of this book, it is also advisable that you have a basic grounding in traditional data warehouse design and business intelligence concepts. For example, you are familiar with facts, dimensions, and star schemas.

Who this book is for

This book is for IT professionals, business analysts, project managers, and/or newcomers to Business Intelligence who wish to learn from self-paced professional guidance and actual implementation experience. Ultimately this book is for anyone who needs a solid grounding in the subject of Oracle Business Intelligence.

Conventions

In this book, you will find a number of styles of text that distinguish between different kinds of information. Here are some examples of these styles, and an explanation of their meaning.

Code words in text are shown as follows: "The following is a list of configuration files based on the central Oracle BI 11*g* instance path of `<FMW_HOME>\instance\instance1\config\`."

A block of code is set as follows:

```
ALTER database [dbname_here] SET SINGLE_USER WITH ROLLBACK IMMEDIATE;
ALTER database [dbname_here] SET READ_COMMITTED_SNAPSHOT ON;
ALTER database [dbname_here] SET MULTI_USER;
```

Any command-line input or output is written as follows:

```
cd C:\Windows\System32\inetsrv
```

New terms and **important words** are shown in bold. Words that you see on the screen, in menus or dialog boxes for example, appear in the text like this: "From the Oracle Business Intelligence (11.1.1.x) Downloads page, scroll down to the **Required Additional Software** section and click on the link for your operating system."

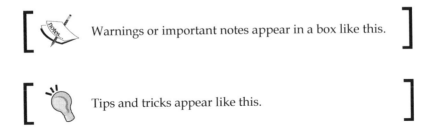

> Warnings or important notes appear in a box like this.

> Tips and tricks appear like this.

Reader feedback

Feedback from our readers is always welcome. Let us know what you think about this book—what you liked or may have disliked. Reader feedback is important for us to develop titles that you really get the most out of.

To send us general feedback, simply send an e-mail to feedback@packtpub.com, and mention the book title through the subject of your message.

If there is a topic that you have expertise in and you are interested in either writing or contributing to a book, see our author guide on www.packtpub.com/authors.

Customer support

Now that you are the proud owner of a Packt book, we have a number of things to help you to get the most from your purchase.

Downloading the example code

You can download the example code files for all Packt books you have purchased from your account at http://www.packtpub.com. If you purchased this book elsewhere, you can visit http://www.packtpub.com/support and register to have the files e-mailed directly to you.

Errata

Although we have taken every care to ensure the accuracy of our content, mistakes do happen. If you find a mistake in one of our books—maybe a mistake in the text or the code—we would be grateful if you would report this to us. By doing so, you can save other readers from frustration and help us improve subsequent versions of this book. If you find any errata, please report them by visiting http://www.packtpub.com/support, selecting your book, clicking on the **errata submission form** link, and entering the details of your errata. Once your errata are verified, your submission will be accepted and the errata will be uploaded to our website, or added to any list of existing errata, under the Errata section of that title.

Piracy

Piracy of copyright material on the Internet is an ongoing problem across all media. At Packt, we take the protection of our copyright and licenses very seriously. If you come across any illegal copies of our works, in any form, on the Internet, please provide us with the location address or website name immediately so that we can pursue a remedy.

Please contact us at copyright@packtpub.com with a link to the suspected pirated material.

We appreciate your help in protecting our authors, and our ability to bring you valuable content.

Questions

You can contact us at questions@packtpub.com if you are having a problem with any aspect of the book, and we will do our best to address it.

1
Understanding the Oracle BI 11*g* Architecture

As with good software suite, a solid architectural foundation is required. In today's marketplace the ability for software to scale well, meet the growing needs of an enterprise, and integrate with an organization's existing **Information Technology (IT)** investments is expected. Having the software be transparent enough for the average IT professional to implement it is definitely a plus. Being simple enough for an end-user to use or consume the product is a must. **Oracle Business Intelligence (Oracle BI)** 11*g* fits within all of these paradigms.

This chapter provides an overview of the Oracle BI architecture and its place in the Oracle **Fusion Middleware (FMW)** stack.

Looking backward and looking forward

Oracle BI has a history forged by acquisition and brilliant advances in both technology and market share (refer to the document called **Magic Quadrants for Business Intelligence Platforms** on Gartner's site at `http://www.gartner.com/id=1531017`). Without going into much historical detail about the early beginnings of the software suite, as a reader, you are either new to Oracle BI or have experienced the tool in one of its former versions. Those versions can be Siebel Analytics or Oracle BI 10*g*.

The old adage of knowing where you've been to know where you are going doesn't much apply to understanding most of Oracle BI 11*g*. From architecture of the **Graphical User Interface (GUI)** the majority of the tool has been rewritten. Although, the principal of the tool remains the same; to provide an end-to-end enterprise analytics solution; the core components of Oracle BI have changed substantially enough for it to feel like a brand new tool to those familiar with its previous versions. With that being said, let's talk about Oracle BI 11*g*'s architecture.

Let's look at the big picture

The following illustration shows some of Oracle BI 11g's infrastructure components from a core architecture perspective:

- **Oracle BI Domain**: It is the core architecture of Oracle BI 11*g*.

- **WebLogic Server**: It is the chosen application server for Oracle BI 11*g*.

- **Java components**: These are the components which have been written in Java for Oracle BI 11*g*. They are deployed to the application server and WebLogic Server.

- **System components**: These are the components which have been written mainly in C++ for Oracle BI 11*g*. They are managed by the Oracle Process Management and Notification Server. (OPMN)

- **Oracle BI relational repository**: It is a set of database schemas (BIPLATFORM and MDS) that store metadata related to a specific Oracle BI 11*g* instance.

- **Oracle BI filesystem**: It is the instructional set of physical files and directories containing configuration, logs, and metadata concerning the Oracle BI 11*g* instance:

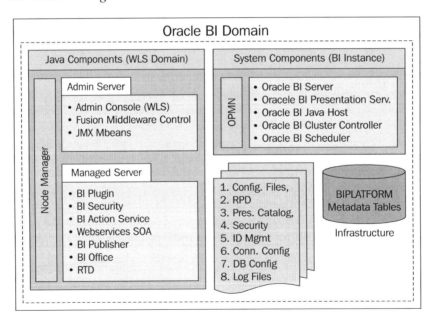

Once Oracle BI 11*g* is installed and configured, the architecture seen in the preceding illustration will exist. The components, pointed out in the preceding illustration, will be the areas where most of the backend, or day-to-day platform maintenance, and troubleshooting takes place. Some IT resources may already have insight into maintaining some of these components if they have experience in working with other Oracle products in the FMW stacks such as WebLogic, WebCenter, SOA, and so on. However, to most Oracle BI aficionados, this environment will be new.

What is Oracle Fusion Middleware?

Oracle Fusion Middleware is taking on the enterprise challenge of bringing together the Oracle database and Oracle applications stacks. It is the middle-tier between them. **Fusion Middleware** is Oracle's go-forward foundation for the fusion of products between the database and application stack. Oracle has acquired many companies over the last decade for their technology or market share. This has taken them to a position of having excellent software. Oracle didn't communicate effectively before that. To achieve interoperability, a common layer had to be formed to fuse together the existing technologies, create efficiencies, and provide consistent delivery of software applications. The following image illustrates the main categories of products, making up the current Oracle product stack:

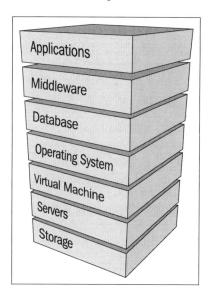

The Fusion Middleware product category contains Oracle **Fusion Middleware (FMW)**, which forms the core of Oracle's **Application Integration Architecture (AIA)**. It is the foundation for Oracle's fusion applications and software suites, such as Oracle BI 11*g*, Oracle Hyperion EPM, and so on.

An application server by any other name

In previous versions of Oracle BI, the default application server delivered with the product suite was **Oracle Container for Java (OC4J)**. This Java application server was actually a slimmed-down version of the better-known **Oracle Application Server (OAS)**. However, with the release of Oracle BI 11g—as with the mass majority of the Oracle Fusion Middleware applications—**Oracle WebLogic Server (WLS)** became the core application server. Previously, it was known as BEA WebLogic.

The WLS is a robust and scalable Java application server and it has been ranked as one of the top application servers in the market. Oracle has made a strong investment in WebLogic Server's atlas-like position as the foundation to which its Fusion Middleware stack is raised. With the current Oracle BI 11.1.1.6 release, the consideration to leverage IBM WebSphere as an alternate application server is under review. However, no guidance has been provided by Oracle on this topic. For prior releases of Oracle BI 11g, no other Java application server has been certified. So, an application server by any other name just won't do.

A database repository – for what?

Oracle BI 11g is a system that has evolved—and continues to evolve—based on expansive user requests, a market that dictates stronger integration points, and more powerful BI tools. As such, Oracle BI 11g now incorporates, or better yet, requires a relational database repository to hold metadata concerning the installation, report scheduling, usage tracking, auditing, and other aspects of the environment.

Actually, the Oracle BI 11g installation process cannot begin until these repositories are created by the **Repository Creation Utility (RCU)** and accessible on a database server. *Chapter 2, Installing the Metadata Repository*, goes into greater detail about this crucial repository structure, better known by two database schemas—**Metadata Services (MDS)** and **BIPLATFORM**. The installation and configuration of these two repositories are required primarily for integration of Oracle BI 11g with the Oracle Fusion Middleware stack.

 One interesting fact to note, however, is that the Oracle metadata repository (RPD) is still file based.

The **RPD** is the metadata storage mechanism in which Oracle BI developers model and map physical data sources to logical business representations in order for the resulting analytics to be easily consumed by the end users.

Overall components

There are a lot of components that comprise Oracle BI 11*g*. Oracle BI 11*g* can categorize these components by classifying them based on the programming languages in which they were developed. The programming languages are mainly either Java or C++. In comparison with previous versions of Oracle BI, where it seemed to be a somewhat compact environment, Oracle BI 11*g* is much more integrated into the larger platform of Fusion Middleware, which adds both value and complexity. Some of the similar legacy components' names persist. However, it should not be taken lightly because most of the legacy components have been renamed, removed, or placed under new management processes.

The following diagram provides a high-level overview of the main components that comprise the Oracle BI 11*g* architecture. The components are clearly segmented by the processes in which they are managed, each of which ultimately comprises the Oracle BI Domain:

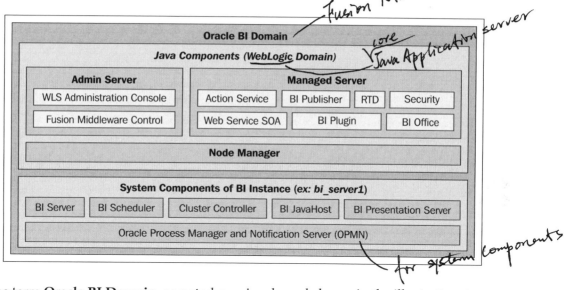

The term **Oracle BI Domain**, as noted previously and shown in the illustration, is used as a way to group all Oracle BI 11*g* components within the Fusion Middleware architecture. This should not be confused with the WebLogic Application Server domain which is given the default name, `bifoundation_domain`, while following the default Oracle BI 11*g* installation options. The latter is a WebLogic Java Application Server term. The former is a Fusion Middleware term. Since Fusion Middleware is so closely related with the WebLogic Application Server, it is good to keep it in mind from a technical perspective.

When learning about the overall component composition, a very important detail to keep in mind is the matter in which the components are managed. Since WebLogic Server is a Java application server, it manages all of the Oracle BI components developed in the Java programming language. Another management system, the **Oracle Process Management and Notification (OPMN)** system, handles the other components, which are referred to as the System Components.

Java components

In relation to Oracle BI 11g, the Java components are those which have been developed in the Java programming language. Those components are as follows:

- **Action service**: Primarily used by the Action Framework it executes actions on behalf of Presentation Services and Oracle BI Scheduler. Actions may be invocations of third party web services, or invocations of user supplied Java code executed as **Enterprise JavaBeans (EJB)**.

- **Administrative components**: **Java Management Extensions (JMX)** and **Managed Beans (MBean)** allow dynamic **Application Programming Interface (API)** functionality for managing, configuring, and administering Oracle BI 11g.

- **Web Service SOA**: This provide a web service interface to the contents of the Oracle BI Presentation Catalog. The tree of objects in Oracle BI Presentation Catalog is exposed as a tree of web services, defined by a **Web Services Inspection Language (WSIL)** tree with **Web Service Definition Language (WSDL)** leaves.

- **Oracle BI Office**: It provides integration between Microsoft Office and Oracle BI 11g.

- **Oracle Real-time Decisions (RTD)**: RTD provides a decision making rules engine that enables real-time business intelligence predictions and outcome analysis.

- **Oracle BI Presentation Service plugin**: Presentation Services run as a process, not as a web server, and does not communicate using any web server plugin API. The Oracle BI Presentation Services plugin forwards HTTP requests to Presentation Services. The HTTP requests are the requests from the browser-based user interface, or SOAP requests. This is ultimately just a servlet.

- **Oracle BI Publisher**: It is the enterprise reporting solution used for authoring and delivering highly formatted documents.

- **Security Services**: It provides standards-based authentication and population services. It enables the Oracle BI server to integrate with the Fusion Middleware security platform which includes the Credential Store Framework and the Identity Store.

System components

In relation to Oracle BI 11*g*, the system components are those which are developed in a non-Java programming language. Most of the system components have been developed in the C++ programming language as mentioned in the previous section. Here is a list of those components:

- **Oracle BI Server**: This is a C++ process that performs the data manipulation and aggregates data from data sources. You can configure multiple Oracle BI Server processes, which share the load. No session replication takes place between the Oracle BI Server processes.

  The Oracle BI Server does not maintain a user session state. For high availability deployments, query results are cached in the global cache.

- **Oracle BI Presentation Server**: This is a C++ process that generates the user interface pages and renders results sets on behalf of the Oracle BI Scheduler. You can configure multiple Presentation Services, which share the load. No session replication takes place between the Presentation Services.

  Presentation Services are almost stateless. The only significant state is the client authentication. If Oracle BI is configured to use a single sign-on for authentication purposes, users do not have to reauthenticate after a failover. For all other authentication schemas, when failover occurs, clients will have to reauthenticate. The client will see an interruption of service and will be redirected to a login page.

> Oracle BI has some very basic capabilities, which can store the state or current session activity for a user logged in to the system. This is referred to as **Session Management**. Since the BI Presentation Server maintains the authentication state, the users do not have to log in on each subsequent dashboard that they visit. If a system is stateless, the application cannot easily remember the information about the user or actions performed previously.

- **Oracle BI Scheduler**: It is a C++ process that runs the jobs according to a configurable frequency. Jobs can be created by agents in Oracle BI Presentation Catalog, or jobs can be created by the Job Manager. The Oracle BI Scheduler differs from the Quartz Scheduler that the Oracle BI Publisher leverages.

- **Oracle BI JavaHost**: It is a Java process that includes resource-intensive graphs and PDF rendering. It also allows Oracle BI Presentation Services to support Oracle BI Publisher and Java tasks within the Oracle BI Scheduler. You can configure multiple JavaHost processes, which share the load. No session replication takes place between the JavaHost processes. JavaHost is a stateless process.

- **Oracle BI Server Cluster Controller**: It is a C++ process, which manages the population of Oracle BI Servers and Oracle BI Schedulers. It also distributes the requests to the Oracle BI Server and ensures that requests are evenly load balanced across scaled-out Oracle BI Servers in the domain.

In general, it is important to understand how all of the components interact within the Oracle BI environment. Understanding some general concepts, such as "which port numbers are defined to communicate within the default Oracle BI architecture", "how the Oracle BI Administration Tool communicates with the Oracle BI database repository" will be quite helpful in your journey for becoming an Oracle BI professional. The following illustration shows each of the components comprising the core Oracle BI architecture, the communication ports, and the communication direction:

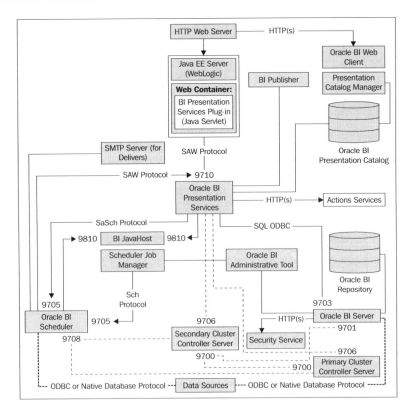

WebLogic Server

Let's talk a little more in detail about the enterprise application server that is at the core of Oracle Fusion Middleware — WebLogic. The Oracle WebLogic Server is a scalable, enterprise-ready **Java Platform Enterprise Edition (Java EE)** application server. Its infrastructure supports the deployment of many types of distributed applications. It is also an ideal foundation for building service-oriented applications.

The WebLogic Server is a robust application in itself. In previous versions of Oracle BI, the Oracle BI administrator and other developers took less effort to modify, configure, or otherwise maintain the Java application server. In Oracle BI 11*g*, the WebLogic Server is more crucial to the overall implementation, not only for installation but also throughout the Oracle BI 11*g* life-cycle. Learning the management components of the WebLogic Server, which ultimately controls the Oracle BI components, is critical for the success of an implementation. These management areas within the WebLogic Server are referred to as the **WebLogic Administration Server**, **WebLogic Manager Server(Servers)**, and **WebLogic Node Manager**.

A few software nuances

Before we move on to the description of each of the management areas within WebLogic, it is important to understand that the WebLogic Server software, which is used for the installation of the Oracle BI product suite, carries a limited license. Although the software itself is the full enterprise version — logically containing 100 percent of the product's functionality — the license that ships with Oracle BI 11*g* is not a full enterprise license for the WebLogic Server. This book hardly deals with software licensing, but here are a few nuances that one should keep in mind as they go about an Oracle BI 11*g* implementation:

- The WebLogic Server license, which is provided with Oracle BI 11*g*, does not grant horizontal scale-out. An enterprise WebLogic Server license needs to be obtained for this advanced functionality.

- The WebLogic Server does not provide a separate HTTP server with the installation. The Oracle BI Enterprise Deployment Guide (`http://docs.oracle.com/cd/E21764_01/doc.1111/e15722/toc.htm`) discusses the separation of the application tier from the web/HTTP tier and suggests **Oracle HTTP Server (OHS)**. OHS is part of the Oracle FMW web tier and must be downloaded separately (`http://www.oracle.com/technetwork/java/webtier/downloads/index.html`). The other web/HTTP servers that can be used are Apache and Windows IIS, which we will discuss in the *Chapter 4, Installation Options*.

These items are simply a few nuances of the product suite in relation to Oracle BI 11*g*. Most software products have a very short list of nuances like the preceding one. However, once you understand the nuances, it will be easier to ensure that you have a more successful implementation. It also allows your team to be prepared for implementations. Be sure to consult your Oracle sales representative to assist you with the licensing concerns.

> In order to learn more about the installation features, configuration options, administration, and maintenance of the WebLogic Server, we recommend that you reference the documentation of the WebLogic Server itself and not just the material on how it relates to Oracle BI 11*g*. The core of the WebLogic Server doesn't change just because Oracle BI 11*g* integrates into it. Understanding this approach should provide you with more efficient results.

WebLogic Domain

The highest unit of management for controlling the WebLogic Server installation is called a **domain**. A domain is a logically related group of WebLogic Server resources that you manage as a unit. A domain always includes, and is centrally managed by, one Administration Server. Additional WebLogic Server instances which are controlled by the Administration Server for the domain are called **Managed Servers**. The configuration for all the servers in the domain is stored in the configuration repository, the `config.xml` file, which resides on the machine hosting the Administration Server. The `config.xml` files, by default, are stored in the path `<FMW_HOME>\user_projects\domains\bifoundation_domain\` where `<FMW_HOME>` is the path on the server to which you have installed Oracle BI 11*g*.

Upon installing and configuring Oracle BI 11*g*, the domain named `bifoundation_domain` is established within the WebLogic Server. This domain is the recommended name for each Oracle BI 11*g* implementation and should not be modified.

WebLogic Administration Server

The WebLogic Server is an enterprise software suite that manages a myriad of application server components mainly focused on Java technology. It is also comprised of many ancillary components that enable the software to scale well, and also make it a good choice for distributed environments and high availability.

Clearly, it is good enough to be at the core of Oracle Fusion Middleware. One of the most crucial components of the WebLogic Server is the WebLogic Administration Server. When installing the WebLogic Server software, the WebLogic Administration Server is automatically installed with it. It is the Administration Server that not only controls all subsequent WebLogic Server instances called Managed Servers, but also controls aspects such as security, Persistence Stores, and other application server-related configurations.

The WebLogic Server gets installed on the operating system and ultimately runs as a service on that machine. The WebLogic Server can be managed in several ways. The two main methods are via the **Graphical User Interface (GUI)** web application called the WebLogic Administration Console or via the command line using the **WebLogic Scripting Tool (WLST)**. You can access the WebLogic Administration Console from any machine using a web-based client (that is, web browser) that can communicate with the WebLogic Administration Server through the network and/or firewall.

The WebLogic Administration Server and the WebLogic Server are basically synonymous. If the WebLogic Server is not running, the WebLogic Administration Console will be unavailable as well. If the WebLogic AdminServer is not running, no administrative tasks can be made to the system, although concessions are made for a High Availability configuration.

WebLogic Managed Server

Web applications, **Enterprise Java Beans (EJB)**, and other resources are deployed on to one or more WebLogic Managed Servers in a WebLogic Domain. A WebLogic Managed Server is an instance of a WebLogic Server in a WebLogic Server domain. Each WebLogic Server domain has at least one instance which acts as the WebLogic Administration Server which we have just discussed. Only one Administration Server per domain must exist, but one or more Managed Servers may exist in the WebLogic Server domain. Having one or more managed servers, allow for deployed JEE applications to be logically delineated. They also provide a means to independently configure application server port numbers and they provide a barrier for runtime issues such as a server crash. You can deploy applications, EJBs, and other resources on the WebLogic Managed Servers and use the WebLogic Administration Server only for configuration and management purposes.

In a production deployment, Oracle BI 11*g* is deployed into its own Managed Server. The Oracle BI 11*g* installer comes with three installation types—simple, enterprise, and software. The latter two installation types configure two WebLogic Server instances, the Administration Server and another Managed Server called `bi_server1`. Oracle BI 11*g* is deployed into the Managed Server called `bi_server1` and is configured by default to resolve to port 9704. The simple installation type configures only the administration server, deploys Oracle BI 11*g* into it, and resolves to port 7001. For the simple installation type, only one WebLogic Server instance exists.

> The simple installation type is not recommended for anything more than sandbox, test environment development, or demonstrations.

When administering the WebLogic Server via the Administration Console, the WebLogic Administration Server instance appears in the same list of servers that also includes the Managed Servers. The WebLogic Administration Server should be used only for configuration and management of the WebLogic Server and should not contain any additionally deployed applications, EJBs, and so on.

> One thing to note is that the Enterprise Manager Fusion Control is actually a JEE application deployed to the Administration Server instance, which is why its web client is accessible under port 7001. It is not necessarily a native application deployment to the core WebLogic Server, but gets deployed and configured during the Oracle BI 11*g* configuration. In the deployment's page within the Administration Console, you will find a deployment named `em`.

WebLogic Node Manager

The general idea behind the Node Manager is that it takes on somewhat of a middle-man role. That is to say, the Node Manager provides a communication tunnel between the WebLogic Administration Server and any WebLogic Managed Servers configured within the WebLogic Domain. When the WebLogic Server environment is contained on a single physical server, it may be difficult to recognize the need for a Node Manager. However, its real power comes into play when Oracle BI 11*g* is scaled out horizontally on one or more physical servers. Each scaled-out deployment of WebLogic Server will contain a Node Manager. If the Node Manager is not running on the server on which the Managed Server is deployed, then the core Administration Server will not be able to issue start or stop commands to that server. As such, if the Node Manager is down, communication with the overall cluster will be affected.

The following diagram shows how machines A, B, and C are physically separated—each of them contains a Node Manager. You can see that the Administration Server communicates with the Node Managers and not directly to the Managed Servers:

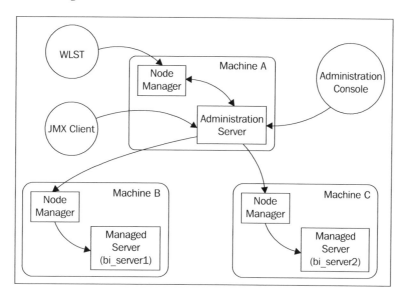

System tools controlled by WebLogic

We have briefly discussed the WebLogic Administration Console which controls the administrative configuration of the WebLogic Server Domain. This includes the components managed within it such as security, deployed applications, and so on. The other management tool which provides control on the deployed Oracle BI application ancillary deployments, libraries, and several other configurations is called the **Enterprise Manager Fusion Middleware Control**.

This seems to be a long name for a single web-based tool. As such, the name is often shortened to **Fusion Control** or **Enterprise Manager**. Reference to either abbreviated title in the context of Oracle BI should ensure fellow Oracle BI teammates understand what you mean.

To discuss the vast amount of individual configuration points contained within the WebLogic Administration Console and Fusion Control, you can warrant an entire chapter devoted to this subject. In fact, a subsequent chapter, *Chapter 5, Understanding the Systems Management Tools* is dedicated to it.

Oracle Process Management and Notification system

The **Oracle Process Management and Notification (OPMN)** system is not a new concept or tool within the Oracle product line. It has acted as a management service in many other Oracle products for years and is now a fitting utility for the cross-platform deployment architecture that Oracle BI 11g allows. The OPMN controls the Oracle BI 11g system components. Those are the components primarily developed in the C++ programming language. The OPMN not only allows each of the five system components to be started and stopped by calling a single command, it will also monitor those system component processes at runtime. It can even attempt to restart a component if it detects a failure. To start and stop the system components, you can use the Oracle Enterprise Manager Fusion Middleware Control or a command-line interface. The following screenshots represent the status retrieval of the System Components using the Fusion Middleware Control GUI and command-line interface, respectively:

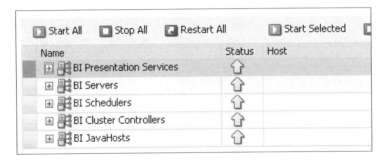

The command-line executable is deployed with the Oracle BI 11*g* installation. It resides in the default filesystem directory locations — `/u01/FMW/Instances/instance1/bin/opmnctl` or `C:\oracle\fmw\instances\instance1\opmnctl.bat`.

The Enterprise Manger Fusion Middleware Control, as per the default Oracle BI 11*g* installation, is accessible via the URL – `http://<bi_server_name>:7001/em`.

Either approach used for stopping, starting, or checking the status of the system components is valid. Either approach will work properly, however it is recommended — whenever possible — to leverage the Fusion Control interface for these actions in order to achieve the most consistent results.

Security

It would be difficult to discuss the overall architecture of Oracle BI 11*g* without at least giving some mention to how the basics of security, authentication, and authorization are applied. By default, installing the Oracle WebLogic Server provides a default **Lightweight Directory Access Protocol (LDAP)** server referred to as the **WebLogic Server Embedded LDAP server**.

This is a standards-compliant LDAP system which acts as the default authentication method for out-of-the-box Oracle BI 11*g*. Integration of secondary LDAP providers, such as **Oracle Internet Directory (OID)** or **Microsoft Active Directory (MSAD)** is crucial in order to leverage most organizations' identity management systems.

The combination of multiple authentication providers is possible, it is in fact common. For example, a configuration may wish to have users that exist in both the Embedded LDAP server and MSAD to authenticate and have access to Oracle BI 11*g*.

Oracle BI 11*g* security incorporates the Fusion Middleware Security model — **Oracle Platform Security Services (OPSS)**. This is a positive influence over managing all aspects of Oracle BI 11*g* as it provides a very granular level of authorization and a large number of authentication and authorization integration mechanisms. OPSS also introduces, to Oracle BI 11*g*, the concept of managing privileges by application role instead of directly by user or group. It abides by open standards to integrate with security mechanisms that are growing in popularity. Those security mechanisms are **Security Assertion Markup Language (SAML)** 2.0 and so on. Other well known single sign-on mechanisms such as SiteMinder and Oracle Access Manager have already preconfigured integration points within the Oracle BI 11*g* Fusion Control.

Chapter 5, Understanding the Systems Management Tools will go into an exercise for creating new users, groups, and assigning application roles, but for now, here are a few key concepts to know about security:

- Oracle BI 11g security is managed completely in a different way from the previous versions, although the Oracle BI 10g security model is still allowed for backwards compatibility.

- An Oracle BI 11g best practice is to manage security by Application Roles.

- Understanding the differences between the Identity Store, Credential Store, and Policy Store is critical for advanced security configuration and maintenance.

The following sections discuss these few key concepts at a high level. Understanding these concepts is not critical at this moment for you to continue with the remainder of the book, however, once you complete the book and are ready to engage in more advanced discovery, you will need to research and understand these items to be more versed in managing Oracle BI 11g security.

Backwards compatibility

Let's first disclaim that the best practice for Oracle BI 11g security is to use the default Oracle Fusion Middleware security model. However, the legacy approach to manage security via the Oracle BI metadata repository (RPD) is still allowed. This backwards compatibility for security allows environments running on previous versions of Oracle BI (for example, Oracle BI 10g) to leverage the investments in complicated metadata repository architectures or unique identity solutions while still taking advantage of Oracle BI 11g's new functions and features.

This backwards compatibility can potentially provide a false sense of comfort. However, since the official Oracle BI roadmap is only to support the Fusion Middleware security model, backwards compatibility merely bridges a gap in migrating to Oracle BI 11g where rearchitecture of security would otherwise delay, or prevent, some organizations from taking advantage of the new offering. There are certain requirements to leverage this backwards compatible security architecture. The Oracle BI 11g product documentation discusses the right way to incorporate this technique in a section called **Alternative Security Administration Options** (http://docs.oracle.com/cd/E21764_01/bi.1111/e10543/legacy.htm#CHDCEFBC).

Managing by application roles

In previous releases of Oracle BI security, groups and the relationship of a managed Identity Store's (that is LDAP or custom relational table) users with an Oracle BI group was managed within the RPD. A group was the highest level of organization for specific sets of users. This goes for both the metadata repository and the Web Catalog. This legacy approach was limited to a single software solution, Oracle BI.

In Oracle BI 11*g*, the default security model is the Oracle Fusion Middleware security model which has a much broader vision and scope. General Information Technology security administration best practice is to set permissions or privileges to a specific point of access on a group and not individual users. The same idea applies here except there is another enterprise level of user/group aggregation called an **Application Role**. Application roles can contain other application roles, groups, or individual users. Access privileges to a certain object such as a folder, web page, or column should always be assigned to an application role. Application roles for Oracle BI 11*g* can be managed in the Oracle Enterprise Manager Fusion Middleware Control interface.

Security providers

Fusion Middleware security can seem complex at first, but knowing the correct terminology and understanding how the most important components communicate with each other it becomes easier. The application at large is extremely important as it relates to security management. Oracle BI 11*g* uses three main repositories for accessing authentication and authorization information, all of which are explained in the next sections.

Identity Store

This is the authentication provider. A simple mnemonic here is that this store tells Oracle BI how to identify any users attempting to access the system. An example of creating an Identity Store would be to configure an LDAP system such as the Oracle Internet Directory or Microsoft Active Directory to reference users within an organization.

Credential Store

The credential store is ultimately for advanced Oracle configurations. You may touch upon this while establishing an enterprise Oracle BI 11*g* deployment, but not much thereafter unless integrating with the Oracle BI 11g Action Framework, or something equally complex. Ultimately, the Credential Store does exactly what its name implies—it stores credentials.

Specifically, it is used to store credentials of other applications, which the core application (that is, Oracle BI) may access later without having to re-enter said credentials. An example of this would be integrating Oracle BI 11g with the **Oracle Enterprise Management (EPM)** suite. In this example, let's pretend that there is an internal requirement at Company XYZ for users to access an Oracle BI dashboard. Upon viewing said dashboard if a report with discrepancies is viewed, the user requires the ability to click on a link which opens an Oracle EPM Financial Report containing more details about the concern. If all users accessing the Oracle BI dashboard do not have credentials to access the Oracle EPM environment directly, how could they open and view the report without being prompted for credentials? The answer would be that the credential store would be configured with the credentials of a central user having access to the Oracle EPM environment. This central user's credentials (encrypted, of course) are passed along with the dashboard viewer's request and hey presto, access!

Policy Store

The policy store is unique to Fusion Middleware security and leverages a security standard referred to as **eXtensible Access Control Markup Language (XACML)**, which ultimately provides granular access and privilege control for an enterprise application. This is one of the reasons why managing by application roles becomes so important. It is the individual application role to which assigned policies are defining access for the information within Oracle BI. Stated another way, the application privileges, such as the ability to administer the Oracle BI 11g RPD, are assigned to a particular application role, and these associations are defined in the policy store. The following illustration shows from where each area of security management is controlled:

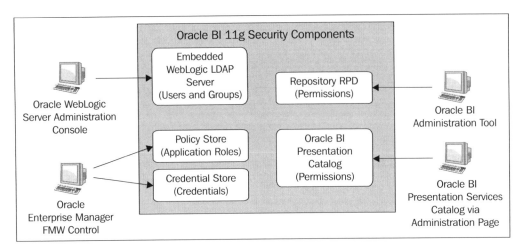

These three types of security providers within Oracle Fusion Middleware are integral to the Oracle BI 11*g* architecture. A chapter or more could be written on each provider but that is outside the scope of this book. Further recommended research on this topic would be to look at Oracle Fusion Middleware Security, OPSS, and the **Application Development Framework (ADF)**.

System requirements

The first thing to recognize with infrastructure requirements prior to deploying Oracle BI 11*g* is that its memory and processor requirements have been increased since previous versions. The Java application server, WebLogic Server, gets installed with the full version of its software (though under a limited/restricted license as already discussed). A multitude of additional Java libraries and applications are also deployed. Ultimately, the authentication **Application Development Framework (ADF)** used to develop much of the platform accounts for a larger overall footprint. Be prepared for a recommended minimum 8 GB **Read Access Memory (RAM)** requirement for an enterprise deployment and a 4 GB minimum requirement for a developer workstation deployment. Other system requirement information can be found within the Oracle documentation at `http://docs.oracle.com/cd/` `E23943_01/doc.1111/e15722/overview.htm#CJAHADHD`.

Client Tools

Since release 11.1.1.5, Oracle BI 11*g* has a separate Client Tools installation that requires Microsoft Windows XP or a more recent version of the Windows OS. The Oracle BI 11*g* Client Tools provides the majority of client to server management capabilities required for normal day-to-day maintenance of the Oracle BI repository and related artifacts. The Client Tools installation is usually reserved for Oracle BI developers who design and maintain the Oracle BI metadata repository, better known as RPD, which stems from its binary file extension (`.rpd`). Compared to previous versions of the product, there are two tools now, which have been removed from the Client Tools installation:

- Oracle BI ODBC Manager
- Oracle BI Catalog Manager (available with version 11.1.1.6)

The Oracle BI 11*g* Client Tools installation provides each workstation with the Administration Tool, Job Manager, and all command-line Application Programming Interface (API) executables.

Multiuser Development Environment

One of the key features of Oracle BI development is the ability for multiple metadata developers to develop simultaneously. Although the use of the term "simultaneously" can vary amongst the technical communities, the use of concurrent development within the Oracle BI suite requires Oracle BI's **Multiuser Development** (**MUD**) environment configuration.

The configuration itself is fairly straightforward and ultimately relies on the Oracle BI administrator's ability to divide metadata modeling responsibilities into projects. Projects—which are usually defined and delineated by logical fact table definitions—can be assigned to one or more metadata developers.

In previous versions of Oracle BI, a metadata developer could install the entire Oracle BI product suite on an up-to-date laptop or commodity desktop workstation and successfully develop, test, and deploy an Oracle BI metadata model. The system requirements of Oracle BI 11*g* prevent developers from installing the full Oracle BI 11*g* server suite on a legacy workstation as the minimum memory requirement is 4 GB. Most of the 32-bit workstations operate with 3 GB or less requirement.

If an organization currently leverages the Oracle BI MUD environment, or plans to leverage with the current release, this raises several questions:

- How do we get our developers to the best environment suitable for developing our metadata?
- Do we need to procure new hardware?

Most of the developers' desktop workstations or laptops run 32-bit Microsoft Windows XP or Windows Vista. Microsoft Windows is a requirement for the Oracle BI Client Tools. However, the Oracle BI Client Tools does not include the server component of the Oracle BI 11*g* environment. It only allows for connecting from the developer's workstation to the Oracle BI server instance. In a multiuser development environment, this poses a serious problem as only one metadata repository can exist on any one Oracle BI server instance at any given time. If two developers are working from their respective workstations at the same time and wish to see their latest modifications published in a **rapid application development (RAD)** cycle, this type of iterative effort fails as one developer's published changes will overwrite the others in real time.

To resolve the above issue there are two recommended solutions. The first is an obvious localized solution. This solution merely upgrades the Oracle BI developers' workstations or laptops to comply with the minimum requirements for installing the full Oracle BI environment on said machines. This upgrade should be both memory (RAM) and processor (MHz) centric. A dual-core processor and a 4 GB plus RAM are recommended.

However, in order for a Windows operating system to acknowledge and use more than 4 GB memory, a 64-bit operating system kernel is required. Without an upgraded workstation, from which to work, Oracle BI 11*g* metadata developers will sit at a disadvantage for general iterative metadata development and especially be disenfranchised if interfacing within a multiuser development environment.

The second solution is one that takes advantage of **virtual machines (VM)**. The virtual machines have become a staple within most IT departments as they are versatile and allow speedy proposition of server environments. For this scenario, it is recommended to create a virtual machine template of an Oracle BI 11*g* environment, from which individual virtual machine images for each metadata developer on the Oracle BI development team can be duplicated or stood up. This solution effectively provides each metadata developer with their own Oracle BI development environment server which contains the fully deployed Oracle BI server environment. Then, developers have the ability to develop and test iteratively by connecting to their assigned virtual server without fear that their efforts will conflict with another developer's. The following diagram illustrates how an Oracle BI 11*g* MUD environment can leverage either upgraded developer workstation hardware or VM images to facilitate development:

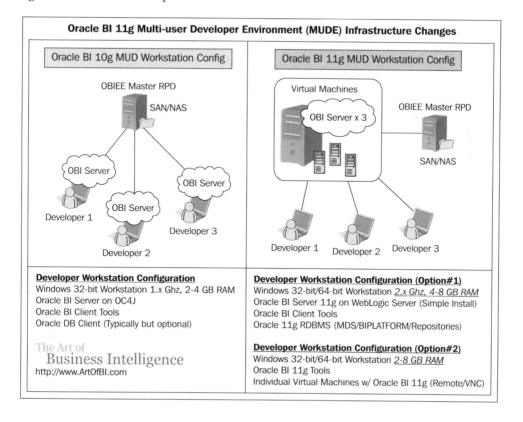

This book does not cover the installation, configuration, or best practices for developing in a MUD environment. However, the Oracle BI development team deserves a lot of credit for documenting these processes in unprecedented detail. The Oracle BI 11g MUD environment documentation provides a case study (`http://docs.oracle.com/cd/E21764_01/bi.1111/e10540/case_study.htm#CHDGIBBD`), which conveys best practices for managing a complex Oracle BI development lifecycle. When you are ready to deploy a MUD environment, it is highly recommended to peruse this documentation first.

The information in this section seeks to convey these best practices in facilitating a developer's workstation when using a MUD environment, but the mentioned resources will delve further into this.

Certification matrix

Now that the Oracle BI 11g is part of the larger enterprise Fusion Middleware stack, the Oracle BI tool suite complies largely with the overall Fusion Middleware infrastructure. This common foundation allows for a centralized model to communicate with operating systems, web servers, and other ancillary components which are compliant. The certification matrix for Oracle BI 11g can be found on the Oracle website at `http://www.oracle.com/technetwork/middleware/ias/downloads/fusion-certification-100350.html`.

The certification matrix document is usually provided in a Microsoft Excel format and should be referenced before you begin any project or deployment of Oracle BI 11g. This will ensure that infrastructure components such as the selected operating system, web server, web browsers, LDAP server, and so on will actually work when integrated with the product suite.

Scaling out Oracle BI 11*g*

There are several reasons why an organization may wish to expand their Oracle BI 11g footprint. This can range anywhere from requiring a highly available environment to achieving high levels of concurrent usage over time. The number of total end users, the number of total concurrent end users, the volume of queries, the size of the underlying data warehouse, and cross-network latency are even more factors to consider.

Scaling out an environment has the potential to solve performance issues and stabilize the environment. When scoping out the infrastructure for an Oracle BI 11g deployment, there are several crucial decisions to be made. These decisions can be greatly assisted by preparing and properly using Oracle's recommended guides for clustering and deploying Oracle BI 11g on an enterprise scale.

Preconfiguration run down

Configuring the Oracle BI 11*g* product suite, specifically while involving scaling out or setting up **high availability (HA)**, needs preparation. Proactively taking steps to understand what it takes to correctly establish or preconfigure the infrastructure required to support any level of fault tolerance and high availability is critical. Even if the decision to scale out from the initial Oracle BI 11*g* deployment has not been made and if the potential exists, proper planning is recommended. Proper planning for HA can be achieved by following the Oracle Enterprise Deployment Guide for Oracle BI at `http://docs.oracle.com/cd/E23943_01/doc.1111/e15722/toc.htm`.

Shared storage

We would remiss the most important concepts of scaling out Oracle BI 11*g* if we do not highlight it, specifically for high availability—shared storage. The idea of shared storage, is that in a fault tolerance environment there are binary files and other configuration metadata that needs to be shared across the nodes. If these common elements are not shared, then if one node is to fail there is a potential loss of data.

Most importantly, in a highly available Oracle BI 11*g* environment, there can be only one WebLogic Administration Server running for that environment at any instance in time. An HA configuration makes one Administration Server active while the other is made passive. If the appropriate preconfiguration steps for shared storage (as well as other items in the high availability guide) are not properly completed, one should not expect accurate results from his/her environment.

Clustering

A major benefit of Oracle BI 11*g*'s ability to leverage the WebLogic Server as the Java application server tier, is that for every default installation, Oracle BI gets established in a clustered architecture. There is no additional configuration necessary to set this architecture in motion. Clearly, installing Oracle BI 11*g* on a single server only provides a single server with which to interface, however, upon doing so Oracle BI is installed into a single node clustered application server environment. Then, additional clustered nodes of Oracle BI 11*g* can be configured to establish and expand the server either horizontally or vertically.

Vertical expansion versus horizontal expansion

With respect to the enterprise architecture and infrastructure of the Oracle BI 11g environment, a clustered environment can really expand in one of the two ways—horizontally and vertically. A horizontal expansion is the typical expansion type when clustering. It is represented by installing and configuring the application on a separate physical server with reference to the main server application. A vertical expansion is usually represented by expanding the application on the same physical server under which the main server application resides.

There are benefits to both scaling options. A vertical scale out can provide an advantage of a single machine's processor or memory power and save the cost of a separate physical machine. Horizontal scale out provides the advantages of failover, multiple machines, and redundancy. The decision to scale out in one way or the other is usually predicated on cost of additional physical servers, server limitations, and peripherals such as memory, processors, or an increase in usage activity by the end users. Some considerations, which may be used to assess which approach is the best for your specific implementation, might be as follows:

- Load balancing capabilities and need for an Active-Active versus Active-Passive architecture (suggests horizontal scaling)
- Need for a failover or high availability (suggests horizontal scaling)
- Cost for processor and memory enhancements versus cost of new servers (suggests vertical scaling)
- Anticipated increase in concurrent user queries (horizontal or vertical scaling)
- Realized decrease in performance due to an increase in user activity (horizontal or vertical scaling)

Oracle BI Server (system component) Cluster Controller

When discussing scaling out of the Oracle BI server cluster, it is a common mistake to confuse the WebLogic Server application clustering with the Oracle BI Server Cluster Controller. In an attempt to clarify, it helps to remember that the Oracle BI Server System Component is the service or server engine controlled by the OPMN. There is also an Oracle BI Managed Server which is controlled by the WebLogic Server. Currently, Oracle BI 11g can only have a single metadata repository (RPD) reference associated with an Oracle BI server deployment instance at any single point in time. Because of this, the Oracle BI server engine leverages a failover concept to ensure some level of high availability that exists when the environment is scaled out.

In an Oracle BI scaled out and clustered environment, a secondary node, which has an instance of Oracle BI 11*g* installed, contains a secondary Oracle BI Server engine. From the main Oracle BI Managed Server containing the primary Oracle BI server instance, the secondary Oracle BI server instance is established as the failover server engine, using the Oracle BI Server Cluster Controller. This configuration takes place in the Enterprise Manager Fusion Control console. Based on this configuration, the scaled-out Oracle BI Server engine acts in an Active-Passive mode. That is, when the main Oracle BI 11*g* server engine instance fails, the secondary or passive Oracle BI server engine then becomes active to route requests and field queries.

Failover and high availability

With high availability, it is often very hard to achieve multiples of nine (that is, 99.999 percent) for uptime of any server or application server environment. High availability is the type of architecture associated with an environment when attempting to maintain a high level of application availability and minimize downtime.

Failover is the process that takes place when a server node in a cluster fails and application traffic, otherwise intended for the down server, flows to the other active clustered server nodes. Failover also requires some level of load balancing and the concept can vary depending on the desired architecture within an organization, but the general concept should be roughly the same in most topologies.

As part of an enterprise deployment strategy, taking failover and high availability into consideration is usually part of the architecture planning process. A step-by-step configuration for HA or a failover environment is an advanced infrastructure topic and is beyond the scope of this book. However, it is important to note that because Oracle BI 11*g* is part of the Fusion Middleware stack, it has the ability to capitalize on all fault tolerance features offered by that common architecture.

Enterprise deployment guide

In an effort to relay best practices and strategic deployment of a large-scale enterprise, Oracle BI deployment, Oracle lends a big helpful hand and provides a topology referred to as the **Enterprise Deployment Guide** (**EDG**). This guide should not be taken lightly. When deciding on major factors of a full-scale enterprise wide Oracle BI deployment, this topology is the one that should be referenced first. Use the EDG to plan for required resource skills, procurement of hardware, and as a gauge to estimate the effort involved in achieving the architecture that your requirements demand. The topology includes pertinent information regarding load balancing, virtual IP addresses, separation of HTTP servers from application servers, and other fully vetted infrastructure recommendations. It is especially recommended to view this guide before embarking on any deployment involving extranet access to your Oracle BI implementation or a large user base of an internal deployment.

Directory folder structure

As you get started with installing, configuring, and deploying Oracle BI 11g in the subsequent chapters, you will see several references to files inside the Fusion Middleware folder structure and the Oracle BI home folder structure. Again, taking advantage of a common architecture, Oracle BI 11g leverages the Fusion Middleware foundation to organize the filesystem structure. This consistency is a benefit for all implementers and administrators that will eventually maintain the platform. It is recommended that, as you progress in your learning of Oracle BI 11g, you should note the folders which contain files pertinent for modifying the environment, or assisting with troubleshooting efforts. The following diagram illustrates the standard logical deployment structure for Oracle BI 11g:

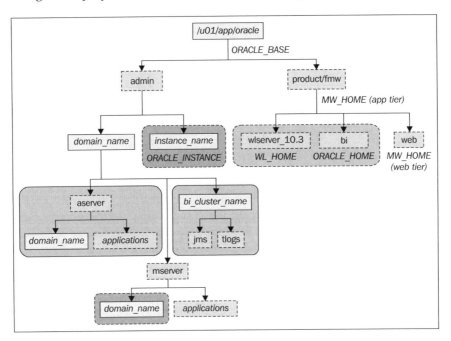

Log files (diagnostics)

As you begin developing and deploying your Oracle BI 11g solutions, you will eventually run into some issues down the road. Face them, you are implementing a technology! Issues, no matter how minor, are bound to arise. No one plans for them. But here is a list of log files' locations where it is best to begin troubleshooting in Oracle BI 11g:

```
<OBI_LOGS> = /u01/fmw/instances/instance1/diagnostics/logs
```

Log Name (`.log`)	Location
NQQuery	`<OBI_LOGS>/OracleBIServerComponent/coreapplication_obis1`
NQServer	`<OBI_LOGS>/OracleBIServerComponent/coreapplication_obis1`
NQSAdminTool	`<OBI_LOGS>/OracleBIServerComponent/coreapplication_obis1`
NQSUDMLExec	`<OBI_LOGS>/OracleBIServerComponent/coreapplication_obis1`
RPD migration utility	`<OBI_LOGS>/OracleBIServerComponent/coreapplication_obis1`
SAW log	`<OBI_LOGS>/OracleBIPresentationServicesComponent/coreapplication_obips1`
JavaHost	`<OBI_LOGS>/OracleBIJavaHostComponent/coreapplication_obijh1`
NQScheduler	`<OBI_LOGS>/OracleBISchedulerComponent/coreapplication_obisch1`
NQCluster	`<OBI_LOGS>/OracleBIClusterControllerComponent/coreapplication_obiccs1`
ODBC	`<OBI_LOGS>/OracleBIODBCComponent/coreapplication_obips1`

All logs regarding the OPMN system can be found at the following centralized location:

```
<OBI_LOGS>/OPMN/opmn/
```

Configuration files

Those who are familiar with the previous versions of Oracle BI might be surprised that several legacy named physical configuration files still reside in the Oracle BI 11*g* architecture. These files can still be manually manipulated to configure the Oracle BI 11*g* environment. However, much of the basic configuration is handled via the Oracle BI Enterprise Manager which will be discussed in more detail in *Chapter 5, Understanding the Systems Management Tools*. If there is a need to locate these configuration files, they can be found at the following location:

```
<FMW_HOME>\instance\instance1\config\component_type\bi_component_name
```

The following is a list of configuration files based on the central Oracle BI 11*g* instance path of `<FMW_HOME>\instance\instance1\config\`:

- `\OPMN\opmn\opmn.xml`

- `\OracleBIClusterControllerComponent\coreapplication_obiccs1\ccslogconfig.xml`

- `\OracleBIJavaHostComponent\coreapplication_obijh1\logging_config.xml`

- `\OracleBIPresentationServicesComponent\coreapplication_obips1\instanceconfig.xml`

- `\OracleBISchedulerComponent\coreapplication_obisch1\instanceconfig.xml`

- `\OracleBIServerComponent\coreapplication_obis1\logconfig.xml`

A review – what I should now know!

For a self review and recap of this chapter, here are a few questions based on important topics covered in this chapter. There is no answer key. These questions are for your own reflection on the chapter material.

1. What is Oracle Fusion Middleware?

2. What are some of the reasons to scale out an Oracle BI deployment?

3. List each of the Oracle BI system components. How many are there?

4. What is the name of the guide that should be referenced while planning an enterprise deployment of Oracle BI 11*g*?

5. What is the purpose of the Identity Store?

Additional research suggestions

The following list would help you to continue your learning:

- Oracle BI 11*g* Enterprise Deployment Guide: `http://download.oracle.com/docs/cd/E21764_01/doc.1111/e15722/toc.htm`

- Multiuser Development Environment: `http://download.oracle.com/docs/cd/E21764_01/bi.1111/e10540/lifecycle.htm#CIAFAFGE`

- A case study: `http://download.oracle.com/docs/cd/E21764_01/bi.1111/e10540/case_study.htm#CHDGIBBD`

Summary

This chapter provided a high-level overview of the Oracle BI 11*g* architecture. Oracle BI 11*g* is an overhaul to prior versions of the tool. This chapter discussed how Oracle Fusion Middleware has made Oracle BI 11*g* an extremely robust tool incorporating open standards and best practices where possible. An effort was made to discuss topics, which are high on the priority list for most organizations, such as security and scaling out the architecture. Recommendations were provided around these topics where possible. Although there is a lot more detail that could be written into each subject section of this chapter, the chapter conveyed enough information to capture the bulk of the Oracle BI 11*g* architecture, so that you can speak intelligently about the subject after reading this chapter.

The architecture described in this chapter discussed the core foundation of Oracle BI 11*g* and did not discuss Oracle Real-time Decisions (RTD), the Oracle decision making engine, nor will the remainder of this book discuss it (an entire book could be devoted merely to this subject; so, we chose to leave it out of this).

The next several chapters take you on a journey through setting up Oracle BI 11*g*, prepping data sources, modeling a custom analytics solution, and getting to know Oracle BI intimately. Keep the momentum going and just know that by the end of this book, you'll be well on your way to becoming an Oracle BI aficionado.

2

Installing the Metadata Repository

Before installing an **Oracle Business Intelligence Enterprise Edition (OBIEE)** 11*g* system, you will need to prepare a database, not for end user reporting but for the OBIEE system itself.

This database will hold some of the vital metadata about your setup, allow for audit tracking, and hold tables ready to accept activity data, for example scheduling information. Not all metadata is held in a database form, as we will see later in the book. So, this chapter will cover how to install the required database components for your Oracle BI system to use them.

In this chapter, you'll learn how to customize the installation to change the options available, and how to use the silent installation. You cannot afford to skip this chapter if you're installing your own development system! It's crucial to understand what is possible so that you can advise the database administrators, who will be managing your production environments.

Repository Creation Utility (RCU)

The first task when installing an Oracle BI EE 11*g* system is to run the **Repository Creation Utility (RCU)**. This will create schemas and tables to hold metadata in a database, which the Oracle BI EE products and the Fusion Middleware components will use at runtime. These tables are collectively known as **metadata repositories**.

A repository represents a specific schema, or set of schemas, that belong to a specific Oracle Fusion Middleware component (for example, Oracle BPEL Process Manager or Oracle Internet Directory). A metadata repository was a feature of many Fusion Middleware products and components for some time, and the Oracle BI 11*g* issue of Oracle BI EE incorporated a new repository in the RCU.

What is the metadata store?

In order to understand the use of the metadata repository in the Oracle Fusion Middleware Business Intelligence system, we need to understand what metadata is and how it is applied.

The term **metadata** is commonly defined as a data about data, but it can also be used in various other contexts, such as data about applications. It is this second definition which is more relevant to a business intelligence system.

Warehouse guru Ralph Kimball divided metadata for databases into three categories:

- Technical metadata
- Business metadata
- Process metadata

Technical metadata

Technical metadata defines the objects in the BI system. Technical metadata includes the system metadata which defines the data structures in the database and includes tables, columns, indexes, and partitions. Technical metadata also defines the data model and the way in which it is displayed for users, including reports, schedules, distribution lists, and user security rights.

This category of metadata is common to every warehouse project I have experienced, and relates to Codd's rule number 4—a good database holds data about its structure in the metadata form, normally in tables within the database that can be easily read.

Business metadata

Business metadata is a content from the data warehouse described in more user friendly terms. The business metadata explains what data is there, where it comes from, what it means, and what its relationship is to other data in the data warehouse. An example of this might be describing what a dashboard page contains and where the data is sourced from.

Users who browse the data warehouse will primarily be viewing the business metadata. So, it may also serve as documentation for the DW/BI system.

Process metadata

Process metadata is used to describe the results of various operations in the data warehouse, such as data loading (also known as ETL) runs and running dashboard. For example, when running an ETL process, all key data from tasks such as start and end times, processed rows, and logged errors. This data is useful when analyzing the ETL or reporting performance.

The Oracle Fusion Middleware product is metadata-driven and uses all three of the above categories to some extent. Metadata is used throughout the wide range of Fusion Middleware components to represent and affect application logic, which reduces the reliance on code-driven processes.

The applications are affected by metadata in various ways, for example:

- **Process definition**: Event definitions, process rules, logging, and so on
- **Runtime configuration**: Configuration files, datasource definitions, and so on
- **User interaction**: Page layouts, security of objects, availability of data, and so on

The Oracle BI EE suite is one of the Fusion Middleware products that use all three types of metadata. For example, the technical metadata incorporates the definitions of the physical tables that Oracle BI EE will report against, and might also include items such as the definition of an alert. The descriptions of the pages, reports, and dashboards used to present reports are examples of business metadata, and the usage tracking data, that is log records of dashboard runs by a user, is process metadata. Some of the metadata used in the OBIEE suite is stored in binary files, and some of the metadata is held in database schemas, which are described in more detail in the next sections. Later in the book, we will discuss the other metadata storage mediums.

Oracle Metadata Services (MDS)

To ensure that the metadata is consistent and can be reliably accessed, it is held in the Oracle **Metadata Services** (**MDS**) repository. The MDS allows for common management tools such as the Enterprise Manager and RMAN backup, and also helps in the deployment process, ensuring that the design is used at runtime. The use of the MDS enables the customization of the Fusion Middleware system without any need to update the underlying code. These customizations are held safely and can be used in deployments.

The metadata, accessed and managed by the MDS, can be either a file based repository or a database repository, but use of a database is the preferred option. The current certified databases for the MDS are Oracle (10.2 and above), SQL Server, and DB2. It is possible to install the RCU on an Oracle XE database, although you will receive a warning that it is not supported in a production environment.

The MDS supports versioning and sandboxing—this is where multiple changes can be tested before being committed to the current version.

In order to ensure good performance, the MDS also supports the caching of data into the application, as well as the use of indexes. This enables faster live user access.

Repository schemas

The MDS is just one of the many schemas that are installed by the RCU.

The various components of Oracle Fusion Middleware require many different schemas, with the MDS schema being the core schema, it is common to all products. Oracle BI EE requires one schema which will be used for the Scheduler, BI Publisher, Usage Tracking, Real-time Decisions, and the new Scorecard product.

The Repository Creation Utility is a common tool for any Fusion Middleware installation, not just for Oracle BI EE. It will, therefore, provide the option to install all of the following types of repository schemas, some of which could be useful for your installation:

- Common schemas
- **Enterprise Content Management (ECM)**
- **Enterprise Performance Management (EPM)**
- Identity management
- **Oracle Data Integrator (ODI)**
- Oracle Business Intelligence
- Portal and BI
- SOA and BPM infrastructure
- WebCenter suite
- WebLogic Communication Services

The Business Intelligence Platform schema is often referred to as **BIPlatform** as that is the default name, although you can call it whatever you like.

For a standard Oracle BI EE installation, it is only the MDS (part of the Common schemas) and the Business Intelligence Platform that are essential, but you may also choose to include the Audit schema. The Audit schema is used to store user activity in various applications, such as in the BI Publisher tool. Testing will need to be done with the use of the audit service to ensure sufficient performance.

As suggested in the preceding list, you can also choose to install your Oracle Identity Management, EPM, and ODI into the same database. This may be useful for a development machine, but it's unlikely that you would want to install them all into the same production database.

Non-repository metadata

It is worth reiterating that not all configuration and system metadata for Oracle BI EE is currently being held in a database schema. For example, the page definitions used to create a dashboard page at runtime are not in the store. The BI system's main repository is also not in the store yet. This may change in future versions, but would need a major development for Oracle to undertake.

It is possible to develop your own schema containing all of your BI server repository objects, and to deploy these objects using XUDML (UDML in version 10*g*). I have developed one such system and used it on many of my projects. This can be useful for large scale, multi-country developments, or where the underlying table names might change. Although not supported by Oracle in previous versions, this method is fully supported in version 11*g* and we will look at the basic concepts in *Appendix A*.

Downloading the software

The choice of site from which to download your RCU software will depend upon whether you are installing a new machine or upgrading an existing installation:

- For upgrades, refer to the Oracle Support site: `http://www.orace.com/support/`
- For a clean installation, consult the main Oracle website: `http://www.oracle.com`

There are several Oracle website pages that currently allow the downloading of the RCU.

For a generic starting point to find the software, you can either use the **Oracle Technology Network (OTN)** or e-Delivery (the ex-Siebel download site):

- `http://www.oracle.com/technetwork/middleware/repository/downloads/index.html`
- `http://edelivery.oracle.com/`

The software can be downloaded for free by signing up to `www.oracle.com`, and accepting the OTN License Agreement, as shown in the following screenshots.

From the Oracle Business Intelligence (11.1.1.x) Downloads page, scroll down to the **Required Additional Software** section and click on the link for your operating system:

> Note that the operating system relates to the one you will run the RCU on, not the one the database is running on.

Required Additional Software

Repository Creation Utility (11.1.1.5.0):
⬇ **for Microsoft Windows (32-bit)** (323,925,499 bytes) (cksum 2130853384)
⬇ **for Linux x86 (32-bit)** (398,173,821 bytes) (cksum 490866219)

Sign in to the Oracle system with your account details. If you don't have an account, you can create one for free.

Once your software is downloaded, you will need to extract the files using an unzip application. My preference is to use the 7-Zip File Manager as it usually performs without any corruption.

Running the RCU

The RCU needs to be run as a user with SYSDBA or administrator privileges. For most organizations this will entail asking the **Database Administrator (DBA)** to run the RCU for you. It is, therefore, worth making sure that they understand the system and what it does, otherwise they will probably object to running in your production environment.

Try to understand what processes the RCU is going through and how you (or the DBA) can keep to corporate guidelines or protocols on your project.

The RCU is supported on 32 bit and 64 bit Windows or Linux.

There are two running methods—normal and silent. The normal method will present the user with a step-by-step guide which prompts the parameters required, whereas the silent method will require all the parameters to be included in the command line.

Setting up your database

The installation provides flexibility to create custom schemas and tablespaces. The default settings provided out of the box are normally sufficient, particularly for a development environment. However, you may want to have control over how the schemas are installed:

- You can choose to install multiple tablespaces (the default setting) or have one for all repositories.
- Creating users (schema) prior to running the RCU is not required, and could cause an installation error.
- Creating tablespaces prior to running the RCU is not required, but can be done without causing any issues. This allows the DBA to create the tablespaces in their normal way.

One other optional database setup task could be to create a user account with the privileges in place to create the users (schemas) and tablespaces. This is not a difficult requirement, but the DBA may prefer this for using SYS.

Oracle

If you are installing an Oracle database and want to run the RCU with a user other than SYS, you will need to grant the user permissions as follows:

```
GRANT execute on sys.dbms_lock to user_name with grant option
```

For example, if you have a user OBI_SYSTEM, the user permission will be as follows:

```
GRANT execute on sys.dbms_lock to obi_system with grant option
```

MS SQL Server

If you are planning to install an MS SQL Server database, you will need to execute the following scripts:

```
ALTER database [dbname_here] SET SINGLE_USER WITH ROLLBACK IMMEDIATE;
ALTER database [dbname_here] SET READ_COMMITTED_SNAPSHOT ON;
ALTER database [dbname_here] SET MULTI_USER;
```

You will also need to run the script, as shown in the following screenshot:

```
ALTER database rcudev SET SINGLE_USER WITH ROLLBACK IMMEDIATE;
DECLARE @collate    sysname
              SELECT @collate = convert(sysname, serverproperty('COLLATION'))
              IF ( charindex(N'_CI', @collate) > 0 )
              BEGIN
                select @collate = replace(@collate, N'_CI', N'_CS')
                exec ('ALTER database rcudev COLLATE ' + @collate)
              END
ALTER database rcudev SET MULTI_USER;
  GO
```

Executing all these scripts will ensure that the errors shown in the following screenshot do not occur during the prerequisite checks in step 3 of the installation:

```
RCU-6083:Failed - Check prerequisites requirement for selected component:MDS
Please refer to RCU log at C:\Downloads\rcu\rcuHome\rcu\log\logdir.2011-11-03_21-40\rcu.log for details.
-----------------------------------------------------------------------------------
Component    : MDS
Error        : Repository creation check failed.
Cause        : Database: 'rcudev' is not configured correctly.
Action       : Alter database to turn on the READ_COMMITTED_SNAPSHOT option.
               Ensure you have DBA priviliges. Also the DBA should not have
               multiple logins on this database - else it will result in a
               lock error.
Command      : ALTER database rcudev SET READ_COMMITTED_SNAPSHOT ON
-----------------------------------------------------------------------------------

-----------------------------------------------------------------------------------
Component    : MDS
Error        : Repository creation check failed.
Cause        : Database: 'rcudev' is not configured correctly.
Action       : Alter database to apply the correct collate to the database.
               Ensure you have DBA priviliges. Also, the DBA should not have
               multiple logins on this database - else it will result in a
               lock error.
Command      : DECLARE @collate   sysname
               SELECT @collate = convert(sysname, serverproperty('COLLATION'))
               IF ( charindex(N'_CI', @collate) > 0 )
               BEGIN
                 select @collate = replace(@collate, N'_CI', N'_CS')
                 exec ('ALTER database $(DATABASE_NAME) COLLATE ' + @collate)
               END
               GO
-----------------------------------------------------------------------------------

RCU-6092:Component Selection validation failed. Please refer to log at
C:\Downloads\rcu\rcuHome\rcu\log\logdir.2011-11-03_21-40\rcu.log for details.
```

Preparing for your installation

In some operating systems, a number of updates are required to ensure that the installation will run.

Linux

In Linux, log in to SQLplus and issue the following commands:

```
alter system set processes = 500 scope=spfile;
alter system set open_cursors = 800;
alter system set sessions = 250 scope=spfile;
```

The following screenshot shows the logging in and running of the required commands:

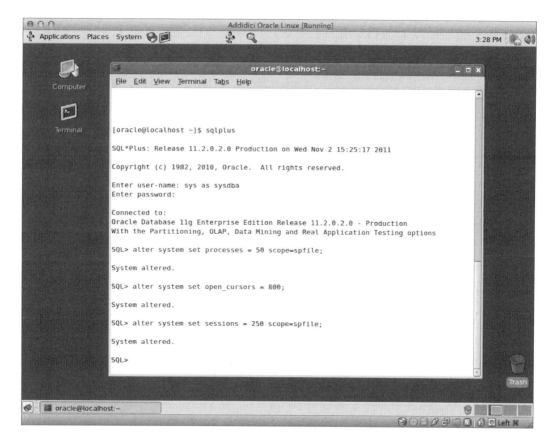

You will then need to restart the database for the updates to take effect.

64 bit Linux

On 64 bit Linux operating systems, you will need to run the following command before starting the RCU:

```
set linux32 bash
```

This will set your bash shell environment to use 32 bit libraries.

Standard installation steps

This section shows the steps involved in running the RCU in normal interactive mode. It is worth understanding the steps even if you are planning on using the silent mode.

Next procedure shows how to install the RCU on Windows into an Oracle database:

1. Locate the **rcu.bat** file in your installation folders. It is held inside the rcuHome\BIN folder. For example, on Windows the path will be C:\downloads\rcu\rcuHome\BIN\rcu.bat:

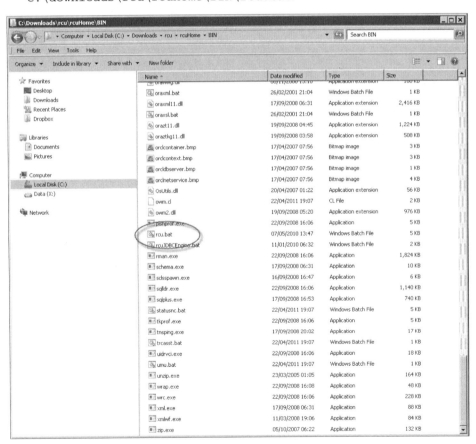

2. Then, you will see the **Welcome** screen:

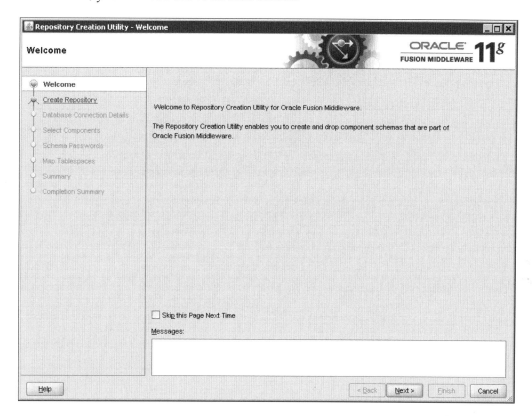

Note that you can customize the message on this screen if you feel it necessary. This can be useful when you have lots of environments to manage and you need to check which one you are running each time. This is done by editing the configuration files held in the RCU folders.

3. Next, you will be presented with the database options. You have to choose from three database types: Oracle, SQL Server, and DB2.

4. In the example shown in the following screenshot, the installation is done into an Oracle database which is running on a local machine. I have used the **SYS** account to create the schema, as shown in the following screenshot:

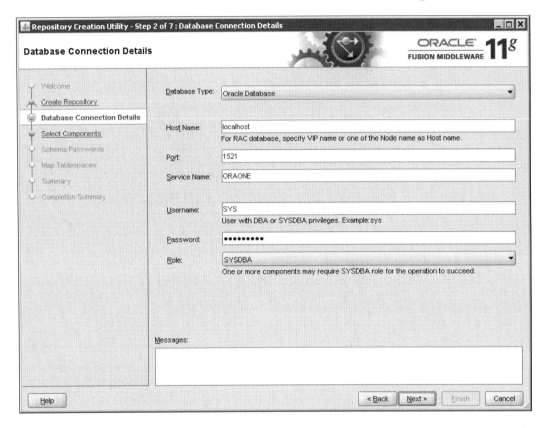

5. The following screenshot shows the dialog box to be completed when you choose **Microsoft SQL Server** as **Database Type**. It is similar to the dialog box for Oracle, but with the added option of **Unicode Support**:

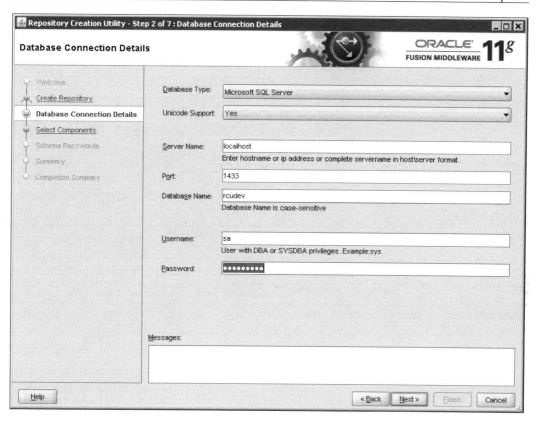

6. Once you complete the details required, the system will run a series of pre-requisite checks. These checks are shown in the following screenshot:

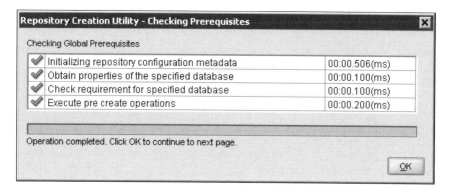

At this stage, you may receive a couple of messages which could be ignored.

If you try to install into an Oracle XE database, you will receive a warning about product versions, but you can still complete the installation. The XE version is not supported for a production installation but it is very useful for **Proof of Concept (POC)** and development environments.

The other message relates to character sets. Again, this can be ignored, but preferably not in a production environment.

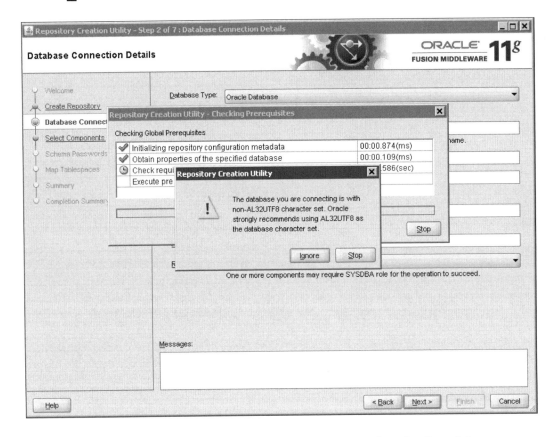

7. After the prerequisite checks, you will be presented with a list of the available repositories to install. Out of the box, you have the option of a long list of schemas to install, but you only need to install **Metadata Services** and **Business Intelligence Platform** (we will discuss some ways to change the list of available schemas later in this chapter).

Note that if you are installing by using the procedure in this chapter, you should also consider including the **Audit Services** schema. This can also be added later, if you prefer to run the standard installation first.

8. Enter a prefix that denotes the environment you are building. In the example shown in the following screenshot, I have used **DEV**. If you have already installed DEV, you must enter a new prefix. Be careful, not to make this prefix too long and note that the RCU requires the use of an underscore (_):

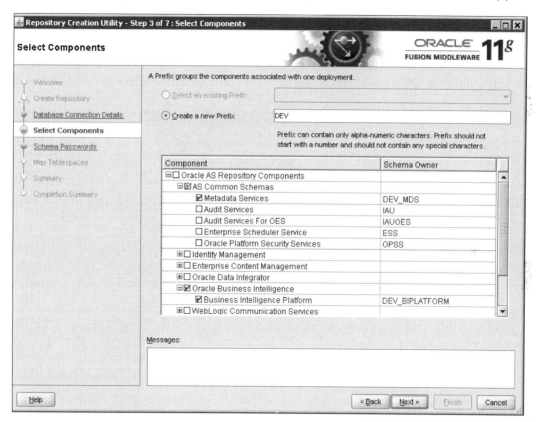

As this is the first time of running the RCU, there is no option called **Select an existing Prefix** (installing **Audit Services** into an existing schema will be discussed later).

9. For each selected repository, another prerequisite check is run, as shown in the following screenshot:

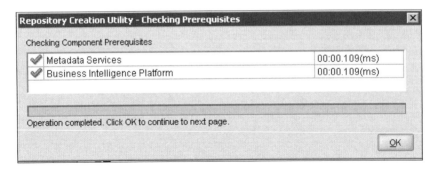

10. When you reach the **Schema Passwords** page, you are required to enter a password for your schemas. For simplicity you can choose to have the same password for each schema:

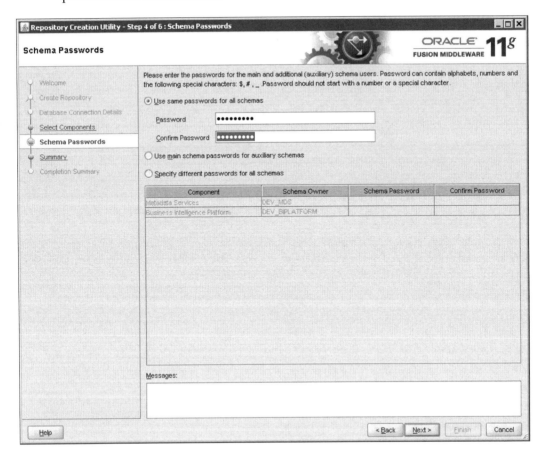

11. For an Oracle installation, Step 5 in the installation is to **Map Tablespaces**. This step is skipped for the SQL Server. You have the choice to enter an existing tablespace, or to specify a new one and have the RCU create the files for you. In the following screenshot you will see that you can chose to accept the default settings for a new tablespace. Then, click on **Next**, or click on **Manage Tablespaces**. Selecting this option means you can be very specific about sizes and file locations:

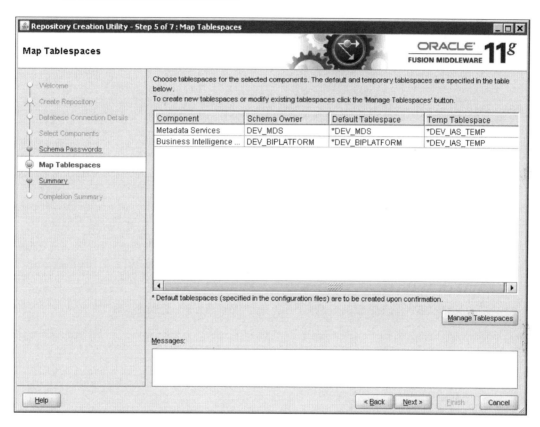

12. If you click on **Manage Tablespaces**, you will be presented with the following screenshot:

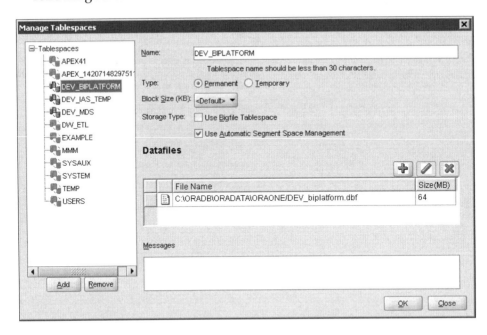

13. By clicking on the edit (pencil) symbol, you can open the **Edit Datafile** page. Here you can give precise size information for your datafile:

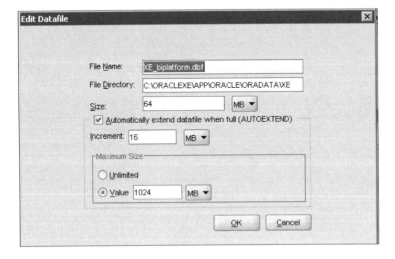

Some DBAs do not support the auto-extension on tablespaces. You can switch it off at this stage, and manually set your datafile size.

14. Once all the settings have been entered, you will see the **Summary** page. This is your final chance to review what is being installed. Once you are happy with it, all you need to do is click on **Create**:

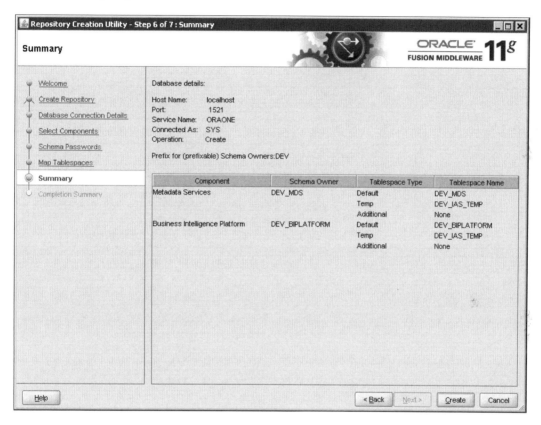

15. Now, you will see the **Completion Summary** page of your installation, as shown in the following screenshot. This will include the location of your log file:

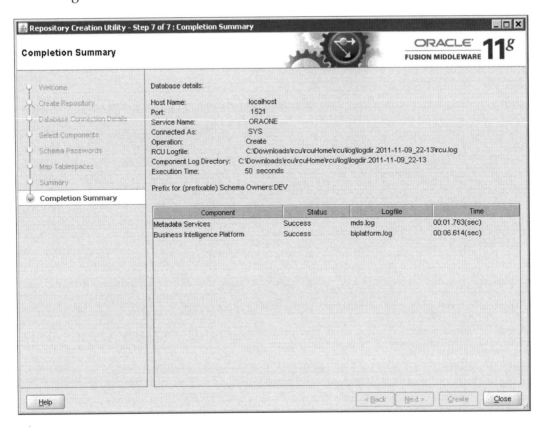

16. You have now completed a standard installation using the RCU and will be able to check that your schemas are created, and that the tables are in place.

 Note that few of the tables will actually contain data at this point.

The following screenshot shows a selection of the repository tables created in an Oracle XE database installation:

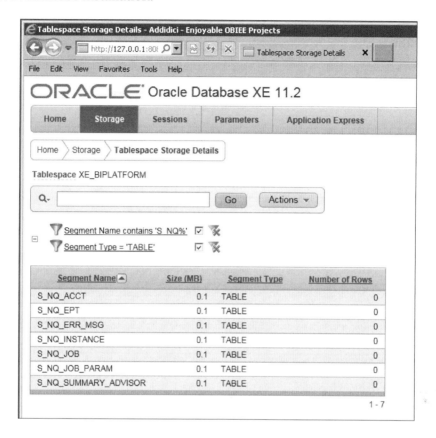

The list of tables shown is a small subset, that is, just those beginning with s_NQ. The s_NQ% tables are related to alerts or usage tracking (refer to *Chapter 16, Usage Tracking*).

There are 152 tables in the BIPlatform schema alone. Some of the created tables and their use are described in the following table:

Table Name	Use
S_NQ_ACCT	Stores usage tracking information (refer to *Chapter 16, Usage Tracking*)
S_NQ_SUMMARY_ADVISOR	Stores information that is used by the summary advisor
S_NQ_DB_ACCT	Stores usage tracking information related to the physical SQL sent to a database when queries are run.

Table Name	Use
S_NQ_JOB	Lists jobs, aka alerts (previously known as iBots)
S_NQ_JOB_PARAM	Provides parameters for jobs
S_NQ_INSTANCE	Keeps a record of a job that has been run, including when it was run and the status
S_NQ_ERR_MSG	If a job fails the error details are logged here
CP%	All the tables prefixed with CP relate to the Essbase tool
CALC%	All the tables prefixed with CALCMGR relate to the hyperion Calculation Manager tool
QRTZ%	All the tables prefixed with QRTZ relate to the BI Publisher Scheduling tool (Quartz)
RTD%	All the tables prefixed with RTD relate to the Real Time Decisions tool

Adding repositories

One of the repositories that you may want to install on an Oracle BI project is the Auditing Services Common Repository. The Oracle Fusion Middleware Audit Framework is a new feature released in version 11g, for monitoring "who does what" on your system. Monitoring can include the Oracle BI screens, and can be reported on using BI Publisher or OBIEE.

Let's use the Audit Services Repository as an example of adding an existing set of schema created by RCU:

1. Run the RCU as usual and proceed to the **Select Components** page.

2. Select an existing prefix.

3. Select the **Audit Services** schema:

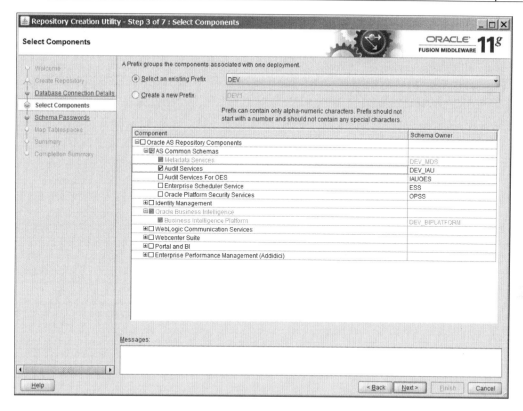

We will look at the ways in which we can report against the audit data in *Chapter 12, Developing Reports Using BI Publisher*.

Customizing your installation

The Database Administration team on your project may want to understand what the RCU is doing, and will probably want to have complete control over what it does. Hopefully, they will use the RCU to install other Oracle systems and will be happy to run the product as it is. However, if you need to re-assure them or allow them to influence the way RCU works, then you will need to review various configuration metadata files that RCU uses.

It is possible to control how the RCU installs the schemas, tablespaces, and tables by changing the settings in the configuration files. The relevant configuration files are as follows:

- `rcu.properties`: Used for runtime options of the RCU (in the `/rcu/config` folder)

- `componentinfo.xml`: Controls which repositories are available for installation

- `biplatform.xml`: Manages the repository creation for the Business Intelligence Platform (located in the `/rcu/integration/biplatform` folder)
- `storage.xml`: Sets the default options for tablespace creation
- **Scripts**: Various folders of sql scripts, specific for each type of database, for example `rcu/integration/bipublisher/scripts/oracle/create_user.sql`

The following code blocks are some extracts from the configuration files and examples of what you can change.

The following `rcu.properties` file:

```
ENABLE_ORACLE_ONLY=false
```

Can be changed to:

```
ENABLE_ORACLE_ONLY=true
```

This removes the option to install the RCU into a SQL Server or DB2 database:

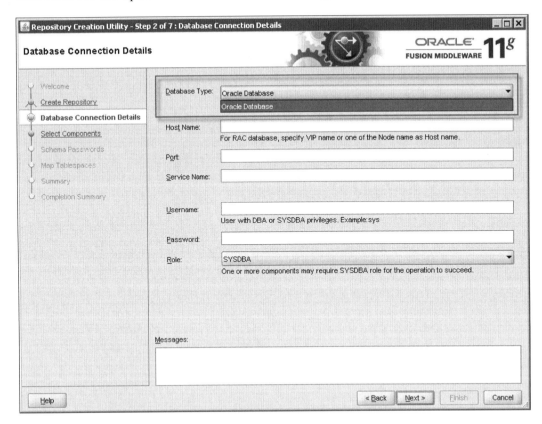

The following line in the code:

```
PRODUCT_NAME=Oracle Fusion Middleware
```

can be changed to:

```
PRODUCT_NAME=Oracle Fusion Middleware (Addidici Standard OBIEE Install
v1.0)
```

Making this change will have no major effect on the file, but can help to ensure that you have the right configuration file version checked out of your code repository (for example, .svn). The right configuration file is ComponenInfo.xml.

All of the nonessential schemas can be removed so that you are just left with the OBI and MDS schemas. You can also set the name of the schema and make it a fixed setting (that is not editable by the installation user).

Other common changes

You can remove all the nonessential schemas, leaving just the MDS and BIPlatform. Refer to the following code snippet:

```
<!-- AS Common GROUP START -->
<Component ID="AS_COMMON" IS_GROUPING_COMPONENT="TRUE">
  <Display NLS_ID="AS_COMMON_ID">AS Common Schemas</Display>
</Component>
&mds;
<!-- AS Common GROUP END -->
<!-- BI_SUITE START -->
<Component ID="BUSINESS INTELLIGENCE" IS_GROUPING_COMPONENT="TRUE">
  <Display NLS_ID="BUSINESS INTELLIGENCE">Oracle Business
  Intelligence</Display>
</Component>
&biplatform;
<!-- BI_SUITE END -->
```

Refer to the following screenshot, which shows the **Select Components** step:

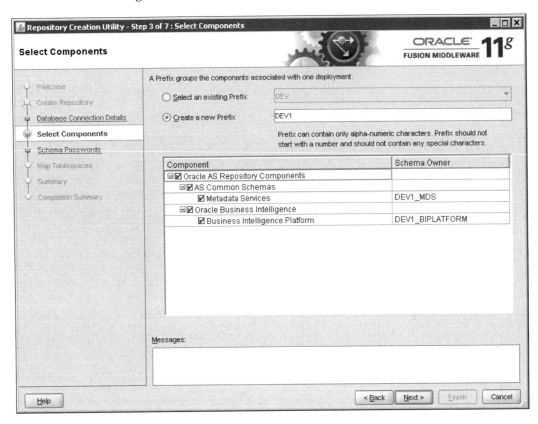

Specific installation files related to the storage options and tablespaces are held in the file under the main folder $rcuHome\rcu\integration. For example, within the biplatform folder you will find the following files:

- biplatform_ComponentInfo.xml: Change the Schema User setting to fix the name of the installed user (schema).

  ```
  <SchemaUser PREFIXABLE="TRUE" USER_EDITABLE="TRUE">BIPLATFORM</
  SchemaUser>
  ```

  The preceding code line should be changed to:

  ```
  <SchemaUser PREFIXABLE="FALSE"USER_EDITABLE="TRUE">OBIEE</
  SchemaUser>
  ```

  This change can be extremely useful for ensuring that settings are consistent from one environment to another. It also reduces the need for user input at installation time.

Another option is to provide your own default tablespace name:

```
<Tablespace TYPE="DEFAULT_TABLESPACE">
<Prompt NLS_ID="DEFAULT_TABLESPACE">Default Tablespace</Prompt>
<TablespaceName>STD_OBI</TablespaceName>
</Tablespace>
```

- `biplatform.xml`: No changes are required in this file. It is possible to remove the SQL Server and DB2 code if you want to be extra cautious in an Oracle environment.

- `biplatform_Storage.xml`: This is used to set the default values when installing tablespaces:

```
<?xml version="1.0" encoding="UTF-8"?>
<!-- BIPLATFORM -->
  <TablespaceAttributes NAME="BIPLATFORM" >
    <DatafilesList>
      <DatafileAttributes
      ID="%DATAFILE_LOCATION%/biplatform.dbf">
        <Size UNIT="MB">64</Size>
        <Reuse>True </Reuse>
        <AutoExtend>True </AutoExtend>
        <Increment UNIT="MB">16</Increment>
        <Maxsize UNIT="MB">1024</Maxsize>
      </DatafileAttributes>
    </DatafilesList>
  </TablespaceAttributes>
<!-- End of BIPLATFORM -->
```

One of the common changes that the DBA may want to make to the installation of the tablespace is to turn off the default automatic size increase setting. To do this, you simply need to update the status:

```
<AutoExtend>False</AutoExtend>
```

Schema installations

The main scripts for creating the objects for the BIPlatform are held under the relevant database folder in the `biserver` folder. For example, there are `biserver` scripts to run in DB2:

- `rcuHome\rcu\integration\biserver\scripts\oracle`
- `rcuHome\rcu\integration\biserver\scripts\db2`
- `rcuHome\rcu\integration\biserver\scripts\mssql`

Oracle CREATE USER Script

The CREATE USER script is as follows:

```
CREATE USER &&1 identified by &&2 default tablespace&&3 temporary
tablespace&&4;
   grant resource to &&1;
   grant connect to &&1;
   grant create sequence to &&1;
```

You should update these script files if you need to add extra options, for example, more grants or limitations.

Silent installation

The RCU can be used to create your repositories without any need for the user input. This silent method is normally used when creating downstream environments, such as test, preproduction, production, and disaster recovery. Having a silent installation in your code armory enables speedy and consistent creation of environments.

Another advantage of silent installation is that the Environments team (sometimes known as Change Management) is more likely to accept your project deliveries, and will be able to respond in a timely manner.

The command for silent installation is as follows:

```
rcu-silent <command><options>
```

There are two main commands:

- `createRepository`
- `dropRepository`

To create a repository, you should use the following options (those in the square brackets are optional):

- `[-compInfoXMLLocation<location of ComponentInfo xml file>]`
- `[-storageXMLLocation<location of Storage xml file>]`
- `[-databaseType<database type - [ORACLE|SQLSERVER|IBMDB2]>]`
- `-connectString`
- `Oracle Database: host:port:service`
- `SQLServer and IBM DB2 Database: Server name/ host:port:databaseName`

- -dbUser<database username>

- [-dbRole<database role>]

- [-unicodeSupport< Yes | No This is applicable only for database type - SQLSERVER.>]

- [-skipCleanupOnFailure< Yes | No - default is No. This allows user to skip cleanup on failure.]

- [-useSamePasswordForAllSchemaUsers<true | false> - default is false]

- [-selectDependentsForComponents<true | false> - default is false]

- [-variables <comma separated variables in variablename=value format. Should be specified before the components>]

- [-schemaPrefix<prefix to be used for the schema. This is optional for non-prefixable components.>]

- -component <component name>

- -tablespace<tablespace name for the component.Tablespace should already exist if this option is used.>

- -tempTablespace<temp tablespace name for the component. Temp Tablespace should already exist if this option is used.>

To drop a repository, you can use the following options (those in square brackets are optional):

- [-compInfoXMLLocation]

- [-storageXMLLocation]

- [-databaseType]

- -connectString

- -dbUser

- [-dbRole]

- [-unicodeSupport]

- [-variables]

- [-schemaPrefix]

- -component <component name>

The variables that the RCU picks up from the environment are as follows:

- - <RCU log location(Default is $ORACLE_HOME/rcu/log/):RCU_LOG_
- - <Creation of timestamped directory (directory name: logdir.
  yyyy-MM-dd_HH-MM format) for RCU logs(Default is true):RCU_
  TIMESTAMP_LOG_DIR>
- - <RCU log name(Default is rcu.log):RCU_LOG_NAME>
- - <RCU log level(Default is ERROR):RCU_LOG_LEVEL - [SEVERE|ERRO
  R|NOTIFICATION|TRACE] >

Example creation

The following Linux code example will create three repositories in a local
Oracle database:

```
/home/oracle/Desktop/rcuHome/bin/rcu -silent
-createRepository
-databaseType ORACLE
-connectString localhost:1521:orcl
-dbUser SYS
-dbRole SYSDBA
-unicodeSupport
-skipCleanupOnFailure No
-useSamePasswordForAllSchemaUsers true
-selectDependentsForComponents true
-variables RCU_LOG_LOCATION=/tmp/rculog/,RCU_TIMESTAMP_LOG_
DIR=true,RCU_LOG_NAME=addi_dev.log,RCU_LOG_LEVEL=TRACE
-schemaPrefix ADDIDEV
-component BIPLATFORM
-component MDS
-component IAU
```

This example will prompt the user for all the required passwords, SYS, and new
schemas. There is also an option for providing the passwords in a file by adding
-f < passwords.txt to the command, as shown in the following code snippet:

```
/home/oracle/Desktop/rcuHome/bin/rcu -silent
-createRepository
-databaseType ORACLE
-connectString localhost:1521:orcl
-dbUser SYS
-dbRole SYSDBA
-unicodeSupport
```

```
-skipCleanupOnFailure No
-useSamePasswordForAllSchemaUsers true
-selectDependentsForComponents true
-variables RCU_LOG_LOCATION=/tmp/rculog/,RCU_TIMESTAMP_LOG_
DIR=true,RCU_LOG_NAME=addi_dev.log,RCU_LOG_LEVEL=TRACE
-schemaPrefix ADDIDEV
-component BIPLATFORM
-component MDS
-component IAU
-f < dev_passwords.txt
```

The `dev_passwords.txt` file needs to hold the passwords in the same order as the components specified, with one per line. For example:

```
sys_database_password
biplatform_password
mds_password
iau_password
```

The file is in clear text format and is not removed automatically after installation, so you may need to delete it after the silent RCU is run successfully.

Useful scripts

The installation includes the creation of tables for usage tracking and scheduling. In case you need to reproduce them, the table creation script for usage tracking is given in the following section. You can also update the SQL files directly in the `scripts` folder.

Usage tracking script

This script file creates the `S_NQ_ACCT` table. You can rename this table to one that is more suited to your environment. I normally call my usage tracking table `W_USAGE_TRACKING` and give it a synonym of `S_NQ_ACCT`:

```
ALTER SESSION SET CURRENT_SCHEMA=&&1;
create table S_NQ_ACCT
(
  USER_NAME VARCHAR2(128),
  REPOSITORY_NAME VARCHAR2(128),
  SUBJECT_AREA_NAME VARCHAR2(128),
  NODE_ID VARCHAR2(15),
  START_TS DATE,
  START_DT DATE,
```

```
    START_HOUR_MIN CHAR(5),
    END_TS DATE,
    END_DT DATE,
    END_HOUR_MIN CHAR(5),
    QUERY_TEXT VARCHAR2(1024),
    QUERY_BLOB CLOB,
    QUERY_KEY VARCHAR2(128),
    SUCCESS_FLG NUMBER(10,0),
    ROW_COUNT NUMBER(10,0),
    TOTAL_TIME_SEC NUMBER(10,0),
    COMPILE_TIME_SEC NUMBER(10,0),
    NUM_DB_QUERY NUMBER(10,0),
    CUM_DB_TIME_SEC NUMBER(10,0),
    CUM_NUM_DB_ROW NUMBER(10,0),
    CACHE_IND_FLG CHAR(1) default 'N' not null,
    QUERY_SRC_CD VARCHAR2(30) default '',
    SAW_SRC_PATH VARCHAR2(250) default '',
    SAW_DASHBOARD VARCHAR2(150) default '',
    SAW_DASHBOARD_PG VARCHAR2(150) default '',
    PRESENTATION_NAME VARCHAR2(128) default '',
    ERROR_TEXT VARCHAR2(250) default '',
    IMPERSONATOR_USER_NAME     VARCHAR2(128) default '',
    NUM_CACHE_INSERTED   NUMBER(10,0) default null,
    NUM_CACHE_HITS               NUMBER(10,0) default null
);

create index S_NQ_ACCT_M1 on S_NQ_ACCT
(START_DT, START_HOUR_MIN, USER_NAME);

create index S_NQ_ACCT_M2 on S_NQ_ACCT
(START_HOUR_MIN, USER_NAME);

create index S_NQ_ACCT_M3 on S_NQ_ACCT
(USER_NAME);
```

A review – what I should now know!

For self review and recap of the chapter, here are a few questions based on the topics covered in this chapter:

1. What is the RCU used for?

2. What is a silent installation?

3. Where does the usage tracking table reside?

4. Is all OBIEE metadata held in a database?

5. How do you configure tablespaces in the RCU?

Summary

Oracle includes the standard repository build method in the Oracle BI 11*g* release. In this chapter, we discussed how to run the installation, in interactive mode. We have also discussed how to customize the installation to suit our project, and how to run it in silent mode.

One component that is useful for installation is the Audit services, which are standard components in the Oracle Fusion Middleware system.

Not all metadata is held in a database form and I expect this may change in future versions but for now MDS and BIPlatform is the minimum you need to install before moving to the next chapter, which will cover the software application installation.

3
Installing on Windows Server 2008

This chapter will serve to provide step-by-step instructions for installing Oracle BI 11*g* (release 11.1.1.6 at the time of writing and it should be consistent with all 11.1.1.x versions) on Windows Server 2008. We've assumed that most readers will have skills around and have access to a Microsoft Windows environment, which is why the Windows operating system was chosen for the book. *Chapter 4, Installation Options* will highlight some advanced installation options and some post-upgrade options that you may find of interest once you've worked through this chapter's first-timer installation. The Oracle Fusion Middleware GUI installation wizard is the default interface for the Oracle BI 11*g* installation and provides a consistent installation experience regardless of the operating system.

This installation will walk you through the Enterprise installation of Oracle BI 11*g*, which is one of the three possible installation options. This installation option will give you the best of all worlds for an Oracle BI 11*g* platform implementation. It will allow you to work/play with all of the features seen in a production Oracle BI 11*g* environment. During this installation of Oracle BI 11*g*, we will make reference to the repository schemas created by the **Repository Creation Utility (RCU)**, which we have discussed in *Chapter 2, Installing the Metadata Repository*.

So let's get started!

Installation media

For both 32-bit and 64-bit operating system versions, there are five files that you need to download from the Oracle website.

The screenshots following the installation which you'll see in this chapter are from a 64-bit Windows Server 2008 installation. The exercises in this book are applied to work on both 32-bit and 64-bit kernels. If you are using a 64-bit server, download the files from the Windows x86-64 option.

Download the five installation files either from the **Oracle Technology Network (OTN)** at `http://www.oracle.com/technetwork/middleware/bi-enterprise-edition/downloads/index.html` or on the Oracle Delivery Cloud at `http://edelivery.oracle.com`. You will have to log in to these sites to download the files from either location, but the software is free to be used for education or development purposes. The following screenshot shows the files ready for download from the OTN:

Once you have downloaded these files, unzip them to a temporary location on your server, using the Windows native zip utility or a utility like 7zip File Manager (`http://7zip.org`). Oracle also recommends using 7zip File Manager to compress and decompress Oracle BI related artifacts when migrating between environments.

Make sure you have enough space to store the downloaded files. Also make sure that your system meets the minimum disk space requirements for the installation as follows:

- Total size of ZIP files: 5.42 GB
- Total size of unzipped files: 5.47 GB
- Recommended free disk space: 20 GB

This is mentioned because if you attempt to perform this installation on Amazon's EC2 service, you are allocated 30 GB of space initially. You will have to add a second disk if you want to install all the components (database/RCU and OBIEE) on a single machine.

Unzip each downloaded ZIP file one at a time, starting with the downloaded Disk 1 ZIP file. Extract the ZIP files into the root location of the temporary directory where the ZIP files are stored. You may be prompted to overwrite some files for each subsequent disk extracted. Be sure to accept the overwrite prompt.

Do not unzip each downloaded ZIP file into its own directory as the goal is to have the extracted files built upon themselves and to create a single directory called `bishiphome`.

Ultimately, you'll have five sub-directories labeled **Disk1** through **Disk5** underneath **bishiphome**. The following screenshot shows the resulting **Disk1** folder inside of the **bishiphome** folder created during the manual ZIP extraction process. **Disk1** houses the `setup.exe` file that will launch the installation process:

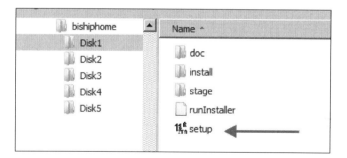

System requirements

For a complete list of system requirements such as hardware, software, operating systems, and so on refer to the guide available at `http://www.oracle.com/technology/software/products/ias/files/fusion_requirements.htm`.

That page links to the most up-to-date requirements and certifications documents.

Here's a quick checklist of items before you get started installing and configuring Oracle BI 11*g*:

- Ensure that the RCU has been run and you have the connection information at the BIPlatform and MDS schemas. If needed, refer to *Chapter 2, Installing the Metadata Repository* to recap the importance of the RCU installation.
- Ensure that the database, where you ran the RCU, is running.
- Verify that the _JAVA_OPTIONS environment variable is not set.
- This variable should not be set. If this is a fresh server created for this installation, it won't be set. If you are unsure, or if it is set, refer to the documentation available at http://docs.oracle.com/cd/E21764_01/bi.1111/e10539/c4_installing.htm#CEGHHFDD.
- This environment variable is set during the installation and ultimately used to manage the Java JVM heap size and other settings used by the WebLogic Server at runtime.
- Ensure that you have sufficient privileges to install the software.
- You should potentially have the ability to right-click on the install executable to use the **Run** option as the Administrator option to conduct the installation.
- It is recommended to use a local user within the Administrator's group to conduct the installation. Do not use a service account or network account.
- Check whether your machine is using DHCP or it has a static IP address.
- The instructions in this chapter are for a static IP. If you are using DHCP and have the Oracle database running on the same server, you'll need to install a Loopback Adapter. For instructions on installing the Loopback Adapter, refer to the document available at http://technet.microsoft.com/en-us/library/cc708322(WS.10).aspx.

Network gotcha

In our experience, one of the most common issues with installing a self-contained Oracle BI 11*g* environment (that is, database and OBIEE are co-existing) on a Windows operating system seems to come from one simple thing—forgetting to install the Loopback Adapter. This will present itself in the configuration phase of the installation, typically on the CreateASInstance (step 13) phase. Avoid this by configuring the Loopback Adapter as per the instructions given in the document available at http://docs.oracle.com/cd/B19306_01/install.102/b14316/reqs.htm#BABGCEAI.

However, for advanced users, there is the potential to use the hosts file on the server which is located at C:\Windows\System32\drivers\etc\hosts.

Installation

Now that you've got the prerequisites quickly out of the way, you are ready to begin the core installation of Oracle BI 11*g*:

1. In the `<temp directory>\bishiphome\Disk1` directory, where you are conducting your unzip operation, you'll find a file called `setup.exe`.

2. Double-click on that file.

3. If you have **Windows User Access Control (UAC)** turned on, you'll be greeted with the following screenshot:

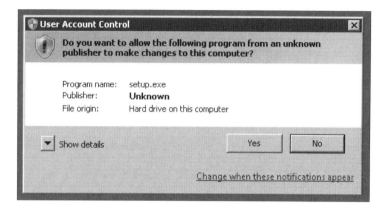

4. Click on **Yes**.

5. You'll then be greeted with a pop-up command shell. It performs some basic system checks:

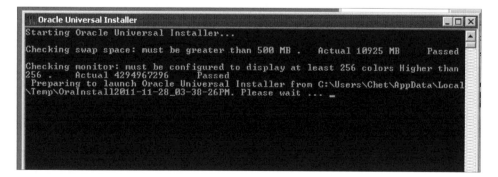

6. After a few seconds, the initial installation **Welcome** page appears. After you read it, click on the **Next** button:

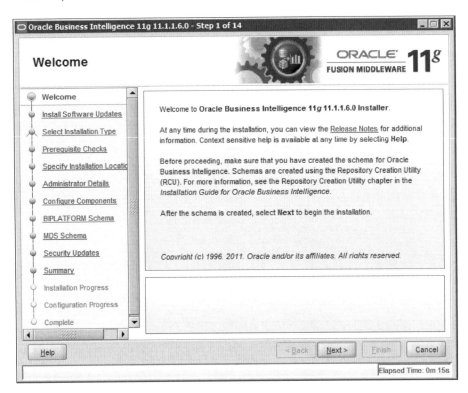

7. For this exercise, we will select **Skip Software Updates**.

8. You can sign up with your **My Oracle Support (MOS)** account and receive updates if you want. Optionally, you can download any patches to the disk and install them from there (you can select the **Search Local Directory for Updates** option).

9. If you choose to skip the software updates, you will be greeted with a pop up asking **Are you sure?**. Select **OK** and click on **Next**:

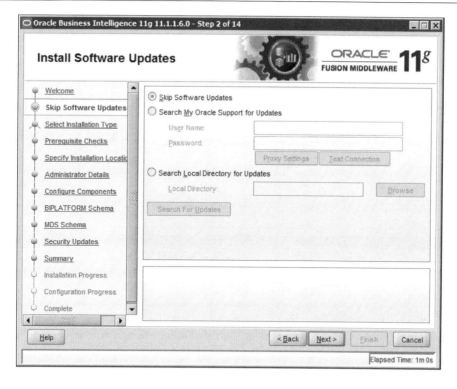

10. There are three types of installation scenarios:

    ° **Simple Install**: This option Installs the most basic components. This allows you to install OBIEE on a single computer as a single node. It is great for a sandbox type environment. This option does not allow for scaling out your Oracle BI 11*g* environment.

    ° **Enterprise Install**: This is the installation type we will be using in this book's installation walkthrough. As the name implies, this is for enterprise use, which means you can create a new enterprise deployment or scale out an existing deployment.

    ° **Software Only Install**: This installs all the binaries for OBIEE. Then, you can use the configuration wizard which gets installed along with the OBIEE binaries post-install to set up your instance.

In Oracle BI 11*g*, **Simple Install** and **Enterprise Install** options conduct the installation of the OBIEE binaries and the configuration of the Oracle BI 11*g* instance, including installation of the WebLogic Server, in the single installation session. When choosing the **Software Only Install** option, you must first have downloaded separately and installed a clean **WebLogic Server (WLS)** instance on the same server you intend to install Oracle BI 11*g*. The WLS then acts as the Fusion Middleware home into which Oracle BI 11*g* gets installed.

11. Select **Enterprise Install** and click on the **Next** button:

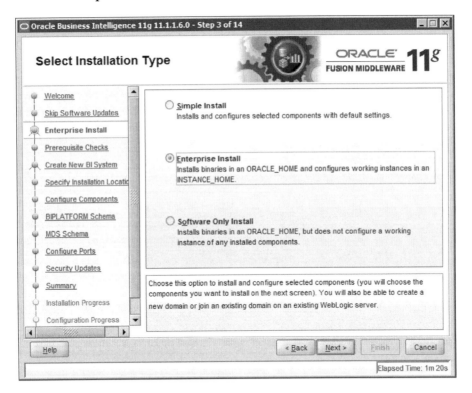

12. In the next screen, **Prerequisite Checks**, the installation wizard ensures that your operating system is certified and that you have enough physical memory. On a Linux installation, it checks to make sure you have the correct libraries and kernel parameters set.

13. Once it completes, click on the **Next** button:

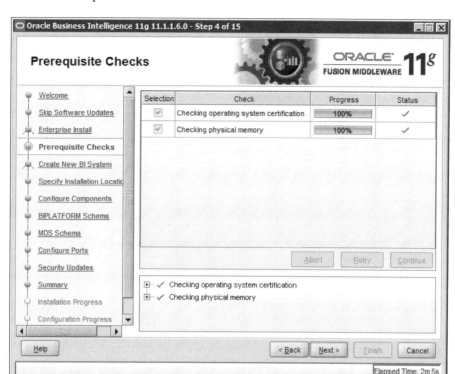

14. After the checks have been performed, you are prompted to **Create New BI System** or **Scale Out BI System**.

15. Select the **Create New BI System** option to continue.

16. In the **User Password** field, enter a password that is easy to remember, for example, Welcome1. The default **User Name** should remain the default, **weblogic**, as this has become a best practice for installing Oracle BI 11*g*. You can remove this user or create a different administrative user for the WebLogic Server after the installation, if you desire. Although, removing the user completely for a demo or sandbox environment is not recommended.

17. Re-enter the password in the **Confirm Password** field and then click on the **Next** button:

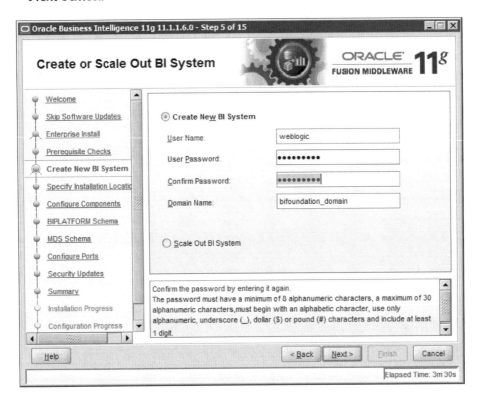

18. The **Specify Installation Location** page of the wizard seeks for you to define the Fusion Middleware home for the Oracle BI 11*g* installation. This is where all Oracle BI 11*g* and common files related to the WebLogic Server will reside.

19. Create a directory named `c:\obiee` and the wizard will install into it. You may choose to create a folder close to the root of your hard drive such as `c:\Oracle` or something similar. Whatever directory name you create just be sure to use underscores instead of spaces in the path name as that may cause issues down the road. We commonly see installations using a path such as `D:\Oracle\FMW\`.

20. Enter the path you've created (for example, `c:\obiee`) in the **Oracle Middleware Home Location** field. You will see the other location fields below it changing accordingly to reflect the base **Oracle Middleware Home Location**.

21. Leave the **Oracle Instance Name** field as it is, by default it is filled with **instance1**. The instance name will become apparent in advanced configurations such as scaling out an Oracle BI 11*g* architecture. Subsequently, scaled-out Oracle BI 11*g* instances are incremented by a value of one. In addition, when integrating other Fusion Middleware softwares such as Oracle HTTP Server with your implementation, its instance name also gets incremented. For example, if scaling out your Oracle BI 11*g* implementation to three separate servers, the last server added to the cluster would be **instance3**.

22. Click on the **Next** button:

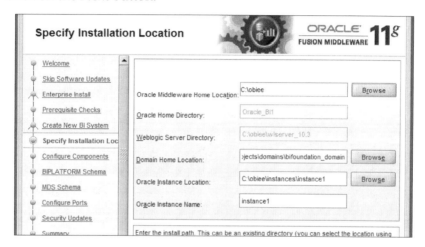

23. It is not recommended to install Oracle BI 11*g* on to a FAT filesystem. Most likely, your server is set up for NTFS, which is recommended. When attempting to install on a FAT filesystem, you will receive the error message after setting the installation location, carried out in the preceding step. If you get the warning message, as shown in the following screenshot, click on the **Yes** button to continue with the installation. Doing so will not harm or cause any issue with the installation:

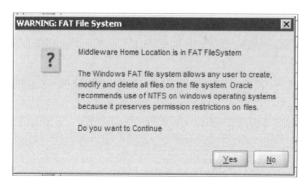

If you would like to read more about these differences between a FAT and NTFS filesystem, check out the document available at `http://www.ntfs.com/ntfs_vs_fat.htm`.

24. On the next step in the wizard, you get to select the components to be included in your implementation. We will not cover the **Real-Time Decisions** application component as it is beyond the scope of this book. It is a new integration to OBIEE which currently does not have a seamless integration path. Deselect it, as shown in the following screenshot. Click on the **Next** button to continue:

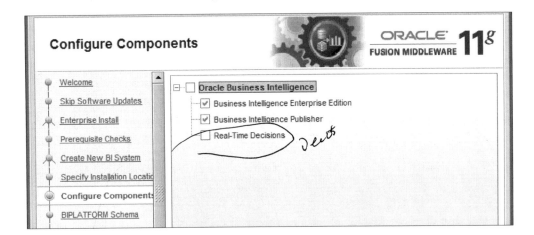

 The other configure component options are linked. That is to say that selecting the option **Business Intelligence Enterprise Edition** automatically selects the option for **Business Intelligence Publisher**. However, you can potentially install **Business Intelligence Publisher** without installing **Business Intelligence Enterprise Edition**.

25. In the next two screens, **BIPLATFORM Schema** and **MDS Schema**, enter the usernames and passwords used during the creation of the repositories in *Chapter 2, Installing the Metadata Repository*.

26. Enter the following information in the **BIPLATFORM Schema** step:

    ○ **Database Type**: **Oracle Database**

    ○ **Connect String**: Insert the value as <server>:<port>:<SID>

For example, **localhost:1521:oraone**

- ○ **BIPLATFORM Schema Username**: DEV_BIPLATFORM
- ○ **BIPLATFORM Schema Password**: Type the password created in *Chapter 2, Installing the Metadata Repository*

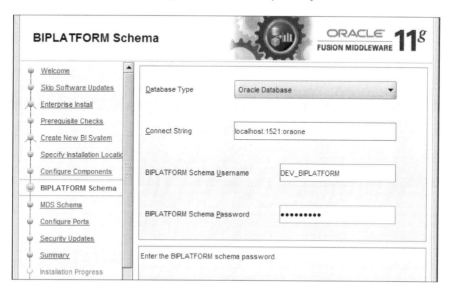

27. Click on the **Next** button to proceed to the **MDS Schema** step.

28. The values are carried over from the previous screen, including the username with MDS in place of BIPLATFORM.

29. Click on the **Next** button to continue:

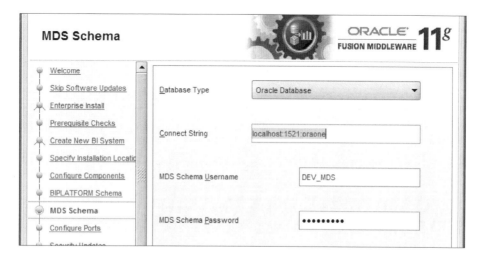

30. If you want to customize your ports, you can do so in the **Confiure Ports** step, as shown in the following screenshot. This is an advanced implementation option that we'll discuss in *Chapter 4, Installation Options*. This exercise will use the default ports.

31. Click on the **Next** button:

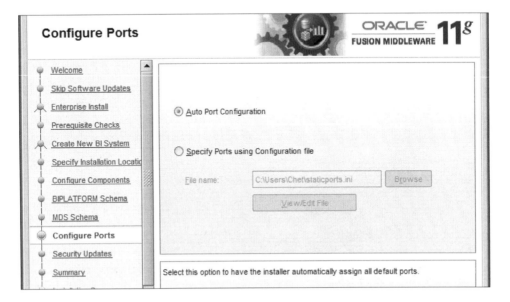

32. After clicking on the **Next** button, the Windows Firewall (if turned on) will prompt you to allow access to the Java platform.

33. Click on the **Allow access** button, if prompted:

 If the Windows Firewall is turned on, the Oracle BI 11*g* installation/configuration process will prompt several more times. So, it is recommended to stand by and monitor the installation while the process is running.

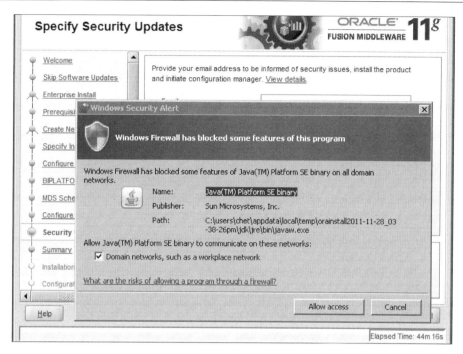

34. On the **Specify Security Updates** page, uncheck the **I wish to receive security updates via My Oracle Support** checkbox. For testing/sandbox purpose skipping, this is absolutely fine. However, you may wish to receive updates for a production environment, in that case you will need to fill in the relevant information:

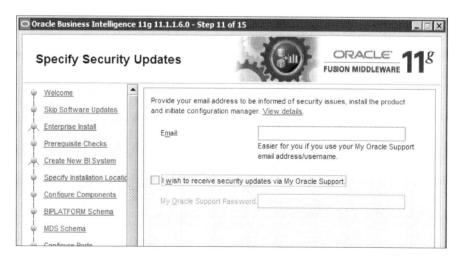

35. Click on the **Next** button to continue.

36. If you unchecked the box to receive security updates, you will be prompted for the certainty of your selection:

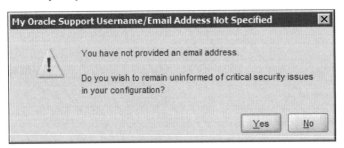

37. Click on the **Yes** button to continue with the installation wizard.

38. Finally, you will be presented with the **Summary** page:

 This will enlist the components that you have chosen in the preceding steps along with the components that will be configured. If you would like to save this for reviewing later, you can do so using the **Save** button. However, this is usually not necessary. Saving this file puts you in the position to have your chosen installation and configuration options populated automatically in the subsequent environments by incorporating them with the silent installer command-line option for Oracle BI 11*g*.

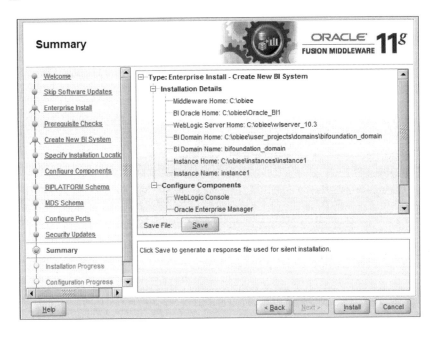

39. Once you are satisfied with the review, click on the **Install** button to begin the installation/configuration process.

40. The following screenshot shows the **Installation Progress** page. This is different from the **Configuration Progress** step, which is the subsequent step that the installation wizard will execute. The **Installation Progress** page indicates the progress of the installation of the binaries with output to the screen, showing exactly which actions are being performed:

41. The installation wizard will automatically switch from installing the necessary Oracle BI 11*g* binaries to configuring the system based on the options you've chosen in the wizard.

42. If the configuration is successful, the **Abort, Retry**, and **Continue** buttons will be inactive and the **Next** button will become active:

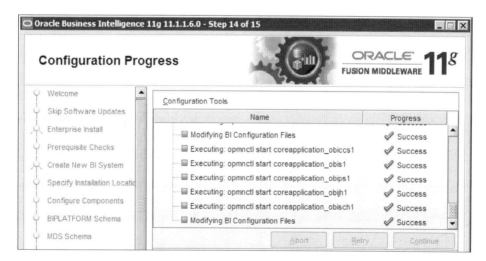

43. Click on the **Next** button to reach the **Complete** step in the wizard.

44. Similar to the **Summary** page of the installation wizard, on the **Complete** page, you will be presented with the details of the installation and configuration process. Here you also have the option of saving these details to a file by clicking on the **Save** button. Once you are satisfied with the review, click on the **Finish** button:

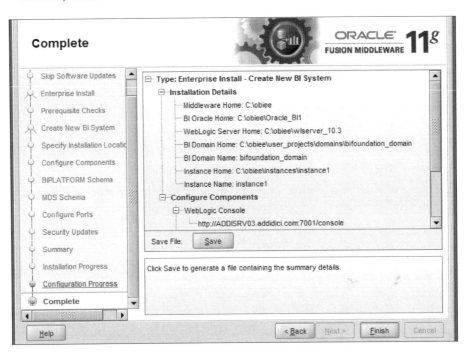

45. After clicking on the **Finish** button, the installation setup wizard will close and your default browser will open up and attempt to render the Oracle BI 11*g* **Sign In** page, as shown in the following screenshot. In many circumstances, the Oracle BI Presentation services component that controls the dashboards and reporting portal is still starting up in the background, even though the web page attempts to open in the browser. This premature launch will cause the web browser to show an error page. Waiting a few extra minutes and refreshing the browser should produce the login page after the component has fully started:

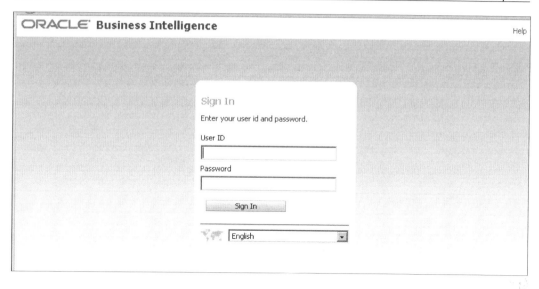

46. Reaching the **Sign In** page clearly indicates that the installation was a success.

A review – what I should now know!

For self review and recap of the chapter, here are a few questions based on important topics covered in this chapter:

1. Which folder under the `bishiphome` directory, created by the ZIP files extraction process, contains the `setup.exe` file?

2. How many installation options are available for Oracle BI 11*g*? What are they? And how does each one differ?

3. What is a Loopback Adapter?

Summary

In this chapter, we conducted an Enterprise Install of Oracle BI 11*g* on Windows Server 2008 after downloading the files from the Oracle website. During the installation, we were able to view several installation options and the many configuration points that potentially make Oracle BI 11*g* a highly configurable enterprise application suite. As we conducted the exercise in this chapter, we were also able to view several tips and notes about installing Oracle BI 11*g* and where special attention should be paid.

This chapter gave a very straightforward step-by-step instruction on how to get your sandbox environment up and running in order to complete the main exercises in this book.

In the next chapter, we will discuss several other installation options that are essential to be aware of when working to establish an Oracle BI 11*g* environment on another operating system such as Linux. We'll also learn how to automate the start-up/shut down of the Oracle BI 11*g* environment and other advanced configuration topics such as **high availability (HA)**, scaling out environments, using port 80, and conducting silent installations.

4
Installation Options

In the previous chapter, the steps for installing Oracle BI 11*g* on a Windows Server 2008 operating system were highlighted. The Enterprise Install option was used. This installation gives you a fully functioning Oracle BI 11*g* foundation to work and develop with. The installation conducted in *Chapter 3*, *Installing on Windows Server 2008*, is perfect for a sandbox or a development environment. Several other advanced configuration options and many production environment considerations may be made using the Software Only Install option. These additional installation and environment configuration options are what we will cover in this chapter.

We will discuss how to configure several of these options, step-by-step, while some of the more advanced options will be discussed at a high-level. Ultimately, the idea in this chapter is for you to be well informed about the capabilities of setting up a production-ready Oracle BI 11*g* environment.

Oracle BI on its own server

For most implementations, Oracle Business Intelligence will run on its own physical or virtual server. That is to say that no other enterprise application suite(suites) would run on the same machine competing for server resources. Often the term "BI Server" or "BI Box" is used as a moniker for this server. In a high availability or failover architecture, the number of servers is multiplied in order to handle the on slaught of consumption that is anticipated.

Each server is a node in a cluster of servers. Each node gets classified as an instance of Oracle BI. Typically, each Oracle BI instance will run on a physical server in production (plausibly in test or **quality assurance (QA)** environments as well) but usually on a virtual machine in a development or sandbox environment.

In a distributed server environment, the application tier (WebLogic Server) where the Oracle BI server and its many Java-based components run are on one server and the web (HTTP) tier (Oracle HTTP Server, IIS, or Apache) are on a separate server per each environment (that is, test, production, and so on). Of course, the database server should be on a separate machine as well. A distributed server environment is just one of the architectural prerequisites to configure Oracle BI 11*g* in a high availability architecture, which we will cover briefly in the next section.

Before installing Oracle BI, we recommend that you should first understand the architectural needs of the implementation. If you require a single Oracle BI instance per each environment, there isn't much to worry about the way it is installed. The instructions provided in *Chapter 3, Installing on Windows Server 2008*, will suit you well. However, if failover, high-availability, or vertical scaling (increasing the nodes on a single machine) is needed, you will need to make several environment architecture calls as part of an installation planning process.

High availability and failover planning

Getting any enterprise environment to **high availability (HA)** is an advanced process. It requires several technical components involving both hardware and software. The hardware components are classified under server hardware, load balancers, and firewall. The software components are classified as database, application tier, web tier, **identity store (LDAP)**, and shared storage via SAN/NAS.

One important part which is most commonly missed while setting up an Oracle BI 11*g* HA environment is the preconfiguration process. This is where a network administrator is required to set up shared storage locations on a NAS/SAN and configure the web tier and the load balancer (that is, virtual servers, virtual IPs, and DNS). The network administrator, during this process, sets up the correct shared storage locations and mapped paths/mounts, which are critical for installing Fusion Middleware into an HA environment. If it is not conducted correctly, the failover effect being sought may not function properly. The preconfiguration steps are detailed in the Oracle BI **Enterprise Deployment Guide (EDG)** document at `http://www.obi11gbook.com/u/2`.

Oracle provides the EDG which illustrates a basic HA environment topology. This document also highlights the additional installation and configuration processes so that your organization can leverage the best practices and recommended setup for Oracle BI HA. Attempting to create an HA environment for Oracle BI without following these instructions is not recommended. The complete Oracle BI EDG can be found at `http://www.obi11gbook.com/u/3`.

Simple versus Software Only Installation

In *Chapter 3*, *Installing on Windows Server 2008*, we used the Enterprise Install option and briefly talked about the other two available installation options—Simple Install and Software Only Install. There are a few more details we'd like to share for your understanding on when and why you'd want to use either of these options.

Software Only Install

It is important to state that during the execution of the Simple Install and Enterprise Install options, the installation of the necessary Oracle BI and Fusion Middleware (that is, WebLogic) binaries and the configuration is conducted in a single process. The Software Only Install option is quite different and considered the more advanced installation option. The Software Only Install option breaks up the installation and configuration process due to the extra flexibility that this option provides.

The primary reasons to use the Software Only installation are as follows:

- For configuring a high availability environment
- Using a separate Java Development Kit version than what is delivered out of the box
- Gaining better control of the installation process
- Deploying Oracle BI 11g into an existing WLS environment (for example, Hyperion)
- Potentially leveraging some functionality, which is not included with the other installation types such as the Paste Binary option.

Installing your own JDK

Fusion Middleware runs on Java. Not all Java engines are created equally though they succeed in a common goal. There are several different Java, **Java Virtual Machine (JVM)**, and **Java Development Kit (JDK)** vendors. Sun Microsystems was the first but other JVM and JDK branches, most notably OpenJDK, HotSpot, and JRockit now exist.

JRockit seems to be the Oracle BI architects' favorite due to a GUI interface that comes with a JVM monitoring and performance tool—Mission Control. The WebLogic Server can be configured to use the JDK of your choice but it should be done at the initial installation for which you will need to run the Software Only Install option.

The JDK desired to use on your environment must match the bit architecture of the system on which you are installing, as Oracle BI does not support it. For example, a 32 bit JDK will not work on a 64 bit machine and vice versa.

Simple Install

This install type is the shortest path for getting an Oracle BI 11*g* environment ready to use. However, with this speedy type of installation, there are both positives and negatives that come with it. Here is a short list of pros and cons in no particular order:

- It is good for a sandbox or quick development environment, not for production.
- It is combined with the WLS Administration Server, so all requests to the analytics application are directed to the same port. There is no separate Managed Server, all applications are deployed to the same server as the WebLogic Administration Console and Enterprise Manager which is not a best practice.
- All general functionality of the tool exists including BI Publisher, Delivers, and so on.
- It cannot be scaled out (horizontally or vertically) and is limited to a standalone instance.

Ultimately, if any of the cons listed here go against the implementation you seek, then you would need to use a different installation type. We find it best to use the Simple Install option only for sandbox or demonstration environment efforts.

Silent installation

Just like the RCU installation, there is a silent installation component that can be used in Oracle BI 11*g*. This option is great for streamlining installations or when attempting to simplify a production control change management process. There you are required to hand-off an installation process and/or document to a change management team who then would commence with the installation without your involvement. This idea may seem difficult and unfamiliar at first.

The easiest way to create a silent installation script is to start the Oracle BI 11*g* installation wizard, setting the necessary configuration options and preferences as if conducting the installation for real. But on the last step in the installation wizard, **Installation and Configuration Summary**, click on the **Save** button to create a `response` file. Once the `response` file is saved to a location that can be assessed later, with a name that marks the occasion, you can exit the installation wizard without actually completing the installation. This `response` file can then be used against the installation wizard command-line executable and scripted into a batch file located in the `Disk1` folder of the extracted installation files, `\bishiphome\Disk1\`. For example, `runInstaller –silent –response C:\downloads\obi11gResponseFile.txt`.

The deinstallation process can be conducted in a similar fashion using the silent method. For more information on the silent install method, please refer to the Oracle documentation at `http://www.obi11gbook.com/u/4`.

Custom static ports

Fusion Middleware products are riddled with configuration preference options and perhaps that is what makes these tools so great. Another option that is available to you during the Oracle BI installation process is the ability to modify default ports that are assigned to Oracle BI and Fusion Middleware for accessing their applications. For example, if you want to change the default port for Oracle BI Presentation services, from 9704 to 8000, you can do that at the **Configure Ports** step in the installation wizard, as shown in the following screenshot:

In *Chapter 3, Installing on Windows Server 2008,* we glossed over this step by clicking on the **Next** button and the default options were used. It is highly recommended to stick with the default options whenever possible.

Keeping with the default options should be rather easy as most Oracle BI implementations should be the single Oracle BI tenant on the server on which it is installed. Therefore, there should be no port conflicts. If you want to change the port for the Oracle BI analytics application to port 80, which is the default web port that requires no port number to be entered for the URL, in the browser address bar, then you shouldn't use this option but rather you should use a web tier server to handle that proxy for you.

Compatible web tier servers or Oracle BI 11*g* are IIS, Apache, or the Oracle HTTP server. Configuring IIS as the web tier is discussed later in this chapter. However, if it is an absolute must for you to modify the ports of the WLS or Oracle BI components, then you may do so at this step in the wizard. In order to do so you'll need to:

- Obtain a copy of an example `saticports.ini` file
- Configure the `staticports.ini` file to represent the port numbers for the Oracle BI or Fusion Middleware applications, whose ports will be changed
- Reference the file in the **Specify Ports using Configuration file** text field

These steps are discussed in detail in the next sections.

Creating your own staticports.ini file

You can borrow the configuration file from the example ports and make it your own by conducting the following steps. This section merely provides a reference instruction for a future installation of Oracle BI 11*g* that you might conduct and is not necessary for the remainder of the exercises in this book:

1. From the `/bishiphome/Disk1` directory where you launched the Oracle BI 11*g* installation process, locate the `/stage/response` directory.
2. Copy the `staticports.ini` file and paste it in a location on the same server machine, for example `C:\Temp\`.
3. This file contains all of the default values that are leveraged in a general installation.
4. Open the copied `staticports.ini` file using a text editor such as WordPad in Windows or VI in *Nix.

5. Uncomment the line under the application section header corresponding to the application or component listen port that you desire to change. Uncomment the line by removing the hash symbol (#) in front of the line in the question.

6. For example, to change the default WebLogic Administration Server listen port from 7001 to 7005, modify the line under the `[WEBLOGIC]` header labeled as `#Domain Port No = 7001` and change it to `Domain Port No = 7005`:

```
[WEBLOGIC]

#The Domain port no. This is the listen port of Weblogic
Adminserver for the domain.
Domain Port No = 7005

#The "content" port for the BIEE apps. This is the Weblogic
Managed Server port on which BIEE applications are deployed.
#Oracle WLS BIEE Managed Server Port No = 9704
```

7. Save the file.

8. Now, after running the Oracle BI 11*g* installation wizard, when you reach the **Configure Ports** step, select the option to **Specify Ports using Configuration file**.

9. Click on the **Browse...** button and locate your modified `staticports.ini` file.

10. Click on the **Next** button and continue with the installation wizard.

After the installation completes, the listen ports that you've modified will be in effect. The three most common listen ports modified using the `staticports.ini` file are the WebLogic Server, WebLogic BIEE Managed Server, and the Essbase Agent. It is recommended not to modify any listen ports unless you are very knowledgeable about the WebLogic and Oracle BI infrastructure and/or have a really good reason for doing so.

 More information about configuring static ports can be found at `http://www.obi11gbook.com/u/5`.

Installing Oracle BI 11*g* on *Nix

One of the obvious options for installing Oracle BI 11*g* is the choice of operating system. *Chapter 3, Installing on Windows Server 2008*, did a fair job of showing the installation of Oracle BI 11*g* on Windows Server 2008. However, on a *Nix (that is, Unix, Linux, and so on) operating system, there are few differences—if any.

On a *Nix environment, you may or may not have the option to log on to the server allocated for the Oracle BI environment. In which case, the *Nix administrator must provide SSH access with display/xhosts options or VNCServer access. This will enable you to use a tool such as Putty or TightVNC to access the GUI-only Oracle BI 11*g* installation wizard. Once you are able to launch the GUI installation wizard for Oracle BI, the installation steps in Linux will be the same as those mentioned in *Chapter 3, Installing on Windows Server 2008*.

This book does not go into extra detail to cover a *Nix OS installation as that would be mainly redundant. However, to provide you with some more insight, we would like to make sure that you know about a Linux-based **Virtual Machine** (**VM**) image that was produced by the Oracle BI Development team with the release of Oracle BI 11*g* (version 11.1.1.5). This VirtualBox-based VM image comes with the complete Oracle BI 11*g* Sample Application and contains all of the necessary environment variables, and so on for a basic Oracle BI 11*g* Linux implementation. The Sample Application is crucial for anyone who wishes to see best practices on reports, dashboards, and the RPD. However, it is not a step-by-step learning resource like this book. The Sample Application may help those who are unfamiliar with a Linux environment. They can begin understanding basic Linux principles in the context of Oracle BI. This could be valuable if you are familiar only with a Windows OS environment and ready to conduct an installation of Oracle BI 11*g* on a *Nix-based OS.

> Information about the Oracle BI 11*g* Sample Application is found at `http://www.obi11gbook.com/u/6`.

Listening on port 80

In the preceding section where we discussed how to create your own static ports, we also discussed the potential for users to access the Oracle BI 11*g* application by entering a URL into the address bar without a port number. So instead of `http://myserver.com:9704/analytics`, you can use `http://myserver.com/analytics`. This configuration is achievable by incorporating what is known as a web (HTTP) tier proxy. In most architectures, the web tier that handles all of the HTTP traffic and the application tier that handles all of the dynamic rendering, database access, and so on, are separated.

Although, usually this is done by means of separate physical servers, it can also be achieved on the same physical server, as long as the server is robust enough to handle the added resource needs of the web tier server.

The web/HTTP servers that are compatible with Oracle BI 11*g* are **Microsoft Internet Information Services (IIS)**, **Oracle HTTP Server (OHS)**, and **Apache Web Server**. OHS is merely a more robust implementation of the open source Apache Web Server solution. Each of these Web Servers can integrate on a Windows operating system but only OHS and Apache can be integrated on a Unix/Linux operating system.

We have already discussed how Oracle WebLogic Server is a robust application server. Although it can definitely handle incoming HTTP traffic like a champ, it does not have all of the features of an HTTP server such as IIS or Apache. One of the nicest features about a web server is that it can compress and cache both static files and dynamic requests from the application server in order to speed up the response time when a user requests information from the server. For Oracle BI, this means that a user's dashboards will render faster in their browser, as well as with any queries they may submit.

Not all client web browsers are created equally. Specifically, **Microsoft Internet Explorer (MSIE)** versions 7 and 8 have a hiccup that causes pages to render slower on them when benchmarked against other web browsers, such as Mozilla Firefox or Google Chrome. This issue potentially affects your Oracle BI 11*g* implementation especially if an organization uses MSIE as the corporate web browser standard.

We can fix this issue by putting a web tier in front of our application tier. It will increase the speed of Oracle BI 11*g* not only in Internet Explorer, but also in other browsers and consumption devices, such as mobile tablets as well. As we are using a Microsoft Windows 2008 Server in this book as our core operating system for the exercise, you will learn how to set up this web tier compression configuration using IIS.

In order to complete any of the other exercises in this book, you do not need to conduct this web tier exercise right now. Here, it is merely a reference and considered as an advanced implementation configuration which should actually take place after your Oracle BI solution has been developed, or in a separate web tier server.

Ensuring IIS web server Role Services are installed

IIS must be installed and available as an option on the Windows Server 2008 machine in order to leverage it as the proxy for port 80.

1. Open **Server Manager** and click on the **Roles** option.

2. Ensure that web services (IIS) are available, installed, and operational.

3. There are several Role Services that belong to IIS. Role Services also need to be installed in addition to the IIS web server. In addition to the Role Services selected by default when IIS is installed, the following Role Services must also be selected:

   ° HTTP Redirection

   ° CGI, ISAPI Extensions

   ° ISAPI Filters

   ° Static Content Compression

   ° Dynamic Content Compression

4. The preceding Role Services are shown in the following illustration:

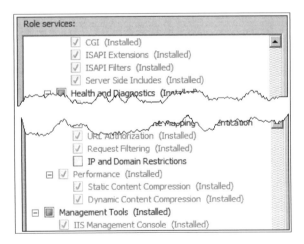

5. Include and install these Role Services. You will need to restart the server, if necessary.

Getting the WebLogic Server Proxy IIS plugins

When WebLogic Server is installed during the Oracle BI installation process, many binaries are installed, which support its interface with other applications. One of these binary file sets is for integration with IIS. Let's locate and copy them to a new folder in order to use them:

1. Create a new folder called **IISPlugins** on the same drive or mount at the root where you have installed Oracle BI 11*g*. For example, D:\IISPlugins.

2. Set this folder to have loose permissions for read and execute operations. Typically, the user running IIS (IIS User) will be conducting the proxy via IIS to that folder.

3. Navigate to the Fusion Middleware Home directory that you declared during your Oracle BI 11*g* installation and locate the folder <FMW_HOME>\ wlserver_10.3\server\plugin\win\x64. For example, D:\Oracle\FMW\ wlserver_10.3\server\plugin\win\x64\.

> If you are running a 32-bit version of Windows Server 2008 then select the folder labeled 32 instead of x64. During the testing of this configuration, we found that only the x64 folder items worked in a 64-bit environment.

4. Copy the contents of the binary specific folder selected and paste them into the IISPlugins folder, which you created in Step 1, for example, D:\IISPlugins\.

5. Next, you need to create a configuration file that the IIS plugin binaries you copied will use as a reference. Open Notepad or another text editor, create a new file, and enter the following information replacing the <server_name> value with the name of the server where the Oracle BI 11*g* application resides:

```
WebLogicHost=<server_name>
WebLogicPort=9704
ConnectRetrySecs=5
WlForwardPath=/
```

6. Save the file as `iisProxy.ini`. The file extension `.ini` is mandatory and is differentiated by an icon with a gear in it when viewed in Windows Explorer, as shown in the following screenshot:

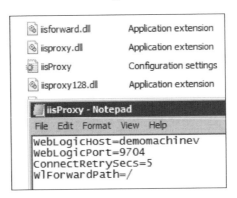

Creating and configuring an IIS Website

In the preceding section we discussed how to get the base files in place for the WLS proxy. Now the configuration within IIS itself begins. In this section, you will create a new IIS website, stop the old one, configure several handlers, and map to the proxy binaries provided by WLS:

1. Open **IIS Manager** by navigating to **Start | Administration Tools | IIS Manager**.

2. Create a new website by expanding the machine node and clicking on the **Add Web Site...** option.

3. Name the new site as **OBI11gAnalytics**, or something relevant to your implementation, in the **Site name** field.

4. Enter the path of the **IISPlugins** folder for the **Physical Path** field under the **Content Directory** section.

5. In the **Host name** field, enter the name of your server. Here, it is ideal to enter a short name for the server (that is, without a domain suffix) first, and enter the full domain name of the server later, using the **Edit Bindings...** option in the **Web Site Properties** pane:

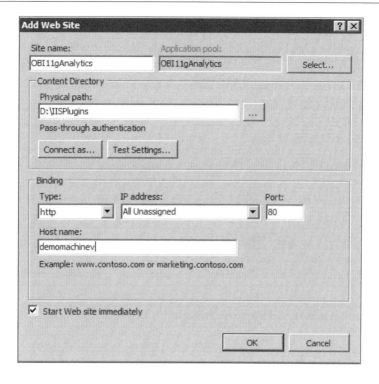

6. Now, you must stop the existing **Default Web Site** once your website is created. Right-click on **Default Web Site** and click on **Manage Web Site | Stop**.

7. Click on the new website that you've created, and then in the middle pane, double-click on the **Handler Mappings** icon.

8. Select the entry named **StaticFile** from the list and edit this entry by changing the **Request Path** value from * to *.*.

9. Click on **OK** to close the **Edit Module Mapping** prompt for **StaticFile**.

10. While still in the **Handler Mappings** area, click on the **Add Script Map...** option, which is under the **Actions** header in the right-hand side pane of the **IIS Manager**.

11. In the **Add Script Map** prompt, enter * in the **Request path** field. In the **Executable** field, enter the path to the `iisproxy.dll` file that resides within the **IISPlugins** folder, for example, `D:\IISPlugins\iisproxy.dll`. In the **Name** field, enter **ProxyWLS**.

12. Click on the **Request Restrictions...** button and make sure the **Invoke Handler** checkbox is not checked.

13. Click on the **OK** button twice to close the **Add Script Map** prompt.

14. Click on the **YES** button when prompted to allow the ISAPI extension.

15. Once again, while still in the **Handler Mappings** area, click on the **Add Script Map...**, which is under the **Actions** header in the right-hand side pane of the **IIS Manager**.

16. In the **Add Script Map** prompt, enter the following values, which are also illustrated in the following screenshot:

    ○ **Request path**: ***.wlforward**

    ○ **Executable**: **D:\IISPlugins\iisProxy.dll**

    ○ **Name**: **wlforward**

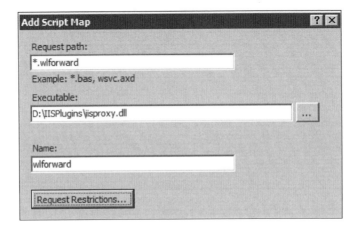

17. Click on the **Request Restrictions...** button and make sure the **Invoke Handler** checkbox is not checked.

18. Click on the **OK** button twice.

19. Click on the **YES** button when prompted to allow the ISAPI extension.

20. Add an ISAPI filter by clicking on the new website you created on the left-hand side pane and then double-clicking on the ISAPI filter's icon from the center pane.

21. Click on **Add...** from underneath the **Actions** header in the right-hand side pane of the **IIS Manager**.

22. In the **Add ISAPI Filter** prompt, enter **wlforward** for the **Filter name** field. Enter the path to the `iisfoward.dll` file residing in the **IISPlugins** folder for the **Executable** field.

23. Click on the **OK** button to create the ISAPI filter.

24. Lastly, modify the ISAPI restrictions globally for the IIS web server by clicking on the web server root (under **Start Page** and above **Application Pools**) in the left-hand side pane of the **IIS Manager**.

25. Double-click on the **ISAPI and CGI Restrictions** icon in the center pane.

26. In the right-hand side pane under the **Actions** header, click on **Edit Feature Settings...**.

27. Check both checkbox options and click on the **OK** button to allow both CGI and ISAPI unspecified module types.

28. Restart the IIS web server to set all changes.

29. Validate the configuration changes you have made by navigating to the analytics application, using the server on port 80 by entering the URL in your browser address bar without a port number, for example, `http://<server_name>/analytics`.

30. Even though you have set your web tier to access the analytics application on port 80, you should still be able to access the application on the default port—9704—if it isn't changed during the installation.

If you are running into issues with the analytics application rendering on port 80 but working on the default port 9704, the culprit is most likely your IIS Application Pool or your `iisProxy.ini` file. Check the IIS Application Pool assigned to the website created by you and ensure that the **Enable 32-bit Application** option is set to **False**, if the IIS Application Pool is running on a 64-bit machine and vice versa. You can set the **Enable 32-bit Application** option to **False** from the **Advanced Settings** of the **Application Pool**.

Also be sure that your `iisProxy.ini` file is indeed an INI file and not a TXT file extension and that the configuration name/value pairs do not have spaces between the equal signs.

Enabling compression in IIS 7.x

Enabling compression on the IIS web server's web tier, comes at the highest recommendation of Oracle. Particularly this configuration solves a problem inherent in the Internet Explorer browsers. However, this compression configuration exponentially optimizes response times for requests sent to the Oracle BI server, and should be conducted in every environment in which you wish to install Oracle BI 11*g*:

1. Open the command prompt on the server where you've been conducting the modifications, specified in the preceding section, to IIS.

2. Change the directory to the location of the core IIS server files, for example:

   `cd C:\Windows\System32\inetsrv`

3. Enter the following text very precisely on the command line and execute. It is recommended to type the syntax in a text editor first to ensure proper spacing and then paste it into the command prompt. Replace `<WebSite_Name>` with the name of the website you've created in IIS:

```
Appcmd.exe set config "<WebSite_Name>" -section:system.webServer/
urlCompression /doDynamicCompression:"True"
```

4. After running the preceding step, a response message should be generated. If it is not, check the syntax of the command you've entered and verify that it is accurate.

5. To set the compression strength settings on IIS, enter the following command:

```
Appcmd.exe set config -section:httpCompression -[name='gzip'].
staticCompressionLevel:9 -[name='gzip'].dynamicCompressionLevel:7
```

6. Restart IIS via the management console or via the Windows Services Manager.

If you've followed the configuration instructions correctly, all requests coming through port 80 on the server will be now proxied to the WebLogic Server and that traffic will be handled with some level of compression. You should immediately see faster response results from Oracle BI, especially if you are using Internet Explorer 7 or 8.

Automate starting and stopping

Some very common questions among the enterprise deployments of an Oracle BI solution are, "how can I have Oracle BI start up when the server boots?" or, "especially with a Windows OS, how can I log off the server where Oracle BI resides and still keep the Oracle BI server application running?"

The solution, or an answer to these questions, is ancillary when compared to the overall architecture, security, and metadata modeling efforts behind the main BI effort. Nonetheless, once this keep-alive solution is implemented, you'll wonder how you did without it.

On a Windows OS, we can take advantage of Windows Services. On a *Nix server, we can take advantage of the `rc.local` or `init.d` and `chkconfig` system startup functions. Either approach involves writing a few short batch (or shell on *Nix) scripts, saving them to the appropriate location on the server, and assigning the scripts to the correct startup and shutdown function delegated for the operating system. Again, since we are using a Windows Server 2008 operating system, this exercise will highlight that operating system and take advantage of Windows Services.

Leveraging the WebLogic Server Windows Service installer command

WebLogic Server comes with a command-line script that allows you to set some parameters and execute them in order to create a Windows Service for the Administration Server or the BI Managed Server. This is a very handy feature and saves you a bundle of time from building a similar process yourself:

1. Locate the file provided with WLS that creates the Windows Service, `<FMW_HOME>\wlserver_10.3\server\bin\installSvc.cmd`, for example, `D:\Oracle\FMW\wlserver_10.3\server\bin\installSvc.cmd`.

2. Back up the `installSvc.cmd` file, because you will need to modify the original in order to add a log file location in the script that captures the standard console output of WLS.

3. Open the `installSvc.cmd` file and modify the last line in the section, which installs the service by adding text for the log switch/argument. The script uses parameterization of variables with `%`, as shown in the following screenshot. Edit the file with the following text and ensure your section appears as illustrated in the following screenshot:

   ```
   -log:"%FMW_HOME%\user_projects\domains\bifoundation_
   domain\%SERVER_NAME%-stdout.txt"
   ```

```
rem *** Install the service
"%WL_HOME%\server\bin\beasvc" -install -svcname:"beasvc %DOMAIN_NAME%_%SERVER_NAME%" -
javahome:"%JAVA_HOME%" -execdir:"%USERDOMAIN_HOME%" -maxconnectretries:"%MAX_CONNECT_RETRIES%"
-host:"%HOST%" -port:"%PORT%" -extrapath:"%EXTRAPATH%" -password:"%WLS_PW%" -cmdline:%CMDLINE%
-log:"%FMW_HOME%\user_projects\domains\bifoundation_domain\%SERVER_NAME%-stdout.txt"

ENDLOCAL
```

4. Save the `installSvc.cmd` file.

5. Create a folder off the root of the main drive/mount where you've installed Oracle BI called `OBIEE11gStuff`, for example, `D:\OBIEE11gStuff\`.

   This will become the folder where you can store scripts and artifacts related to the management of your Oracle BI 11*g* implementation. This is not the same path as the Fusion Middleware Home and this folder should not be placed in that path.

6. Create two empty batch scripts and place them in the folder you just created. Save the batch scripts as `installAdminServerSvc.bat` and `installBIServerSvc.bat`.

   Remember if you are using Notepad, save the file with quotes to ensure the correct file extension.

7. Enter the following code in the `installAdminServerSvc.bat` script. There are several environment specific variables which you need to ensure that they are accurate with your environment:

```
SETLOCAL
    set DOMAIN_NAME=bifoundation_domain
    set FMW_HOME=D:\Oracle\FMW
    set USERDOMAIN_HOME=%FMW_HOME%\user_projects\domains\
    bifoundation_domain
    set SERVER_NAME=AdminServer
    set PRODUCTION_MODE=true
    cd %USERDOMAIN_HOME%
    call %USERDOMAIN_HOME%\bin\setDomainEnv.cmd
    call %FMW_HOME%\wlserver_10.3\server\bin\installSvc.cmd
ENDLOCAL
```

8. Save and close the `installAdminServerSvc.bat` script.

9. Enter the following code in the `installBIServerSvc.bat` script. Again, there are several environment specific variables. So, ensure they are accurate with your environment. Be sure to replace the `<server_name>` value with the name of the server in your implementation for the `ADMIN_URL` variable:

```
SETLOCAL
    set DOMAIN_NAME=bifoundation_domain
    set FMW_HOME=D:\Oracle\FMW
    set USERDOMAIN_HOME=%FMW_HOME%\user_projects\domains\
    bifoundation_domain
    set SERVER_NAME=bi_server1
    set PRODUCTION_MODE=true
    set ADMIN_URL=http://<server_name>:7001
    cd %USERDOMAIN_HOME%
    call %USERDOMAIN_HOME%\bin\setDomainEnv.cmd
    call %FMW_HOME%\wlserver_10.3\server\bin\installSvc.cmd
ENDLOCAL
```

10. Save and close the `installBIServerSvc.bat` script.

11. Right-click on the `installAdminServerSvc.bat` script and select the **Run as Administrator** option.

    This will run the code in that script against the `installSvc.cmd` script, which you modified with the log file parameter earlier.

12. Open the Windows Services Manager to ensure that the Windows Server was created with the name `beasvc bifoundation_domain_AdminServer`:

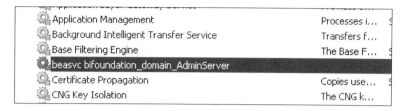

13. Right-click on the `installBIServerSvc.bat` script and select the **Run** option as the Administrator option, and then verify that the `bi_server1` service has been created.

You've successfully set up the core WebLogic Server Windows Services so that, not only start-up and shutdown can be scripted, but also the services can be run under the profile of a different user and not just the profile of the user that is logged on to the Windows Server. There are two steps to be taken in order to fully leverage these new Windows Services under the premise of a user being able to log off the machine with the services still running. You'll need to contact a Network Administrator to create a Service Account under which these new Windows Services will run, and build a script that enables the serialized launch or shutdown of the primary components of Oracle BI 11*g*. We will walk you through the latter step in the next section. However, you will need to work with the Network Administrator to implement the service accounts against the newly created Windows Services, if you want to work in a production environment.

Creating start-up and shutdown scripts

After installing Oracle BI 11*g* on a Windows OS, a method to start and stop the Oracle BI system is provided through the Oracle Business Intelligence menu by navigating to **Start** | **Programs** | **Oracle Business Intelligence**. Although this mechanism is great for testing and development, it lacks the enterprise production-ready capability to restart itself in case of failures, the ability to be scheduled, or agility to continue running if the user who launched Oracle BI via this mechanism logs off the server. Also, the Windows Services you've created, in the preceding sections for WebLogic Server, are only a portion of the components that must be run for Oracle BI 11*g* to function. Creating a start-up script gives you control over launching the specific programs required to support Oracle BI 11*g* and the order in which they are launched.

It is important that the components of Oracle BI, including the WebLogic Server, start in a particular sequence which allows for satisfaction of dependencies. You'll need to create two more scripts in the OBIEE11gStuff artifacts folder (for example, D:\OBIEE11gStuff\) that you created in the previous section and associate the variables in the new scripts with the correct references to your environment.

The order, in which processes for the Oracle BI 11*g* system are started, is very important:

- Node Manager
- WebLogic Server
- BI Server (Managed Server)
- OPMN (Oracle BI System Components)

To shutdown the Oracle BI 11*g* system, the reverse order of the start-up process is executed:

1. Create two batch scripts—OBI11g_Startup.bat and OBI11g_Shutdown.bat.

2. Edit the OBI11g_Startup.bat script and enter the following code into it and make sure that you edit the script placeholders such as <server_name> with the correct values from your environment.

```
SETLOCAL
  SET SERVER_PATH=D:
  SET SERVER_NAME=<server_name>
  SET FMW_HOME=%SERVER_PATH%\Oracle\FMW
  CD %SERVER_PATH%
  %SERVER_PATH%
  echo Starting Oracle BI 11g System...
  START %FMW_HOME%\wlserver_10.3\
  server\bin\startNodeManager.cmd
  net start "beasvc bifoundation_domain_AdminServer"
  @ping %SERVER_NAME% -n 300 > NUL
  net start "beasvc bifoundation_domain_bi_server1"
  @ping %SERVER_NAME% -n 80 > NUL
  net start "Oracle Process Manager (instance1)"
  @ping %SERVER_NAME% -n 60 > NUL
  echo Start up Script Complete!
ENDLOCAL
```

3. Save and close OBI11g_Startup.bat.

4. Edit the OBI11g_Shutdown.bat script and enter the following code into it:

```
SETLOCAL
  SET SERVER_NAME=<server_name>
  echo Begin OBI System Management / Application Shutdown...
  net stop "Oracle Process Manager (instance1)"
  @ping %SERVER_NAME% -n 60 > NUL
  net stop "beasvc bifoundation_domain_bi_server1"
  @ping %SERVER_NAME% -n 60 > NUL
  net stop "beasvc bifoundation_domain_AdminServer"
  @ping %SERVER_NAME% -n 60 > NUL
  echo Shutdown Script Finished!
ENDLOCAL
```

5. Save and close OBI11g_Shutdown.bat.

As a quick description of the preceding code, the start-up script contains a serialized execution of mainly Windows Services, except for the very first call which launches the Node Manager. Both scripts contain statements that begin with @ping, which is merely a very primitive way to create a pause or wait in the script by pinging the local server for -n seconds. These batch scripts can now be plugged into a scheduler system such as Windows Task Scheduler, and so on, to automate the start-up or shutdown of your Oracle BI 11*g* system.

> The Node Manager execution can also be started as a Windows Service. We've seen this method vary in some installations and you may consider using the Node Manager Windows Service, instead of this direct command file execution call used in the start-up script. Currently, if you do not have a Node Manager Windows Service after your installation of Oracle BI 11*g*, you can create one by running the installNodeManagerSvc.cmd script from the same path that created the Administration Server Windows Service.

Creating desktop shortcuts

You will want to have a quick means to start or stop the Oracle BI suite, if you log on to the server directly. This is easily accomplished by navigating to the folder where you are storing your Oracle BI artifacts, D:\OBIEE11gStuff\. Then, right-click on the start-up script, OBI11g_Startup.bat, and select **Send to | Desktop (create shortcut)**. Do the same for the shutdown script, OBI11g_Shutdown.bat.

It is very important that the scripts used to serialize the start-up and shutdown of the Oracle BI suite, reside on the same drive/mount as the Fusion Middleware Home. There are some drive/mount specific references made by the WLS Node Manager that may have erratic behavior otherwise.

Creating boot.properties files

Lastly, when automating the WebLogic Server or Managed Server start-up, WebLogic requires an administrator's credentials. As a matter of fact, the above Windows Services will not work properly for starting up the services until you conduct the steps to create the `boot.properties` files. By default, WebLogic prompts for credentials to start and stop the server. In order not to have the interface prompt you for these credentials each time, the credentials can be stored in a properties file. A file needs to be created for each Managed Server, as well as the Administration Server instance of the WebLogic Server:

1. Navigate to the Fusion Middleware Home path, `<FMW_HOME>\ user_projects\domains\bifoundation_domain\servers\`, for example, `D:\Oracle\FMW\user_projects\domains\bifoundation_domain\servers\`:

2. Open the Administration Server/security folder. If the folder does not exist then create it.

   The path should be `<FMW_HOME>\ user_projects\domains\bifoundation_domain\servers\AdminServer\security`.

3. There may, or may not be, a `boot.properties` file in this folder depending on the steps you've taken thus far in your new environment.

4. Create the file, `boot.properties`, using your favorite text editor if it does not already exist.

5. Open the `boot.properties` file for editing and enter the information, as shown in the following screenshot, to provide the credential values for the WebLogic username and password replacing the placeholder values with your environment's credentials:

   ```
   username=<username>
   password=<password>
   ```

6. Save and close the file.

7. Conduct steps 2 through 4, to create the `boot.properties` file in the BI Server Managed Server folder, `bi_server1` at `<FMW_HOME>\user_projects\domains\bifoundation_domain\servers\bi_Server1\security`. For example, `D:\Oracle\FMW\user_projects\domains\bifoundation_domain\servers\bi_server1\security`.

When creating the `boot.properties` file using Notepad, the extension is best preserved correctly when you save the file name with quotes, as seen in the following screenshot:

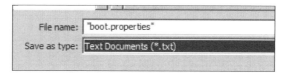

Now, the `boot.properties` files exist. When the respective WebLogic Server and BI Server is started, the credentials in these files will get encrypted so that they are no longer plain text as you've entered them.

Now, you may use the start-up and shutdown scripts, and validate the effort. In case you need the log files, they are in the log path that you set earlier with the log switch when creating the Windows Services for Administration Server and BI Server.

This section provided you with the means to provide an automated way to start and stop the Oracle BI 11g system and avoid the need for a particular named user to be logged on to the Oracle BI physical server at all times.

Ancillary application integration awareness

Oracle BI 11g is marketed as a product which can be connected and configured with several enterprise products such as Oracle Enterprise Performance Management (EPM) to view existing financial reporting and Oracle MapViewer to incorporate geographical spatial analytics into reports and dashboards. Although these are great concepts and ideal for many organizations, they are not set up by default. They are not considered as out-of-the-box integrations where you may flip a single switch to introduce them into your Oracle BI 11g implementation. Some of these integration points such as EPM, require configuration of the Oracle BI Action Framework (discussed in *Chapter 11*, *Agents and the Action Framework*) which requires additional modification to a physical configuration file on the server and a credential key configuration via the WebLogic Server Administration Console. Other consoles require configuring a separate application and potentially a database, such as that involved with incorporating Oracle MapViewer.

We mention that you should not make judgment on Oracle BI 11*g* as a tool, but you should be aware of some additional efforts required to hook in all the bells and whistles of Oracle BI 11*g*. This also gives you a sense of how straightforward or how complex you can make your Oracle BI implementation. From a project management perspective, milestones are crucial when laying out your Oracle BI 11*g* project. From a technical perspective, there's a lot of amazing stuff you can do with this tool—expanding your skill set or getting some outside assistance will be key for meeting those milestones on time.

Recommendations for further learning

This chapter gave an idea about the additional installation options for Oracle BI 11*g*. You read brief discussions on a few topics that we would have loved to include but were either too advanced or too lengthy in sophistication to cover. Here are a few recommended topics for you to investigate further on your own to continue your learning:

- **Shared Storage Preconfiguration**: http://www.obi11gbook.com/u/2
- **IIS URL Compression**: http://www.obi11gbook.com/u/8
- **Oracle BI 11*g* Sample Application Virtual Machine Image**: http://www.obi11gbook.com/u/6
- **IIS Proxy Configuration**: http://www.obi11gbook.com/u/7

A review – what I should now know!

For self review and recap of the chapter, here are a few questions based on important topics covered in this chapter:

1. Is high availability an option available in the Oracle BI 11*g* installation wizard or an architectural configuration?
2. How can the Oracle BI 11*g* application, analytics, listen on port 80 to be accessible from the network using a URL such as http://<server_name>/analytics?
3. When should the listen ports of any Oracle BI or WebLogic component be changed from its default?
4. Which install type must be used in order to leverage a specific JDK?

Summary

In this chapter, we highlighted some of the most common installation options and discussions heard in many real world implementations that we've experienced. The sections in this chapter aimed to provide both a step-by-step explanation and a bit of food for thought on how to strategically approach hurdles confronted by most organizations implementing Oracle BI. An attempt was made to focus on items surrounding the installation process itself and illustrate the means which are possible for controlling the Oracle BI application in the environment, which it will install. Although most of the discussions and exercises in this chapter, do not have any bearing on the immediate success of the hands-on exercises that you will conduct later in this book, it will act as a reference for any future Oracle BI 11*g* installation planning you may be a part of.

Get ready for the next chapter, which focuses on educating you on managing the entire Oracle BI and WebLogic system via the System Management Tools.

5

Understanding the Systems Management Tools

Oracle BI 11*g* is an enterprise application suite and is comprised of several major application components that ties it all together. Together the components operate as a system. These components typically run on the server and are configured by using a web client interface, an API library, or a command-line interface. These tools that configure the system are referred to as **system management tools** as they coordinate the operation of the entire Oracle BI 11*g* system. The WebLogic and Fusion Control administration interfaces were briefly discussed in the previous chapter.

This chapter goes into greater detail about each. We'll explain what these components are, what they do, and how they work together. We will dive into the navigation of these tools so that you will become more familiar with the interfaces and learn what components are specific to Oracle BI 11*g*. We will also explore which key controls are used to maintain the Oracle BI 11*g* environment.

Lastly, this chapter is crucial to the remainder of the book as it contains the security exercises for creating the users and groups that will be used to access the Tennis Repository dashboards and reports, which you will develop in subsequent chapters.

Let's talk about management tools

Oracle BI 11*g* is based on the Fusion Middleware Architecture that provides two core applications—**WebLogic Server (WLS)** Administration Console and the **Enterprise Manager (EM)** Fusion Middleware Control.

WLS and EM manage configurations that have a systematic impact. Basically, if those applications aren't online and available, neither is your Oracle BI 11*g* deployment. Yes, there are other management consoles that allow for the specific control of the individual applications such as Oracle BI 11*g* server, BI Publisher, MapViewer, and so on. Those consoles are referred to as the **Application Administration Tools**, all of which are part of a larger system which is managed by the System Management Tools, which is the topic of discussion for this chapter.

WLS and EM can be accessed through a standard web-based **Graphic User Interface (GUI)** as well as through command-line and programmatic means. Access points for managing the system can be broken down into two classes—GUI and programmatic.

Here are the main programmatic interface tools which are also referred to collectively as the **Oracle BI Systems Management Application Programming Interface (API)**:

- **WebLogic Scripting Tool (WLST)**: It is a command-line interface included with the WLS installation that provides a way to manage WLS domains, its objects, and artifacts. WLST leverages the Jython programming language and WLST-specific commands to script logic that executes against WLS.

- **Java Management Extensions (JMX) / Managed Beans (MBeans)**: They provide the functionality to manage Java resources such as applications, services, devices and also to dynamically monitor the resources. An individual resource is controlled by one or more MBeans, which are registered to a managed object server called the MBean server.

WebLogic Server Administration Control

If you have any WLS experience, you will understand that WLS is an application in its own right and a server that runs other applications. If you don't have any WLS experience, don't be discouraged by the number of options and configuration points that it offers. At the moment, concern yourself only with the WLS components that relate to the operation of the Oracle BI 11*g* environment.

The goal of this section is for you to familiarize yourself with the Oracle BI 11*g* System Management Tools. You'll review the main areas of the system, which an Oracle BI administrator frequents and gain a better sense of how Oracle BI 11*g* fits together with Fusion Middleware. After completing the Oracle BI 11*g* installation, follow the steps provided in the following subsections.

First access and checkpoint

Let's begin by getting into the WLS Administration Console. This is fairly straightforward, so follow the next steps:

1. Navigate to the WLS Administration Console via the URL, `http://<server_name>:<default port>/console/` (default port is typically 7001), where `<server_name>` is the name of the server where you've installed Oracle BI 11g. \ *computer/machine name*

2. Once logged in, you will see a navigation index on the left-hand side pane of the GUI. You can use this navigation panel to move around WLS for these walkthrough exercises:

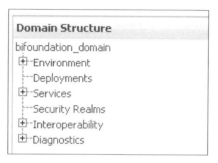

If your login procedure was successful, continue with the steps mentioned in the next sections. If not, make sure that your WebLogic Server has been started. We are operating under the premise that the Oracle BI 11g installation succeeded and all is operational.

Let's Get It Started!

As shown at the end of *Chapter 3, Installing on Windows Server 2008,* the Oracle BI 11g system launches in the default browser after the installation completes. At this time, the entire system including WLS is up and running. If you have restarted the machine since then, the easiest way to get Oracle BI 11g started on a Windows OS is to navigate to **Start** | **All Programs** | **Oracle Business Intelligence** | **Start BI Services**.

Several command windows will appear on the screen once this option is clicked. Do not close any of those command prompts at any time otherwise you will shutdown part of the Oracle BI 11g system, instead minimize the command windows. Using this method a default browser will open once the system has successfully started.

You'll stay inside of the WebLogic Server Administration Console during this walk through until otherwise stated.

Servers

As an indication of how the Oracle BI 11*g* environment was installed and what scaled-out servers have been included in the post-installation configuration, the **Servers** page provides great insight into the current state of the infrastructure. No matter what installation type you choose, **AdminServer(admin)** will always be found in this list. If an Enterprise or Software Only installation of Oracle BI 11*g* takes place, you should expect to see the **bi_server1** Managed Server in this list as well:

1. Expand the **Environment** node under **bifoundation_domain** in the navigation pane.

2. Click on the **Servers** link.

3. Click on the **bi_server1** Managed Server name:

☐	Name ⌃	Cluster	Machine	State	Health	Listen Port
☐	AdminServer(admin)		ADDISRV03	RUNNING	✔ OK	7001
☐	bi_server1	bi_cluster	ADDISRV03	RUNNING	✔ OK	9704
New Clone Delete					Showing 1 to 2 of 2 Previous	Next	

4. Notice the tabs and options available to you on the **Settings** page for **bi_server1**. The **Configuration | General, Keystores, SSL sub-tabs**, and **Monitoring** tab is where most of the advanced configuration for the Oracle BI 11*g* Managed Server will take place.

5. On the **General** tab, you can see a position where the ability to change the default port numbers for Oracle BI 11*g* analytics exists.

Next, let's talk about the WLS domain cluster for Oracle BI 11*g*.

Clusters

A WLS domain cluster establishes the context for the scalability and reliability that comes from adding one or more Managed Servers to the domain. An Enterprise or Software Only installation of Oracle BI 11*g* creates a default cluster in WLS. This cluster refers to a WLS domain cluster which has the goal of redundancy and high availability. This domain cluster configuration is for the application server nodes themselves. This should not be confused with clustering the Oracle BI server system components. A domain cluster is required for scaling-out Oracle BI 11*g*. The term scaling-out typically refers to either scaling-up vertically on the same server or scaling-out horizontally to one or more separate servers.

Expand **bifoundation_domain | Environment | Clusters**, to see the default cluster configuration established during the default installation configuration of Oracle BI 11*g*. The name of the cluster is **bi_cluster**. The default configuration for the cluster should be left alone unless an advanced implementation specifically requires modifying it:

	Name ⌃	Cluster Address	Cluster Messaging Mode	Migration Basis	Default Load Algorithm	Replication Type	Cluster Broadcast Channel	Servers
☐	bi_cluster		Unicast	Database	Round Robin	(None)		bi_server1

Next, we'll look at where the identifying address of the Oracle BI 11*g* server(servers) resides in WLS.

Machines, IP address, or DNS

Knowing where and how an installation recognizes the server, on which it resides, is important. During a scale-out, the WLS Administration Console keeps track of its immediate location, as well as any other nodes in the cluster. Any changes, to a server's IP address, or DNS after an installation, can be painful to correct, so avoid doing so if possible. In a horizontal scale-out, Oracle recommends using a load balancer and virtual IP address to handle this complexity:

1. From the left-hand side pane navigation menu, expand **bifoundation_ domain | Environment | Machines**.

2. In the **Machines** table list, you should see the name of the server on which you have installed Oracle BI 11*g*.

3. In a horizontally scaled-out environment, multiple machine names would be listed in this table.

4. Click on the name of the machine in the **Machine** list.

5. Under the **Configuration** tab, click on the **Node Manager** subtab.

6. Notice that this area provides insight into the Node Manager, which should reside on each Managed Server associated with a WLS domain. By default the Node Manager communicates over SSL on port 9556. *Chapter 4, Installation Options*, discussed how this port could have been modified using the advanced custom ports' configuration during the installation of the software.

7. Click on the **Monitoring** tab and then click on the **Node Manager Log** subtab.

8. In the **Node Manager Log** page, you can see the status and log information for the Node Manager on that machine. This is often helpful for diagnosing more advanced integrations and modifications made to the SSL or ports' configurations.

Next, let's explore the easily overlooked data source connection settings that are seldom modified, if at all, for a standard implementation.

Data sources or JDBC connections

WLS is a Java application server. One of the biggest benefits of hosting JEE applications (such as BI Publisher and other Oracle BI related applications) through WLS, is the performance gain achieved by reducing the opening and closing of database connections via leveraging connection pools. WLS controls the connection pooling. The deployed JEE applications typically access the JDBC data source connections created in the **Data Sources** area of WLS by calling the JNDI name associated with the JDBC connection:

1. From the left-hand side pane navigation menu, expand **bifoundation_domain | Services**.

2. Click on **Data Sources**.

3. The resulting page is the **Summary of JDBC Data Sources** management area. Here are the application server registered data sources, which can be leveraged by one or more applications deployed on the WebLogic Server.

4. In the **Data Sources** table, look at the **Targets** column. As you can see, each of these data sources are deployed to (that is, accessible from) the server names listed in the **Targets** column. **bi_cluster** is listed as one of the targets, which mean that any Managed Server included in that cluster is a candidate.

The default web-based applications and/or libraries deployed to the same target(targets) as the JDBC connections, such as Oracle BI and BI Publisher, are programmed to reference these default data sources. For example, the **mds-owsm** connection is set up as a default connection, which we know is a reference to the MDS metadata repository created by the RCU. BI Publisher and Oracle BI both communicate with that schema in some way. Although you may not see a configuration setting for the connection within the Oracle BI application itself, the underlying program code has a reference.

5. The following screenshot shows the default connections list configured during an installation. The **JNDI Name** column is usually the specific reference to this data source used within the application code. So, do not modify any of these names or settings. The only two repository schemas deployed during the Oracle BI 11*g* installation, via the RCU, are BIPlatform and MDS:

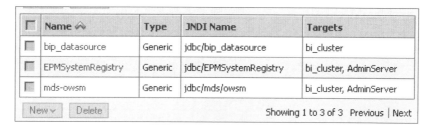

	Name ⌂	Type	JNDI Name	Targets
☐	bip_datasource	Generic	jdbc/bip_datasource	bi_cluster
☐	EPMSystemRegistry	Generic	jdbc/EPMSystemRegistry	bi_cluster, AdminServer
☐	mds-owsm	Generic	jdbc/mds/owsm	bi_cluster, AdminServer

New ⌄   Delete   Showing 1 to 3 of 3   Previous | Next

6. Click on the **bip_datasource** data source under the **Name** column.

7. Click on the **Configuration** tab and then on the **Connection Pool** subtab.

8. Scroll down to the URL input field and notice the connection string that was established during the installation and configuration process.

9. Scroll down a bit further and you will see the **Properties** box.

10. Here you can see that an explicit reference to the BIPlatform schema is made. The data source you clicked on is used for BI Publisher and the reference to this schema is due to the fact that several tables hold meta data specific to BI Publisher, such as scheduler information.

11. Click on the **Monitoring** tab in this section. Then click on the **Testing** subtab.

12. Click on the radio button in the **Server** table corresponding to the Managed Server on which this data source is deployed:

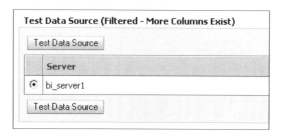

Test Data Source (Filtered - More Columns Exist)

Test Data Source

	Server
⦿	bi_server1

Test Data Source

13. Click on the **Test Data Source** button.

14. A connection success message should appear above the tabs of this section.

Next, we'll take a look at exactly how and where the Fusion Middleware security model for Oracle BI 11*g* is managed.

Security realms

Management of the over-arching system security will take place in the security realms area. A **security realm** is basically a configuration area to manage the protection of WLS resources. This is where you configure users, groups, and other security profiles that determine how access to applications deployed, on the WLS and the WLS Administration Console itself, is achieved. More than one security realm can exist, but only one can be set up as the active realm from which the security configuration for the application server is sourced. Thus, during the Oracle BI 11g installation and configuration, only one security realm called myrealm is created. It is within this realm where we will configure and manage authentication providers such as a company's LDAP directory, and so on.

> Note that WLS itself contains an embedded LDAP directory. This is also referred to as DefaultAuthenticator. It follows the open standard LDAP v3 protocol and could indeed support custom built directories for a small organization to host users (10,000 or fewer) and groups.
>
> Although most organizations use a more enterprise LDAP standard, such as those offered by Microsoft or Oracle, it is always good to know the capabilities of a tool.

Later in this chapter, we will conduct a step-by-step exercise in assigning an enterprise LDAP directory — **Microsoft Active Directory (MSAD)** — as a WLS identity provider to show how an organization's core network identity authentication repository can be used with the Oracle BI 11g Fusion Middleware architecture. But first, let's take a look at navigating through **Security Realm** to understand where the key points of activity will take place:

1. From the left-hand side pane navigation menu, expand **bifoundation_domain** | **Security Realms**.

2. Click on the solo security realm, **myrealm**, under the **Name** column in the **Realms** table.

3. The default landing subtab is **General** under the **Configuration** tab. This area highlights a few of the global security realm settings which can be left alone for a basic Oracle BI 11g configuration.

4. Click on the **Users and Groups** tab, then click on the **Users** subtab.

5. This will show the WLS embedded LDAP server users. There should be three users established during the installation and configuration by default. These users are **weblogic** (or whatever you decide to call this administrative user during the installation), **OracleSystemUser**, and **BISystemUser**.

6. Additional users can be added to this list at any time by clicking on the **New** button and completing the resulting **Add New User** form:

	Name ⌄	Description	Provider
☐	Adrian	OBI Developer	DefaultAuthenticator
☐	BISystemUser	BI System User	DefaultAuthenticator
☐	Christian	Oracle BI ACE	DefaultAuthenticator
☐	OracleSystemUser	Oracle application software system user.	DefaultAuthenticator
☐	weblogic		DefaultAuthenticator

New   Delete   Showing 1 to 5 of 5   Previous | Next

If an upgrade from a previous version of Oracle BI to Oracle BI 11*g* has been conducted, this section will list all explicitly defined Oracle BI users (and groups in the **Group** tab) previously defined within the legacy RPD. This is due to the Oracle BI 11*g* roadmap which standardizes the management of user and group security using WLS, in order to comply with the Fusion Middleware Security model, instead of the RPD.

7. Click on the **Groups** subtab.

8. Similar to the users established by default within the WLS embedded LDAP directory, several groups are also established. The default installation propagates three core Oracle BI 11*g* groups—BIAdministrators, BIAuthors, and BIConsumers.

9. Click on the **Providers** tab. Ensure the **Authentication** subtab is selected as the default. If not, click on it.

10. You should be able to see the two default identity providers, **DefaultAuthenticator** and **DefaultIdentityAsserter**. Both are defaults for the WLS installation. You can find them under **Providers | Authentication**, where we will configure our MSAD LDAP directory, which is discussed later in this chapter:

	Name	Description	Version
☐	DefaultAuthenticator	WebLogic Authentication Provider	1.0
☐	DefaultIdentityAsserter	WebLogic Identity Assertion provider	1.0

11. Click on the **Migration** tab.

12. Here you can see that the possibility to import and export security provider information is available. This is good to know when copying some security credentials from one server environment to another.

Security migration using the open source project called Project Amelia, will be discussed later in this book. If leveraging the SampleApp developed by the Oracle BI development team, part of that installation configuration process leverages this WLS Migration functionality to synchronize security with the sample environment.

WebLogic Server is its own application

When working with WLS in the context of Oracle BI 11*g* for the first time, it is easy to miss the fact that WLS is its own Oracle product. As an example, a company may license WebLogic Server Enterprise Edition just to serve their internally developed application deployment needs. The following are a few items that often get overlooked:

- As mentioned above, after the default Oracle BI 11*g* installation, a default set of users and groups is created in the WLS embedded LDAP. The users and groups established by default are a mix of users and groups for Oracle BI 11*g* and the WebLogic Server application itself. Looking at the list of groups within the **Groups** table you can see groups named **Administrators** and **BIAdministrators**.

- The **Administrators** group is specific to the WLS application. That is to say that a WLS user belonging to this group will have administration rights to log in to the WLS administration console and manage it.

- The **BIAdministrators** group signifies a bucket for users established within the WLS embedded LDAP directory that should have access to certain administration rights within the Oracle BI 11*g* application.

- The weblogic user exists in both the **BIAdministrators** and **Administrators** groups by default, which is why that user is the "God-like" user on the system. If you recall from *Chapter 4, Installation Options*, the name of this user is created during the installation and is arbitrary-based although the default and recommended name is **weblogic**.

- WLS contains an embedded LDAP directory and as such it can be accessed via standard LDAP browsing tools. Leveraging an open source tool, such as JXplorer, will allow you to view information about the repository, such as its users and groups.

After conducting the preceding walkthrough in the WLS Administration Console, you can clearly see that there are many tabs and configuration sections available to manage the application server. Most of the other sections and tabs, which are not mentioned, are for advanced configurations. Any sections that were not mentioned in the preceding walkthrough are most likely not crucial to a basic Oracle BI 11*g* configuration or administration routine.

Using WLST

Eventually, the need will arise to use some advanced features against the application server—WLS—that hosts Oracle BI 11*g* in order to automate or reduce the work of repetitive functions. The **WebLogic Scripting Tool (WLST)** is one of the ways in which you can interface with the application server.

WLST is fairly straightforward to use. Its command-line interface is launched from a directory underneath the FMW installation root, typically on the server for which the installation resides. However, when WLST is located on a networked server, it may communicate with any other WLS located on the network.

Let's conduct a quick exercise that will show you how to launch the WLST interface. In addition, you'll run a few quick commands to return some simple data from the WLS in this section:

1. Launch WLST from a terminal or command prompt window on the server where Oracle BI 11*g* is installed, using the path and command `<FMW_HOME>\ oracle_common\common\bin\wlst.cmd`. For example, `C:\obiee\oracle_ common\common\bin\wlst.cmd`:

2. On a Nix OS, launch WLST using the `./wlst.sh` command in the similar path, `<FMW_HOME>/oracle_common/common/bin/`.

3. The script first attempts to load a series of environment variables into the terminal session so that the WLST's required libraries can be assessed. This is a part of the program's procedure before the WLST engine can be ready on the command prompt or terminal for use. As the launch message states, it can take up to a few minutes in order for the WLST prompt to ready itself for use.

4. Once the environment variables have been loaded you will be presented with a command prompt cursor and you will be ready to access the WLST program in offline mode.

 Be sure to launch the WLST command from the file path specified in the previous step. There are other ways to launch WLST but those methods will not provide you with the access that you need for Oracle BI 11*g*.

5. At the command prompt, connect to the WLS by entering the following and pressing *Enter*:

```
connect('weblogic', '<password>','<server_name>:7001');
```

For example:

```
connect('weblogic', 'Admin123','localhost:7001');
```

```
Connecting to t3://localhost:7001 with userid weblogic ...
Successfully connected to Admin Server 'AdminServer' that belongs
oundation_domain'.

Warning: An insecure protocol was used to connect to the
server. To ensure on-the-wire security, the SSL port or
Admin port should be used instead.

wls:/bifoundation_domain/serverConfig> _
```

6. If the WLS is running and credentials are valid, a successful connection message will be returned. Now, with a successful online connection, there are many commands that could be entered to explore the WebLogic Server, and to a small degree, the Oracle BI 11*g* server. To keep your first trek into WLST simple but powerful, let's programmatically create an embedded WLS LDAP user.

7. Enter the following code lines into the command prompt, each line break should be entered on a new line by pressing *Enter*:

```
dauth=cmo.getSecurityConfiguration().getDefaultRealm().lookupAuthe
nticationProvider("DefaultAuthenticator")
dauth.createUser('obi11gbook','Admin123','OBI11g Book User')
```

The result should be the silent (that is, no response message) creation of a new user within the WLS embedded LDAP directory.

By quickly breaking down the preceding code block, the first line instantiates the look up function call for the identity provider defined as the argument. As we saw when walking through the WLS Administration Console there are two default identity providers; one of which is named `DefaultAuthenticator`.

The second line in the preceding code block makes reference to the instantiated `dauth` object and calls the `createUser` function passing three arguments to the parameters—username, password, and username alias.

Syntax errors are bound to happen when working with WLST as the code is case-sensitive. One note is that the majority of WLST commands comply with the camel-case coding convention.

Open the WLS Administration Console and navigate to the **myrealm** security realm. Click on the **User and Groups** tab. Refresh the page if you want to see the new user that you just created:

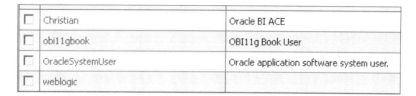

☐	Christian	Oracle BI ACE
☐	obi11gbook	OBI11g Book User
☐	OracleSystemUser	Oracle application software system user.
☐	weblogic	

You can nearly manage all operations of WLS via WLST. There is an entire document, which comes with the WLS offering from Oracle, at `http://docs.oracle.com/cd/E15523_01/web.1111/e13813/toc.htm` dedicated to WLST. The information that we've offered, gives you a practical insight into how to get started, as well as giving you an idea of what else it can do for you. For quick assistance, you can always use the `help()` command from the WLST prompt to get more information on using the tool.

Enterprise Manager Fusion Middleware Control

WLS Administration Console's complementary web-based console, rounding out the System Management GUI tools, is the **Fusion Middleware Control (Fusion Control)**. It is the main interface to configure basic Oracle BI 11*g* frontend presentation options, as well as the primary means for deploying an RPD and setting the active Presentation Catalog.

Presentation Catalog is a new term in Oracle BI 11*g*. It replaces the legacy term Web Catalog referring to the Oracle BI Presentation Services' artifacts file repository.

This section will guide you through the Fusion Control console and explain each section as you navigate through it. Let's start by logging in to the console to have a look around.

Getting around in EM

The Fusion Control console is not WLS. It is a completely separate application. You'll learn how to log in to the console and navigate around the interface in the following steps:

1. Navigate to the URL `http://<server_name>:7001/em`.

2. Enter the weblogic user credentials in the prompt and click on the **Login** button:

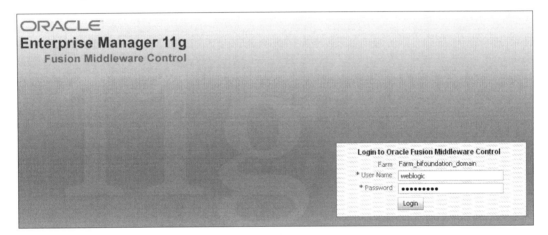

BI Foundation Domain dashboard

The main page provides an overview of the management console and all paths from which you may reach more insight about the environment. The dashboard is broken into the left and right panes. The right pane always contains the main content while the left pane is used for navigation:

1. Expand **Farm_bifoundation_Domain | Business Intelligence** from the
    left pane:

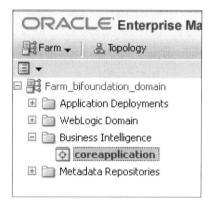

2. Click on **coreapplication**.

Coreapplication

This section is specific to the **Business Intelligence** node under which the navigation
is labeled. Since this is context-specific to the Oracle BI 11*g* application, this is where
many configuration changes will be made. This page opens up the tabs that were last
in use by the user.

Click on the **Overview** tab:

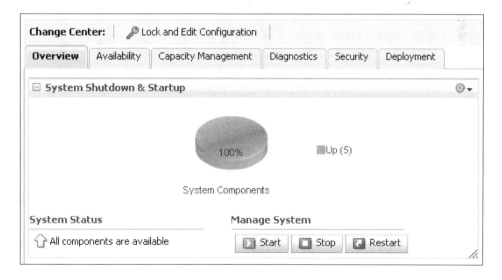

The Overview tab

The **Overview** tab provides a quick glance at the status, most recent errors and warnings, and responsiveness of the Oracle BI 11*g* instance(s). Here you also have the ability to initiate the start, stop, or restart operation of the Oracle BI 11*g* System Components. Initially there will not be much to do from this page, but it is good to know that once the environment begins the activity, this is a good resource for getting a high-level status.

Click on the **Availability** tab.

The Availability tab

The **Availability** tab is a section that the Oracle BI 11*g* Administrator will see quite frequently during development. Two subtabs are available under this tab—**Processes** and **Failover**.

Process

The **Processes** subtab provides information regarding the status of each individual System Component along with their deployed port and instance. More importantly, this is the area of the management console where you can stop, start, or restart one or all of the Oracle BI System Components as an alternative of using the command-line opmnctl utility.

Failover

The **Failover** tab highlights the current redundancy status of the environment by listing potential points of failure, either from not having the environment scaled-out or not using the Oracle BI server's application clustering option.

Click on the **Capacity Management** tab.

The Capacity Management tab

This tab has three subtabs. These subtabs are **Metrics**, **Scalability**, and **Performance**.

Metrics

The **Metrics** subtab provides a useful snapshot of system metrics, which may give insight to the current system performance. There are more detailed means to get the detail underlying these metrics, and those means are discussed later in this chapter.

Scalability

The **Scalability** subtab allows a visual representation for which Oracle BI 11*g* system components are scaled-out either horizontally or vertically within the configured architecture. In the default installed environment, this shows only one instance and only one set of system components. Upon scaling the environment, you must use this subtab section to manage the scaled-out components.

Performance

For context specific to the Oracle BI 11*g* application, the **Performance** subtab allows several of the main performance related configurations to be modified. Applying changes in this section transparently updates the Oracle BI `instanceconfig.xml` configuration file per each Oracle BI 11*g* instance. Although there are many other configurations that could manually be adjusted in the physical `instanceconfig.xml` files, this GUI interface captures basic performance configuration settings deemed most useful to any organization's basic needs from the application.

Click on the **Diagnostics** tab.

The Diagnostics tab

There are two subtabs under this tab. These subtabs are **Log Messages** and **Log Configuration**.

Log Messages

This subtab shows all errors and warnings related to all underlying components of the Oracle BI 11*g* application. Viewing this section is very useful when experiencing any issues within the Oracle BI 11*g* environment. In addition, it is this section that you will visit when you want to access log files critical to the Oracle BI environment, such as the Oracle BI Server or Presentation Services log files. The section at the bottom, **View / Search Log Files**, provides the starting point to launch the Log Viewer for all or only one specific log.

Log Configuration

This section, **Log Configuration**, is quite essential to the way log files, accessible from the **Log Messages** subtab, are built. This section enables you to manage a log file's size and length of time in which each log file can be written. Most importantly, the **Log Levels** section on this subtab allows management to control the amount of detail each log file will store as it is being written. By controlling the level of file storage granularity, the log file size will grow or shrink, but the more granular the logging; the more detailed will be the diagnostic information.

Click on the **Security** tab.

The Security tab

This section allows you to manage the Single Sign-On system configuration for Oracle BI. It also provides navigation links to other parts of the Oracle BI 11*g* System Management tools in order to manage user, groups, application policies, or application roles.

Click on the **Deployment** tab.

The Deployment tab

This tab has five subtabs under it. These subtabs are **Presentation**, **Repository**, **Sheduler**, **Marketing**, and **Mail**.

Presentation

It is one of the least used sections. The **Presentation** subtab allows you to modify global settings that relate to the dashboard, analysis development, or overall Presentation Services environment.

Repository

This section contains one of the most frequented sections of the Fusion Control console. Here you have the ability to change the Presentation Catalog, which is currently referenced by the Oracle BI 11*g* application. Also, this is the section where the Oracle BI administrator will deploy the Oracle BI RPD to the Oracle BI Server. The interface is fairly straightforward and we will conduct an exercise on deploying the RPD and Presentation Catalog later in this chapter. Conducting operations, such as deploying the RPD through Fusion Control, makes physical changes to the NQSConfig.INI file.

 If you open the NQSConfig.INI file from the server filesystem, you will see comments in several places noting that a configuration is managed by Fusion Control. If you attempt to modify a configuration in the file directly where this comment exists, the configuration will be overwritten when the system components start for the next time. An advanced configuration allows you to turn this Fusion Control management off, but it is not recommended.

Scheduler

This section provides the means to register the database repository location for the Oracle BI 11*g* Agents (iBots). Fortunately, as per the default installation, this information is automatically configured to the default BIPlatform schema established during the Oracle BI configuration. Note, however, that if the BIPlatform schema credentials change at any time, the connection information will need to be entered manually in this section in order to pick up the change by the BI Scheduler.

Marketing

This section is used to reference the location of the Siebel CRM Content Server.

Mail

This section allows for the **Simple Mail Transfer Protocol** (**SMTP**) configuration in order for an Oracle BI Agent to send an e-mail with the content from Oracle BI Delivers. Credentials and the SMTP server used within your organization can be configured here, along with ancillary attributes such as leveraging SSL or limiting the number of sending retries before failing the sending of an e-mail.

Managing Oracle BI 11*g* artifacts

All core transferable objects to a software application such as Oracle BI 11*g* are defined as artifacts. These artifacts for Oracle BI 11*g* are items such as the RPD, Presentation Catalog, and so on. Since these are a few of the most critical artifacts to the operation of Oracle BI, this section shows you how to deploy them within the GUI. In the Fusion Middleware Control console, under the **Deployment** tab, the OBI administrator will upload the latest RPD to the Oracle BI server, create a new Presentation Catalog, or change the Presentation Catalog.

All of the exercises in this section will be done from the Fusion Middleware Control console under the **Business Intelligence | coreapplication**. Log in to the Fusion Middleware Control console with the weblogic user's credentials, by accessing the URL—`http://<server_name>:7001/em`—and navigating to the **Repository** subtab location:

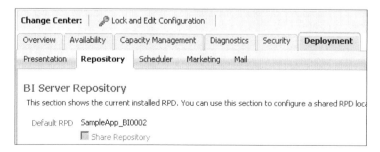

Creating a new Presentation Catalog

The easiest way for you to create a new Presentation Catalog, as an Oracle BI administrator, is by using the Fusion Middleware console.

1. Log in to the Fusion Middleware Control console by navigating to the URL—`http://<server_name>:7001/em`.

2. Navigate to **Business Intelligence | coreapplication | Deployment | Repository**.

3. After clicking on the coreapplication link in the left pane navigation, it may take a few minutes for the main page area to render. This is a known (and annoying) issue with the Enterprise Manager console.

4. Click on the **Lock and Edit Configuration** button above the main tabs:

 The **Lock and Edit Configuration** button is a toggle to create a serialized means of administration for Fusion Control. It allows you to make changes and later commit or activate those changes in a somewhat formal change control manner.

5. Close the confirmation prompt, if prompted.

6. Then, the **Change Center** button changes to two different buttons—**Activate Changes** and **Release Configuration**.

 When you click on the **Activate Changes** button, it will save/confirm any modifications you apply to the immediate tab you are working in.

When you click on the **Release Configuration** button, it will discard any immediate modifications. It is basically a cancel or revert button.

7. Scroll down to the bottom of the **Repository** subtab section. You will see the **BI Presentation Catalog** section.

8. In the long filesystem path, move the cursor at the end of the path to expose the final directory of the path, **SampleAppLite**.

9. Change the **SampleAppLite** text to **OBI11gbook**.

10. Click on the **Apply** button in the upper-right corner within the **Repository** subtab.

11. Click on the **Activate Changes** button in the **Change Center** section (where you clicked on the **Lock and Edit Configuration** button a few steps back).

12. After clicking on the **Activate Changes** button, the modification will process behind the scenes and will prompt you when it is complete.

13. Close the prompt showing success.

14. A new button called **Restart to apply recent changes** will be placed next to the **Lock and Edit Configuration** button.

15. At this point not all Oracle BI System components need to be restarted. Only the Presentation Services components need to be restarted.

16. Navigate to **Availability | Processes**. *Capacity Management |*

17. Click on the **BI Presentation Servers** row to highlight it.

18. Click on the **Restart Selected** button to restart that specific component.

19. Accept all prompts and cancel all success prompts when finished.

20. When restarted successfully, navigate to the filesystem location on the server where the Presentation Catalogs are stored.

The default location for the Presentation Catalogs is `<INSTANCE_HOME>\bifoundation\OracleBIPresentationServicesComponent\coreapplication_obips1\catalog\`, where `<INSTANCE_HOME>` is `C:\obiee\instances\instance1\` based on the installation conducted in *Chapter 3, Installing on Windows Server 2008*. You should see that a new catalog folder has been created with the name that you provided in step 9:

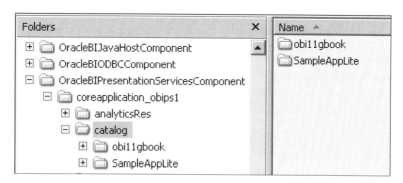

Deploying an existing Presentation Catalog

Every now and then you may need to replace the existing catalog with one from another environment, or perhaps one with examples from the Oracle BI development team such as the full `SampleApp` catalog. The swap is fairly straightforward.

Let's revert back to the `SampleAppLite` catalog as if it was a different catalog that was just delivered. The `SampleAppLite` catalog already exists in the `catalog` folder on the Oracle BI server. This is the same place where you would put any additional web catalogs coming from another environment.

Follow the procedure mentioned in the preceding section and this time revert the catalog path value (refer to step 9 in the preceding procedure) from **OBI11gbook** to **SampleAppLite**. Be sure to click on the **Lock and Edit Configuration** button, swap the directory path in the catalog path location under the **Deployment** tab, click on the **Activate Changes** button and restart the Presentation Catalog system components after changing the directory path as instructed.

Deploying an RPD

One of the new functions of Oracle BI 11*g* and the Fusion Middleware Control console is the ability to deploy the RPD metadata repository file to the Oracle BI server from the remote web-based GUI. Previous versions required this to be a manual network transfer (for example, FTP) process. The capability for automatic versioning of the RPDs that are uploaded is included with this new functionality. Each uploaded RPD is suffixed with a globally (specific to an instance of the Oracle BI 11*g* server) incrementing integer in order to identify it amongst the other RPD files uploaded to the server. Unfortunately, there is no automated clean up, so all uploaded RPDs will remain on the filesystem for historical reference unless manual intervention takes place.

Follow the next procedure for deploying an RPD:

1. Click on the **Lock and Edit Configuration** button:

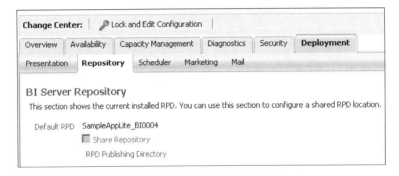

2. Close the prompt indicating the locking was successful.

3. In the **Deployment** subtab content area, look at the current **Default RPD** value above the **Share Repository** checkbox. This value is typically the name of the saved RPD suffixed by `_BI####`. This value will change once we have completed the final step.

4. In the **Upload BI Server Repository** section, click on the **Browse...** button. Notice how the file browser dialog box is looking on the immediate local machine where you are running the GUI in order to find an RPD file to be deployed. It is a local file selection operation.

   If you are currently accessing the Fusion Middleware Control console on the same machine where you have installed Oracle BI 11*g*, or have access to the remote server's filesystem via network share, then continue to step 6 in this procedure.

   If you are on a remote machine using the GUI, you will need to go to step 5 in this procedure and transfer the RPD from the server where Oracle BI 11*g* is installed on your local machine.

5. Using your favorite FTP (we like FileZilla) utility or a simple manual network transfer via Windows Explorer or any other browser, move the `SampleAppLite.RPD` file from the `<INSTANCE_HOME>/bifoundation/OracleBIServerComponent/coreapplication_obis1/repository/` path on your server, to a temporary folder or desktop on your local workstation.

6. In the dialog box for uploading the file, navigate to the **SampleAppLite.RPD** file on your location machine and select it.

7. Enter the password for the RPD in both the **Repository Password** and **Confirm Password** fields. The default password for `SampleAppLite.RPD` is `Admin123` (no period and it is case-sensitive).

8. Click on the **Apply** button in the upper right-hand corner in the **Repository** subtab section.

9. Notice how the Default RPD label above the **Shared Repository** checkbox changes. It has now been incremented by positive one. If you missed it, you can reselect the RPD again by repeating the instructions.

10. Click on the **Activate Changes** button.

11. The **Change Center** button should revert back to the **Lock and Edit Configuration** button. Then, a **Restart to apply recent changes** message link will be shown.

12. Click on the **Restart to apply recent changes** link.

13. You will be redirected to the **Overview** tab.

14. Click on the **Restart** button in the **System Shutdown & Startup** section.

15. Accept all prompts and wait for a completed prompt notification to be returned. Once this notification is returned and the status of all system components show green arrows pointing upward, it is safe to assume that the system components have been restarted. Now, you may verify that the entire system still works correctly by accessing Presentation Services and the Oracle BI Dashboards, using the URL—`http://<server_name>:9704/analytics`.

> There is a deployment option to configure a shared repository location which is typically used when scaling-out the Oracle BI architecture. The same deployment concepts are applied for a shared repository location configuration. However, the exercise on scaling-out is an advanced topic and beyond the scope of this book.

Starting/stopping system components

There are two main ways to stop, start, or restart the Oracle BI system components. One way is to use the GUI as achieved in the preceding section. The other is to use the command-line interface using an executable that installs with Oracle BI 11*g*.

In the Fusion Middleware Control console, restarting all components simultaneously, using the **Restart All** button, as we discussed in the preceding section, ensures that the Fusion Middleware control will handle all serial communication with the OPMN in order to stop and start the system components correctly in the necessary order.

However, there is a more advanced approach that can be achieved. It is by calling an executable on the server where Oracle BI 11*g* is installed. This executable is located at the location `<FMW_HOME>/instances/instance1/bin/` and is called `opmnctl.bat` (`opmnctl.sh` on Nix). The system components can be started by calling the command `opmnctl startall` from the command line. They can be stopped by calling `opmnctl stopall` from the command line.

This approach is recommended only for administrators having access to the Oracle BI 11*g* physical server. This approach is often restricted for Oracle BI 11*g* developers, because when you execute the following steps, we will have you stick with using the GUI to restart the system components:

1. Navigate to the **Availability** tab.

2. Click on the **Restart All** button above the system component items table.

3. Accept all prompts and wait for a completed prompt notification to be returned. Once this notification returns and the status of all system components will show green arrows pointing upward. Then, it is safe to assume that the components have been restarted. You may now verify that the entire system still works correctly by accessing Presentation Services and the Oracle BI Dashboards.

> Another way to restart the system components via the GUI, is to click on the **Stop All** button and wait for the services to stop. Then, click on the **Start All** button. Some readers may feel this provides a greater sense of comfort as they can explicitly see the status of the components getting recycled, which is not the case when using the **Restart All** option.

Checking the logs

Oracle BI 11*g* allows almost every crucial log file regarding the runtime of its artifacts to be visible from the Fusion Middleware Control console. This is very important when diagnosing issues as you don't need to navigate to the Oracle BI 11*g* filesystem in order to locate the respective service's log files. Oracle BI 11*g* does something very clever with its log files by using an **Execution Context ID (ECID)** which ties all log files together around one transaction or event. This way, a single error or failure will allow you to look across all components based on a particular event, using the ECID, to determine what caused an issue. Use the following steps to get some basic Oracle BI log information:

1. Navigate to **Diagnostics | Log Messages**.

2. Here, you will see the most recent warnings and error messages across all system components.

3. Scroll towards the bottom of this subtab section and notice the header **View / Search Log Files**.

4. Click on the **Server Log** link.

5. This will take you to the Log Viewer specifically predicated on the Oracle BI server logs.

6. If no records are shown immediately, change the **Date Range** fields to **Most Recent 20 Days**, or modify the day filter to a range that would have captured data since your Oracle BI 11*g* installation.

7. Click on the **Search** button.

8. Notice that the results section is now populated. Scroll through the results looking for both errors, if any, and warnings. There should always be few warnings — most of which can be ignored.

9. Above the log table is a drop-down button labeled as **Export Messages to File**. Click on the drop-down button and select the **As Oracle Diagnostic Text (.txt)** option.

10. The log file contents from the search will process and a save file prompt will appear asking you to download or open the file.

11. Download this file for using later, while making a snapshot of issues or reporting issues to Oracle Support:

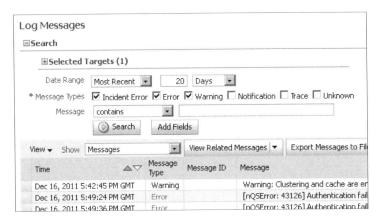

 The Log Viewer is predicated on the selected target. In this case, **Server Log**, as selected in step 4 in the preceding procedure. In order to change or add other Oracle BI 11*g* log perspectives, click on the plus icon of the **Selected Targets** option below the **Search** header under the **Log Messages** section to expand the ability to add or remove other target types such as Presentation Services.

Creating the Tennis users, roles, and associations

You've taken a look at the WLS embedded LDAP server and you have also completed an exercise using WLST to create a new user via scripting. There is one other operation that is integral to managing users and groups within Oracle BI 11*g* — application roles.

Application roles provide a means to associate universal privileges to users and groups, regardless of which identity provider they may stem from. That is to say, we can assign an embedded WLS LDAP user, and a user from our active directory LDAP, to a single application role. Then, we can assign certain privileges within the Oracle BI 11*g* application to that application role. In addition, you can assign application roles to another application role in order to provide a hierarchy of authorization.

Oracle BI 11*g* comes out of the box with four broad range core application roles that should not be deleted or modified — BISystem, BIAdministrator, BIAuthor, and BIConsumer. The names are quite indicative of what each role's capabilities are except — maybe — BISystem.

BIAdministrator has administrative ability over the Oracle BI environment, BIAuthor may read/write reports, and a BIConsumer can read reports. BISystem is a trusted role that controls the ability to impersonate users and it provides intercomponent communication with the Oracle BI system. As an administrator, in Enterprise Manager, you can create new application roles from scratch or you can mimic the properties from any of the default application roles to assume those capabilities into your own custom application roles.

Creating users and groups in WLS

In this exercise, we are going to create several users and groups in WLS. Then, we will navigate to the Enterprise Manager Fusion Control console and associate those users and groups with application roles that we will create from scratch:

1. Launch the WLS Administration Console.

2. Log in using the WebLogic administrator credentials.

3. Navigate to **Security Realms** | **myrealm** | **Users and Groups** | **Groups**.

4. In the **Groups** subtab, click on the **New** button to create a new group.

5. On the **Create New Group** page:

   Enter **Coaches** in the **Name** field.

   Select **Default Authenticator** from the **Provider** drop-down list.

   Click on the **OK** button to save the new group.

6. Using the same technique as in steps 4 and 5, create the following groups:

   ° West USTA

   ° East USTA

7. Navigate to **Users and Groups** | **Users**.

8. Under the **Users** subtab, click on the **New** button to begin adding a user.

9. On the **Create New User** page:

    ○ Enter **Tommy Racquet** in the **Name** field.

    ○ Select **Default Authenticator** from the **Provider** drop-down list.

    ○ Enter `Password1` in the **Password** and **Confirm Password** fields.

    ○ Click on the **OK** button to save the new user.

10. Using the same technique as in steps 8 and 9, using the same password, `Password1`, create the following users:

    ○ `Jill Twoshoes`

    ○ `Frank Forehand`

    ○ `Adam Aceit`

    ○ `Orlando Ontheline`

    ○ `Coach Volley`

11. Verify in the **Users** subtab if six new users exist.

12. Verify in the **Groups** subtab if three new groups exist.

13. After more users are added, the **Users** subtab page table will paginate at 10 records per page:

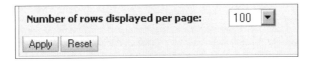

 To change this, click on the **Customize this table** link above the **Users** table to expand the option. Then change the value in the **Number of rows displayed per page** drop-down list to a higher value.

Assigning users to groups

Now, let's assign the users to groups in order to make the full WLS security associations.

1. On the **Users** subtab, in the **Name** column of the **Users** table, click on the name **Tommy Racquet**.

2. This will open **Properties Editor** for the user.

3. Click on the **Groups** tab within the **Settings for Tommy Racquet** page.

4. Assign the **West USTA** group by placing a check in the checkbox of the **West USTA** option in the **Available** box.

5. Using the middle arrows, click on the right-hand side arrow so that it appears in the **Chosen** box.

6. Click on the **Save** button.

7. Navigate to **Users and Groups | Users**, by using the breadcrumb navigation at the top of the page under the **Home, Log Out, Preferences** menu.

8. Repeat steps 1 to 6 to assign the remainder of users to groups using the following matrix to guide you:

Users	Groups
Coach Volley	West USTA, Coaches
Tommy Racquet	West USTA
Jill Twoshoes	West USTA
Frank Forehand	East USTA
Adam Aceit	East USTA
Orlando Ontheline	East USTA

Creating and assigning application roles

The users and groups have been created and properly associated with one another based on the matrix provided in the preceding section. This would be the same type of relationship that is already established in an organization's LDAP directory. Here we are simply leveraging what is built into WLS, in order to showcase that using the embedded LDAP is a solution for managing a small number (really up to 1,000, it is still quite functional) of users. For the remainder of our assignments, associating groups to application roles will be conducted in the Fusion Middleware Control.

For creating and assigning application roles, follow the next steps:

1. Navigate to Fusion Middleware Control and log in with the WebLogic administrator user's credentials.

2. Use the left-hand side pane to navigate and right-click on **Business Intelligence | coreapplication**.

3. Select **Security | Application Roles**.

4. On the **Application Roles** page, if no roles are shown:

    ○ Select **obi** from the **Application Stripe** drop-down list.

    ○ Click on the play image button on the right of the **Role Name** field.

5. Now, the default OBI application roles should appear.

6. Click on the **Create...** button above the **Application Roles** table.

7. On the **Create Application Role** page:

    ○ Enter **Tennis Match Administrator** in the **Role Name** field.

    ○ Below the **General** section, locate the **Members** section and find the **Roles** subsection.

    ○ Click on the **Add Group** button in the **Roles** subsection.

    ○ Click on the green play button to reveal all groups from the WLS identity provider(providers).

    ○ Check the checkbox next to the **Coaches** option and using the right arrow in the middle, click on the move arrow so that **Coaches** appears in the **Selected Groups** box.

    ○ Click on the **OK** button.

    ○ Click on the **OK** button in the upper-right corner of the **Create Application Role** page:

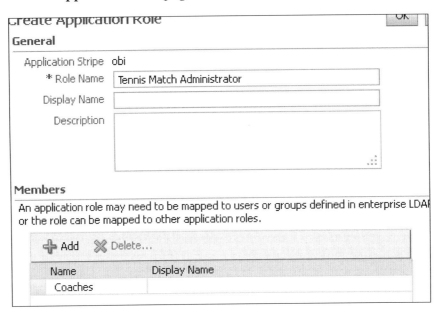

8. Repeat steps 4 to 6 to create the application roles and assign the appropriate embedded WLS groups, using the following table:

Application role	Group name
West USTA Player	West USTA
East USTA Player	East USTA

9. The final application roles' list should look similar to the following screenshot:

BIAdministrator	BIAdministrators
BIAuthor	BIAuthors, BIAdministrator
BIConsumer	BIConsumers, BIAuthor, authenticated-role
Tennis Match Administrator	Coaches
West USTA Player	West USTA
East USTA Player	East USTA

Now, we have wrapped up with the security assignments that we needed to create in order for our Tennis users to access the reports and dashboard, which you'll create in *Chapter 10*, *Creating Dashboards and Reports*.

Configuring an LDAP identity provider in WLS

In just about every Oracle BI 11*g* implementation, the organization already has an existing Identity Store established. This is typically an LDAP-based store containing the users within the organization, which has each user's responsibilities organized into a set of groups, and so on. This is common place. WebLogic allows an Oracle BI 11*g* implementation to leverage the existing structuring of users by adding it as an Identity Store provider. The LDAP store can then determine who can authenticate, or gain entry, into Oracle BI 11*g*, and who cannot. Along those same lines, the groups stemming from LDAP will also assist in determining which users have specific privileges once they have gained entry into the application. LDAP will determine who can authenticate into the application. Authorization will be controlled mainly by application roles, as discussed in the previous section.

One of the most popular LDAP providers is **Microsoft Active Directory (MSAD)**. This section steps through the tasks required to incorporate a MSAD LDAP system into the WLS environment. The net result of this configuration will be that users existing in the MSAD LDAP repository will be able to log in to the Oracle BI 11*g* portal by leveraging their credentials which reside inside the LDAP repository. For those who are not familiar with LDAP, these credentials would typically be the same as those that are used for a user to log in to an organization's network.

There are some best practices to establish configuration of an LDAP provider within WLS as it relates to FMW and Oracle BI 11*g*:

- **Establish LDAP service accounts**: An organization may use a different LDAP server per environment. For example, LDAPServerDev, LDAPServerQA, LDAPServerProd. This potentially requires different attribute changes and bind user credentials to access those servers. Since Oracle BI 11*g* requires the configuration of an LDAP account to represent the directory as an Oracle BI system account, an LDAP service account user should be created by the network administrator in each LDAP environment specifically for this purpose. The association to this service account is made in the Fusion Middleware Control console for each environment. Each service account created should have a unique name per LDAP environment in order to differentiate its purpose. Examples would be SVCBIDEV, SVCBIQA, SVCBIPROD, and so on.

- **Work with the network administrator**: The person within the organization that controls access to the LDAP server information is your friend. You will need to ensure that you are able to request the necessary LDAP connection information from them before you begin this identity provider configuration process. A basic list of the attribute items that you will need are shown in the table in the next section.

- **Manage by application role**: Although the organization's LDAP directory currently contains users and group associations, your Oracle BI environment has the potential to require different control over groups of users. Keep in mind that ultimately privileges and permissions within the presentation catalog, the RPD, and so on, will be set by assigning application role privileges and not individual users or LDAP groups. Keep this in mind as you are working to develop your role-based security strategy for Oracle BI 11*g*.

Now, let's actually walk through the steps of adding an MSAD LDAP server to WLS.

Setting up the identity provider

This section is here, primarily for advanced users and is not a pre-requisite for any of the other chapters or segments of this book. Consider this as a step-by-step reference with a walkthrough rationalizing each configuration action so that you can be knowledgeable of this integration in case you need to leverage it for your project:

1. Log in to the WLS Administration Console.

2. Click on the **Security Realms** link from the left-hand side pane.

3. Click on **myrealm** under the **Security Realms** link.

4. Click on the parent tab, **Providers**, and then click on the **Authentication** subtab.

5. Only the two default providers, **DefaultAuthenticator** and **DefaultIdentityAssertor** should exist in the table list.

6. Click on the **Lock & Edit** button from the left-hand side pane under the **Change Center** section:

7. Click on the **New** button at the top of the **Authentication Providers** table.

8. Now, it should be active after the **Lock & Edit** button was selected.

9. Enter an arbitrary alias name, **MSADAuthenticator**, into the **Name** field.

10. Select **ActiveDirectoryAuthenticator** from the **Type** drop-down menu.

11. Click on the **OK** button.

12. Click on the **Reorder** button at the top of the **Authentication Providers** list.

13. In the **Reorder** page, check the box next to the new identity provider, **MSADAuthenticator**, and use the up arrows on the side of the panel to move it to the top of the list:

14. Click on the **OK** button.

15. Click on the **DefaultAuthenticator** link in the table, to access this provider's specific properties. Navigate to **Configuration | Control** and change the **Control Flag** drop-down box to the **SUFFICIENT** value:

16. Click on the **Save** button.

17. Navigate back to the **Providers** tab under **Security Realms** and conduct the same operation for the **MSADAuthenticator** provider.

18. The result of this step is that both providers are set to SUFFICIENT.

 Control Flag is used to determine a waterfall-like authentication scenario or restrict it to a serialized authentication process. This flexibility allows functionality such as the ability to authenticate with one or more providers, which is of course the aim of this exercise.

19. Navigate back into the **MSADAuthenticator** provider's properties by clicking on its link from the **Identity** table.

20. Navigate to **Configuration | Provider Specific**.

21. Enter the information regarding your LDAP server in the available fields. For this example the information required, which must be updated in this page in order to connect to our example MSAD LDAP server, as provided by our network administrator, is as follows:

Attributes	Value
Host	Companyxyz.com
Port	389
Principle	CN=Administrator,CN=Users,DC=companyxyz,DC=com
Credentials	Enter the password of the Principle user
User Base DN	OU=obi11gbook,DC=companyxyz,DC=com
User From Name Filter	(&(sAMAccountName=%u)(objectclass=user))
User Name Attribute	sAMAccountName
User Object Class	user
Group Base DN	OU=obi11gbook,DC=companyxyz,DC=com
Group From Name Filter	(&(cn=*)(objectclass=group))
GUID Attribute	objectguid

22. The following image shows how the fields are edited to reflect the LDAP connection information provided by the network administrator:

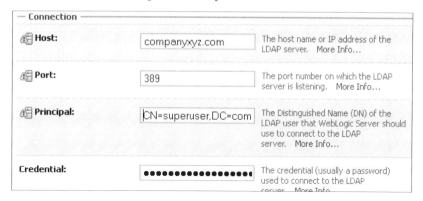

23. Click on the **Save** button to ensure that the modifications to the **MSADAuthenticator** provider are applied.

24. Click on the **Activate Changes** button in the left-hand side pane to solidify the changes on the WLS server:

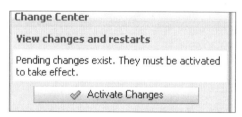

A message will appear after changes have been activated stating that several services need to be restarted. This is true, but we will conduct another step within the Enterprise Fusion Control first, and then restart the Oracle BI system after that step is completed.

Establishing Fusion Middleware Control security linkage

Although you've configured the MSAD provider, now you need to link it as a valid identity provider for the Fusion Middleware system that communicates with Oracle BI. In this section you will add three attributes, which do just that. A virtualized attribute set to TRUE allows the Identity Store to be virtualized in order to recognize more than one identity source. The other two attributes allow Oracle BI to understand the main user variable that will be passed around the system once a user is authenticated via the provider.

For MSAD, this is typically `sAMAccountName`. The default LDAP provider variable is `cn`, which is the default for Oracle Internet Directory but not MSAD.

1. Open the Fusion Middleware Control console by navigating to the URL—`http://<server_name>:7001/em/`.

2. In the left-hand side panel menu, navigate to **Security Provider Configuration** by expanding the **WebLogic Domain** folder and right-clicking on **bifoundation_domain**. Select **Security | Security Provider Configuration**, as you can see in the following screenshot:

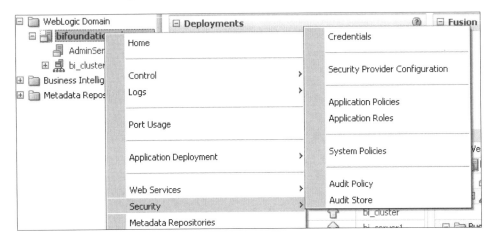

3. On the resulting **Security Provider Configuration** page, click on the **Configure...** button under the **Identity Store Provider** subsection:

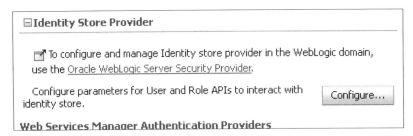

4. In the **Custom Properties** table, one entry should already exist for
    CONNECTION_POOL_CLASS. We need to add three more. Click on the
    green plus for add button to enter the following properties and values:

Property name	Value
user.login.attr	sAMAccountName
username.attr	sAMAccountName
virtualize	TRUE

5. Click on the **OK** button to save the changes.

6. In the left-hand side panel, right-click on **bifoundation_domain**
    under the **WebLogic Domain** folder again and navigate to select
    Security | Credentials.

7. On the resulting page, expand the **oracle.bi.system** folder.

8. Click on the **system.user** row and click on the **Edit...** button above the
    Credential Store Provider table.

9. Change the **User Name** field to that of the LDAP service user for the
    environment. In this example our user is **SVCBIPROD**.

10. Enter the respective credentials:

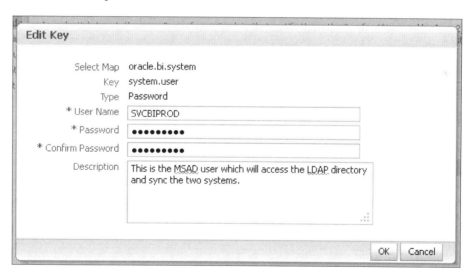

11. Click on the **OK** button on the form to save and close.

Restarting the WebLogic Server and Managed Server

Now, we can feel comfortable, when we restart the servers that our configurations will be in place. Two main assertions will take place after restarting the WLS Administration Server and the Managed Server, `bi_server1`. The first will be to validate that the LDAP configuration was indeed configured properly. The second will be that we are able to assign the LDAP service user to the BISystem application role. It is important to bring down the services in the correct order, especially when making a systematic change such as with the identity provider. So, first bring down the Oracle BI system components and then the WLS Administration Server and Managed Server:

1. In the Enterprise Manager Fusion Control console, stop all Oracle BI system components, using the GUI. Refer to the *Starting/stopping* system components section in this chapter, if you do not recall how to do this and for other caveats.

2. In the Fusion Control console, click on **Business Intelligence | coreapplication** from the left-hand side panel. Then on the main page, navigate to the **Overview** tab.

3. Click on the **Stop** button under the **System Shutdown & Startup** section.

4. Accept any prompts that appear.

5. Switch to the WLS Administration Console and navigate to **Environment | Servers** using the left-hand side pane.

6. Click on the **Control** tab on the resulting page.

7. Check both checkboxes for each server in the **Servers** table. Then, in the **Shutdown** drop-down list, select the **Force Shutdown Now** option.

8. Accept the **Server Life Cycle Assistant** confirmation prompt by clicking on the **Yes** button.

9. WLS will take a few minutes to shutdown. Once confirmed that WLS service is no longer running, start the service, using the methods explained earlier in this chapter. The command-line option or the GUI option (Windows OS only) should do the trick.

10. Verify that WLS has started by accessing the WLS Administration Console.

11. Start the Managed Server, **bi_server1**, using the WLS Administration Console GUI.

> If it is unclear to you how to start WLS and the Managed Server individually and you are using a basic Windows OS installation, you may use the **Start** | **All Programs** | **Oracle Business Intelligence** | **Start BI Services** option. Conversely, use the **Stop BI Services** option to stop the BI system all at once.

12. Once the WLS Administration Console is accessible, navigate to the **myrealm** Security Realm. Click on the **Users and Groups** tab.

13. Here, you should see the list of your LDAP users. The **Provider** column distinguishes the identity provider for each user:

	Name ⌄	Description	Provider
☐	Adrian	OBI Developer	DefaultAuthenticator
☐	BISystemUser	BI System User	DefaultAuthenticator
	chet.ace		MSADAuthenticator
☐	Christian	Oracle BI ACE	DefaultAuthenticator
	christian.ace		MSADAuthenticator
☐	obi11gbook	OBI11g Book User	DefaultAuthenticator
☐	OracleSystemUser	Oracle application software system user.	DefaultAuthenticator
	SVCBIPROD		MSADAuthenticator
	tennis.pro		MSADAuthenticator

14. If you've configured the identity provider correctly the LDAP groups should be shown in the **Group** tab as well.

> There are a few considerations on this assessment, which determine if you have configured your LDAP identity provider correctly. If you see LDAP users in this list, you are good to go. But, perhaps you are not seeing the correct list of users. Or, perhaps you are seeing no LDAP users at all but only the embedded WLS LDAP users as before.
>
> In either case, the best diagnostic would be to download a free LDAP browser such as JXplorer, and test the LDAP attribute values and connection information that you were provided with. That will quickly allow you to assert the LDAP credentials and validate which forest or **Organizational Unit (OU)** is needed to return the correct set of users on the **Users and Groups** tab.

Assigning the LDAP Service Account Role Privileges

Since the LDAP user and groups are now successfully being retrieved in WLS, the LDAP service user called SVCBIPROD needs to be provisioned with two administration roles in order to complete the communication between all system components. The first provision is conducted within WLS and the other in the Fusion Middleware Control. These administration roles provide the necessary connectivity between FMW Security and Oracle BI application security:

1. While still in the WLS Administration Console, click on **Security Realms | myrealm | Roles and Policies**.

2. In the **Roles** table, expand **Global Roles | Roles**.

3. On the row where the Admin name resides, under the **Role Policy** column, click on **View Role Conditions**.

4. Click on the **Add Conditions** button.

5. Select **User** from the **Predicate List** drop-down list and click on the **Next** button.

6. Enter the LDAP service user name (or equivalent) — SVCBIPROD — in the **User Argument Name** field and click on the **Add** button.

7. Click on the **Finish** button and then the **Save** button to save your modifications.

8. The resulting configuration should look similar to the following screenshot:

Next, let's add the SVCBIPROD service user to the BISystem application role:

1. Open the Enterprise Manager Fusion Middleware Control console.

2. Navigate from the left-hand side panel menu to expand the **WebLogic Domain** folder and right-click on **bifoundation_domain**.

3. Select **Security | Application Roles**.

4. In the **Search** section, check the radio button for the **Select Application Stripe to Search** and change the value to **obi** in that drop-down list:

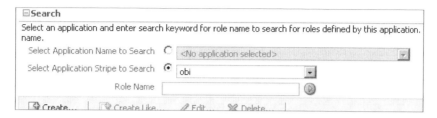

5. Leave the **Role Name** field blank and click on the play button next to the **Role Name** field to show all application roles for **obi**.

6. Click on the **Result** row containing the BISystem role name to highlight the row.

7. Click on the **Edit...** button above the **Search Results** table to edit the BISystem role.

8. Scroll towards the bottom of the **Edit Application Role** page to the **Users** section and click on the **Add User** button with the green plus sign.

9. In the **Add User** prompt, click on the green play button next to the **Username** field to search for all users.

10. Find the user in the **Available Users** column, or use a wildcard search in the **Username** field to find the LDAP service user, **SVCBIPROD** (or equivalent).

11. Move the user to the right-hand side column called **Selected Users** by using the right-arrow sign in the middle area between the two columns:

12. Click on the **OK** button to save your changes and close the prompt.

13. Click on the **OK** button in the upper-right corner of the **Edit Application Role** page.

14. Confirm that the **SVCBIPROD** user is now associated with the BISystem application role:

Role Name	Members
BISystem	BISystemUser, SVCBIPROD
BIAdministrator	BIAdministrators
BIAuthor	BIAuthors, BIAdministrator

JMS modules for BI Publisher communication

There is technically one last configuration which reflects the JMS modules communication for BI Publisher. This communication is mainly used for the robust BI Publisher Scheduler system. If you've used an LDAP system and replaced the BISystem user with an LDAP user, as in the steps mentioned in the preceding section you will need to complete the following steps as well:

1. Open the WebLogic Administration Console.
2. Navigate to **Services | Messaging | JMS Modules**.
3. Select **BIPJmsResource** from the list.
4. Click on the **Security** tab and then the **Policies** subtab.
5. Add a new condition for the user **SVCBIPROD** and save the entry.

This completes the steps for establishing an LDAP identity provider. Next, just refresh the GUIDs as explained in the next section and you are ready to log in to Oracle BI 11*g* in accordance with the FMW Security standard.

Refreshing Presentation Catalog GUIDs – sync it up!

After configuring the LDAP server as an identity provider and lining up both WLS and Enterprise Manager so that security is synchronized between those applications and the Oracle BI 11*g* application, a final step is to refresh the presentation catalog GUIDs. This will ensure proper running of Oracle BI 11*g* after a fresh installation; or indeed any other type of installation, such as after an upgrade from Oracle BI 10*g*, which we'll discuss in *Chapter 6, Upgrading the RPD and Web Catalog to 11g*.

The process of synchronizing the GUIDs revolves completely around the fact that user identities are stored atomically within the Presentation Catalog, not by username but by a **globally unique identifier (GUID)**. In certain circumstances, specifically when moving between environments with different identity providers or changes to users within those providers are made, the GUIDs can get out of synchronization. Following this process of GUID synchronization allows the catalog to stay organized.

At this point, the Oracle BI 11*g* system components should still be stopped or made offline as we have not started them since the restart to WLS. Check Enterprise Manager and confirm that all system components are stopped. If not, go ahead and stop all system components.

Two core configuration files must be modified for this synchronization exercise—NQSConfig.INI and instanceconfig.xml. Please make back-up copies of these files before making any modifications so that you maintain the ability to revert:

1. Navigate to `<ORACLE_INSTANCE>/config/OracleBIServerComponent/coreapplication_obis1/` and open the NQSConfig.INI file for editing.

2. Locate the text FMW_UPDATE_ROLE_AND_USER_REF_GUIDS parameter and change its value to YES as follows:

   FMW_UPDATE_ROLE_AND_USER_REF_GUIDS = YES;

3. Save and close the file.

4. Open the instanceconfig.xml file for editing. This file is located at, `<ORACLE_INSTANCE>/config/OracleBIPresentationServicesComponent/coreapplication_obips1/`.

5. Locate the Catalog XML element which should contain only the UpgradeAndExit subelement.

6. Add a new subelement to the Catalog element called UpdateAccountGUIDs with a value of UpdateAndExit.

   ```
   <Catalog>
     <UpgradeAndExit>false</UpgradeAndExit>
     <UpdateAccountGUIDs>UpdateAndExit</UpdateAccountGUIDs>
   </Catalog>
   ```

7. Save and close the file.

8. Start all Oracle BI system components using the Enterprise Manager Fusion Middleware Control GUI.

9. Presentation Services should fail to come up but should not throw any errors. If an error is presented to you in the resulting start-up prompt, you most likely have a syntax error resulting from editing of the configuration files.

> Presentation Services won't start up after setting the element value in the `instanceconfig.xml` file. This is by design. If you look at the newly added subelement in the `instanceconfig.xml` file, the value is `UpdateAndExit`, which gives some insight that the account GUIDs are updated, but then an exit occurs before any other processing can happen.

10. While the other services are started and the Presentation Services system component is down, open the `NQSConfig.INI` file again for editing.

11. In the `NQSConfig.INI` file change the value of `FMW_UPDATE_ROLE_AND_USER_REF_GUIDS = YES;`to `FMW_UPDATE_ROLE_AND_USER_REF_GUIDS = NO`.

12. Save and close the `NQSConfig.INI` file.

13. Open the `instanceconfig.xml` file again for editing.

14. Modify the `instanceconfig.xml` file by changing the value of the recently added `UpdateAccountGUIDs` subelement from `UpdateAndExit` to none:

```
<Catalog>
   <UpgradeAndExit>false</UpgradeAndExit>
   <UpdateAccountGUIDs>none</UpdateAccountGUIDs>
</Catalog>
```

15. Save and close the file.

16. Restart all system components using the Enterprise Manager GUI.

17. Once the system components have been started, open the analytics portal using the default URL, `http://<server_name>:9704/analytics/`.

18. Login with the WebLogic administrator's credentials.

19. The log in should be successful. If so, log out.

20. Next, log in with any of the MSAD LDAP users. Even the `SVCBIPROD` user should be able to log in. This is a quick acid test because if both the WLS embedded LDAP user—WebLogic—and an LDAP service user are able to log in to the Oracle BI portal—you have success!

Now, we've completed the LDAP identity provider's setup exercise, let's read some more about the advanced security features available to you in Oracle BI 11*g*.

JMX, MBeans, and Java

Similarly to WLST, when there comes a time for automating processes that interface with WLS or Fusion Control, there is an opportunity to look at the System Management API leveraging JMX, MBeans, and some Java programming. Again, using a handy IDE such as NetBeans or JDeveloper, which can put together a custom Java program that can be executed via command line, is a cinch for a Java programmer. The Oracle BI 11*g* System Management API documentation (`http://docs.oracle.com/cd/E14571_01/bi.1111/e10541/admin_api.htm`) provides several code examples of creating and running Java code to interface with WLS. Those examples include programmatically checking the status of the Oracle BI system components, restarting the system components, and scaling-out the servers.

Migrating FMW Security to other environments

In previous versions of Oracle BI, migrating all components of security and other Oracle BI artifacts was done simply by moving the RPD and/or Web Catalog from the source to the target server. Oracle BI 11*g* is much broader in scope and does not come with such a luxury. This section takes a glance at the files that comprise FMW Security within the System Management tools, leveraging the WebLogic security import/export utility, and leveraging an open source project called **Project Amelia**, to aid in simplifying security migration.

FMW core security files

Security configuration within Fusion Middleware is ultimately stored by several configuration files that maintain the necessary metadata regarding the environment. The file that stores the application roles and policy configurations shown via the Fusion Control GUI is the `system-jazn-data.xml` file. This is the file-based Policy Store for FMW. The `system-jazn-data.xml` file and other files residing in the same folder path, `<FMW_HOME>/user_projects/domains/bifoundation_domain/config/fmwconfig`, revolve around XACML and OPSS concepts discussed earlier in this chapter. It is good to know where and why these files exist purely from a technical administration perspective.

 For now, just keep in mind that this is the location of the Policy Store. As an advanced note, the Policy Store can be placed in an LDAP system, currently only OID, but that is a much more advanced configuration that is seldom used.

This file contains two major configuration sections. The first contains the application role definitions themselves (that is BIAdministrator, and so on) and which principals (users, groups, and other application roles) are assigned to those application roles. The second contains the policies (permission-based points of access to certain items or resources within the Oracle BI application) and which application roles and principals can access those policies. An example of a policy resource item would be `oracle.bi.server.manageRepositories`, which can control permissions to manage the RPD. You can learn more about these technologies and how they are applied by learning more about the Oracle Application Development Framework, which is the Java framework controlled by Oracle that was partially used to develop Oracle BI 11*g*, if interested.

Project Amelia

Project Amelia is an open-source initiative that allows for easier migration of basic security changes from a source environment, usually development or test, to subsequent environments such as production. The power of Project Amelia is that it can be executed via command line on any operating system where Oracle BI 11*g* is implemented. Project Amelia can be downloaded for free from its open source repository on GitHub at `https://github.com/artofbi/Oracle-FMW-Amelia`.

The following exercise steps show how to execute Project Amelia and migrate basic security from a source to a target environment. Project Amelia can be used to provide snapshot documentation of your Oracle BI 11*g* environment's Fusion Middleware Security. This is perfect for project documentation that can enable quick recovery from a certain point in time. The only prerequisite for using Project Amelia is that the Java JDK needs to be installed on your machine. The path to the Java home should be set as an environment variable, which can be referenced readily from the command line.

Downloading Project Amelia

Follow the next steps to download Project Amelia:

1. Download Project Amelia from `https://github.com/artofbi/Oracle-FMW-Amelia/downloads`.

2. Extract the ZIP or `tar.gz` file to a local temporary directory, for example, `C:\Temp\`.

3. Navigate inside the folder structure to **OBIEE11g_Amelia | dist**.

4. Copy the JAR file from the `/dist/` folder to a base folder on the Oracle BI 11*g* server that will be accessible from a command prompt, for example, `C:\Temp\`.

5. Open a command prompt and change the directory to `C:\Temp\`.

Getting the FMW Security file

For this purpose you can follow the next steps:

1. Locate the `system-jazn-data.xml` file on the Oracle BI 11*g* server. This file is located at `/<FMW_HOME>/user_projects/domains/bifoundation_domain/config/fmwconfig/`.

2. Copy the `system-jazn-data.xml` file to the `C:\Temp\` folder.

Running the script and generating the WLST script

For this purpose you can follow the next steps:

1. Execute the following command from the command prompt:

```
java -jar OBIEE11g_Amelia.jar "C:\Temp\system-jazn-data.xml" "C:/
Temp/" weblogic Admin123 localhost 7001
```

2. The resulting file, `OBI11gSecurityMigration.py`, has a `.py` extension that contains pure WLST syntax.

There are six arguments that can be passed in to the program. The first is the location of the `system-jazn-data.xml` file and the second is the output directory path, which must contain a trailing slash. The remaining arguments are the credentials for the administration of the target WLS. Since the resulting script is obtained by running the preceding code that is executed on the target machine using the WLST, the target server's credentials are entered in WLST so that they appear in the resulting `.py` script. Respectively, the remaining arguments are the WLS admin username, WLS admin password, WLS name, and WLS port.

Migrating the security script and running it on the target server

For this purpose you can follow the next steps:

1. An FTP or a manual network transfer operation sends the `OBI11gSecurityMigration.py` file to the target WLS where the subsequent Oracle BI 11*g* environment resides.

2. For example, the target server would be QA or UAT, if the file is coming from the Development Server, and so on.

3. Place the file in an easily accessible folder location such as `D:\Amelia\`.

4. Start the WLST command-line engine by launching the program from the location found in our previous exercise, using WLST, which is at `<FMW_HOME>\oracle_common\common\bin\wlst.cmd`. Execute the following command from the command line once the command prompt appears—`execfile(<full file path location of the .py file>)`:

   `execfile(D:\Amelia\OBI11gSecurityMigration.py)`

5. The script will execute and the Fusion Middleware security will be updated.

6. Open the Enterprise Manager Fusion Control console and navigate to **Security | Application Roles** management area to confirm that the Application Role assignments have been transferred successfully.

Be sure that you have a grasp of each environment that you are managing before executing the WLST script. When running the WLST script against a clean target Oracle BI 11*g* server environment, the amount of manual effort required for moving the application role assignments can be reduced. Project Amelia is not perfect and at present it only migrates the application role assignments for users, groups, and other application roles. As of the latest release, it does not capture or migrate advanced configurations such as custom application policies. For capturing both application roles and application policies, although only in binary file format, you will need to use the WLS Import/Export utility.

FMW Security Import/Export utility

Although Project Amelia is a time-saver and safe alternative for conducting basic migration of security, the WebLogic Server provides a mechanism for exporting a full security realm, that is users, groups, and provider configurations, and so on, for purposes of backup or migration to another security realm. Remember, the security realm, `myrealm`, handles the Identity Store portion of FMW Security but the Enterprise Manager Fusion Control handles the configuration of the Policy Store. So, another utility is provided to migrate the Policy Store from one environment to another, its function is called via WLST, `migrateSecurityStore`.

Using the Security Realm Migration utility

When migrating security, there are only two scenarios proposed to artifacts on your target environment—clean or dirty. If you have already done a clean migration (that is for the first time) to your target once then the environment is now dirty. So, subsequent migrations must take into consideration the possibility of overwriting or replacing existing items. Regarding security realm migration, the WLS Security Realm Migration utility handles all of this for you. For example, if you export a security realm from a Development environment and it contains a group named BIAdministrators that also exists in the Production environment already, the import into Production will not overwrite the BIAdministrators group already existing there. To understand how to migrate the default security realm from one environment to another follow the next steps:

1. Open the WLS Administration Console and navigate to **Security Realms | myrealm**.

2. Click on the **Migration** tab.

3. Click on the **Export** subtab.

4. Enter a temporary path on the physical server where the Oracle BI 11*g* implementation resides, for example C:\Temp\, in the **Export Directory on Server** field:

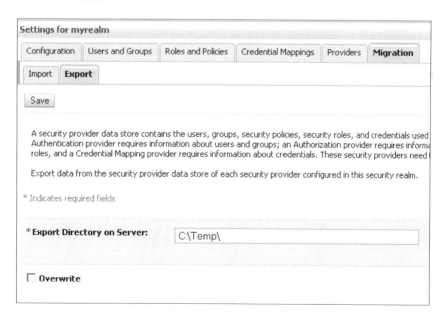

5. Click on the **Save** button.

6. A success message should appear. The resulting directory should have several DAT files now placed inside of it and should appear similar to the following screenshot:

Filename △	Filesize	Filetype
📁 ..		
📄 DefaultAuthenticator.dat	6,234	DAT File
📄 DefaultCredentialMapper.dat	372	DAT File
📄 exportIndex.dat	670	DAT File
📄 XACMLAuthorizer.dat	158,338	DAT File
📄 XACMLRoleMapper.dat	35,964	DAT File

7. To import this security realm's exported metadata to a target system, copy all DAT files to the target environment and place in a similar location, for example `C:\Temp\`.

8. Open the WebLogic Administration Console in the target environment and navigate to **Security Realms | myrealm**.

9. Click on the **Migration** tab and then click on the **Import** subtab.

10. Enter the folder path on the target server where you placed the exported files from the source environment in the **Import Directory on Server** field.

11. Click on the **Save** button.

Following the preceding steps, you will successfully migrate a single security realm from one environment to another. Unless you check the **Overwrite** checkbox, when you export the security realm, WLS will automatically conduct a difference algorithm to ensure that no users, groups, and so on, are overwritten in the target environment.

Using the migrateSecurityStore function via WLST

This book recommends using the `migrateSecurityStore` function of WLST, only if you have modified application policies within the Fusion Control environment of your Oracle BI 11*g* implementation. If only application roles have been created or modified, we suggest using Project Amelia, as discussed in the preceding section. However, for completeness, use the following syntax for calling the `migrateSecurityStore` function from WLST in offline mode:

```
migrateSecurityStore(type="appPolicies",srcApp="obi",
configFile="<jpsConfigFile>", src="<srcJpsFile>", dst="<dstJpsFile>",
overwrite="false")
```

In the preceding syntax, `<jpsConfigFile>` is the `jps-config.xml` file located in the same configuration directory as the `system-jazn-data.xml` file. `<srcJpsFile>` is the source environment's `system-jazn-data.xml` file and `<dstJpsFile>` represents the target environment's `system-jazn-data.xml` file.

This approach has several limitations. It may require additional post-migration configurations and additional manual sanity checks, even though it is the primary means of Policy Store migration from Oracle. No automated mechanism is provided out of the box to conduct this migration.

Oracle BI Publisher system management

Oracle BI Publisher can be embedded within Oracle BI 11*g* or stand on its own as a solo installation. Following this book's guidance, the result of the installation discussed in *Chapter 3, Installing on Windows Server 2008*, is the former. As per that configuration, BI Publisher's system management tools are primarily the same as those used for Oracle BI 11*g*. The WLS Administration Console and Fusion Control console are used to monitor, deploy, and set data source configurations for BI Publisher. *Chapter 12, Developing Reports Using BI Publisher* covers several details concerning the administration of BI Publisher.

Monitoring system performance

Ideally an application server environment will monitor and regulate itself to optimize performance and resolve any issues automatically if one is to occur. However, this is of course just wishful thinking! But luckily, WLS at least provides mechanisms to monitor the environment. The ability to monitor WLS is available from the WLS Dashboard. This can be a very helpful means for gauging request loads, most active applications, and peak load times. All of these can contribute to a better understanding of when and in which direction to optimize the server(servers).

Another approach for monitoring Oracle BI is under the analytics server itself. By entering the URL, `http://<bi_server>:9704/analytics/saw.dll?Perfmon`, a diagnostic view is displayed. This information provides insight into current activity and peak uses within the Oracle BI system components. Taking this information into account, combined with information from the WLS Dashboard, and possibly other sources such as Windows Server's perfmon logs, the load balancing servers, and database monitoring services, you should have enough data to make an informed decision on tuning the Oracle BI 11*g* environment for optimal performance.

Have a backup plan!

It's hard to get out of a chapter about managing a system without discussing backing up and disaster recovery. Again, an entire chapter could be filled with content on this subject, but that would be beyond the scope and intent of this book. Let's first be aware that backing up the FMW folder structure is a good thing. The frequency is the choice of each organization, but once a week at a minimum is a good recommendation. Each application delivered with the Oracle BI 11*g* suite has its own backup consideration. Though OBIEE, OBIP, and RTD comprise the Oracle Business Intelligence Enterprise Edition software, they have some common metadata elements and some that are sole references.

The gross loss of effort after your Oracle BI 11*g* environment has been established will usually stem from any development which has occurred in the RPD or Presentation Catalog artifacts. The `.rpd` file and the Presentation Catalog folder should be continually backed up inline with the development and deployment life cycle. From a database perspective, the relational schemas created during the Oracle BI 11*g* installation by the RCU will also need to be backed up. Typically this falls inline with other backups conducted on the database server where these schemas reside. Using Project Amelia to backup the basic security principals and application role assignments is also a good measure to take.

 Ultimately, a full monthly backup of the entire FMW folder structure is simply the minimum that should be done in any enterprise production deployment of Oracle BI 11*g*.

Recommendations for further learning

This chapter looked at the basic points to advanced aspects of the Oracle BI system management components. There were a few sections which were limited in coverage because of the advanced nature of the topics. As a step in the right direction, please explore the following recommendations for a chance to expand your learning further:

- **WebLogic Scripting Tool**: `http://docs.oracle.com/cd/E17904_01/web.1111/e13813.pdf`

- **Understanding Oracle BI Security**: `http://docs.oracle.com/cd/E15586_01/bi.1111/e10543/install.htm#`

- **BIESC768 JXplorer**: `http://jxplorer.org/`

- **LDAP Configuration**: `http://download.oracle.com/docs/cd/E14571_01/bi.1111/e10541/toc.htm`

- **Oracle BI SampleApp**: `http://www.oracle.com/technetwork/middleware/bi-foundation/obiee-samples-167534.html`

- **System Management API**: `http://docs.oracle.com/cd/E14571_01/bi.1111/e10541/admin_api.htm`

A review – what I should now know!

For self review and recap of the chapter, here are a few questions. There is no answer key. These questions are for your own reflection on the chapter:

1. From which console do you deploy the Oracle BI RPD and Presentation Catalog?

2. Name the two Oracle BI 11*g* System Management APIs.

3. How many security realms are configured with the default Oracle BI 11*g* installation?

4. What are the key files that need to be backed up for Oracle BI 11*g*?

5. In WLS, what is the WLS embedded LDAP directory?

6. Under which main tab and section of the WLS Administration console do all user and group directories get configured and reside?

Summary

In this chapter, we explored the system management tools required to administer the core components of the Oracle BI 11*g* environment. We discussed each main section of the WLS Administration and Enterprise Manager consoles. We provided insight and an example on how the APIs can be interfaced with Oracle BI 11*g* to manage the environment programmatically. Although an optional exercise and instruction was provided for how to configure an organization's LDAP system with FMW Security in order to authenticate users with Oracle BI 11g. Finally, we took a look at deploying the core Oracle BI metadata components, migrating security, and monitoring performance. These management concepts should have provided you with an above average understanding of how to administer your Oracle BI 11*g* environment and speculate on future activities that you may need to facilitate within your organization.

In the next chapter, you will learn how to migrate legacy Oracle BI 10*g* artifacts to Oracle BI 11*g* and discover the nuances that come with that effort.

6
Upgrading the RPD and Web Catalog to 11*g*

At this point, you should have installed the software and major components, and used the RCU to create the database schemas that are required for 11*g*. Now, we can look at the upgrade process for the most fundamental parts of the system from a version 10*g* implementation to 11*g*.

The upgrade process for this is extremely straightforward, as Oracle has provided an easy-to-use upgrade tool that we will step through in this chapter.

If you are upgrading a current live implementation, then we must consider the wider implications of the upgrade, especially the possible effects on current functionality. Therefore, in this chapter we will also touch upon the thinking and planning that is needed prior to a full upgrade for a current live implementation.

Upgrading an RPD and Web Catalog

Before attempting an upgrade, ensure that you have the necessary files and the correct administrator details for the following:

- 10*g* RPD
- 10*g* Web Catalog (in 11*g* you will find that this is now more commonly referred to as the Presentation Catalog)

You should also consider the following before the upgrade:

- Check that, the new 11g system has the correct database connectivity setup for the newly upgraded 10g RPD. For example, on an Oracle database, this would mean configuring the TNSNames.ora file on the new system.

 Remember that 11g utilizes its own TNSnames.ora file rather than requiring a separate Oracle client installation. It was the case in 10g. The path for this is: [middleware home]/[oracle home]/Oracle_BI1/network/admin.

- Note that any configuration files that have been changed must have these changes reapplied in the 11g system as the Upgrade Assistant does not perform this. This includes NQSConfig.ini and instanceconfig.xml.

- If you have other customizations on your current 10g implementation, you will also need to reapply these. This may include CSS files to change the look and feel of the frontend, or enhanced functionality via JavaScript files. Also, rather than reapplying, you may actually need to redevelop customized styles and skins. You can ascertain this by testing your old customizations during the regression cycle that we will go through at the end of this chapter.

Before embarking on the upgrade of these components, also check that you have started up all of the relevant 11g services. These services are as follows:

- BI services
- WebLogic Server
- Enterprise Manager

You can test this by logging in to the following links (the port numbers will be different if you have changed these in your initial installation):

- **Enterprise Manager**: http://localhost:7001/em
- **Weblogic Server Console**: http://localhost:7001/console
- **OBIEE Answers**: http://localhost:9704/analytics

 IMPORTANT

Please note that the upgrade takes place online and against a live system. Any current Web Catalog or RPD that has already been installed in the new 11g environment, will be superseded and replaced by the upgraded components (although the previous files will be automatically stored safely).

Upgrade Assistant

Oracle provides a simple and straightforward utility called **Upgrade Assistant**, for upgrading an RPD and Web Catalog to 11*g*. This section will take you through the steps for upgrading an RPD and Presentation Catalog simultaneously, using the Upgrade Assistant. Later in this chapter, we will also cover the upgrade of the BI Scheduler database schema via the same Upgrade Assistant.

So let's start upgrading an RPD and Presentation Catalog, using the Upgrade Assistant:

1. Double-click on the executable file to start the Upgrade Assistant. On a Windows machine, this can be found at: `\INSTALL_LOCATION\Oracle_BI1\bin\ua.bat`.

2. On Linux, you can run the `ua` command from the same file location:

    `./ua`

3. Upon initiation, the first screen is the **Welcome** page. Click on **Next** to continue.

4. In this example, we are upgrading both the Oracle BI RPD and Presentation Catalog. So in the **Specify Operation** screen, choose the first option, as you can see in the following screenshot and click on **Next**:

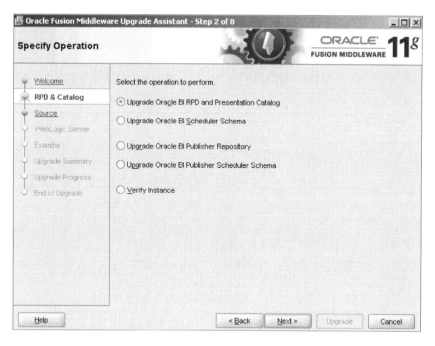

5. In the **Specify Source Details** screen, ensure that the boxes for **Upgrade Repository (RPD)** and **Upgrade Catalog** are checked.

6. Enter the locations of the 10*g* RPD and catalog.

7. Enter the administrator credentials for the old RPD.

8. In the **Password** and **Confirm Password** boxes, enter a new password for the upgraded RPD. This has to have a minimum length of eight characters and include at least one numeral:

> Note that in the next screenshot, we have not stipulated the exact location of the Deliveries Directory in the Web Catalog. This is because the Upgrade Assistant will recursively scan the location and will continue as long as it finds a Deliveries Directory folder, even if that folder is empty.

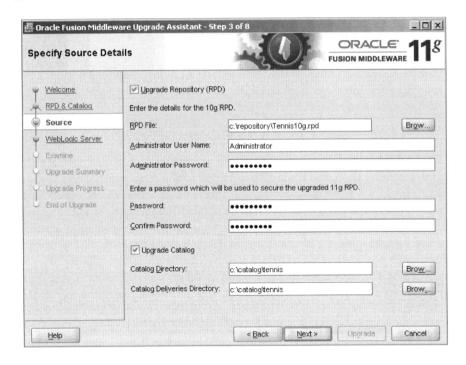

9. Next, in the **Specify WebLogic Server** screen, enter the administrator's **User Name** and **Password** details of the WebLogic Server Administration Console. The default **Port** is **7001**, unless this has been changed in the installation.

10. Click on **Next**:

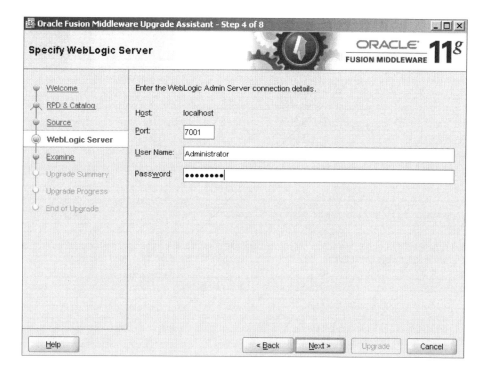

11. The Upgrade Assistant will now run a sanity check of the location details for the RPD and Web Catalog.

If the directories exist and the files are accessible that is, not read-only, you will see the **succeeded** message underneath the **Status** heading. You can see an example of this in the following screenshot.

Instead if there are failures, you will see the **failure** message under the **Status** column. Then, you can inspect the log file and seek to remedy the issues found. The log location can be found at the bottom of the **Examining Components** screen, as shown in the following screenshot.

12. Click on **Next**:

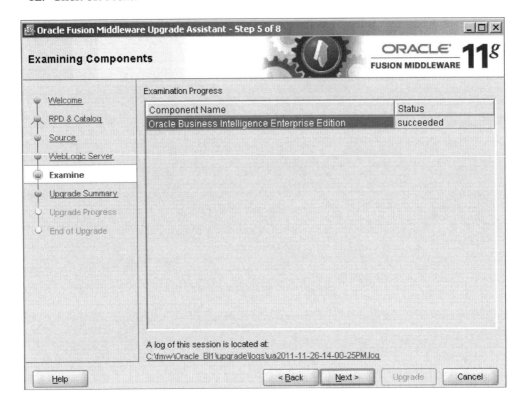

13. In the **Upgrade Summary** window, you'll see a summary of the components to be upgraded, as you can see in the following screenshot:

 As highlighted at the beginning, the upgrade takes place within a live system. So, we must ensure that we are happy at this point, as cancelling the process after clicking on **Upgrade**, may leave the new 11g system in an uncertain state.

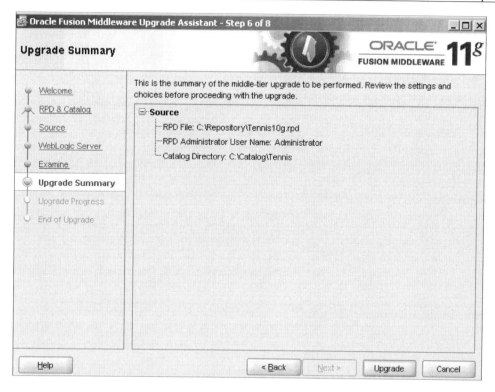

14. Once the **Upgrade** button on the previous screen is clicked, the listed objects will be upgraded. The process will take a few minutes, and you will see the screen, as shown in the following screenshot, while this takes place. This will give you an indication of how much time is left and what percentage has been completed for the upgrade.

15. If you have succeeded until this point, the upgrade should run smoothly. However, if any errors appear, consult the log file to ascertain what has gone wrong. Most commonly, any problems that occur are to do with OBIEE services that have not started:

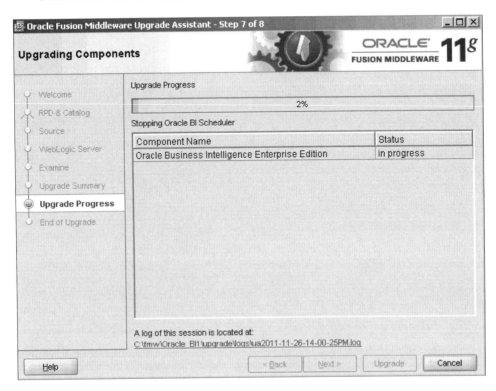

16. Once the upgrade process has finished, you will see the screen, as shown in the following screenshot. This shows that 100 percent of the upgrade process has been completed and you will see the **succeeded** message under the **Status** column.

17. At this point you can actually click on **Close** as there are no further processes to run. However, it is worth clicking on **Next** as this will give you a summary of what has taken place:

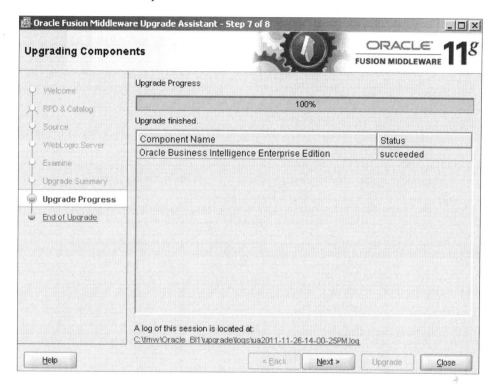

18. The first summary screen is the **Upgrade Success** screen, as shown in the following screenshot. It will provide you the location of a text file containing the details of what has taken place during the upgrade.

It will also provide you with a list of optional post-upgrade tasks. An example, which we will cover later on, is about rerunning the Upgrade Assistant in order to upgrade the scheduler, if you have iBots/agents in your current system.

Other common post-upgrade tasks include recreating CSS files and skins, and upgrading a cluster:

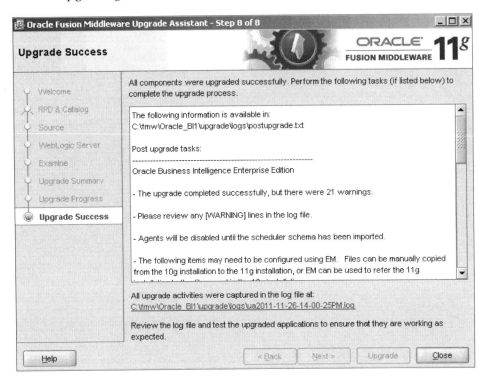

19. Check the log for any warnings and rectify appropriately.

For example, there are various alphabetical characters that are invalid when naming users or groups. These are ", +, =, \, <,>, ; ,and .. If a user or group has one of these characters in its name, you must recreate that object in the newly upgraded 11g RPD as it will not get copied over from the previous 10g version.

Other warnings link in with the post-upgrade tasks that we mentioned previously. In the preceding screenshot, you can see that we are being told that agents will be disabled until the relevant schema has been imported. So, if we were using agents (iBots) in 10g, we should proceed to import this schema:

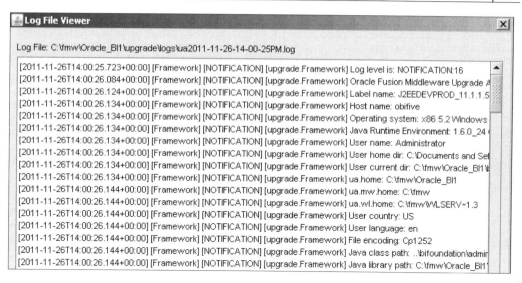

Verification

Now, we have successfully upgraded the 10*g* RPD and Presentation Catalog files into ones that can be run in 11*g*. At this point, the upgraded components should live in our 11*g* system, replacing the previously incumbent files. We can verify this by logging in to Enterprise Manager and checking that our 11*g* system is indeed referring to the newly upgraded components.

As shown in the following screenshot, if we log in to Enterprise Manager and look at the **Deployment** tab, we can see that the current live RPD and Web Catalog are the ones that we have upgraded through the Upgrade Assistant.

The newly upgraded RPD will be located at `/INSTALL_LOCATION\instances\ instance1\bifoundation\OracleBIServerComponent\coreapplication_obis1\ repository`.

It is also possible to return to the Upgrade Assistant and choose **Verify Instance** at the **Specify Operation** stage, in order to check if the upgrade has run successfully. This option should be checked in order to see whether your OBIEE services are running (for example, the BI server) and whether the components have been upgraded or not:

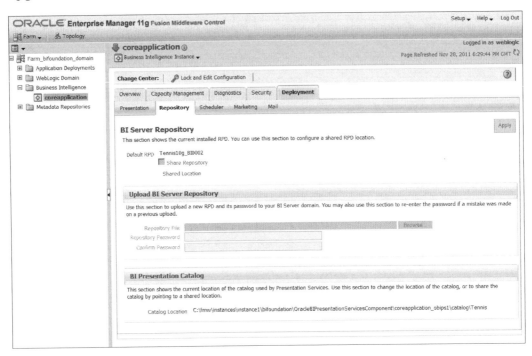

You can also check the RPD and Presentation Catalog by logging in to our dashboards, and connecting to the RPD in online mode using the OBIEE Administration Tool. If you are new to OBIEE and not sure what this means, don't worry for now as we will be covering this in depth during the rest of the book.

Upgrading BI Scheduler

The metadata for agents (previously named in 10g as iBots) is stored in the Web Catalog. This metadata has been upgraded in our previous run of the Upgrade Assistant. However, as you would expect with such an aptly named service, the scheduling and management of jobs is carried out by the BI Scheduler. The data for this is stored in a separate database schema.

The Upgrade Assistant connects to the original 10*g* schema and in effect runs an extract, transforms it, and loads the process into the new target 11*g* scheduler schema.

Again the process is simple and merely requires the connectivity and authentication details for the legacy and new scheduler schemas. We will briefly take a look at these steps now:

1. Return to the Upgrade Assistant, but this time, select the **Upgrade Oracle BI Scheduler Schema** option at the **Specify Operation** stage, as shown in the following screenshot:

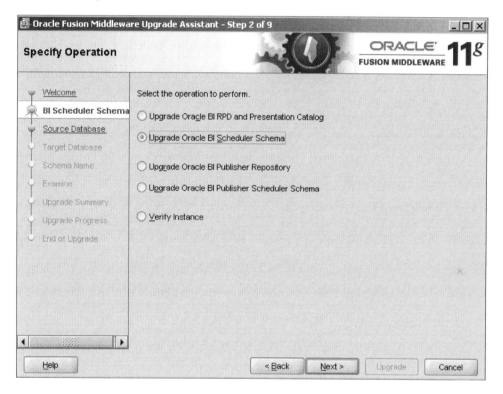

2. Enter the appropriate information for the source 10*g* scheduler schema in the **Specify Source Database** window, as shown in the following screenshot.

3. Click on **Next** and the Upgrade Assistant will attempt a connection with
    these details. If it is successful, you will move on to the next **Step 3 of 9**
    screen, where you will have to specify the target schema's details:

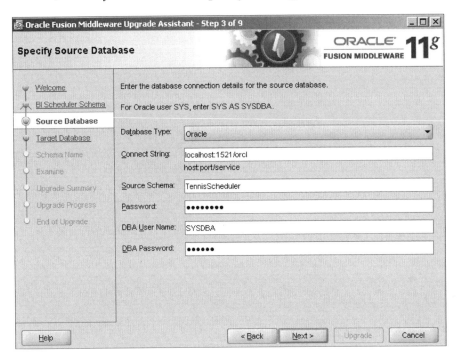

4. The same information must be entered for the target scheduler schema in the
    Specify Target Database screen. This time, the information is split across
    two screens. The first screen prompts for the database connectivity and
    authentication details.

5. Once you click on **Next**, you will be prompted for the **Target Schema User Name** and **Password**. Again click on **Next**:

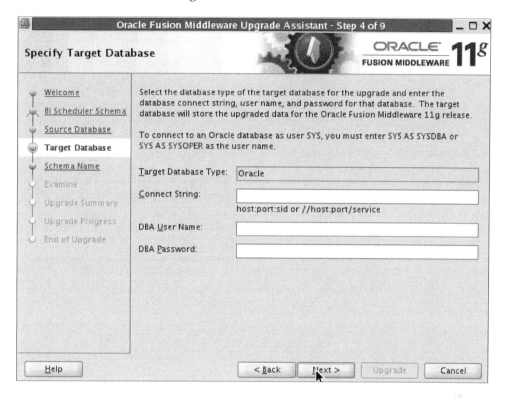

6. Next, the Upgrade Assistant will do a connectivity check for both databases and also proceed to do a column check for both schemas. If they get successfully validated, the status will appear as **succeeded**, just as in the upgrade of the RPD and Web Catalog.

7. The process from then onwards is exactly the same as for the previous components. Click on **Next**, the upgrade takes place and when it is successful, provides us with a summary of what has been done. Again, we should check the log file in order to ensure that there have been no issues.

 Note that the assistant can also be used to upgrade the BI Publisher schema. This is carried out step-by-step in a way that is very similar to that of upgrading the BI Scheduler schema as we have done now.

Manual migration

Before embarking on any testing of reports, make sure that you have manually migrated or recreated objects that are not part of the automatic process initiated via the Upgrade Assistant. As mentioned previously, these objects include:

- Any configuration changes to initialization files for example, `instanceconfig.xml`, `NQSConfig.ini`

- Custom style sheets and changes to the look and feel of the web frontend

- Custom images

- Custom JavaScript files that are referenced

The directory structure for CSS and skins has radically changed in 11*g*. So, for more information on the new structure refer to *Chapter 13, Customizing the Style of Dashboards*.

Clustered environments

Note that the upgrade will create a single OBIEE node. So, if you need a clustered 11*g* environment, you will need to scale out your 11*g* deployment separately.

If you are upgrading the BI Scheduler, you may have to manually amend the following settings in the 11*g* system:

- Scheduler script path

- Default script path

Consistency check

At this stage, a consistency check of the RPD should also be run. During each iteration of OBIEE (and previously Siebel Analytics/nQuire), the Consistency Check has become rather more strict and more comprehensive in its validation rules. This means that any modeling in the 10*g* RPD that was incorrect or not inline with best practice and was not caught previously, may be highlighted.

This may be flagged as a show stopping error that must be solved before the RPD can go live. For example in 11*g*, the validation rules are rather more stringent about correct logical column mappings. The naming rules are also stricter, so there cannot be leading or trailing spaces. Both of these issues will flag errors that will stop validation of a whole section of an RPD.

Other issues may produce warnings. These will not hinder deployment but ideally should be resolved. An example of this is that the Consistency Check will now flag up a connection pool that is being used for both report queries and as an initialization block for variables. This is because it can create a potential problem with resource contention.

The key message is that, an RPD upgrade should be run well in advance of a go-live date, to give a developer enough time to sort through any unforeseen issues.

Security

As part of this upgrade, all users, their passwords, and groups are moved from the RPD to the Weblogic Server. This is also the place where all future creations of security objects takes place. Other things to take note of are as follows:

- Groups are now replaced by application roles that can be managed via the WebLogic Server Administartion Console, as we demonstrated in *Chapter 5, Understanding the Systems Management Tools*.

- You will find that LDAP security mappings and variable initialization blocks remain in the upgraded RPD. This is fine, but to simplify administration or to utilize Oracle Identity Management you would be best advised to move these into WebLogic and the Oracle Platform Security Service.

- Note that there is now no administrator user for the RPD. This is replaced by the default weblogic WLS admin user.

- Before going live you should perform a sanity check for all security settings in WebLogic, and make sure that application roles are set up as required. This will form part of the regression test cycle that we will discuss in a moment.

- In the upgraded Web Catalog, catalog groups retain the same access rights and privileges as in the previous 10*g* version.

Outside of this component upgrade that we are conducting through the Upgrade Assistant, and as part of a larger upgrade project, you should be looking at the wider implications of the new 11*g* security model.

As we discussed through the security tutorials in Chapter 5, *Understanding the Systems Management Tools*, 11g provides a far more scalable security model than what was previously available, with a much easier method of administering it via WLS. It also has far more advanced embedded functionality, such as the embedded LDAP server in WebLogic that can be used as the Identity Store for Authentication. Weblogic also supports 3rd party commercial identity management products such as Active Directory and SiteMinder. In addition, the Authorization side is far more integrated with the general Oracle Fusion Middleware security architecture through Enterprise Manager.

If your project currently does not use LDAP and other more sophisticated tools or has other Fusion Middleware products, it is well worth exploring these new inherent 11g security capabilities, and spending some time to see how your project can better leverage these new possibilities and look at adopting this new 11g approach towards security.

Regression testing

Unlike other IT systems that tend to have very defined procedural or coded steps, Business Intelligence systems have an inherent complexity due to the query engines that form a large part of the system. OBIEE is no different, and with an upgrade like this, it is vital that we should test the system before releasing it live to our business users. In addition to the extra validation rules in the Consistency Check, there are changes to the query engine that can subtly alter queries that have been modeled identically in both 10g and 11g. 11g is quite a change from 10g and the BI server contains a lot of upgraded capability that can affect currently implemented functionality and reports. Also, due to the upgrade and changed functionality in the Web Catalog, upgraded reports may show changed behavior. This can range from missing labels to reporting aggregates producing results different from those previously expected.

The basic stages of a full regression test are described in the following sections.

Unit test

Once the upgrade has been completed as mentioned, a Global Consistency Check should be run on the RPD and if any errors occur, they should be noted and solved. Individual reports should be sanity checked by the technical team to ensure that results are being presented and that there are no other errors, for example, database connectivity or server errors, discrepancies in results, and visualization errors.

The behavior of customizations such as the performance of any custom JavaScript should also be checked. This will enable you to decide if any report actually needs to be rebuilt completely.

If you have updated the scheduler, then agents (previously known as iBots) should be run to check for error.

Full regression testing

A test team should be used to see whether the datasets being generated by reports are the same as before the upgrade.

As we mentioned the security model has changed in 11g. Tests should also check security rules and visibility. This will involve logging in to dashboards/reports with different users and checking if the appropriate object and/or data is being displayed for that user and user group. This is even more important if you have decided to make radical changes to your security model in order to better utilize the changes to security functionality and capability that arrive with 11g.

User Acceptance testing

The final stage of testing will be User Acceptance testing by the end business users to ensure that they are happy that the system is fit for purpose, and inline with the requirements for the previous implementation. This will also include testing of agents and ad-hoc answers' requests.

If the project is well run, the scripts for all of these tests should be available from the last iterative implementation in the project's lifecycle. If not, we cannot stress enough how important it is to create a robust set of scripts that have been created in conjunction with the business and end users.

At each stage of testing, errors should be tracked and dealt with by a developer.

To aid a robust test cycle, you may wish to do further research into third party test automation tools such as HP LoadRunner or the open source Selenium.

A review – what I should now know!

In addition to understand how to utilize the Upgrade Assistant in order to migrate some of the core components to 11*g*, you should also have an understanding of the following issues before you embark on an upgrade of your current implementation:

- Understand the original 10*g* architecture and plan how you will migrate across. This is especially important if the current implementation is in a clustered environment or has a lot of customizations.

- Understand and plan for the new skill sets required when implementing and supporting 11*g*. For example, WebLogic is a new middleware component in 11*g* that was not part of the product set before.

- It may be necessary to create a proof of concept, and/or at the very least carry out a dry run. This will give you an opportunity to perform Consistency Check for the upgraded RPD. If this highlights new issues in the RPD and Web Catalog, a better understanding of how much time/resource is needed to fix these will be reached.

- Agree acceptance criteria with the business and with management.

- Document the full upgrade with a list and instructions on migrating customizations.

- Document and implement a comprehensive testing strategy. This will incorporate everything from testing individual reports to checking security rules and privileges.

- Provide training and manage expectations for end users. Both the look and feel, and functionality is radically different in 11*g*. Users, especially power users, will need training on the new features.

- Work out a pathway on how to utilize the new features and capabilities of 11*g*.

Summary

As we have demonstrated in this chapter, the actual upgrade process using the Oracle provided Upgrade Assistant is very simple. However, around this, there are many other issues that we have touched upon, and these issues need to be looked at if an upgrade is to be successful. These include regression testing and exploring changes to the overall system such as in security.

Ultimately, the message is, "Plan, Plan, Plan!" The added value that a competent developer can add to this process is a comprehensive understanding of the scope of the upgrade process and the need for business involvement as well as an implicit comfort with the technical detail.

Now, we are ready to dive in and start to build a new 11*g* implementation from scratch. In the next chapters, we will discuss how to do this and create a brand new RPD and new fully working dashboards.

7
Reporting Databases

No book on Oracle BI would be complete without introducing the concepts of the reporting database.

Just to be clear, **Oracle Business Intelligence Enterprise Edition (OBIEE)** is neither a database nor a storage system for data. OBIEE grabs data from a source (which is normally a database), and sends it to your screen (or e-mail, PDF, and so on) in a presentable format.

As discussed in previous chapters, the source data can be held in a variety of formats including spreadsheets, tables, and XML. However, for most large implementations, a database is the only suitable source. If there are millions, or even billions of data items, a database is crucial. Moreover, a well-structured and well-maintained database is essential for the survival of an OBIEE project. Size matters when it comes to designing the database. The bigger the database, the better are the design needs — otherwise it will be impossible for your clients to run reports.

This chapter can only introduce the main concepts of a reporting database, because the process of creating an efficient database is the subject of dozens of books and blogs (see the recommended reading list). However, the details in this chapter should provide enough information to create a database that is fit for using in an Oracle Business Intelligence system.

The chapter is split into three parts:

- A brief introduction to the theory
- Guidelines for creating a warehouse
- Creating a warehouse example

Theories and models

It is said that creating a database is more about art than it is about science. I tend to agree with this. However, a number of theories and rules have evolved over the last 40 years that are worth understanding before attempting to build a database for an Oracle Business Intelligence system.

From an overall design perspective, there are two scientific types of database:

- Transactional databases
- Reporting databases

A **transactional database** is designed for the input and updating of data, usually in small but high volume changes to the data; whereas the **reporting database** is designed for fast access to the data, which can be transformed into useful information for decision-making. The common name for a reporting database is the **data warehouse** (a phrase originally coined by Bill Inmon).

The following diagram shows how tables in a transactional model are laid out. It shows a small extract of the system that will be used throughout this book, and is based on a Tennis statistics system:

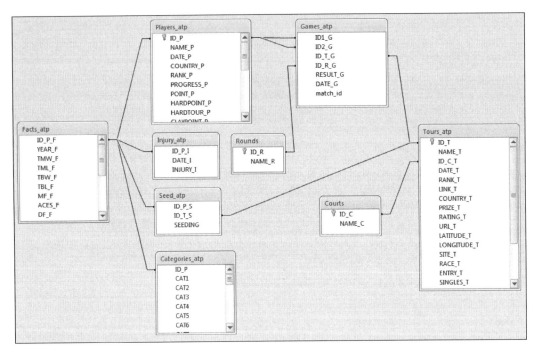

The following diagram shows more of the links involved in our transactional database, but not all of them. If all of the links were to be shown at once, the image would have become so complex that it would have appeared as blur lines and tables:

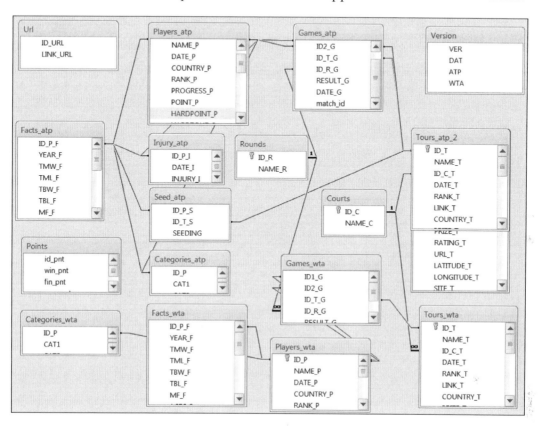

Reporting databases

There are two main theories for the design of a reporting database:

- Relational modeling
- Dimensional modeling

Relational modeling

The layout of tables in relational modeling is similar to that of a transactional system, that is, of Third Normal form. These types of warehouse are normally intended to populate smaller databases for operational reporting, or an **Operational Data Store (ODS)**. An ODS is a type of database that is usually used as an interim storage area prior to loading a corporate warehouse or for processing data and then loading data back into a source system. They are often multidepartmental levels and typically data is checked against a set of rules, and updated in batches. They do not contain history and are not designed for large scale reporting.

A note on normalization

The early development of theories on database design is dominated by E. Codd, whose works inspired a generation of new databases including Oracle, in the 1970s. In 1969, Codd proposed a relational model, which essentially ensured that tables in the database contain specialist data, such as customer names or sales orders, and that these tables relate to each other using a key field. In 1970, he expanded the theory to include normalization. The process of normalizing a database consists of reducing tables down to their smallest size, both in columns and rows, breaking them down into smaller tables. The objective is to remove data replication.

Codd's theories on normalization and the 12 rules of database construction that he created in the 1980s still apply today. I recommend that, anyone serious about building large scale Oracle BI systems should read his work, or at least the summaries!

Sources:

http://en.wikipedia.org/wiki/E.F._Codd

http://en.wikipedia.org/wiki/Database_normalization

http://www.dbnormalization.com/difinitions-of-the-normal-forms

http://en.wikipedia.org/wiki/Relational_model

Dimensional modelling

Dimensional modeling was proposed by Ralph Kimball in the mid 1990s as a method of speeding up report production and simplifying the database layer. The model is a response to the large complex relational databases (also known as **entity relational (ER)** databases).

Kimball published papers which showed why ER databases are not suitable for reporting:

> *However, in our zeal to make transaction processing efficient, we have lost sight of our original, most important goal. We have created databases that cannot be queried! Even our simple order-taking system creates a database of dozens of tables that are linked together by a bewildering spider web of joins.*

You can refer to the article called **A Dimensional Modeling Manifesto**, by Kimball, at `http://www.kimballgroup.com/html/articles_search/articles1997/9708d15.html`.

The main advantage of dimensional modeling is that it reduces the number of joins, which in theory results in a faster query runtime and a much simpler model for report developers to work with.

Dimensional modeling actually consists of tables of dimensions and a table of facts:

- The **dimension tables** hold information that is largely non-numeric, that is, descriptive text, dates, references, and so on. The records are related to an entity, such as a Tennis Player and usually represent an aspect of the data stored in the fact table.
- The **table of facts** holds data that can be aggregated, for example, counted, summed, averaged, or other calculations. The facts records are normally transactional or activity-related, such as a Person Holiday record.

The **Date table** is an example of a table of type dimension. It contains a list of dates, each of which is defined by a number of descriptive fields, or attributes, which could include month name and year, for example.

Dimension tables can also contain columns that are structured to represent a hierarchy, that is the relationship between different attributes within the dimension. For example, one possible hierarchy in the Date table is represented by the fields Year Number, Quarter Number, Month Name, and Date. This hierarchy has four levels, with Year at the top and Date at the bottom (most detailed) level.

An example of a fact table is a table recording daily sales by a store. In this example, the fact table might contain three columns recording the Date, Store Name, and Sales Amount.

Tables in a dimensional database are normally joined together by linking the dimensions to the facts. This is known as a **Star Schema** model, and is shown in the following diagram. The joins between the tables use key fields. The key fields on the dimension will be the primary key for that table, and the key fields on the facts are foreign keys.

As you can see, dimensional modeling establishes a much less complicated layout than the relational modeling system, and has fewer joins. The dimension tables (labeled with the suffix "D") only join to the fact table, which is located centrally:

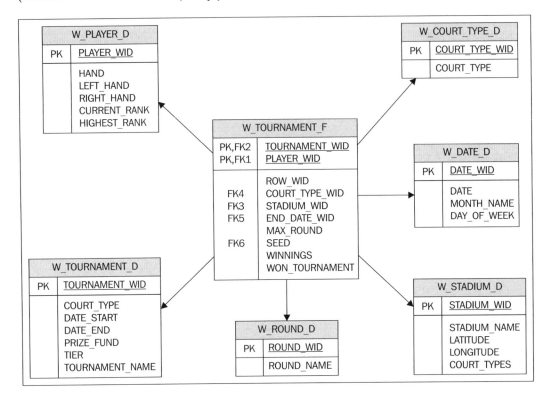

Why is database theory important?

The introduction to the theories behind the relational database may seem a little dry, and you may be wondering why we are looking at the theories of databases in an OBIEE book. But for every single project you undertake, it is essential that you have a good understanding of the data structures that you will be using, particularly when designing the OBI Repository. If you want your project to succeed, speed is crucial; but this is only achievable with the correct design. Therefore, choosing the correct design is crucial, which means understanding the theory.

Later in this book, you will be using dimensional modeling in the OBIEE configuration. It is also worth mentioning that there are other models which can help certain types of reporting. These types include the OLAP cube models and column-based databases, both of which are worth reading on, but are not covered in this book.

Designing your database – objectives, rules, and goals

Whenever you create a data warehouse for reporting, you have to consider that there are finite resources. There is never enough space to store data, never enough time to populate the database, and never enough processing power to use a fully normalized source. Even with the latest superfast technologies, such as Oracle Exadata, there is a limit to the amount of data that can be stored or processed in a given time period (ETL window).

The primary objective should always be to speed up the report production, which means using a dimensional model, particularly when storing a large amount of data. As discussed in the *Theories and models* section, using an entity relational database would reduce the redundancy of data and, therefore, reduce the amount of data stored and the time taken to load it. However, the report production time would increase.

It is always necessary to establish a trade-off between data volume (which improves speed of reporting), load speed (to minimize the amount of time loading a database), and read speed (to produce faster analysis). Each of these factors affect the other, as indicated in the following diagram. If the amount of data stored is increased, read speed will be minimized (good) but the load speed will be increased (bad):

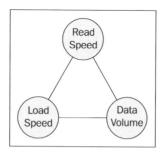

In order to ensure a good balance between data volume, load speed, and read speed, you should use a set of objectives, rules, and goals in your designs.

Objectives

My objectives when building a warehouse, in no particular order of importance, are as follows:

- Objective 1 – fast reporting
- Objective 2 – fast data loading
- Objective 3 – minimize data volume
- Objective 4 – accurate reporting

I believe that fast reporting is better than fast data loading. A delay in the availability of the system (while it uploads new data) is acceptable for a time, but if it takes an inordinate amount of time to run reports, the users will soon switch off. However, this does not mean that the system can be offline for the update process when the users require access on an ongoing daily basis. If this happens, your users will decide to look elsewhere for their reports.

 Note that if loading time is an issue, you could explore the use of a dual warehouse solution—load one warehouse while you are using the other, then switch warehouses.

Rules

In order to achieve the database objectives listed in the preceding section, there are a number of rules that must be adhered to:

- Rule 1 – complete dimensions
- Rule 2 – build generic tables
- Rule 3 – partition large tables
- Rule 4 – prudent indexing
- Rule 5 – aggregate everything
- Rule 6 – constant analysis of usage and accuracy
- Rule 7 – manage statistics
- Rule 8 – understand the granularity

These rules emphasize the use of **performance data**.

A note on performance data

Performance data is the data created in a warehouse that <u>makes reports run faster</u>. This not only includes the data that make queries use less data (aggregation tables), but also the data that reduces the number of joins in queries.

Types of performance data are as follows:

- Roll up data (aggregated data)
- Subsets
- Star fields
- Mini dimensions
- Flat tables
- Indexes
- Materialized views (for prejoined or precalculated tables)
- Calculated data

Rule 1 – complete dimensions

A complete dimension has two aspects:

- Complete in terms of number of rows
- Complete in terms of number of attributes (fields) *columns*

If you have a fact table that has a field related to a dimension (for example a Sales Order fact contains Order Taken Date, which links to the Date table), then the dimension table must contain a row which corresponds to every date within the fact. The ultimate way to enforce this is to add a <u>referential integrity rule</u> to your tables. However, this should not be generally done as it <u>impacts on load speed.</u>

Similarly, any attributes assigned to the dimension must be complete. For example, you may have a Shops table, which lists shops and includes contact details. Each shop will have a location (city, town, village, and so on) that must be included in the Shops dimension table. With this kind of scenario, there is a choice to be made—you can either apply a relational model, or add the relevant data to the Shops table's attributes. If you choose to follow a relational model, the Location table can be joined to the Shops table for reporting purposes, which is a very simple process. However, my preference is to bring the relevant data into the Shops table's attributes (fields). These attributes might include Location Name, Address, Country, and Postal Code.

Rule 1 fulfills Objectives 1 and 4, but at the cost of Objectives 2 and 3. Using a relational join for the location attributes helps with Objectives 2 and 3 but undermines Objective 1.

Rule 2 – build generic tables

It is vital to ensure that your model can cope up with the reporting requirements, both at present and in the future. Building a table just to suit a particular report might be great in terms of getting the job done quickly. However, you will inevitably end up with rewriting large amounts of the database, ETL, and the reporting system whenever any changes to requirements occur. Take an example of a Contracts table that has been built specifically to handle monthly salaried shop and head office employees. Later, if the client requires reports on sales achieved by temporary Saturday morning staff on weekly contracts, what will you do? You can build another dimension for these contracts or rewrite the Contracts table to accommodate both sets of staff. But then what about the sales team who were acquired this month, carrying their own contracts? It is much better to build the generic tables in the first place that will be able to satisfy a wide range of datatypes and user requirements.

Rule 3 – partition large tables

Partitioning is a way of breaking down large tables into smaller sets of records. Large tables can be partitioned by a single field value, such as Player Gender. This should really be an obvious thing to do, even if your database does not have the option to partition tables automatically. If you are using Oracle's partitioning capability, you will require an extra license, but it is worth investing in as it overcomes the need to create and maintain a manual partitioning system. My own working method is to apply a partitioning solution as soon as the number of records in a table exceeds 10 million, but you can partition smaller tables too. Once I encountered a project which had a table with 1.6 billion rows and no partition.

Rule 4 – prudent indexing

Prudent indexing ensures that Objectives 2 and 3 are not undermined. Indexes can be helped with joins and data filters, and can be the difference between a working database and one that has no value whatsoever. Unfortunately, there is often a tendency to over-index. When building a database, in the first instance you should only add indexes to fields that are used in the joins. Over time, you can analyze usage patterns and then decide whether more indexes are required to improve reporting performance or not. Removing unnecessary indexes will save time in the loading process and may even improve reporting performance. The Oracle database system now includes an option to monitor index usage, which can be very revealing (to implement add monitor usage to the index definition).

Rule 5 – aggregate everything

My motto is that if it can be aggregated, aggregate it! If you have a Daily Sales fact, why not create a Monthly Sales fact? And how about Annual and Weekly facts? Provided that the aggregation is used in the analysis, the report performance will usually be significantly better when accessing smaller datasets. Aggregating is, therefore, great for Objective 1. The downside is that all the aggregates need to be populated and stored, which is contrary to Objectives 2 (loading time) and 3 (amount stored). Again, a balance needs to be struck.

Aggregations need not be applied only to facts, they can also be applied to dimensions. If you take the Date table, which may have tens of thousands of rows, and aggregate these to a year level, this could result in only a couple of hundred records. Then, this table can be used to join to the Year Aggregate Sales fact. The two combined will have a huge performance benefit over the Date table joining to the Daily Sales fact and grouping by Year.

Rule 6 – constant analysis of usage and accuracy

You should analyze usage and accuracy constantly, because no matter how quickly your database is loaded, if the reporting system is slow to produce reports, your customers will soon lose interest and your project will collapse. It is crucial to know if a report is slow, and preferably before your customers know! Make sure that you have excellent feedback about the speed of reports from your reporting system, and also the speed of loading and, as far as possible, the accuracy of data in the warehouse.

My personal favorite way to do this is to create a dashboard showing usage, performance, and data items. The monitoring systems are often forgotten during the development stage and can be difficult to acquire funding for them at a later stage. Make sure you factor them in from the starting stage. If this is the only thing that you take from this chapter, remember that monitoring will make things so much easier — monitoring and performance data.

Rule 7 – manage statistics

Managing statistics is not just about gathering statistics each night, it's about ensuring that your queries are tuned for the tables that they run against. When building queries, we will use Oracle's Explain Plans feature to let you know what it plans to do. Automatically creating new statistics on your table each night can interfere with Explain Plans, which is the last thing you will want when you find one statistic that really suits your purposes. The best way I have found to avoid this, is to save the statistics for a table and then import them to the table after each load.

This ensures that the Explain Plan that you want to use, will be used. It is also possible to work with managing Explain Plans in a similar way. The statistics will still need to be reviewed regularly when the table size changes significantly, but the monitoring tools that you have put in place will tell you when a table has changed size, or when a query is slowing down over time.

Rule 8 – understand the granularity

Last, but certainly not least, don't compromise with data granularity. In order to create reports, which use nonrelated information, it can be tempting to break the natural granularity of the data. Consider an example of an employee database recording sickness absence. Here, the granularities are the employee and time (measured in days). An employee could be working on more than one project. If you are requested to produce a report showing absence by project, how can this be done? The tempting thing would be to break the granularity of the data by creating more than one record in the Absence fact table, one for each employee, date, and project. Don't do this. Keep the data stored at its natural granularity and join an Employee/Projects table to the Absence fact table (using the Employee key).

I have seen various methods, which show how to break a single record down into multiple records, allocating the facts across those records. However, I find it best to ignore these theories, and stick to the natural granularity of the original fact.

Goals

Along with rules that should be followed, I have goals that I aim for in the design and on-going upgrade of a warehouse. In an ideal world, we would only work with simple data, have unlimited resources, and have access to an OLTP source system. In the real world, we have awkward datasets (for example, many to many relationships), no way of putting triggers in the source system, and we never have enough computing power. Compromises, therefore, have to be made. But never compromise your objectives, try not to compromise your rules, and keep these goals in mind when responding to difficult design choices:

- Goal 1 – keep it simple
- Goal 2 – minimize the use of type 2 slowly changing dimensions
- Goal 3 – use data, not functions
- Goal 4 – minimize joins
- Goal 5 – reduce snowflaking
- Goal 6 – make it flexible

Goal 1 – keep it simple

This should be self-explanatory, but the goal is to be able to come back to your design (either you or the next consultant who will be editing your code) and quickly understand what it is doing. This entails making fewer objects and keeping code to a minimum.

Goal 2 – minimize type 2 slowly changing dimensions

Slowly changing dimensions are tables where the dimension attributes change over the time. For example, a staff member may get married and then change his/her last name. Then how to record the change? A dimension that includes the current staff member details and a record for his/her previous details is called **type 2 slowly changing dimension (SCD)**. I tend to avoid this wherever possible in the standard reporting stars. If you cannot avoid it, due to the need for reporting dimension changes over time, try to keep the history of a dimension record in a separate table. The dimension history table can still be used in reporting where required, but does not impact every report like the type 2 SCD tables do. Also, if you need to use a dimension history table, be careful about the keys you implement. Make sure that your facts are able to link to each relevant record of the dimension, not just to the dimension record in force when the fact was created.

Goal 3 – use data, not functions

The use of database functions in reporting can have a hugely detrimental effect on the speed of reports. Wherever possible, get the results of the functions into the table as extra fields.

Goal 4 – minimize joins

Joins are normally bad in performance. If data can be held in one table, hold it in one rather than two. Try to follow the Kimball's star schema methodology where it is applicable.

Goal 5 – reduce snowflaking

Snowflakes are not ideal in a warehouse. Snowflaking is normally slower due to an increase in the number of joins, but can also indicate that the dimension has not been built completely.

Goal 6 – make it flexible

Try to ensure that you have not created objects and data that are only fit for the reporting requirements that you already have.

For example, an initial requirement to report games won by a player in a year. The table storing the tennis games won by a player could be at a year level, but what if you want to drill into it by month? Store the data at the month level in the first instance and you can satisfy both requirements.

Design summary

Try to gain a good level of understanding regarding star schema database design, because it will speed up your report performance. However, be aware of the speed and data triangle and, therefore, the need to compromise.

Each data warehouse needs to weigh up the outcomes required against the technical objectives in order to determine which rules and goals are to be observed. This will then lead to a suitable warehouse design.

Whenever you have to make a design choice, score the possible methods against your rules and goals. This usually results in an obvious best approach.

Creating a warehouse

This section of the chapter will lead you through the design and build process for a small warehouse (often referred to as a data mart) used for the reporting examples in the next chapters of this book.

For this book, we have taken a tennis statistics program and created a warehouse for reporting. To achieve this, first of all we need to assess each table in the source system for its type of data in order to determine if it fits into a dimension table, fact table, or another table type. Based upon our assessment of the source tables, we can then design and build the warehouse tables. This is followed by the creation of a process to copy data from the source to the warehouse. Finally, we review and tune the database in order to ensure that we can meet the goals that we have set.

Source system assessment

We will start with a list of the source tables. For each list, we will note which datatype they are, examine the contents, determine if they are required in the warehouse, and consider any other factors that might be significant.

The standard approach is to look at the table from three angles:

- **Physical attributes**:
    - What are the columns and their data types?
    - What restrictions are there?
    - What keys are there?

- **Data content**:
    - Try to get as big a sample of the data as possible
    - Bring it into a system you understand, such as Excel, Access, or a database
    - Finally, try to understand the field contents and numbers involved.

- **Business use**:
    - Find out how the table is used in the source system.
    - If the table is used in an existing reporting system, what reports use the table (and how!)?

The tables in our source system are split into the Men's Tour and Ladies' Tour tables, along with some joint lookup tables, for example Tennis Court Types. A section of the database showing Men's Tennis is shown in the following diagram:

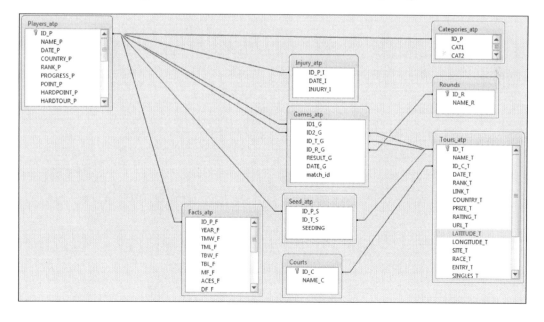

Based on our Tennis Statistics database, the following table demonstrates the typical analysis that should be done:

Source Table Name	Content	Rows	Potential Warehouse Target	Warehouse Notes
PLAYER_ATP	List of male players	23,535	Player dimension	The ATP and WTA source tables will be combined into one warehouse table.
PLAYER_WTA	List of female players	11,769		
ROUNDS	List of tournament rounds	17	Round dimension	
COURTS	List of court types	6	Court type dimension	
TOURS_ATP	List of tournaments for male players	8,381	Tournament dimension and Stadium dimension	The ATP and WTA source tables will be combined into one warehouse table.
TOURS_WTA	List of tournaments for female players	4,500		
GAMES_ATP	Each game played at the tournament, with the result	335,563	Match dimension and Match fact	Create two records in the MatchFact, one for each player in a singles match or four records for a doubles match.
GAMES_WTA	Each game played at the tournament, along with the result	170,844		
CATEGORIES_ATP	Extra information on a male player		Player dimension	Consider keeping in a separate table if the Player table becomes too wide (that is, too many columns).
CATEGORIES_WTA	Extra information on a female player			
FACTS_ATP	Annual statistics for each male player	1,530	Player Year facts	Player's yearly summary can also include stats not in the FACTS_ATP table.
FACTS_WTA	Annual statistics for each female player	0	n/a	

Warehouse design

We can now draw up a design for the warehouse, with a star schema in mind. Our goals are to reduce joins and, therefore, to reduce snowflake designs, and make the design flexible enough for any reporting that we would like to think of. We will also keep in mind the rules laid out in the first section of this chapter.

Warehouse tables

The initial result of our analysis has resulted in the six dimension tables and two fact tables. This is not set in stone, we need to be flexible enough to add more tables later if the report requirements dictate. There are no aggregate tables yet in place, as at this stage we do not know where, if any, there are performance issues. Given that we have designed a star, then the initial performance for a two-million records table should be fine:

Warehouse Table Name	Content	Type	Granularity
W_PLAYER_D	List of players	Dimension	Player
W_ROUND_D	List of rounds	Dimension	Round
W_DATE_D	List of dates	Dimension	Day
W_COURT_TYPE_D	List of court types	Dimension	Court type
W_STADIUM_D	List of stadia	Dimension	Stadium
W_TOURNAMENT_D	List of tournaments	Dimension	Tournament
W_MATCH_F	Matches at a tournament	Fact	Match and Player
W_TOURNAMENT_F	Players at a tournament	Fact	Tournament and Player

These tables can be arranged into the following two star schema layouts, with joins between the tables using the primary keys for the dimensions.

The Match star

The following diagram shows the Match star layout:

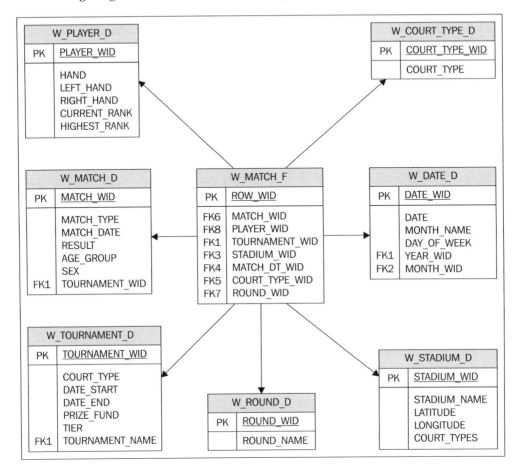

Note the direct connection from the Tournament dimension table (W_TOURNAMENT_D) to the Match fact table (W_MATCH_F). If we model the Tournament table to connect to the Match table (W_MATCH_D) and not have a Tournament_WID field in the Match fact, we will have a snowflake design.

Note that WID is a column name suffix that was introduced with Siebel. It stands for warehouse ID, and is used to name the field, which is normally part of the key for a table. For example, DATE_WID would be used on the Date table and would contain a warehouse derived ID. In the Oracle BI Applications databases, you often see ROW_WID as the primary key on the dimension tables.

The Tournament star

The following diagram shows the Tournament star layout:

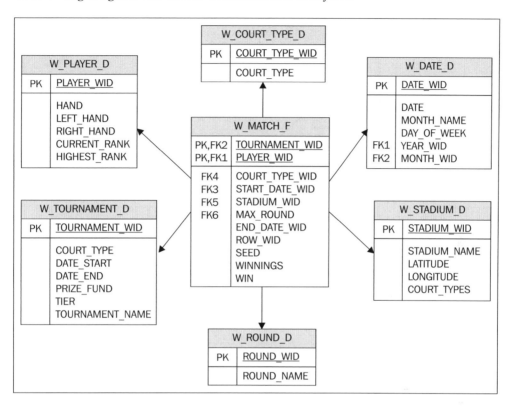

With the two star designs, we are now able to respond to a whole range of analyses, such as how many matches do left-handed players win in the Southern Hemisphere each year on hard courts!

Populate and tune

Having designed your warehouse, it's now time to create the objects.

Creating the tables is straightforward and can be achieved using free tools, such as SQL Developer.

You are now faced with choices over the use of indexes and partitions. The general rule of thumb is to only create what you need. If an index is not going to be assisting in reports, do not create it. If a table has more than 10 million records, it becomes a good candidate for partitioning. The latest versions of Oracle have a useful feature for auto incrementing partitions, which can make the whole process much easier to implement (make sure you have the right license though!).

Primary keys should be added, where suitable, certainly on the dimension tables, but also on the fact tables provided they do not slow down the loading process too much. If you are not able to use a unique key in the fact due to massive amounts of data, it is prudent to check that the dimensions rule is not broken, that is, make sure there are no references in the fact to dimension records that do not exist.

Monitor and maintain

Having created and populated our warehouse, the hard work begins! Once the Oracle BI tool starts to throw requests at our database, we will learn where the bottlenecks are. Monitoring the **ETL (extract, transform, and Load)** and database statistics everyday are vital to ensure that the potential breakages are avoided. This includes understanding how the tables are growing each day, and what the impact is on our allocated disk space.

The latest version of Oracle Enterprise Manager (11*g*) has a substantial set of monitoring processes that makes it an in-valuable tool in your armory.

Implement usage tracking in Oracle BI to understand where your customers are experiencing slow performance and act on the information gathered. This could be adding indexes, performance data, or even changing the way that OBI accesses the star layout.

Usage tracking will be explained in detail later in this book.

Some definitions

Refer to the following table:

ETL	Extract, transform, and load (ETL) is the process of taking data from a source system into the warehouse
SQL	**Structured Query Language (SQL)** is the basic language that databases such as Oracle and the SQL Server understand. SQL is used to create data, create database objects such as tables, and to query data.
Performance data	I use this term to describe any data which helps to speed up the reporting performance. This includes creating the aggregate tables, for example the Tournament fact table. It also includes the use of subsets of data, partitioning of tables, and indexing.
Star transformation	It is a special feature of the Oracle databases. This feature can maximize the performance of a query that uses a star design table layout. Oracle can build a more efficient query than usual, due to the fact that it knows all dimensions join to the fact table.
Hints	Hints are used to help an Oracle database to query the tables in the most efficient manner. This could include telling Oracle to use particular join methods or indexes.
Exadata	It is an Oracle machine that increases performance of the Oracle database by bringing together the storage, processing, and database operating system into one box.
Cubes	A cube is a special way of organizing data so that it can be queried quickly. Data is often aggregated in cubes so that numbers are available to the user without the database having to do any calculations.
Slowly changing dimensions	A dimension record, for example a Player, does not normally change once it has been created. However, if a player gets married and then changes his/her last name, the warehouse designer needs to decide how this is reflected in the dimension table. If you create a new record based upon the player's new details then you have a slowly changing dimension table created.
Indexes	Indexes are used to help a database access data more quickly than simply by looking at the data itself.
Hierarchies	Records in a table can often have a parent-child relationship, which develops into a hierarchy of levels. For example in the Date table we have Date, which has a parent of Month, which has a parent of Year. Then the hierarchy is Year	Month	Date.

A review – what I should now know!

For self review and a recap of the chapter, here are a few questions. There is no answers key. These questions are for your own reflection on the chapter.

1. How is a reporting database structured?

2. How do you set reasonable objectives when building a data warehouse (for example the ETL should run for three hours)?

3. What are the rules for creating efficient warehouses?

4. What are the steps involved in creating a data warehouse from a source OLTP database system?

Summary

In this chapter, we introduced the basic concepts of database design, and which ones are more suited for reporting. We have also seen how a balance between report speed and data loading needs to be struck, given limited resources.

To ensure that your database is useful to its customers, it should achieve certain objectives that are met using rules and goals that you lay down in the initial design phase and follow up in each design choice.

Implementing a database does not stop when the objects are created, but should be followed up with a continuous monitoring and maintenance process.

In the production of this book, we have created a small warehouse for reporting on Tennis statistics. You can find all the database objects and data with the code files supplied with this book or from our public repository on GitHub—`https://github.com/artofbi/`.

8
Developing a BI Repository

Finally we get to the heart of the OBIEE system, the metadata repository that resides within the RPD file. The RPD contains all of the information concerning the physical tables that are held in our database or data warehouse, whether this is from a single source or a heterogeneous set of sources. It stores their relationships, additional business logic for these objects, and the structure of how columns are presented via the frontend to report and dashboard creators. As well as physical database tables, the RPD can also utilize other data sources such as Essbass, Oracle OLAP, and Excel sheets.

The RPD also holds variable definitions, various security and cache settings, and drill/dimensional hierarchies that affect the end functionality of reports. All of these settings and metadata are used by the Oracle BI server in choosing the content and structure of database queries when presented with a request via OBIEE Answers.

Once a system is installed, and gone live, a lot of development time will be spent on the metadata repository. A developer is given a great amount of freedom in modeling and enhancing physical objects in a way that can satisfy the most complex business requirements.

In this chapter, we will cover the development of a simple RPD from tables in a database through to how those objects are presented to us when we move on to create an actual request. This will be carried out via the Oracle BI Administration tool which is the primary method of accessing and modifying an RPD file. This tool provides an inviting graphical interface for developing and administering an RPD file. By the end of this chapter, you will be able to complete the major tasks associated with RPD development. We will also briefly describe some of the more advanced options that are available. This will give you a basis on which you can investigate functionality under your own supervision.

Prerequisites

The example we will be using stems from a Star schema design for a data warehouse. It is expected that you are already familiar with terms such as Star, Snowflake, Fact, and Dimension and that you have an understanding of data warehouse schemas. The vast majority of development projects out there will use such a design as the basis for their Business Intelligence projects. If you are not familiar with this, we would recommend first studying one of the seminal texts on this subject — The Data Warehouse Toolkit by Ralph Kimball.

Repository architecture

Before we embark on developing a new repository, let's have a look at how the RPD is structured. The fundamental structure of a RPD is made up of three layers for modeling data.

Physical layer

This contains the information for example, table/column names and keys, for your data sources, as they exist in their database, and their connectivity details. No data is actually stored in the RPD, just references to your data sources that is metadata is stored in it.

If needed, we can also connect to other data sources, for example, Flat files and Excel files.

Business layer

The main objective in this layer is to create an abstract and simplified model of the physical layer objects. This is especially valuable if we need to combine data from different data sources. The business layer allows us to integrate these different sources and then present them to an end user as a coherent and unified whole.

OBIEE supports federated querying, so we can query and stitch together data from multiple data sources. For example, we may need to combine multiple data sources into one logical object such as Geography or Business Department.

We can add business logic to the set of objects that we have described in the physical layer. We can also restructure them as necessary and enhance them via OBIEE server-based calculations and functions.

The final business model that we produce in this layer should be organized as per your business requirements. It should reflect how your business sees and organizes itself.

Presentation layer

In this layer, we can choose how we present the business layer objects to the end users when they actually create reports. We can customize the view of the business layer for the end users. For example, renaming data objects as they pertain to the end user's business requirements.

That was a brief overview of RPD structure. As we will proceed to actually develop a new project, you will gain more clarity on the role of each metadata layer in the RPD. The example that we will be using is that of a professional tennis series which has collated a large amount of data on its players and their performances in tournaments around the world. Although the subject matter is exotic, it is typical to the type of the project that you will be developing in the industry and for that we will use a data warehouse structure. We will use this structure to create aggregated measures that are reported across multiple dimensions. The tools and techniques that we will teach you in the next chapters can be used in any environment that has a requirement of being able to mine data and generate intelligent insight. So let's start!

Physical layer

Firstly, we will be creating the physical layer of our RPD.

Creating an RPD and importing metadata

The procedure is as follows:

1. Start the **Oracle BI Administration Tool** by navigating to **Programs | Oracle BI | BI Administration**.

As shown in the following screenshot, in **Oracle BI Administration Tool** by click on **File | New Repository...**:

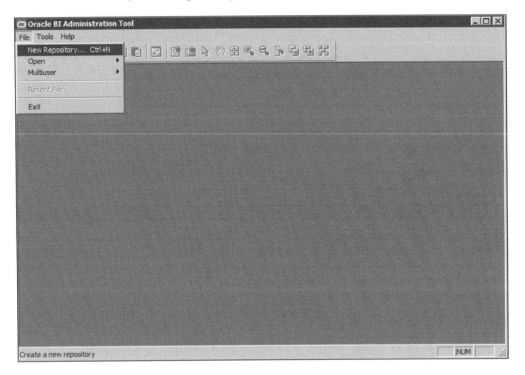

2. This leads us to the start of the **Create New Repository** wizard. The first screen is an input screen for **Repository Information** where you need to input the following information:

- **Name**: Choose something sensible in this field according to the project or subject matter. For our purposes we will name the RPD as **Tennis**.

- **Location**: Leave this field as it is, but this can be changed to anything that you require, such as a shared area or mapped drive.

- **Repository Password**: This has been implemented slightly more stringently in this edition of OBIEE as you must have at least eight characters and one numeral.

- **Retype Password**: Enter the same password that you entered in the **Repository Password** field.

- **Import Metadata**: If you choose **Yes**, you will automatically be prompted to import metadata (physical layer table definitions). If you choose **No**, a completely empty RPD will be created:

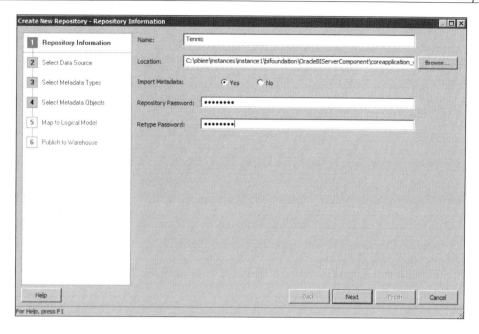

As we have previously chosen to import our metadata, you will be presented with screens enabling you to automatically import physical table definitions, from a data source to the physical layer. We can create all of these definitions manually, using the Administration tool, but a vast amount of time will be saved if the initial set of tables is imported with this method.

Within projects, it is common to initially import a first draft of the schema directly from the database and then to make manual changes when needed as that schema is enhanced.

 The **Import Metadata** wizard can also be instigated at anytime from the Oracle BI Administration tool by navigating to **File | Import Metadata**.

3. In the first screen of the wizard, as shown in the following screenshot, you will need to choose the following:

- **Connection Type**: This can be a native driver for the major databases or via ODBC.

- **Datasource Name**: If we have chosen a native driver, for example Oracle, we will generally need to present this information.

- **User Name**: It is the user information for the data source.

- **Password**: It is needed for the Administration tool so that it can access the data source.

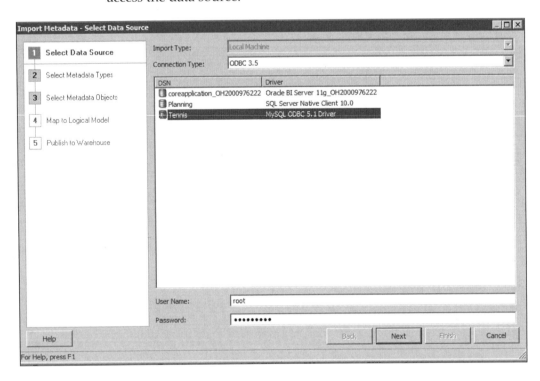

There are other bits of information that are required if you natively connect to other sources, for example Essbase or Oracle OLAP. Have a play and choose other options from the **Connection Type** drop-down, and you will see those other requirements.

For our purposes, we are using a MySQL database and connecting to it via ODBC. This requires us to have MySQL drivers installed on the local machine and a system DSN setup in the ODBC Data Source Administrator in Windows. These are quite common Windows/ODBC tasks, so we will not go into detail on setting this up.

As you can see in the preceding screenshot, we have a Tennis DSN available that connects to our Data Warehouse schema. You have to input your **User Name** and **Password**. Then, click on **Next**.

4. In the next screen, choose which types of objects you want to import into the RPD. These are all common database terms that you should (hopefully!) be familiar with. For example, if you choose **Views**, in the next screen you will be able to import view definitions from the database. If you wish to import joins between tables, choose **Keys** and **Foreign Keys**:

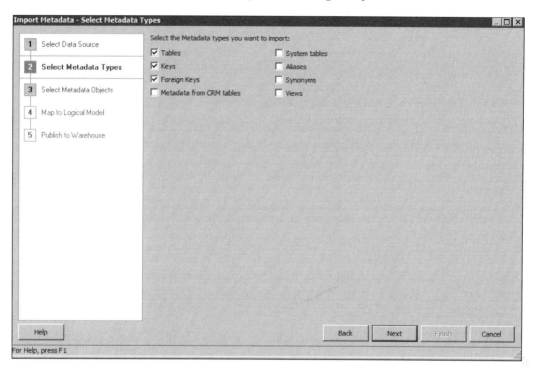

The only nongeneric option is **Metadata from CRM tables**. If it is chosen, after clicking on **Next**, the Administration tool will read the table definitions in a legacy Siebel CRM system, from that CRM system's metadata dictionary. This is as opposed to reading these definitions directly from the database itself. Although this option is not widely used, it is important to note the distinction here. A CRM table may differ in definition at its application metadata layer compared to the implementation in the database, and the project requirements may mean that the CRM application relationships are more pertinent.

For our example, we have a very simple database schema, so we will only need to choose **Tables**, **Keys**, and **Foreign Keys**. All foreign keys have not been set up in the database, so, we will manually have to implement these in the Administration tool as the chapter progresses.

5. Once you are happy with our chosen options, click on **Next**. At this point, in the left-hand side pane, you will see all the objects within the data source, that we have provided details for, filtered by the options chosen in the previous screen:

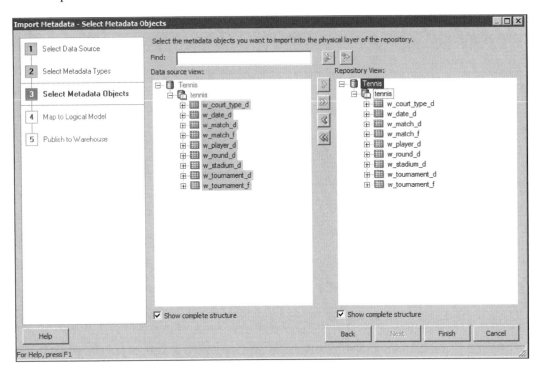

If we were rerunning this wizard in the future, we can selectively choose objects and use the single arrow icon to move them to the right for importing. As we are starting from scratch, we will need all of these tables, so we can use the double arrow button to move everything into the right-hand side pane. Once you do this, you can click on **Finish**, and these table definitions will be imported.

Only import objects that you will actually use. You do not want to confused by, or your workspace made unwieldy to manage, by adding extraneous objects.

6. As shown in the following screenshot, at this point you will be in the main view of the RPD that you will see every time you return to open it. Note the structure, there you will see the base (physical) layer on the right-hand side pane, and the layers that build upon this flow to the left-hand side. Although initially this maybe anti-intuitive to western readers, this order does make sense when you consider how the metadata in the RPD actually works in a live environment. When building reports, we choose objects in the **Presentation** layer. The tool then constructs OBIEE specific logical SQL that filters through the **Business Model and Mapping** layer. This in turn informs OBIEE how to turn that logical SQL into actual physical queries against our sources in the **Physical** layer.

These panes are, of course, empty at the moment but we should see our imported tables in the **Physical** layer, waiting for us to check and finalize details such as the keys and joins:

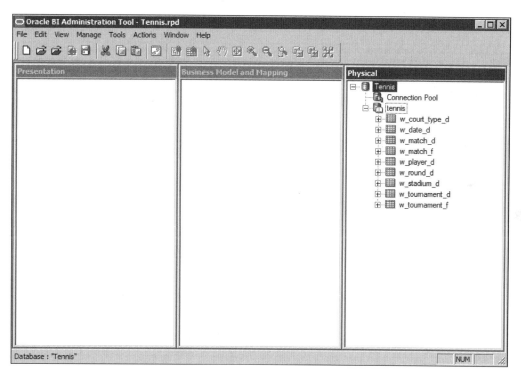

Elements of the physical layer

Before we create joins, let's go through the physical layer objects that have been automatically created by the Import Metadata wizard.

Database object

If you double-click on the topmost object, the **Database** object will open. This is more generically known as the **Datasource**, as we can have different types of source for example, Flat files. Have a look at the following screenshot, in the **General** tab we can set and amend features for that individual database connection. You can change the name of the object and if you decide to use another database type, we can inform OBIEE by changing that definition.

On this tab, there are also some useful advanced features, which we will briefly describe:

- **Allow populate queries by default**: This allows the use of this database to run populate SQL.
- **Allow direct database requests by default**: This allows the execution of actual physical SQL queries directly against this database, by passing the RPD metadata. Be extremely careful with this option, as users will be able to do anything including dropping tables and updating data, if the connection rights in the connection pools (which we will discuss shortly) are too powerful:

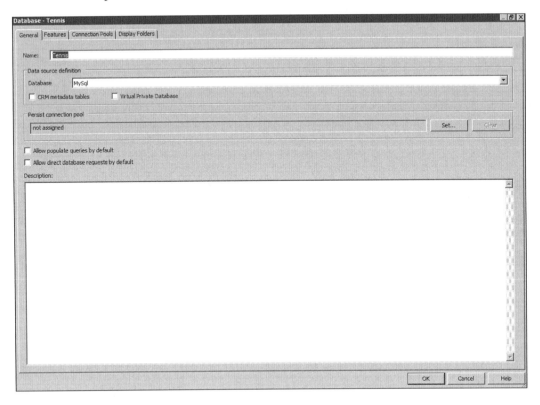

Moving onto the next tab—**Features**. Although it is an advanced part of the RPD, it is well worth quickly exploring this capability in the **Database** object. When we imported our table definitions, we stipulated the database type. The types of query that are supported by this specific database are populated in this tab, as shown in the following screenshot. You can then turn on or off supported types of query capability as you please. This results in the OBIEE server producing SQL that is restricted to the set of chosen features. This is sometimes really useful when fine-tuning queries against a certain database. However, be warned that this is an advanced feature and unless you are an experienced database developer or have DBA support, you should leave the default settings alone:

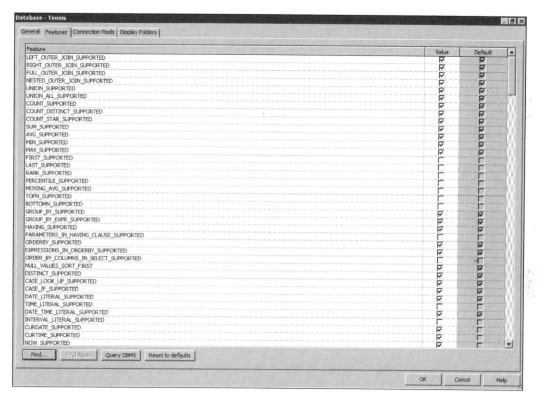

The next two tabs list the child objects of the database object and we will cover these in the following sections.

 Note that you can also manually create a new database object in the physical layer by right-clicking in the white space in that pane, and choosing the **New Database...** option.

Connection pools

Referring back to our physical layer, under the **Database** object we can see an item called **Connection Pools**. This contains authentication details for the database object and allows multiple users to use the same data source. We could also create multiple connection pools for the same data source. This may be helpful if you want to access the same data source but with different users, and their associated rights.

As shown in the following screenshot, in the **General** tab under **Connection Pool**, you can see the following fields:

- **Name**: It contains the name of the **Connection Pool** object
- **Permissions**: This button can be useful if you have multiple connection pools and want to restrict their use to certain groups of users. Be careful with this, as users will be able to access cached reports regardless of the permissions set here.
- **Call interface**: This field describes the method of connecting to the database object.

 Try and use native drivers in **Call interface**, wherever possible. This will be helpful to increase the performance, when compared to ODBC.

- **Maximum connections**: This determines the maximum number of connections that the server can open in the database through this connection pool. Before going live, take some time to get this setting right for your environment. You do not want to allow so many connections that query performance is degraded, or so few that users are frustrated as they cannot run queries.

    You will need to look at the capacity of your database to handle multiple concurrent sessions, and the size/memory of your servers. To get you started, we would say that it is useful to multiply the number of users on the system by the average number of queries on a dashboard.

 For example, a system has 100 users. Typically 20 percent of them will be online, running an average of four reports at a time. So, our **Maximum connections** parameter will be as follows:

(100 x 20 percent) x 4 = 80

Then, amend this number depending on our database capacity and as we assess how the system is used in a production environment.

- **Timeout**: Along with **Maximum connections**, this is an important setting as the time set here affects how often OBIEE opens and closes new connections. It is the field where we can stipulate how long a connection to a data source remains open. If a request is received within the set time, the associated query will use an open connection rather than creating a new one.

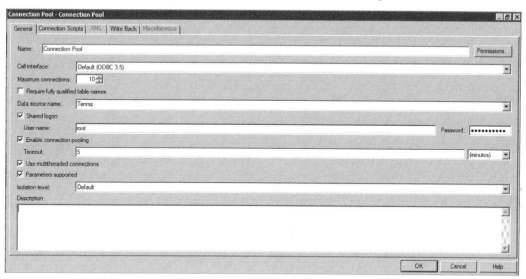

For our purposes, we are happy with the defaults that have been automatically created. Other advanced options are not relevant for our example or most development activities, but it is worth having a look at the **Connection Scripts** tab (refer to the following screenshot). Here, it is possible to run commands on the database before and after the initiation of a query or database connection. This gives an opportunity for enhancing the performance of requests against this connection pool. An example, from a recent project run by the authors of this book, is that we needed to improve the performance of a set of queries running against a specific connection pool. It was found to be really helpful to run the `Alter Session` command on the Oracle database, to allow parallelism for the SQL queries. Again a change, such as this, would be after a very mature period of development and in consultation with your database experts:

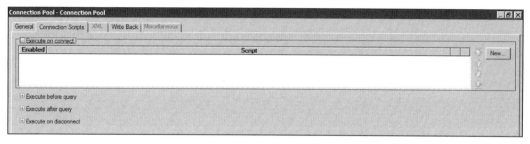

Connection pools can also be created within the **Connection Pools** tab of the **Database** object, or by right-clicking on the **Database** object and selecting **New Object | Connection Pool**.

Physical catalog and schemas

Referring again to the objects that have been created automatically by the Import Metadata wizard, you can see an object called **Tennis**. This is called a **physical catalog**. A catalog contains all of the definition information (metadata) for a particular data source (in our case the database object).

However, if we have vast amounts of metadata and want to organize objects that exist within the same schema in the database, we can optionally create a **Physical Schema** folder.

We have a small set of objects, so it is fine if we continue with the sole catalog, as the Import Metadata wizard has created.

Physical Catalogs and **Physical Schema** (display) folders can be created by right-clicking on the data source. Additionally, **Physical Schema** folders can be created via the **Display Folders** tab within the **Datasource** object. A catalog contains information for a whole database object while a schema contains metadata information for a schema owner. Model this in the same way that your database is designed.

Get your groups organized in advance. It is difficult to amend this afterwards, and if you decide to use folders instead of a catalog, you will not be able to rearrange and create a catalog.

Physical tables

Either of the previous objects will contain **physical tables**. As we have mentioned in the preceding section, these are the definitions of the actual tables within our database. If you double-click on a physical table object, you can see the basic properties of the table.

As with other objects, we can create physical table definitions manually by right-clicking on the catalog or schema folder. We can manipulate the definitions of columns and keys via their associated tabs or by expanding the physical table definitions and double-clicking on the individual columns:

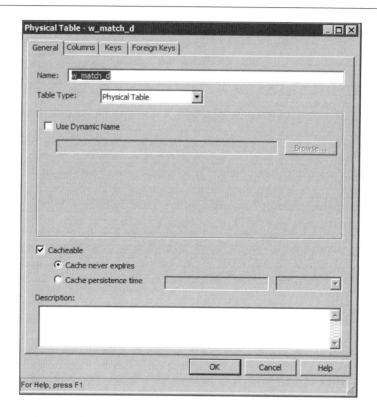

We can also add foreign key relationships via the **Foreign Keys** tab. Let us take a look at the **Columns**, **Keys**, and **Foreign Keys** tabs in the following screenshots placed side-by-side:

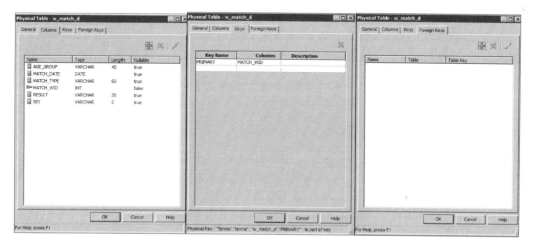

We can see that our column definitions have been imported correctly with a primary key (as denoted by the golden key sign). However, we do not seem to have any foreign keys. So, we will have to create these relationships (also know as **physical joins**) ourselves via the Administration tool.

Physical join

We could create the relationships between the tables by using the **Foreign Keys** tab, but the Administration tool provides a far easier way of changing these relationships. This is carried out via the **physical diagram**. During any development cycle, you will spend a lot of time here. The physical diagram graphically represents relationships between tables. It will show basic cardinalities as with an Entity Relationship Diagram, that is 1:M or 1:1 signifiers.

So, let's open the diagram. We can choose all of the tables that we want to model, then right-click on **Physical Diagram | Selected Objects Only** (actually in this instance any of those final options will suffice). Note that instead of contextual right-click, we could have also used a button on the toolbar that looks like a mini-ERD diagram:

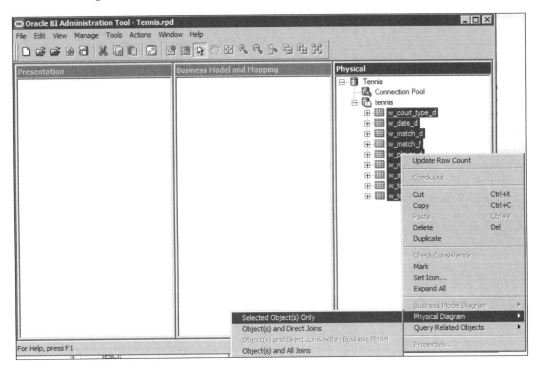

As you can see in the following screenshot, we are now presented with a graphical representation of the table definitions. We can double-click on the tables to open the previous screens that we have described, but the most useful aspect of the diagram is that we can define the relationships between these tables in a visual manner.

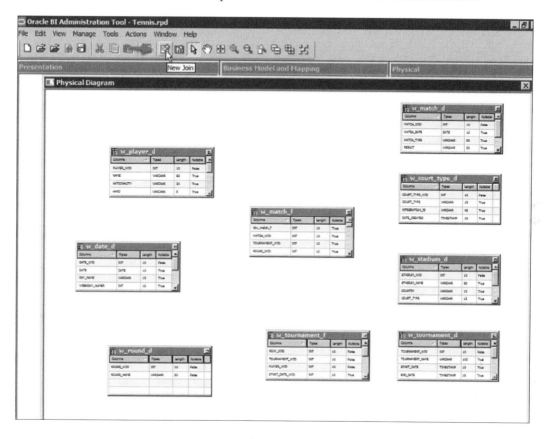

To do this. click on the **New Join** button (as denoted by the tooltip in the preceding screenshot) and then click on our fact table (**W_MATCH_F**) and drag the pointer out to the table for which we want to define a join (in our case, the dimension **W_PLAYER_D**).

As you can see in the following screenshot, a line is drawn representing the relationship that exists between the two tables. The **Physical Foreign Key** screen prompts us. This is where we can stipulate the exact details of the join. OBIEE makes a pretty good guess of the join for single key tables, especially if we have already set up our primary keys properly.

In the following screenshot we can see that it has guessed that we are joining on **MATCH_WID** in both tables. This is correct, but if it had not been, we could easily change this in the **Expression** box. This would definitely need to be done if we were joining on compound keys. As well as we would have to check that the tables, columns, and join information are correct and also have a look at the cardinality. Ensure, that this is inline with your warehouse design, otherwise redo the join:

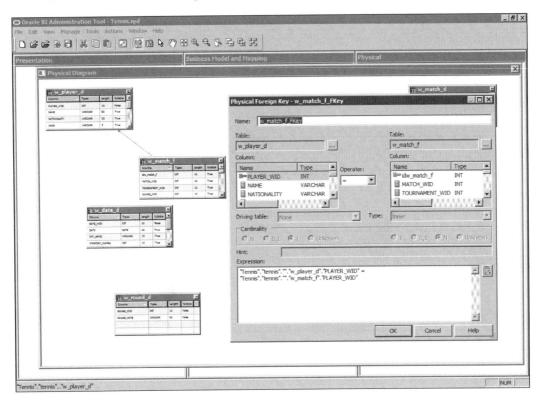

Once you are happy with the settings, you can click on **OK** and proceed to define the joins for all other tables as needed. For each star within a warehouse, we will end up with something looking like we have in the following screenshot. The Physical Diagram is a great tool with which you can model your data. Visualizing your data in this way adds clarity and eases the development process:

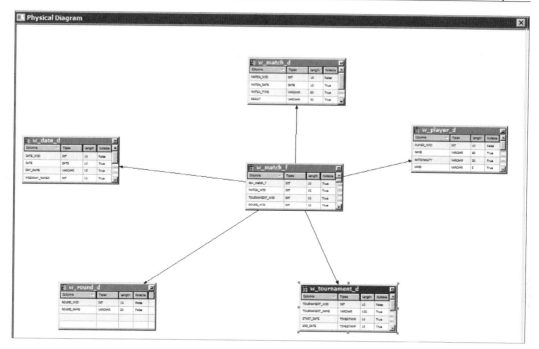

 If you use the Import Metadata wizard for keys and foreign keys, and imported joins rather than creating them manually, double check the results. Ensure that these joins have been imported correctly.

Consistency check

Now we are ready to proceed to the next layer of the RPD. We have set up the objects needed for data connectivity and defined the objects that exist in that data source. Having completed a large amount of work, it is easy to make errors when completing large swathes of development. So we should save and check our work periodically.

To this end, the Administration tool provides what is commonly known as the consistency check, or in Oracle's own documentation as the Consistency Check Manager. We touched upon this in *Chapter 6, Upgrading the RPD and Web Catalog to 11g.* This process will parse all of the detail that we have developed, rather like one of the tasks, a compiler may do for a programming language, and inform us of any errors. It will give us **Errors**, which we must fix before proceeding or it will create **Warnings**, where we can use our own judgment on whether it will impact our development negatively or not. Errors can range from missing object definitions such as column types. Warnings can be a flag, as an example, a join that we have purposely disabled. We can also choose to have the process give us best practice recommendations.

Normally, you will be prompted to run the check when saving your work, but it must be stressed that it is good practice to run this check of your own volition regularly. Let's run the check now. Select **File** | **Check Global Consistency**:

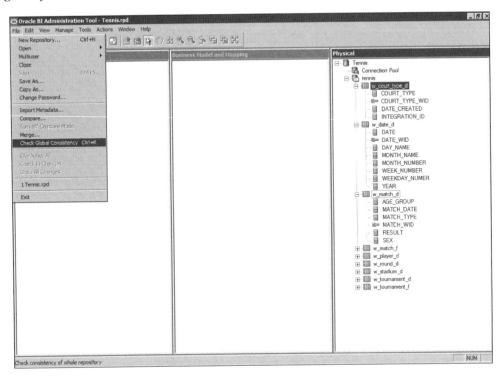

Ideally, next you should see the following message:

Consistency check didn't find any errors, warnings or best practice violations

If not, and you see a list of errors and warnings, you will need to note this and look through your development to rectify these issues. There are too many possibilities to go through here, but as you increase in experience as an OBIEE developer, you will learn to recognize and solve these quickly.

Table aliases and naming conventions

Before we move onto the business layer, let's quickly look at a couple of best practices in developing this layer:

- **Naming conventions**: For ease of use, your objects should have identifiable names. For example, our physical tables have _D and _F suffixes denoting whether they are a dimension or fact.

- **Aliases**: If your physical objects are not appropriately named, you can create aliases by right-clicking on the object and choosing the alias creation option, as you can see in the following screenshot:

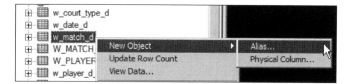

This creates another object, or level of abstraction, that retains its reference to the original source object. Then, we can name this alias in a more appropriate way. Note that the icon for an alias differs:

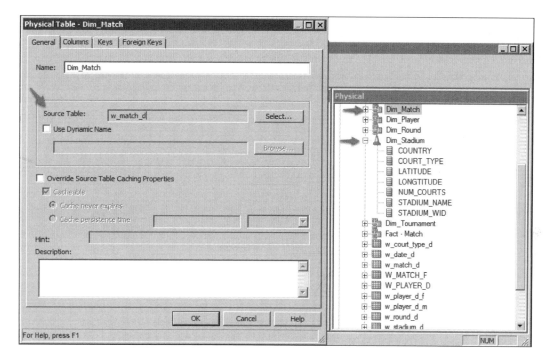

 By right-clicking on the icon, we can also change the icon for an object to a custom setting if that helps to identify key tables quickly. You can see that we have chosen a traffic cone icon for one of our tables in the preceding screenshot.

Aliases are also commonly used to create multiple physical models based on the same base objects. This is sometimes useful if we want to avoid circular joins or just wish to organize our star schemas in a clear manner.

Business layer

In this layer, we are not limited by the constraints of the actual physical tables in the database. We can restructure and consolidate sources that will inform the BI server on how to best handle the end user requests. Most of the metadata, which affects SQL production by the BI server, is handled in this layer.

Business model

The **business model** is the highest level in this layer and contains a business view of the physical schema. You should be able to simplify the physical schema so that in the end you are looking at the business view of the data. Anything we do in this layer, will not affect the work that has been done in the physical layer, and we can create multiple models based on the same physical sources.

To create a business model, right-click on the **Business Model and Mapping** pane in the middle and choose **New Business Model**. Then, we are prompted to give the model a name (as shown in the following screenshot):

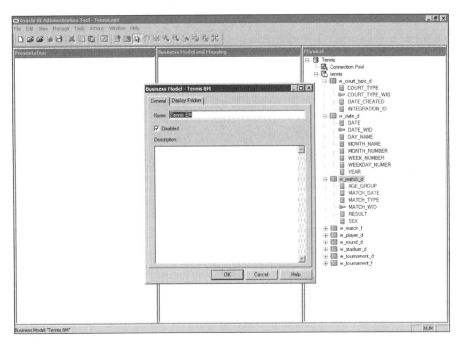

We will name our model as **Tennis BM**, and will keep the **Disabled** flag checked, as this model is not ready to handle any queries. Once we click on **OK**, we will see a new business model created. In the following screenshot, note that the business model icon is supplemented with a no entry sign. This signifies that it is disabled. We are now ready to start adding the logical representations of the tables that we have already added in the physical layer:

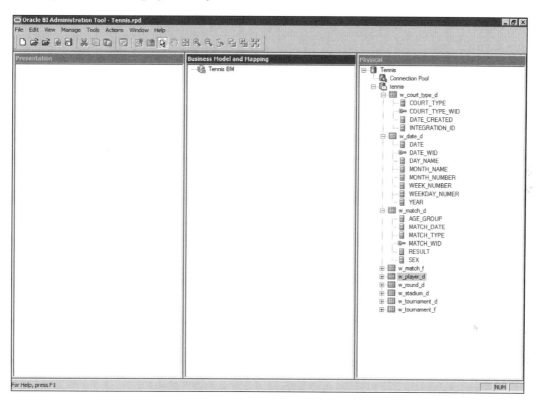

 In general, create different business models for different areas of reporting even if they are from the same source, for example, a separate model for Human Resources and another for CRM data.

Logical tables

Within a business model, the most common object that you will create is called a **logical table**. This is a representation of one or more tables amalgamated into one logical group. A common best practice example would be if we have a snowflake physical schema, we will be able to define that as a star schema in the business model.

A logical table:

- Can be a fact table or a dimension
- Contains at least one logical table source but can have many
- Is a business view of data

Initially, we are going to create a logical table for our match fact. Right-click on the model and select **New Object | Logical Table**:

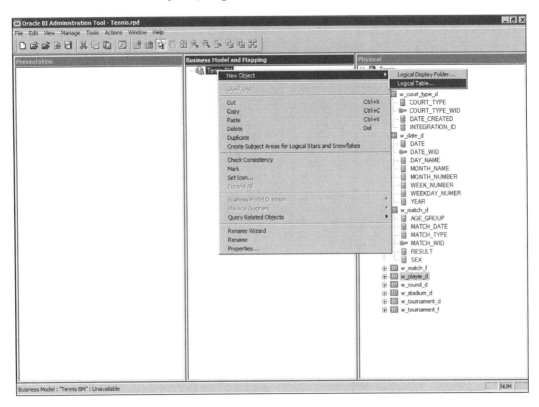

In the following screenshot, note that we have named the new table as
Fact - Matches:

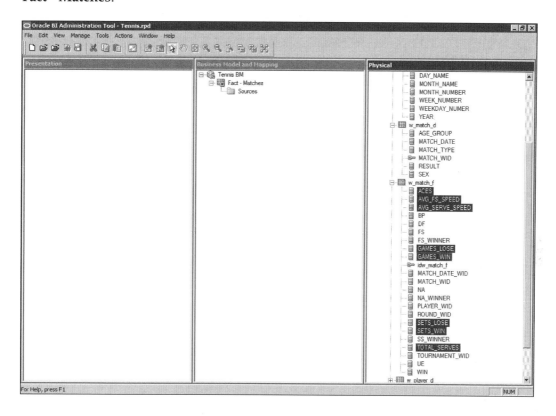

 You can name these tables whatever you want, but it is good
practice to give sensible names that denote their purpose. For
example, a Dim - prefix for dimensions and a Fact - prefix
for facts.

We want this fact to contain measures from the W_MATCH_F table. So, as shown in the
preceding screenshot, we can pick the required columns in the physical layer and
drag them to our new logical table.

 Logical Fact versus Logical Dimension Tables
Ideally, fact tables should only contain aggregated measures and
dimension tables should only contain descriptive attributes.

As demonstrated in the following screenshot, after adding columns to that logical table, the **Sources** folder is now populated with a reference to the physical table that holds these columns. This is known as a **logical table source**:

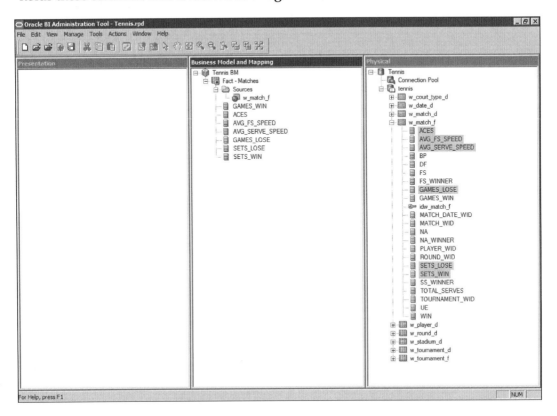

Logical table sources

A **logical table source (LTS)** is where you can map a logical table to one or more physical tables. As we will see later, we can use a LTS to:

- Transform and map data, for example, adding calculations on top of the physical columns
- Define aggregation rules for measures in fact tables
- Add other physical tables for purpose of aggregation or fragmentation

Logical columns

We will cover these LTS scenarios as the chapter progresses, so let us concentrate on our current example. We have bought the measures over, but we need to tell the OBIEE server that these are metrics that should be shown in queries in an aggregated format defined by dimensions.

We do this by double-clicking on a column to get to the tabs shown in the following screenshot:

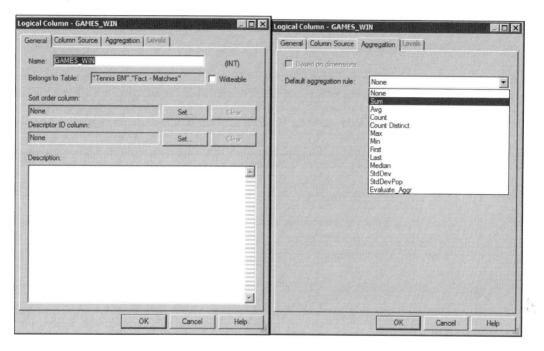

We will rename the column to something that makes more sense from a reporting point of view—**Games Won**. Note that this does not change the name of the physical column, and that the mapping to that column will remain unaffected.

Then, in the **Aggregation** tab, we will set the **Default aggregation rule** field to **Sum**, as this measure is an additive and we want to report on the aggregated number of games won by a player. Note that if we also want to treat this measure in a different manner, for example, an average, we can copy this column and have the aggregation rule set to **Avg**. This would result in two logical columns, although which are mapped to the same physical column, will yield different results in a report due to our varying definitions in the business model:

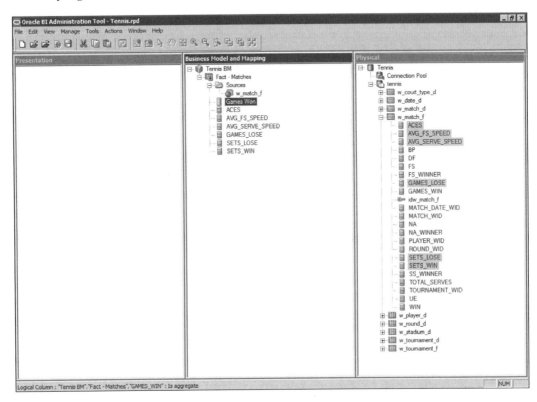

Note that in the preceding screenshot, the name of the logical column has changed (without changing the underlying physical mapping). More importantly, the column is identified by a yellow slide rule icon, which indicates that this column has been defined as a measure. Let's go ahead and repeat this for the other measure columns.

We will also go ahead and add a new logical table for a dimension. Rather than right-clicking as done before, we can use the alternative method of dragging the whole physical table into the business model. Doing this for W_MATCH_D will result in what you can see in the following screenshot:

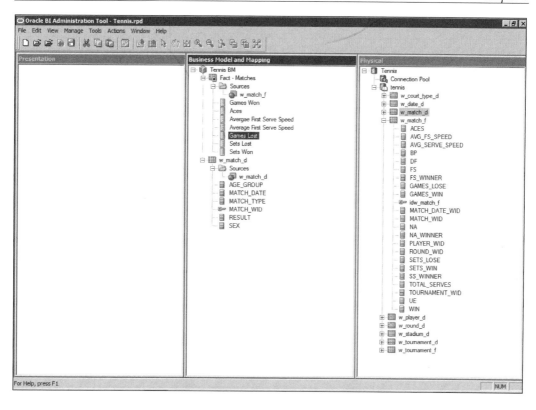

Note that when bringing the dimension table across, it also automatically sets one column (primary key) as a key for that logical table. We should have a logical key but this should be something that has more of a business meaning. We can change this key in the same way that we did for a physical table, by opening the logical table, navigating to the **Keys** tab, and changing the key definition.

Logical keys

Fact tables generally do not need logical keys.

Dimension tables do need a key, but generally the physical key should be deleted from the business model, and a key with more of a business meaning should be set.

Logical joins

With the joins in the physical layer, we must also set the relationships between the logical tables. Again, the Administration tool provides a good visual interface for this.

We can choose our dimension and fact. Right-click and select **Business Model Diagram | Selected Tables and Direct Joins** (as currently we only have two tables in the business layer, any option would have sufficed):

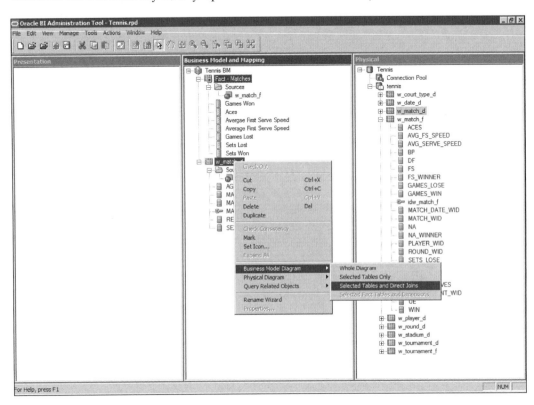

Refer to the way in which we set the joins between the tables in the physical layer. We will create joins in the business layer in exactly the same way. However, take a look at the join detail shown in the following screenshot. Notice that this time there are no columns stipulated in the **Expression** block for the join. This is because we have already set up the physical relationships previously. The OBIEE server will use this information as well as the metadata that we have set up in the logical tables and logical table sources in order to ascertain what type of SQL query it should run:

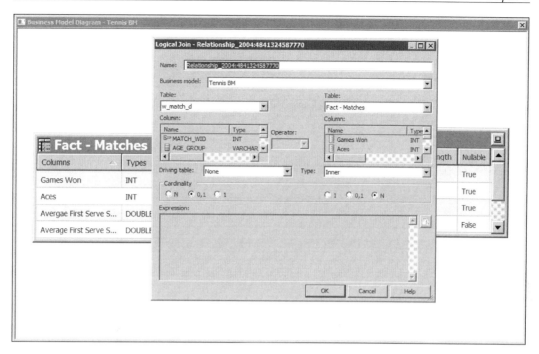

Physical join: It is a join between two physical tables based on an exactly stipulated relationship.

Logical join: It is a join between two logical objects. These objects may be made up of many different physical data sources. This join is a symbolic way of letting OBIEE know that a relationship exists between these objects. The OBIEE server will utilize our settings within these logical objects, and subsequently the physical joins, in deciding how to best generate a query when joining these logical objects in a report.

Again, looking at the information about the logical join in the preceding screenshot, we do have a choice of what cardinality to set between these logical tables. This helps in providing the information to OBIEE on how to create queries. In general, you should leave this setting alone unless you are an advanced developer and understand the ramifications.

Now that we are comfortable with setting up logical facts and dimensions, let's go ahead and bring all of our physical dimensions and facts into the business model:

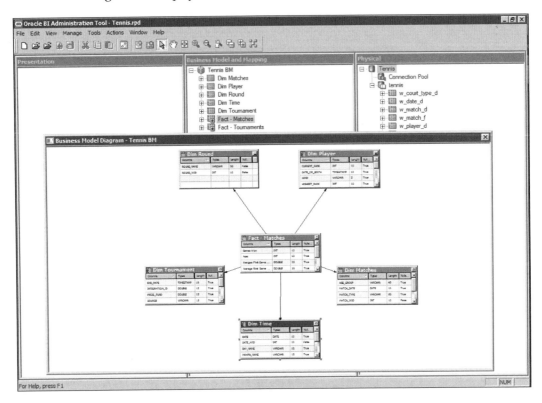

Once we have done this, our RPD should look something like what you can see in the preceding screenshot. Note that we are using easily identifiable names for the logical tables. Also, we can see in the **Business Model Diagram** for one of the stars, that all the tables are joined.

Now, there is a bit more work to do regarding dimensions. We need to create a dimension hierarchy for each logical dimension table.

Dimension hierarchies

At this point you may have been thinking about how to represent levels in a dimension. For example, how do we show that a geography dimension has levels of country, state, and city, or that time has year, month, and day? Well OBIEE allows us to set hierarchies in the business model. The most common hierarchy is level-based. This enables us to:

- Create measures aggregated at a certain level
- Create predetermined drill paths for the end users in reports

These levels will vary from dimension to dimension and will depend on your business requirements. For example, a business may need separate geography dimensions—one with different levels or groupings for their customers and another for their offices or stores.

To create a logical dimension, right click on the logical table for the dimension. Then, select **Create Logical Dimensional | Dimension with Level-Based Hierarchy**. You can see this in the following screenshot:

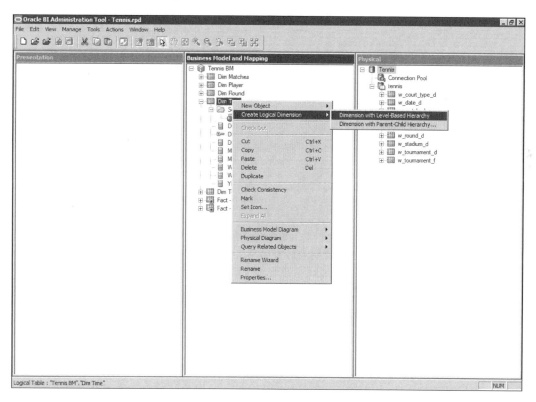

This results in the dimension object that you can see in the following screenshot. Notice that there are only two levels—one for the grand total and another for the lowest level of granularity. We need to have levels that correspond to a year, month, week, and so on. So there is a bit more work for us to do:

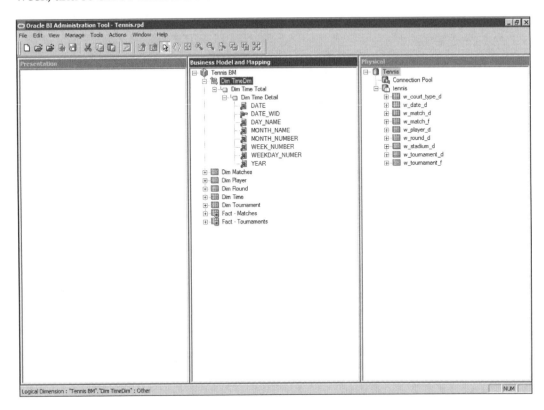

Build up the levels by starting at the lowest level and adding parents between that level and the grand total. We can do this by right-clicking and selecting **New Object | Parent Level...**:

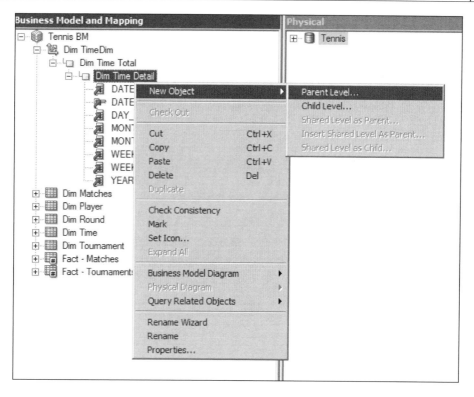

As you can see in the following screenshot, we will be presented with the detail tabs. Our lowest level is **Date**, so we will name this next level up, **Week**. Note that there is an entry called **Number of Elements at this level**. This entry does not affect the results that will be brought back in a query, but when we go on to include multiple table sources (especially aggregates), these figures will help the OBIEE server to optimize that query. Don't be worried about an exact number, all that matters is the ratio between levels. The grand total is defaulted to and system set at **1**. The lower levels should have numbers that are progressively higher than the figure in the level preceding it.

In the example shown in the following screenshot, we are looking at the **Week** level. For our requirements, the next level will be month. So, the final number that we input here will be just above four times of the number that we input at the **Month** level as that is the ratio between the two levels:

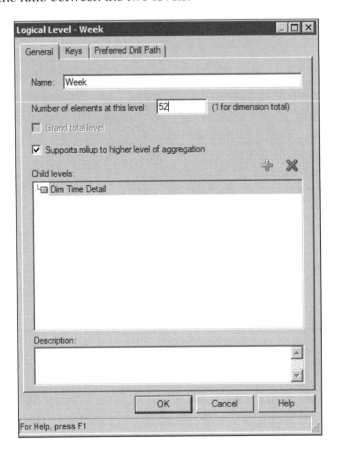

Number of elements

Remember that the ratio between levels matters more than the actual numbers.

If we do this for all of our new levels, we will end up with something that is shown in the following screenshot. However, we also need to inform the OBIEE server about how to identify those levels using the columns that we have brought into the business layer. This requires us to set keys at each level.

Remember that we can also set drill paths within dimensions that can be utilized by the end users. In addition to the level keys, it is at this point that we can set these paths:

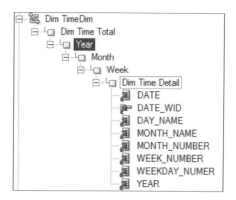

So we need keys that uniquely identify a level, and we should not have columns at a level that differs from their grain. So as an example, for our Time dimension, we have a very straightforward hierarchy of **Year | Month | Week | Date**. We can see that we have unique identifiers such as **MONTH_NUMBER** for the month, **WEEK_NUMBER** for the week, and so on. These will be great for our level keys. Notice, that we also have some descriptive columns, for example, **MONTH_NAME**. We need to ensure that these exist at the right level, so these will have to be moved as well. If we do that for all of the levels, we will get an hierarchy, as shown in the following screenshot:

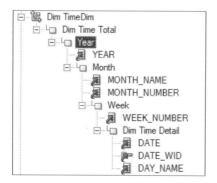

At this point, still we have not stipulated which columns are keys, and which are to be used in a drill path. We can do this by right-clicking on a column and choosing **New Logical Level Key**. We will then get a screen, as shown in the following screenshot. A **Year**, such as 2006, is both a unique identifier and a descriptive that we would be happy to click on and drill down from in a report. Therefore, we will set it as key, and check the **Use for Display** box to indicate that this is what we will be using for drilling in a report:

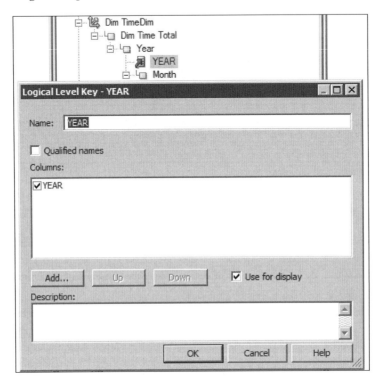

If we do this for all our levels, we will get an hierarchy, as shown in the following screenshot. Note that the icons have changed to a golden key, indicating that these are now keys. The keys that will uniquely identify these levels for optimization purposes are **Year | Month | Week | Date**. The drill path that we have set is **Year | Month Name | Week | Day Name**.

Note that we have also renamed all columns in the logical table to ones with more business meaning, without changing the mapping to their associated physical column:

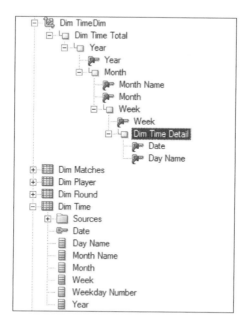

Once we repeat this for all of our dimensions, we are ready for the final part of developing an RPD—the presentation layer.

Presentation layer

If we try to do a consistency check at this point, we will find that it throws up an error, as we do not have anything in the presentation layer. So far, we have mapped our data sources and defined the physical objects. Then, we proceeded to add some business logic, and tell the OBIEE server how to handle the physical objects in a way that relates to our business requirements. Now we need to expose this to our end users.

In this layer, we can customize the view of the business model for the end users. This includes renaming objects sensibly without affecting the logical and physical names that will be used to generate queries. Just to reinforce, the names and definitions of presentation tables are separate from logical tables.

We can also choose to widen or limit the scope of the parts of the business model that can be seen by the end users at any time within a project.

> The presentation layer names will be stored and used as references in the Presentation Catalog metadata when creating reports.

Subject areas

A subject area is a grouping of objects from the business model. This can be a subset if required. We can do this by right-clicking in the presentation layer area, and choosing the option to create a new subject area. We can then drag folders and columns across. We can also automatically create a subject area for the whole Business Model straight from the business layers. We do this by right-clicking in the **Business Model and Mapping** area and choosing **Create Subject Areas for Logical Stars and Snowflakes**:

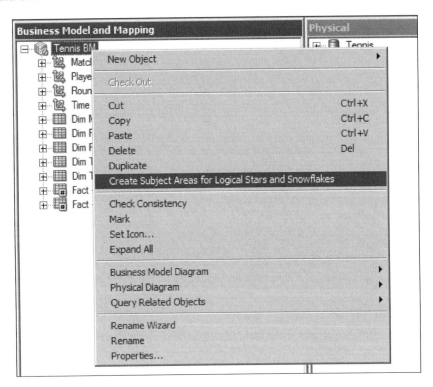

This option automatically creates a separate subject area for each logical star that is detected. This is a new option in 11*g* as compared to previous versions and is a great way to start creating your subject areas.

As you can see in the following screenshot, we have one subject area for our Matches star and another for our Tournaments. Note that our Tennis business model has a green icon, which shows that it has passed the consistency check and is now ready to generate queries:

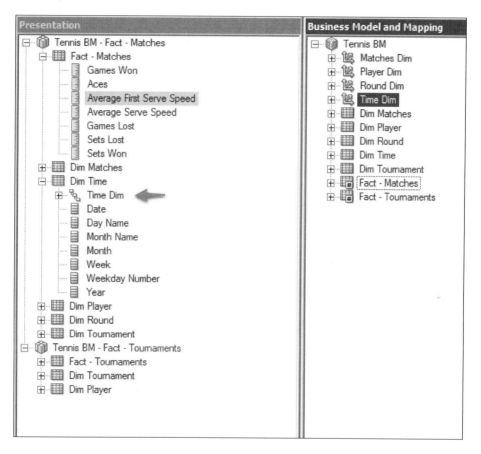

Also note the object in the presentation layer that is arrowed in the preceding screenshot. This is called an hierarchical column and we will discuss this further in *Chapter 10, Creating Dashboards and Reports*.

Best practices in the presentation layer

Development in this layer is not as involved as it is in others. It mostly involves considering how you wish to present your logical columns to the end user. Users will see tables and columns exactly as you arrange/name them in the presentation layer. Due to this flexibility, it's beneficial to go through some of the better practices that we have found through our own experience:

- Keep column names relevant to the business. Try and do this renaming at the business model layer rather than at the presentation layer.

- Order your dimensions and facts in the same way in all subject areas. For example, we would recommend always having Time first. If dimensions appear in multiple subject areas then keep their order same in all of those areas.

- Keep fact tables at the bottom, with dimensions preceding.

- Rename tables to remove dimension and fact prefix indicators that is, remove `Dim` as this looks ungainly to the end users.

- Ensure that every possible combination of columns chosen in a subject area will produce a coherent result. It is not possible to run a query for those errors which occur due to a logical error. If this happens, your credibility in front of users will diminish.

- Keep subject areas as small and as targeted as possible.

If you follow these guidelines with our example RPD, you will end up with something shown in the following screenshot, in the presentation layer:

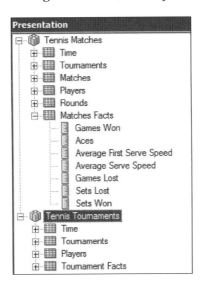

Note that we have removed the `Dim` prefixes. Shared objects now have the same order in both the subject areas and the column now have names with business meanings. We can reorder and rename tables by double-clicking on the subject area and navigating to the **Presentation Tables** tab as shown in the following screenshot:

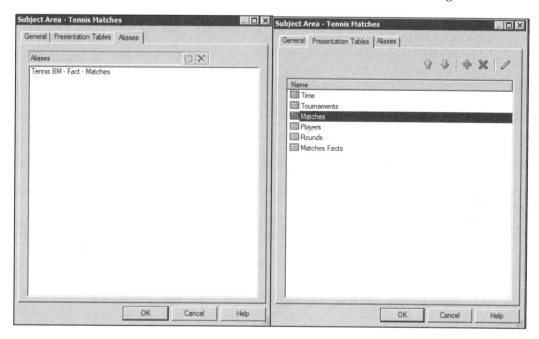

As you can see in the preceding screenshot on the left, we can click on the pencil icon to rename a table. We can use the arrow buttons to reorder them.

Subfolders

We can make subfolder using a hyphen at the start of the presentation table name. This is especially useful as it is common to have an empty fact folder at the bottom with nested tables separating different types of measures.

Aliases

Have a look at the preceding screenshot on the right-hand side. We can see that there is also an **Aliases** tab. Here, we can rename a column without ever losing its mapping to a logical column. However, every time we rename a column or table in the presentation layer, we still retain a reference to the old presentation layer name here. This ensures that if we have already created reports and dashboards using these names, they will not create error using the new names.

However, this also means you cannot create a column/table with the old name unless that alias is deleted. This is a common source of errors, so be aware of this. Presentation aliases are easy to forget about, so you should use these very sparingly and keep in mind the drawbacks of using it. They should not be used as a quick way to fix badly named presentation objects. These have to be agreed with the business beforehand.

Implicit fact

Many times users will try to choose columns from two or more dimensions in a report without choosing a fact. OBIEE will then choose a fact accordingly, however, this may not always be the fact that we desire the query path to run through. An example would be in our current RPD. We have facts for Tournaments and Matches. They currently share conformed dimensions such as Tournament and Player. In our Tennis Match, subject area, we would prefer a query using Tournament and Player dimensions to use the Matches fact. In the Tennis Tournaments subject area, if our user chooses the same two dimensions, we would prefer the query to use the Tournaments fact. OBIEE allows for this by enabling the selection of an implicit fact for each subject area. We do this by double-clicking on a subject area and choosing **Set** for the **Implicit Fact Column**:

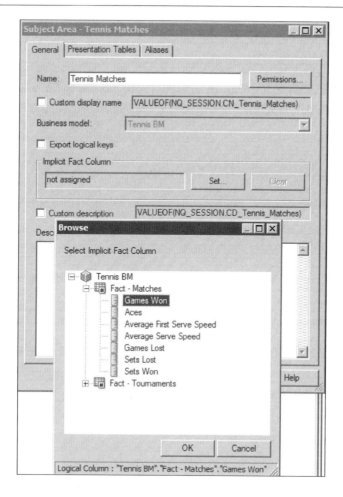

Then, choose any column from the fact that we want our default query to join to. So in the preceding example, you can see that we have opened the **Tennis Matches** subject area and are choosing a column from the **Matches** fact. So whenever we try to run a query in this subject area, which consists solely of dimensions, this column and fact will be used for generating the query.

Note that this is not a mandatory step in development. An important part of a BI project involves educating the end users. Properly educated users generally will not choose queries without a fact. However, if you notice that this does commonly recur, think about implementing this feature.

Calculated measures

Congratulations! We have finally completed the RPD. We have gone through a basic example, which you can use as a starting point in any environment. It's now time to delve into slightly more complicated examples of OBIEE functionality. As well as, giving you a greater insight into the full capability of OBIEE, it will also serve to reinforce the concepts that we have gone through in this chapter.

Logical column calculation

So far, the columns and measures in our example RPD have had a one-to-one relationship with physical columns. We have added aggregation information, but we can also make new columns using the already created logical columns, without the need to create new physical sources in the database.

As an example, we currently have measures from **Games Won** and **Games Lost**, but let's say that we have a requirement to understand what percentage of total games have been won by a player. To do this, right-click on our logical table and choose **New Object | Logical Column...**:

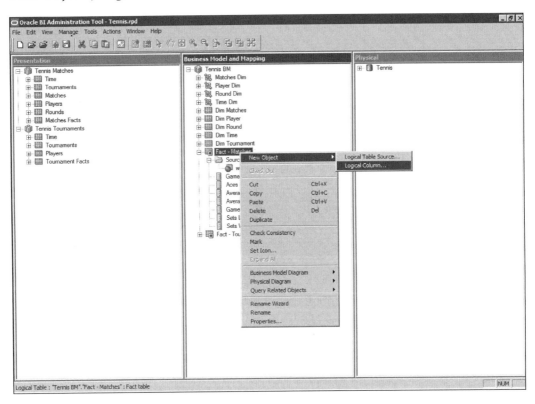

Then you will get the screen, as shown in the following screenshot. In the **General** tab, name our new measure as **% Games Won**. Then, proceed to the **Column Source** tab. Note that there is no physical column mapped. Remember from the preceding section that we dragged object from the physical layer to the business layer, automatically creating logical columns with their appropriate physical mapping:

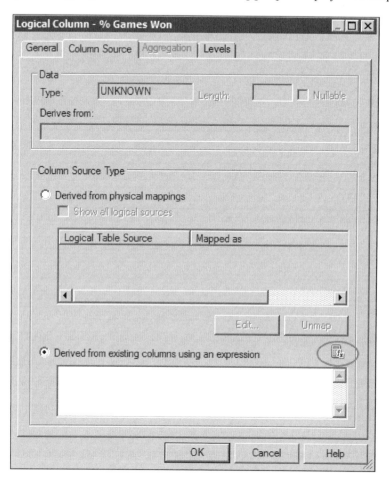

This time, we are creating a column directly in the business layer. We are not worried about physical mappings or columns as we can deduce the information for the new measure from two current logical columns. So, as you can see in the preceding screenshot, we have checked the **Derived from existing columns using an expression** option. If you are familiar with the syntax needed, you can type that into the input box straightaway. Alternatively, you can invoke the Expression Builder by clicking on the icon with the **fx** indicator on the bottom right of the screen shown in the preceding screenshot.

Expression Builder

You will come across the Expression Builder at many places during project development. It exposes functions and methods of manipulating data that the OBIEE server provides. We can use these to create new definitions in a repository, or to manipulate strings in an attribute column, for example, concatenating first name and last name for a customer, or to convert a column data type. In fact, there are many possibilities here and you are well advised to take time to explore the possibilities here. You can have a look at the various functions and objects by changing the choice in the **Category** box on the top left of the screen shown in the following screenshot. Then, you will be given further options in the other two boxes:

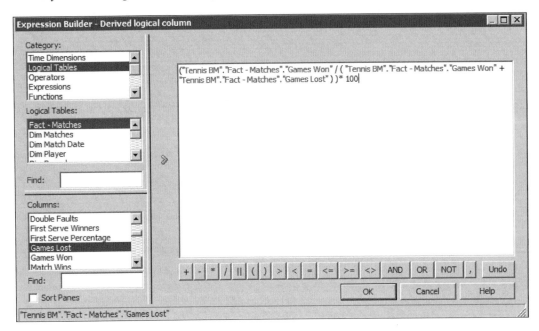

In our case, we want to refer to two logical columns. So choose **Logical Tables** as our **Category** and then choose the table (**Fact - Matches**) and columns that we require. We can then make calculation that represents the percentage of total number of games won. You can see that calculation in the following screenshot:

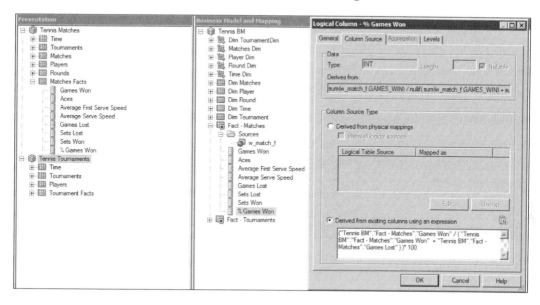

Once you click on **OK**, the Expression Builder will check that our syntax is coherent and then you can proceed to drag this new measure to our physical layer. Note that in the **Column Source** tab, the column automatically gets a data type as INT and the **Aggregation** tab is grayed out. Both of these are derived from our base columns.

So, now we have a new measure that our business can use without having to alter our data source. All the required development has taken place within OBIEE.

Physical column calculation

We can create the same calculation but this time using physical columns, rather than logical columns, as our base. So, we will create a new logical column exactly as before, however, let's name it as **% Games Won (Physical)**. Note that this time we have to set an aggregation rule as we are deriving the information directly from the physical columns. After this, we need to open the logical table source. We can do this via the **Column Source** tab and edit the logical source from the **Derived from physical mappings** section, or we can double-click on the LTS itself. Then, we proceed to the **Column Mapping** tab, as you can see in the following screenshot:

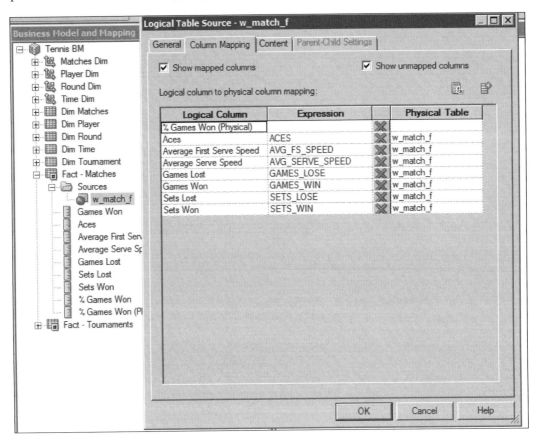

In the preceding screenshot, you can see the mappings from physical to logical columns. If you check the **Show unmapped columns** box, you will see our new logical column. To create the mapping and calculation, choose our new column and again click on the Expression Builder icon:

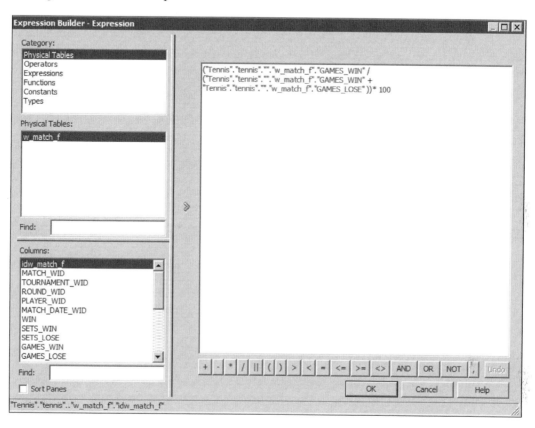

This time we do not have access to the logical columns and tables. The physical tables replace this option, but we have access to the same functions and operators. If our syntax is correct, we can drag this column to the presentation layer.

Although we have discussed two methods to produce the same calculation, you have to be careful while choosing the solution for a live environment. The rather more correct method in this case would be to use a logical calculation. Why? Well, because we want to know the aggregated number of games won and lost before we calculate a percentage. So, it is better that we set an aggregation rule before our calculation rather than setting after as it is in the second case.

Logical calculations: Use when you need an aggregation before your calculation.

Physical calculations: Use when you need an aggregation after your calculation.

However, both of these methods will be utilized as needed according to your project requirements. Ensure that you test the results properly before you expose such development to the users.

Time series measures

OBIEE also provides several functions that allow you to make comparisons between different time periods. For example, we may have a report based on the current month's statistics for games won, but we also want to include a column for last months' statistics as well. OBIEE offers the following time series functions:

- AGO: This is used when we have a requirement such as the one we have just described, that is,. to compare current time periods with previous time periods.

- TODATE: This function is used when you need to aggregate a measure from the beginning of a specified time period to the lowest grain in a report that we have created. For example, an year-to-date calculation.

- PERIODROLLING: This is a new function in 11*g*. Here you can stipulate the length of the period to cover. For example, we could set a period of 3, which would cover three months or three years depending on the grain of the report. This function is useful when you need something like a rolling average in a report.

We are going to create a new measure using the AGO function. Firstly, this requires a slight change to the Time dimension hierarchy that we had previously stepped through the setup. In the preceding section we discussed how to set up a generic dimension hierarchy, however, when we start using time series functions, we need to inform the OBIEE server that this dimension is specifically associated with time.

We do this by double-clicking on the Time dimension hierarchy in the business layer and ensuring that the **Time** box is checked under the **Structure** options. This will then give us the option to set a **chronological key** at each level of the dimension, as shown in the following screenshot:

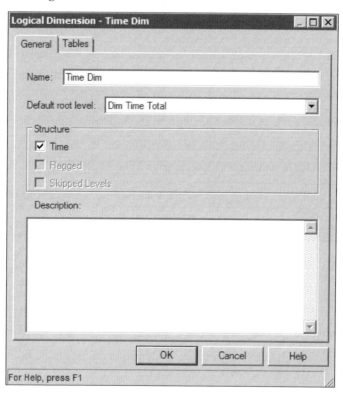

The OBIEE server requires a chronological key to be set for each level of our Time hierarchy. Oracle describes this key as monotonically increasing, which for our purposes means a key that increases in chronological order. This key will enable the server to produce efficient SQL when creating the time series queries:

As you can see in the preceding screenshot, we have opened the detail level of our hierarchy and set the key. Then, proceed to do the same for all of our levels. At this point, we are ready to create our new measure.

First, create a new logical measure in the business layer. Again, we will be doing this in our **Matches** logical fact table. As we have shown you in the preceding section, we will open the Expression Builder to create our calculation. If we choose **AGO** from the time series function, the builder will ask us to create a calculation based on this syntax:

```
Ago(<<Measure>>,<<Level>>,<<Number of Periods>>)
```

The measure we want to make a comparison with is **% Games Won**. Let's say our requirement is to see the previous year's stats. Chose the **Year** level from our Time dimension (as you can see in the following screenshot). The number of periods will be **1** as we wish the time-shift of one year:

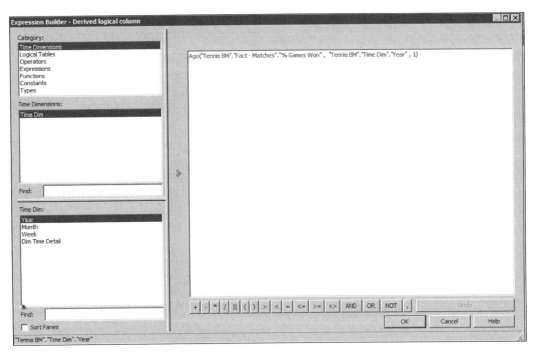

Drag this measure to the presentation layer, and there you go, we have a new measure based on the AGO function. Note that we built this measure upon a column that was calculated from two other logical columns. It shows how you can increase complexity in the business layer without changing physical columns, and how quickly you can increase the sophistication of your offering to the end users:

Level based measure

The AGO measure will show us last year's results for the lowest grain in our report. So if we were looking for a report by Month, that measure would show us the data for the same month last year. How about if we wanted to show data for the whole previous year in spite of the grain that we choose for our report? Well we can leverage our dimensional hierarchy and create a measure that always covers an entire year. This is done by creating a measure and setting its content level to the desired level in one of our dimensions:

Again, we will build upon our previous work. As you can see in the following screenshot, you can copy the whole definition of our AGO measure by right-clicking and choosing **Duplicate**:

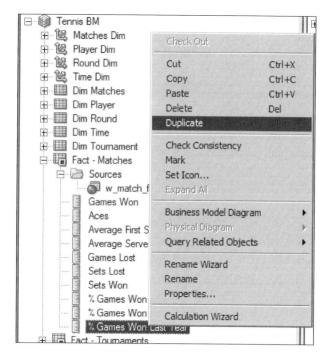

Then open that new logical column, rename it, and navigate to the **Levels** tab. The **Levels** tab shows us all of the levels for the dimensions that we have connected to this logical table:

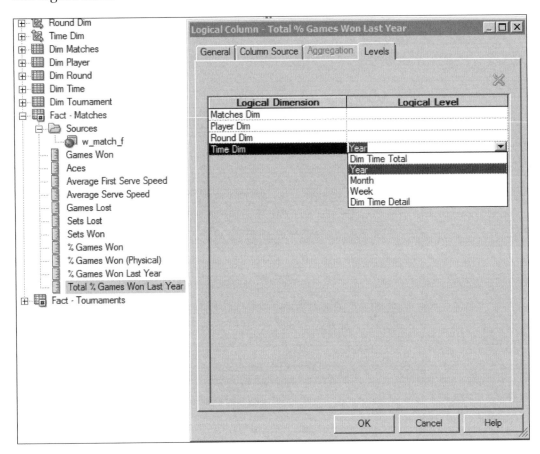

In our case, as you can see in the preceding screenshot, choose the **Year** level from the Time dimension. This means that this measure will always show results for an aggregated level of **Year**. This functionality is extremely useful when dealing with many requirements. For example, a business may have the need to compare the sales performance of a store against that of its parent region, but they are part of different levels in the same dimension. We could create a level-based measure for the parent region and still show results for the store.

Once you have clicked on **OK**, our new measure is created:

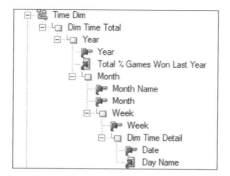

As shown in the preceding screenshot, this new measure now appears in our dimension hierarchy for Time and at the **Year** level. This shows that this column/measure is aggregated at this level of the Time dimension. Note that rather than changing the settings in the **Levels** tab, we could also have dragged this new measure to the **Year** level in the hierarchy. Both methods yield the same end result.

Federated and fragmented content

We have talked a little bit about how we can have multiple logical table sources behind each logical table. This supports the federation and fragmentation of data, and is an extremely important part of OBIEE's capability. This is an advanced topic, but we will provide an introduction to this advanced LTS functionality with an example of fragmentation. There are three main scenarios where we would require multiple logical table sources.

Vertical federation – aggregation or level based

This is used when we have aggregate tables in our schema. An aggregate table is a summary of our base data at a higher level of one or multiple dimensions. This is usually created to improve query performance. We can introduce an aggregate table as a new LTS. As we have done with our previous level-based measure, we can set the content for the whole LTS to the appropriate level in one of our dimensions. Logical columns will be mapped to both sources and OBIEE will then choose to utilize the appropriate source depending on the grain of the query run. This is an extremely common scenario and as such we go into more detail and a step-by-step example of this in *Chapter 14, Improving the Performance*.

Horizontal federation

This is where a fact or dimension has multiple table sources at the same grain, but they contain different column information. Columns will be mapped to one of the sources and OBIEE will choose a single source table or combine both depending on which columns are chosen in the query.

An example of horizontal federation is where we want to combine two sources at the same granularity as one logical table. An example would be that we have financial actuals information and budget figures in different sources, but want to be able to report on them as a whole. These physical sources would not even need to be in the same location that is, we could combine data from two different databases.

Fragmentation

This is where we have multiple physical tables for a dimension or fact, but this time these tables have the same set of columns and they differ in the information or row-set contained in each column. For example, this is quite commonly used when we have set of data that is rarely accessed and we want to save on database I/O.

Fragmentation example – content based

So let's look at a scenario for the content-based fragmentation. Our data warehouse development team have come back to us and said that they would prefer if they present the information for Players in two different tables—one for male players and another one for female players. We have created two new tables—w_player_d_f and w_player_d_m. These supersede the old dimension table of w_player_d. Firstly, we import them and add the appropriate joins in the physical layer as shown in the following screenshot:

Physical Diagram

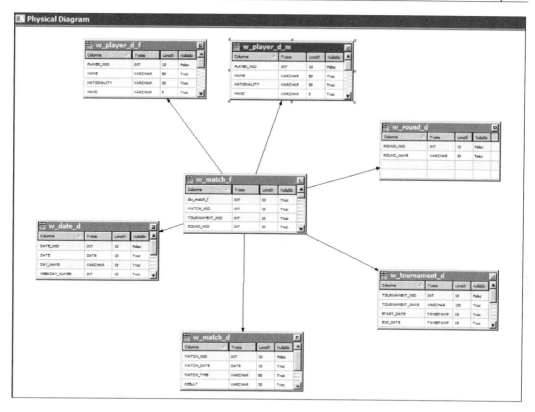

At this point, we could delete the current logical table source for Player in the business model and add the two new tables as two new sources. However, to save a bit of time we can rename and repoint the current source to one of the new tables. As you can see in the following screenshot, we have opened the **w_player_d** table source. Note that in the **Map to these tables** section, we have deleted the reference to **w_player_d** and added a mapping to the new table for female players:

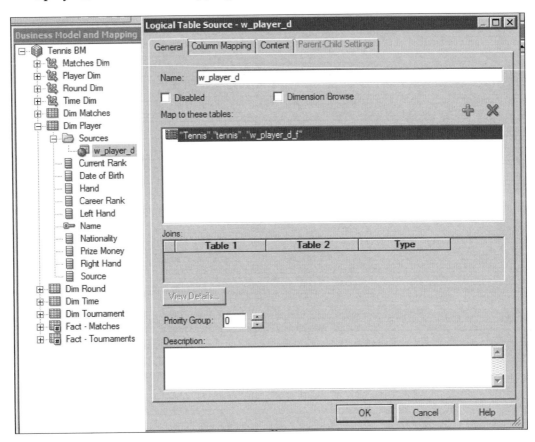

Now we move onto the **Column Mapping** tab and ensure that it is showing both mapped and unmapped columns. The change in the LTS mapping to the underlying physical table means that some columns may not be mapped correctly to a physical column. In fact, you can see exactly that has happened in the following screenshot on the left-hand side. OBIEE will make a best guess by comparing column names, but as we have renamed the logical tables to use names with business meaning, it has struggled to map all of the columns. So we must ensure that all of these columns are mapped successfully:

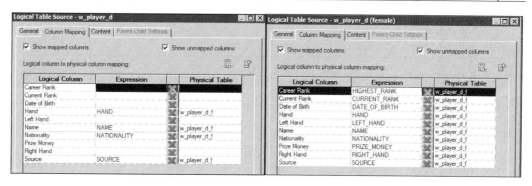

In the preceding screenshot on the right-hand side, we can see that we have now mapped all of the existing columns correctly. Note that we have also renamed the source **w_player_d (female)**,, so that it is clear what this LTS represents.

Now, create a new LTS called **w_player_d (male)** and map it to the **w_player_d_m** table. We can do these by right-clicking on the logical table and choosing **New Object | Logical Table Source**. Name and map it accordingly. As you can see in the following screenshot, we now have two logical table sources for one logical table. Also, if we open a logical column as we have done in the following screenshot, we will see that each one is now mapped to two physical columns. So how does the OBIEE server know which physical table and column to use?

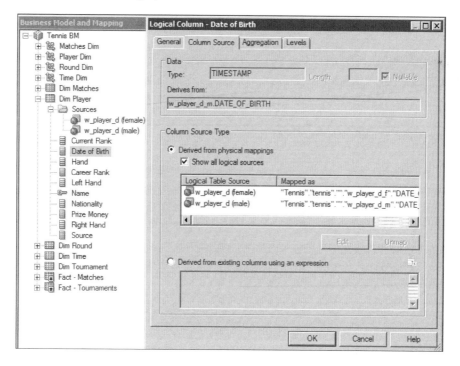

Well, as you may have seen in the **General** tab, that there is a priority option for the LTS. We could set one as a higher priority over another, and the OBIEE server would choose that one first. However, that does not make sense in this case as these tables are of equal priority, they just differ in their data sets. So, we need to give an indication to the server of how they differ. We do this in the **Content** tab of each LTS. We can set a condition based on a column in the **Fragmentation Content** pane. Once this condition is satisfied, the associated LTS will be used in the query. We have added a column called **Sex** that has a value of **F** or **M** to differentiate between the two datasets. Let's bring that in and ensure it is mapped to the two tables, so that we can use it in our condition, and also add it to the presentation layer.

You can see the condition set up in the following screenshot. Note that you can use the Expression Builder to create your condition. Also, we have to do the same for our other LTS but this time the condition will be as follows:

```
"Tennis BM"."Dim Player"."Sex" ='M'
```

This is because we are denoting that this LTS has records for our male players:

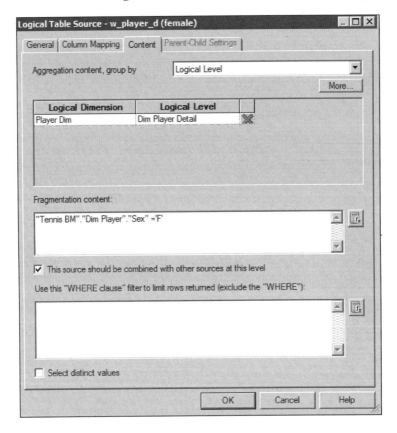

Note that we have ticked the **This source should be combined with other sources at this level** option. This is important as if a query is made that does not filter on sex, we will need OBIEE to combine record sets from both of these sources in order to produce a result.

With that we are done with fragmentation. Note that we, at no point in our example, deleted a logical column. This means that no presentation columns were affected and all of this work was hidden from the end users. It would not have impacted them in any way, and any previously created reports would have worked seamlessly.

Variables and initialization blocks

Outside of the three layers of RPD development, there are also other sections of functionality that help to support the creation of reports and dashboards. The most important of these are the ability to create variables that end users can use in their reports. There are two types of variable:

- **Repository**: Set for the system as a whole and is refreshed at set periods
- **Session**: Individual to the user or session when they login

To create either of these, we need to create what is called an **initialization block** in order to instantiate these variables.

Let's create a repository variable. The first step is to click on **Manage | Variables**:

This brings us to the **Variable Manager** screen. Here, create a new **Init Block** by navigating through **Action | New | Repository | Initialization Block...**:

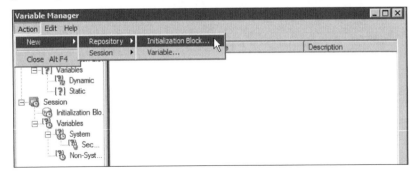

This brings us to the main initialization block screen, where you can set up the data source and actual variables. Provide a name for the block. In our case the name is **initTimeComparison**. You can also set up how often you want the variable values to be refreshed:

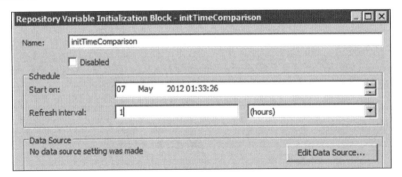

In this screen, first click on **Edit Data Source...**. This opens up the data source screen:

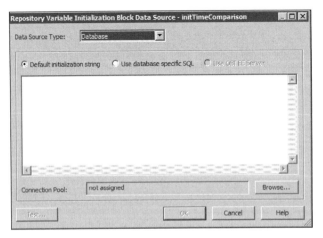

In this area, we need to inform OBIEE about the following:

- **Data Source Type**: It gives the location from where we are getting the data for our variables. In our case this is a normal database.

- **Default Initialization String**: It is a query that we will run on our data source in order to get variable values.

- **Connection Pool**: It is the connection pool in the physical layer against which we will run our query.

As you can see in the preceding screenshot, we have already set our **Data Source Type**. Let's go ahead and chose one of our connection pools by clicking on the **Browse...** button:

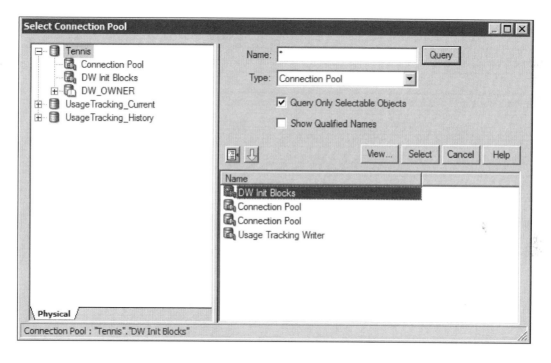

This provides us with a list of our physical layer connection pools. Select a new pool called **DW Init Blocks** that we created especially for this purpose:

Create a separate connection pool solely for variables. This reduces contention with your main connection pools.

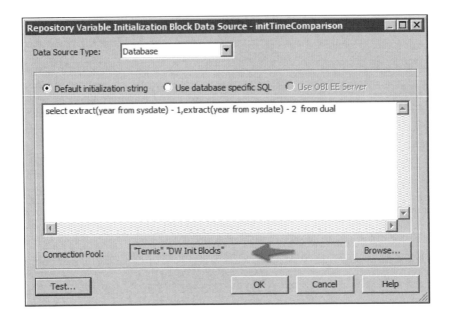

Note that our connection pool has been recorded. We can now write a statement to populate our variables. As you can see in the preceding screenshot, we have written a simple example for an Oracle database. This returns two values retrieving the last two years. We can test that our query and Init Block are working by clicking on **Test**:

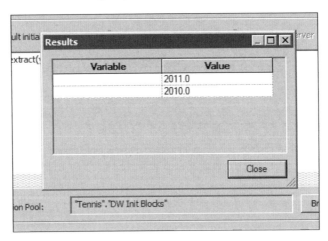

Our values have returned successfully, but we now need to assign them variable names. We do this by returning to the block's main screen and clicking on **Edit Data Target...**:

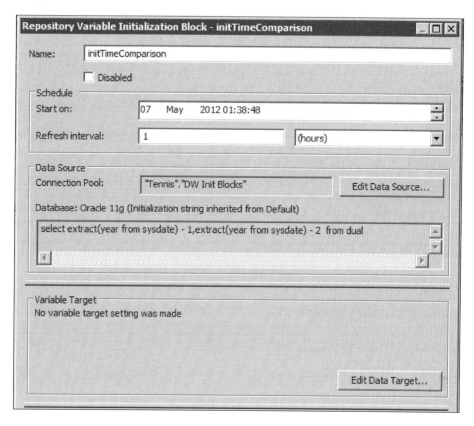

This brings up the **Initialization Block Variable Target** screen. Here, click on **New** and you can proceed to define our variable names. These names will be used as references to the variable when we come to the point for making reports:

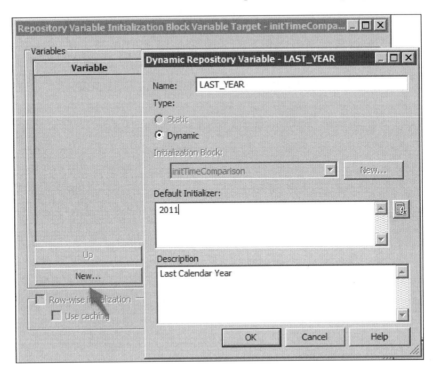

We can also set a default value if we require. Once we have created both variables, make sure that they appear in the same order as the values are returned within our SQL query:

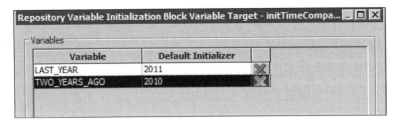

Clicking on **OK**, we can return to a fully completed **Initialization Block** screen:

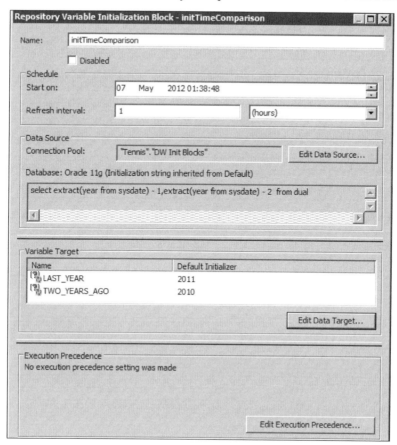

We can click on **Test...** here to check whether the whole block works.

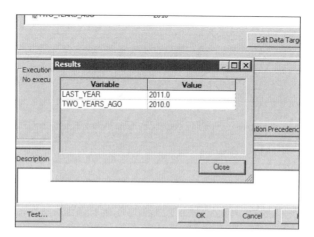

As you can see in the preceding screenshot, our whole block works and the returned values have associated variables.

Returning to the **Variable Manager** screen, you can see our new objects:

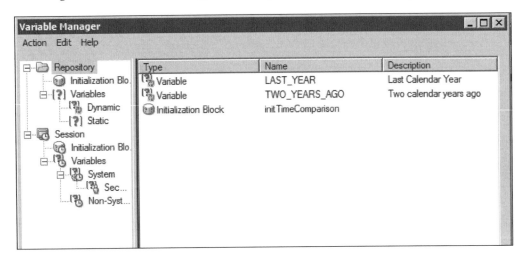

We will see an example of a variable in use when we come to create reports in *Chaprter 10, Creating Dashboards and Reports*.

A review – what I should now know!

For self-review and recap of the chapter, here are a few questions based on important topics covered in this chapter:

1. What are the three layers of an RPD?
2. How do you define physical joins?
3. How do you setup the levels of a dimension?
4. How do you create a level-based measure?
5. What is a way of using functions to compare time periods in a report?
6. How do you ensure that a fact less query is routed properly?
7. How and why do you add multiple table sources to a logical table?
8. How do you check that an RPD is consistent?

Additional research suggestions

Following are some additional research suggestions that may help you in understanding this chapter in more details:

- Help files in the Administration tool
- Oracle documentation at `http://www.oracle.com/technetwork/ middleware/bi-enterprise-edition/documentation/index.html`

Summary

As you can see in the final screenshot, we have covered a lot of ground in this chapter. This will be enough to get a developer going on any project, yet it is hoped that this material has opened your eyes to the fact that there are a vast amount of development options in the RPD, and also that there is massive scope for you to gather further experience and knowledge:

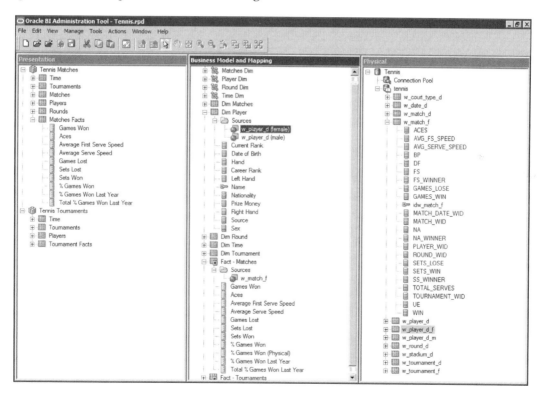

We went through setting up a new project from the physical tables, through to adding extensive business logic, and then configuring the presentation to our end users. We created advanced objects adding layer upon layer of complexity, each time iterating and building upon a previous piece of development. Don't be overawed by the amount of options but take time to experiment and read upon all of the topics that we have discussed in this chapter.

Once you are up to the speed in running the queries (as we will show you later in this book), you can use OBIEE's query log (NQQuery.log) to check how the logical and physical SQL changes as we make RPD changes. This will strongly enhance your understanding of RPD development.

We also talked a lot about best practices. If you wish to become a valuable developer, take the time to develop your projects with this in mind. It is very easy to just drag a bunch of objects in quickly without thinking about the future iterative cycles and requirements. OBIEE has very powerful options, but do not be tempted to just put everything into the RPD.

Take time to understand whether something should be developed in the RPD or pushed down to the ETL or database.

Many times, an advanced metric or solution would perform better in a lower level of the system. Also keep in mind that advanced functionality can add a lot to the server load of your OBIEE installation. Although it can be difficult in a pressurized project, liaise with your ETL and database experts to try and reach the best and most performant solution for your overall system rather than grasping for the easiest option straightaway.

9

Features of the Presentation Catalog

So far, you will have installed all the software, have a database ready, have set your users up, and have a BI server repository ready to go. You are now ready to use the reporting part of the system—the **Presentation Catalog**. The Presentation Catalog is controlled by the Presentation service, which now has a bigger role in managing the Presentation Catalog and the applications that form OBIEE 11g.

This chapter will introduce you to the new interface of the catalog, and the tools that are integrated into the Presentation services. We will also explore the aspects of the catalog administration.

Changes to the way the catalog works is one of the big improvements from the 10g version, with the new and improved Oracle BI system having such a large number of features, we need to examine what they are, before deciding which ones to use.

The Presentation Catalog can be thought of as a comprehensive file management system, which includes folders and files that have attributes such as security controls. The files tend to contain XML and the folders relate to the real folders in your operating system.

The Presentation Catalog is controlled by the Presentation services. This is a web-based system that contains various tools that are integrated with the security of the WebLogic platform and the Presentation Catalog itself. For example, you can use one of the tools to create a report and then save it in the catalog, in a secure folder.

The security of access to the whole OBIEE 11g system is controlled by the Weblogic services; The security of the data available for reporting is controlled by the BI Server, which integrates it's security with the Weblogic security service. The Presentation service also integrates it's security with Weblogic, which enables securing the dashboards, reports and other objects held in the catalog. Later in the chapter we explore the security administration of the catalog.

Integrated tools

Several BI tools are now integrated into the Oracle BI main Presentation Server application. These tools and features that are integrated into the Presentation Server (using the Oracle-defined names) are as follows:

- Analysis
- Dashboards
- Published reporting
- Actionable Intelligence
- Performance management
- Marketing
- Briefing books
- Administration
- Search
- Help
- Mapping
- RSS feeds
- Office integration
- iPad integration

Analysis

Answers are part of the system that enables the creation of analysis objects, which are the requests for the information that returns rows of data from a datasource (such as an Oracle database). The resulting set of records can be presented by the analysis in a variety of layouts, for example in a Table of columns and rows, or as a Chart.

The important point to note is that the request for information is saved in the catalog, not the data. Each time the request is run, it fetches the data in the source system at that time. You can save the results by downloading them as an Excel file, as a PDF, or even as a web page, but OBIEE does not store the result in an analysis.

Analyses are saved for using later by opening them directly or by placing them on a dashboard. They can also be used by the Actionable Intelligence tool (refer to the *Actionable Intelligence* section in this chapter).

Analyses are normally created by the more advanced users of the system, but you do not need to have high technical IT skills—it's mainly click or drag.

The next chapter will go into more detail on how to create analysis objects.

Dashboards

A dashboard is used to present information to users, in a way that is simple to use and that can be bespoke to each user. Dashboards consist of one or more pages (also known as tabs), and can contain analysis, embedded websites, URLs, text, actions, and folders.

The dashboards can be used by thousands of users, with each user seeing a view customized to themselves. The dashboards can be highly interactive, provide end users the ability to drill into the data, and investigate the results in a personalized way.

There is a chapter dedicated to the building of dashboards, as this is the core feature of most OBIEE implementations (refer to *Chapter 10, Creating Dashboards and Analysis*).

Published reporting

My favorite new feature in 11*g* is the integration of the BI Publisher tool into the Presentation services platform. In the previous versions, the BI Publisher security was separate and so was the BI Publisher Catalog of reports. Published reporting is a new way to refer to the BI Publisher Reports in OBIEE 11*g*.

Published reports are highly formatted reports that are normally available for printing. You could use reports for invoices, statements, and pick lists as well as formatted reports on company performance.

Refer to *Chapter 12, Developing Reports Using BI Publisher*, later in this book.

Actionable Intelligence

One of the great uses of OBIEE is to set up a report and have it delivered to your e-mail inbox everyday. Better still, have the report e-mailed to you only if you need to take some action, for example order new stock or chase debtors! The new term for delivering contents to users is named as agents. Agents are scheduled jobs, which decide whom to send the content to, when, and where. For example, you can create a schedule that checks the stock levels in the database for various stores. If a certain level is reached in one store, an e-mail is fired off to the controllers, showing them where the stock is and how old it is.

OBIEE 11*g* takes this idea one step further and enables you to take action directly from a dashboard. An action may be to navigate to another part of the system or to invoke a web service or even some JavaScript. In our example, the action available to the user could be to use a web service that puts an order into the distribution system to move the stock from one warehouse to the store.

Chapter 11, Agents and the Action Framework, is dedicated to the creation of Actionable Intelligence.

Performance management

The Business Intelligence system is mainly used for reporting on the company performance. Performance is measured in terms of financial activity, sales, HR, and other specific business drivers, such as churn rates. Certain measures that we report upon are fundamental to the success of the organization, for example the profit margin on products sold or the acquisition of new customers each month.

These measures are known as **Key Performance Indicators (KPIs)**.

The concept of presenting all KPIs together in one page is called a **balanced scorecard**. These scorecards were designed in the early 1990s and have been widely adopted throughout the world in businesses, governments, and nonprofit organizations.

Oracle has integrated the reporting on KPIs and the creation of scorecards into the Presentation Server and Presentation Catalog. The creation of these is out of the scope of this book, but there are some examples available in the sample application that you can install (available at `oracle.com`).

Marketing

One of the early uses of OBIEE (when it was owned by Seibel) was in the Siebel Marketing Tool. The concept is simple, finding lists of people to send marketing information. The idea is that OBIEE can help to identify customers with certain attributes, for example males over 50 living in London. This initial list is then further reduced by those who already had a letter sent to them in the previous month. Once the target list has been created, it is imported into the marketing system for the fulfillment process (sending out literature by mail or e-mail).

Siebel Email Marketing is still available from Oracle today as part of the Siebel Enterprise Marketing Suite. You can also purchase Marketing Analytics.

Mapping

MapViewer is now integrated into OBIEE 11*g*. End users can now incorporate Map Views into their dashboards without using complex coding and without any extra licenses. Typically, the data involved is address-related, for example postal address, but you can also include custom areas to show on a map. Address type information is normally subjected to geocoding to make it usable by OBIEE. Mapping Data is managed from the administration screen and the definitions are held in the catalog.

To use MapViewer a new type of view has been created, unsurprisingly called the **Map View**. The Map View normally contains a map of a location and this is overlaid with colored shapes or pins. These overlays denote items or measures. For example, sales by state could be three colored to denote low, medium, and high levels. Map Views allow further analysis by allowing users to drill into the data points, or even to use actions.

MapViewer is also available directly with your installation of Oracle BI 11*g*. Try `http://[server]:<port>/mapviewer` on your environment.

Administration

The common interface and use of a single catalog for the reports, analysis, alerts, and lists requires an administration tool for the features, as well as the catalog itself. The web-based administration area is used to control who can access which feature and what settings to use in Mapping Data and BI Publisher. One change from the previous version is that the management of the catalog objects is moved out of the administration area, so that the catalog tool allows you to control who can access which object (report, analysis, and so on).

The administration area also has access to see the current logged in users and the queries that they are running.

Briefing books

If you are out of the office with no connectivity to your OBIEE system, you can use briefing books to take some of your reports with you. Briefing books are a way of gathering analyses together into a PDF or MHTML file and saving locally for using later.

This feature has been made easier to use in 11*g* given that you can get output as useful file formats. This may lead to increased usage as the 10*g* version was not popular due to the need to download a separate tool.

Search

Searching for any object is now much easier—thanks to a common search tool. It is accessible from the common toolbar or from links on the **Home** page. The search system can now use wildcards and can search by the type of object. This is a huge improvement on the 10*g* version.

Help

Getting help is now much easier from all the installation pages of OBIEE 11*g*. The **Home** screen itself has a whole section dedicated for all the information you need. The common toolbar also has a link to internal help and web links to the Oracle documentation. The help is contextual and it decides which help page you need based upon the page on which you are.

Office integration

OBIEE 11*g* is great for presenting the information and enabling further analysis. Most deployments can be managed by using the online data. Sometimes, users need to have their analysis in Excel or PowerPoint, and this release makes that easier than ever. Exporting into Office, PDF, HTML, and XML is quick and easy. You can also use Excel to connect directly to the OBIEE Presentation service.

The Home screen

When you first log into OBIEE 11*g*, you are normally presented with the **Home** page.

Try typing `http://[server]:9704/analytics` into your browser and after the login screen, you should see the **Home** screen.

> Note that your browser version is important. If you install version 11.1.1.5, I advise you to use Firefox 9. Internet Explorer 9 and Firefox 10 will not work. For version 11.1.1.6, you can use Firefox 10, but please refer to the full Certification Matrix for a complete analysis of what is supported.

Looking at the **Home** screen, we can see that it is divided into the areas shown in the following screenshot:

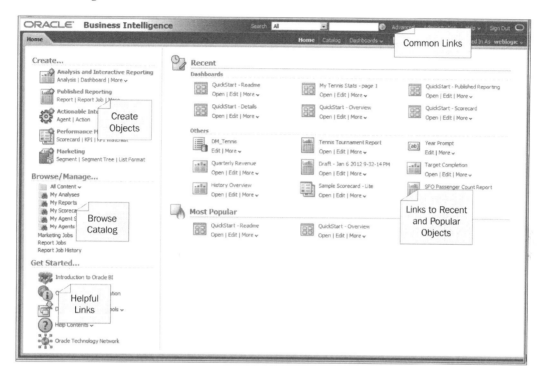

Common links

Most of the integrated tools use a common menu layout, with easy navigation from any part of the system to another. Links are only available to users who have the relevant access rights. This common area is known as the **BI EE Global Header** as it is available on all the tools.

Existing object links

This section contains links to the recently opened dashboards, analysis, briefing books, filters, published reports, and prompts. Basically, it contains any catalog content that you have recently created or edited. You will also see a list of the most popular objects displayed here.

Create objects

You can now create new objects directly from the **Home** page. Along with the major types of objects, such as dashboard, you have access to create related objects, such as prompts, filters, and style templates. You can also use the **NEW** menu item on the common links area.

The only create item links that are visible are the ones for which you have the rights to use.

Browse catalog

A **Quick Link** section mainly contains links that fire off predefined searches. This includes a search for your analyses and reports.

Helpful links

If you need help, you can get it from these links from the local help files that were installed along with the application. Also, in this section, there are links to the main Oracle website. In this section, you will also find links to download the Office Integration client tools.

The BI Desktop tools available to download are as follows:

- **Oracle BI for MS Office**: Enables direct access to OBIEE from Microsoft Office
- **Template Builder for Word**: Creates RTF templates for using in the published reporting
- **Analyzer for Excel**: Enables data to be sent from reports into Excel

Administration

The link to the **Administration** screen is available from the common toolbar.

You can also save a link to the address — `http://[server]:<port>/analytics/saw.dll?Admin`.

The content on the **Administration** screen is also controlled and, therefore, you will only see what the system administrator has privileged for you. A full access user will see six sections on the **Administration** screen:

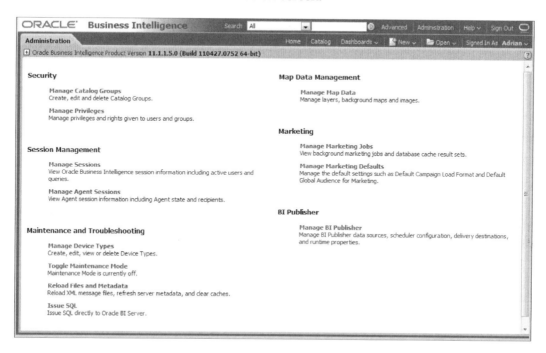

The **Security** section provides links to the administration of the catalog groups and system privileges.

Use the **Session Management** link to view current logged in users and see what they are running. An active request could be cancelled if they are taking too much time.

Groups and users

We have seen in *Chapter 5, Understanding the Systems Management Tools*, that we can create users and groups in our security store (LDAP). The Presentation Catalog uses those groups and users that are already set up, but it also has the facility to create its own groups. This may be useful for certain special access that you want to set up or to group various users or groups together. This is not suitable in your LDAP system. An example of this could be to give some users extra administration rights on a temporary basis, for example for a couple of hours during a deployment. Note, that it is not the best practice to manage security in both the Presentation service and WebLogic Enterprise Manager. So, changes made directly in the Presentation Service Group Administration should be treated as temporary.

Privileges

All of the features of the Presentation service can be secured by allowing access to certain individuals or groups that are using the **Manage Privileges** screen. These privileges are at a more detailed level than those set in the Enterprise Manager. Defining and maintaining the privileges is an important requirement for any OBIEE project. If you do not want to give access to untrained users to certain features or to administration areas, you can choose the users carefully and in advance, the matrix can be created to decide who can use what.

The **Manage Privileges** screen has various sections that relate to the parts of the system that the named users can access or use. You can provide access to groups and/or users, and you can also deny specific groups or users from accessing a particular feature.

The main section to consider is the access rights. The first section of the **Manage Privileges** screen controls general access to the main tools, for example dashboards:

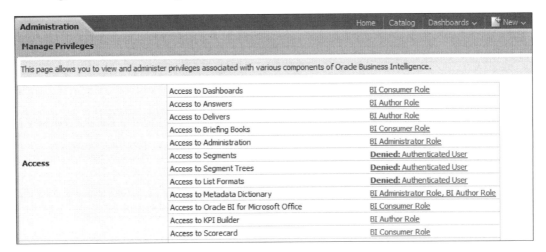

If you click on the link to the right of the item description, you can allocate or deny access. Try clicking on the **Access to Dashboards** link, which currently reads **BI Consumer Role**. Then, you will see a standard pop-up screen for allocating the rights to an object:

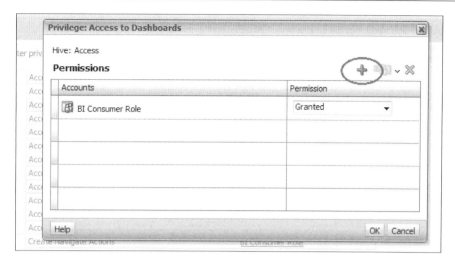

You can now click on the green plus sign to start adding more groups or users. This brings up the **Add Users and Group** form. Search for, and select the role, group, or user to which you would like to give specific access. You can also select the role, group, or user for which you want to deny the access.

Where possible you should aim to assign permissions to roles. If this does not give sufficient granularity, choose groups. Again, if more granularity is required, choose individual users:

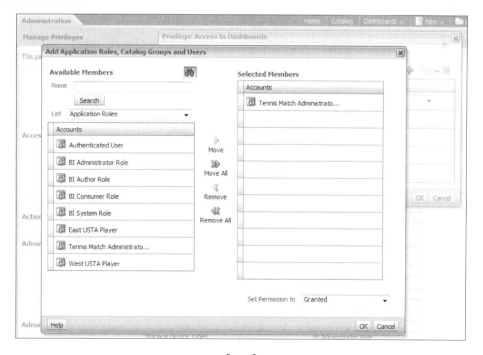

Full privileges list

At the end of this chapter, we have included a list of all the available privileges that can be set. Use the list as a reference to decide what settings to apply on your project.

Session management

On the **Administration** screen, there is a facility to view and manage the current sessions. **Sessions** are simple individuals that have logged in and are running analyses, dashboards, reports, and so on.

Clicking on the **Manage Sessions** link directs you to the session listing screen. At the top of the list, there is a list of the sessions logged in, and below this you will see the recent requests that have been sent to the BI server. The list is also known as the **Cursor Cache** list:

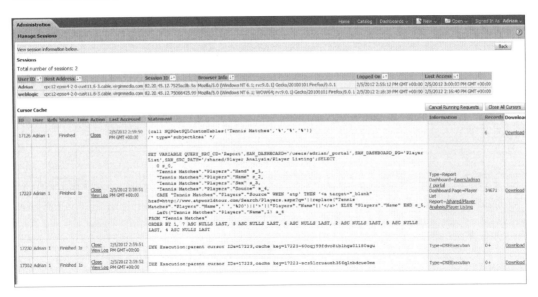

As you can see from the preceding screenshot, the list is showing two logged in users—**Adrian** and **weblogic**. In the **Cursor Cache** section, you can see four cursors and their status. In the column headed as **Action**, you can see highlighted words on which you can click to invoke the action. For running requests, you can click on the **Cancel Running Requests** button to cancel the cursor. For finished requests, you can click on **View Log**, which will bring up a window showing the details of the requests. The level of detail depends upon the logging level that is set for the user.

The following code block shows the log of a request sent by **Adrian**:

```
[2012-02-05T15:34:32.000+00:00] [OracleBIServerComponent] [TRACE:2]
[USER-0] [] [ecid: 76b54503a7a1d074:746fe273:135116de618:-8000-
000000000000bada] [tid: 23fc] [requestid: 31ea0001] [sessionid:
31ea0000] [username: Adrian] #######################################
###### [[
------------------- SQL Request:
  SET VARIABLE QUERY_SRC_CD='Report',SAW_SRC_PATH='
  /users/adrian/Gemini Players';SELECT
    0 s_0,
    "Tennis Matches"."Players"."Name" s_1,
    "Tennis Matches"."Players"."Sex" s_2
  FROM "Tennis Matches"
  WHERE
  ((MONTH("Players"."Date of Birth") = 6 and DAYOFMONTH
  ("Players"."Date of Birth") < 22) OR (MONTH("Players"."Date of
  Birth") =5 and DAYOFMONTH("Players"."Date of Birth") > 21))
  ORDER BY 1, 3 ASC NULLS LAST, 2 ASC NULLS LAST
]]
[2012-02-05T15:34:32.000+00:00] [OracleBIServerComponent] [TRACE:2]
[USER-23] [] [ecid: 76b54503a7a1d074:746fe273:135116de618:-8000-
000000000000bada] [tid: 23fc] [requestid: 31ea0001] [sessionid:
31ea0000] [username: Adrian] -------------------- General Query Info:
[[
  Repository: Star, Subject Area: Tennis BM, Presentation: Tennis
  Matches
]]
[2012-02-05T15:34:32.000+00:00] [OracleBIServerComponent] [TRACE:2]
[USER-18] [] [ecid: 76b54503a7a1d074:746fe273:135116de618:-8000-
000000000000bada] [tid: 23fc] [requestid: 31ea0001] [sessionid:
31ea0000] [username: Adrian] -------------------- Sending query
to database named Tennis (id: <<361301>>), connection pool named
Connection Pool: [[
  WITH
  SAWITH0 AS ((select T875.NAME as c2,
    T875.SEX as c3
  from
    w_player_d_f T875
  where  ( (TO_NUMBER(TO_CHAR(T875.DATE_OF_BIRTH, 'MM'), '99') in
  (5, 6)) and (TO_NUMBER(TO_CHAR(T875.DATE_OF_BIRTH, 'MM'), '99') in
  (5) or TO_NUMBER(TO_CHAR(T875.DATE_OF_BIRTH, 'dd'), '99') < 22) and
  (TO_NUMBER(TO_CHAR(T875.DATE_OF_BIRTH, 'MM'), '99') in (6) or 21 <
  TO_NUMBER(TO_CHAR(T875.DATE_OF_BIRTH, 'dd'), '99')) and
  (TO_NUMBER(TO_CHAR(T875.DATE_OF_BIRTH, 'dd'), '99') < 22 or 21 <
  TO_NUMBER(TO_CHAR(T875.DATE_OF_BIRTH, 'dd'), '99')) )
  union all
```

```
select T862.NAME as c2,
  T862.SEX as c3
from
  w_player_d_m T862
where  ( (TO_NUMBER(TO_CHAR(T862.DATE_OF_BIRTH, 'MM'), '99') in
(5, 6)) and (TO_NUMBER(TO_CHAR(T862.DATE_OF_BIRTH, 'MM'), '99') in
(5) or TO_NUMBER(TO_CHAR(T862.DATE_OF_BIRTH, 'dd'), '99') < 22) and
(TO_NUMBER(TO_CHAR(T862.DATE_OF_BIRTH, 'MM'), '99') in (6) or 21 <
TO_NUMBER(TO_CHAR(T862.DATE_OF_BIRTH, 'dd'), '99')) and
(TO_NUMBER(TO_CHAR(T862.DATE_OF_BIRTH, 'dd'), '99') < 22 or 21 <
TO_NUMBER(TO_CHAR(T862.DATE_OF_BIRTH, 'dd'), '99')) ) )),
SAWITH1 AS (select distinct D2.c2 as c1,
  D2.c3 as c2
from
  SAWITH0 D2)
select distinct 0 as c1,
  D1.c1 as c2,
  D1.c2 as c3
from
  SAWITH1 D1
order by c3, c2
]]
```

Near the top of the preceding code block, you can see information about Request —
in this case, Report has been fired off:

```
SET VARIABLE QUERY_SRC_CD='Report',SAW_SRC_PATH='/users/adrian/Gemini
Players'
```

The actual SQL that was sent to the database is listed after the following line:

```
Sending query to database named Tennis
```

We mainly use logging of the queries to solve the performance problems. The SQL
sent to the database can be examined to check if any bottlenecks exist in the database.
In our example, the logging level has been set to 2, which should provide most of the
information you need.

Maintenance and troubleshooting

This is a section on the **Administration** screen, which contains links to the following system settings:

- Managing mobile devices
- Loading metadata
- Toggling maintenance mode

 Managing the device types is not a common requirement, and in 12 years of OBIEE projects (new Siebel Analytics), I have never had a requirement to send data to a pager or update the OOTB settings.

Loading metadata may be required, if you update the RPD in online mode. It can also refresh the web caches.

Issue SQL

Under the **Maintenance and Troubleshooting** heading, there is a link to a significant feature—**Issue SQL**. The **Issue SQL** option is normally used to test the BI server and is not normally made available to users. The SQL is the OBIEE Logical SQL and not the ANSI SQL, but there is a subtle difference to the Logical SQL that can be run in an analysis. For example, the following statements make use of the * notation to select all fields in the presentation layer tables:

```
SELECT * FROM Players
SELECT * FROM Tournaments
SELECT * FROM TIME
```

The following example uses the SELECT_PHYSICAL statement to query the physical layer object:

```
SELECT_PHYSICAL CALENDAR_DATE FROM "TENNIS"."tennis".W_DATE_D;
```

You can also use the * notation

```
SELECT_PHYSICAL * FROM "TENNIS"."tennis".W_DATE_D;
```

Functions can also be used in the statement. For example, to count the number of records in the Date table:

```
SELECT_PHYSICAL count(*) FROM "TENNIS"."tennis".W_DATE_D;
```

We will cover more details on the Oracle BI SQL (also known as Logical SQL) syntax, later in this book.

The Presentation Catalog

All of the tools mentioned in the preceding sections will store the user-defined objects into a folder structure. This structure is bound together in a Presentation Catalog, also known as a **Web Catalog**. The catalog not only makes use of your operating system file and folder management, but also adds a layer of security and management. Each object is stored with a security reference and properties marker that control when and how the objects are accessible.

The catalog is managed by the web-based administration screens of the Presentation Server or by using a windows-based Catalog Administration tool (also known as the Catalog Manager).

For those familiar with the OBIEE 10*g* system, there is a change in the way items are accessed and managed. In the previous version, managing catalog objects was a separate set of screens to be navigated in the catalog. In OBIEE 11*g*, you can navigate and view the objects in one screen. All properties and controls are available directly in **Catalog View**. The tasks such as copying, renaming, and changing permissions are undertaken while browsing the catalog. There is no longer a separate screen to set the permissions on dashboards, and significantly, there are no dashboard links in the common screen.

Structure of the Presentation Catalog

From a users perspective, there are two main folders that contain the subfolders and stored objects. These folders are as follows:

- Users
- Shared

The users folder contains a subfolder for each user that logs in. This provides a space for the users to store their own analysis and other objects securely. The option to use personal storage folders can be disabled.

> On a recent project, we had up to 50,000 potential users. This could make the user folder very difficult to navigate, so we implemented one of the advanced features, which arranges the user folders into subfolders. In this case, the subfolders were the first two characters of the user name. Users such as Daniel and Dave are available in the DA subfolder. For projects where you have more than 1,000 users, consider adding the parameter HashUserHomeHirectories to the instanceconfig.xml file.

Click on the **Catalog** link on the common menu to explore the catalog.

The default view, shown in the following screenshot, includes your personal folders and shared folders to which you have access:

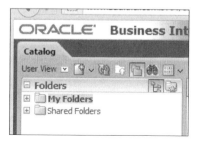

If you have sufficient permissions, you can switch to **Admin View**. Click on the drop-down icon and select **Admin View**. Normal users do not have an option of **Admin View**:

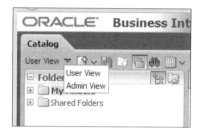

You are now presented with **Admin View**, which starts at a higher level of the Web Catalog—**Catalog Root**. As an administrator, this allows you to see all the subfolders, but you will only be able to navigate into those folders if you have permissions to do so. By default, you do not have permission to navigate into the **User** folder:

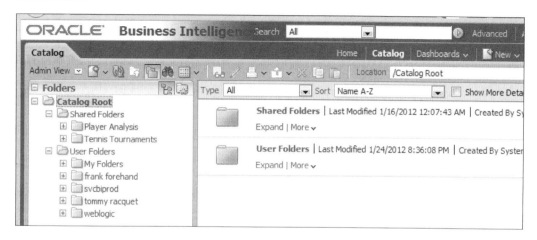

Hidden items

The objects that you create, such as your own analysis or dashboard pages, are visible to you in your own **User** or **Shared** folders. There are also various hidden files that help to control your user experience. For example, users that have accessed the system, using an iPad have their favorites stored in a hidden XML file.

To see the hidden items, tick on the **Show Hidden Items** checkbox on the top right of the screen.

File management

Management of the catalog is undertaken using the Oracle supplied tools, that is the web-based Presentation Server or the Windows-based Catalog Manager. However, you can backup the whole catalog or parts of it, such as a dashboard, using normal operating system tools. On Linux, I tend to use tar to compress a folder and store this as a backup, or copy into another environment.

XML files

The object definitions and hidden files contain XML. Using the Catalog Manager, you can view the XML being used, and can even edit it directly in the Catalog Manager. This is an advanced feature, which is not necessary on most projects, nor undertaken without fully understanding the XML structures.

The XML files are also visible in your normal file explorer and they can be useful, for example, if you want to find which analyses use a particular column from your BI server.

Object copying

The previous versions were able to copy objects, but with version 11*g*, you can also copy dashboards. This feature speeds up the development cycles and encourages greater flexibility.

> I was previously on a 10*g* project that wanted 22 similar dashboards, and now I wish I had 11*g* version! On that project, we had to create each dashboard manually, whereas now you can simply copy the whole dashboard and make any minor changes afterwards.

The new copy method is widely available throughout the catalog, either in the **Tasks** pane (bottom left corner) or under the **More** menu.

Multiple personal dashboards

One of the nice surprises in the new features of 11*g* is the ability to create more than one personal dashboard. For some power users, a single dashboard – My Dashboard – is just not enough. Having said that, it is also possible to create a dashboard in the **Shared** folder and set the permissions so that you are the only person to see it, that is, it has the same effect.

The downside of multiple personal dashboards is that only one dashboard – **My Dashboard** – is listed in the dashboards menu. To navigate to other personal dashboards, you can locate them under **My Folders** in **Catalog View**.

Catalog deployments

One of the challenges we face on every project is how to develop, test, and deploy new dashboards and analysis without breaking the existing ones. Various approaches have been used at various companies that either involve lots of downtime or worse still, no user-developed reporting. My preferred method is to use another part of the production system to create new dashboards and only expose these when the testers have signed it off. This approach minimizes the risks in deploying from one network to another (which include the permission issues and loss of user settings).

OBIEE 11*g* has a neat solution which allows the users to archive their analysis, dashboards, folders, or other catalog objects, and save these archive files on the network. Then, they can be imported (unarchived) into another catalog. This process could be used to copy from a test catalog to a production one for example.

Securing catalog objects

Each folder, dashboard, analysis, and report has permissions attached. In fact, every object in the catalog has a form of permissioning. In the preceding section, we have seen that access to the features in the Presentation Catalog and Presentation Server have permissions (set by the **Privileges** screen), but access to the feature does not automatically allow access to the objects in the feature (for example, a report).

The permissions for the objects can be found under the **More** drop-down menu. The following screenshot shows the **Permissions** link for the folder **Player Analysis**:

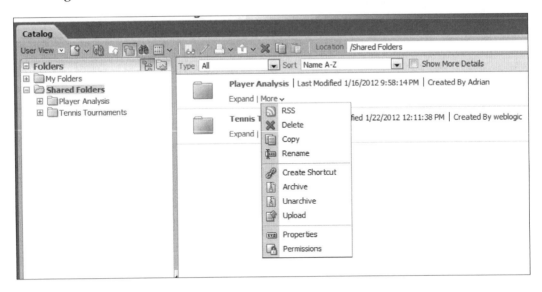

If you click on the **Permissions** link at the bottom of the **More** drop-down menu, you will be presented with the **Permission** form. A standard layout is used for all the objects, as seen in the following screenshot:

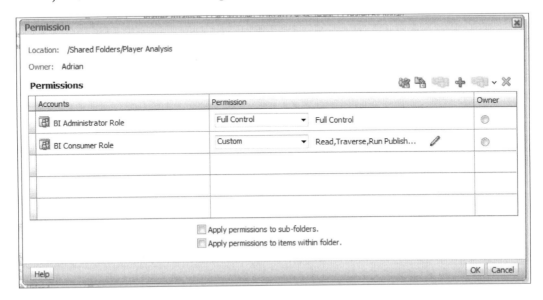

Here, we have set the permission levels (from full control to denied access). Note the options at the bottom of the form — **Apply permission to sub-folders** and **Apply permissions to items within folder**. These are best left in the default mode of not applying (in 10g this often catches out the reports' developers).

 Note that the dashboard sits inside a folder, so changing the folder can change the selection of users that can see your dashboard.

Permission inheritance

When a new object is saved into a folder, it inherits the permissions of that folder. You can overwrite the permission settings if required at the individual level, but in practice this could end up in an administrative nightmare.

Practical steps to object security

For most implementations that I have lead, we have implemented a form of **Access Control List (ACL)**. This would entail creating catalog groups that are assigned access rights. A typical example could be ACL Answers Users. Then, this Web Catalog group can be given the privilege of using answers. So, you can now add users, groups, or roles to the ACL Answers Users, and the people involved will be able to access the Answers tool. In the 11g version, catalog groups are mainly provided for the backward compatibility and, therefore, the recommended approach would be to create the ACL in the WebLogic/Security layer for using as a role.

If you have a great LDAP service, the ACL can be set up as groups in the LDAP and the allocation of people to groups is then controlled by the Security Administration Team. This frees up your team to continue developing. Alternatively, you can manage the administration from the Web Catalog Administration screens:

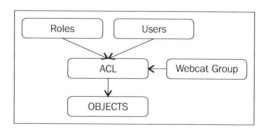

A review – what I should now know!

The following points are very important for you to remember:

1. What features are accessible from the OBIEE **Home** page
2. What security options are available
3. How the Presentation Catalog is organized
4. How to set the parameters and options for the BI tools
5. What administration tools are available

Summary

In this chapter, we introduced you to the new Oracle BI Presentation Catalog, and all its features and tools.

The integration of the published reporting allows for a total reporting solution that fits the needs of each user, all at one place.

Managing security and deployments is simplified with the integration, along with the ability for users to bring the Oracle BI reporting output to their desktops and into their daily routines.

In the next chapter, we will look in more depth at using the analysis and dashboard tool, and later in this book, we will look at the Published Reporting tool.

The next chapters will go into more detail on how to create the analyses and dashboards, as well as use the other great features of the BI Publisher and Alerts system.

10
Creating Dashboards and Analysis

In the previous chapters, we have installed a new system, learned how to administer the system, and developed the metadata for a brand new project. This chapter is the culmination of all that work in that we are finally ready to develop reports that can be delivered to our end-users.

We will cover creating reports (known as Analyses in OBIEE), and how to group them in dashboards. We will also look at the various ways of representing and formatting data that are available, along with advice on best practices gained from implementation experience.

Analysis versus Reporting

For 11*g*, Oracle has changed the nomenclature of a request so that they are now termed as an Analysis throughout the system. This is quite instructive as it points us in the direction of what we should be attempting in creating a Business Intelligence project. In industry when we talk about "Reporting", we are often referring to operational types of reports that contain frequently changing data, or are based on current performance. For example, this type of reporting is used for state of play reports in quick changing retail and transactional environments. Another example would be call center metrics on the performance of individuals and teams in dealing with current call volumes. If modeled and developed appropriately then OBIEE, of course, can be used for this but this would be wasting a lot of the system's rich functionality and potential.

The driver behind OBIEE and other BI tools is to create "Analytical" reports where we are focused on gaining insights that are difficult to pick up in our daily dealings. This often means that we are looking for patterns or information over an historical period in an aggregated format. Using the operational examples, we might want to look at call volumes over a whole year, so that we can make better choices about the staff numbers needed. In retail, we might want to see what types of products sell better in certain countries over a certain time period. So, in essence, we are looking at giving ourselves information that drives more strategic or longer-term decisions rather than those that concern day-to-day matters. This also means that we traditionally would be looking at a dataset that changes less often than that used for operational reporting.

Creating an Analysis

So, we have discussed a little bit of the philosophy behind analytical reporting, and we will cover a bit more later, but let's first look at creating a technical example in OBIEE.

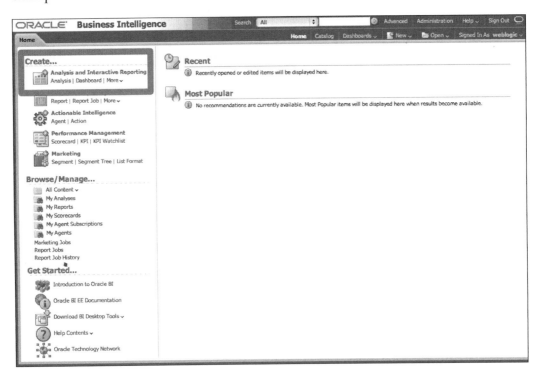

We start with a completely empty **Presentation Catalog**. In the previous chapter, we went through an overview of the catalog, and in this chapter we will be developing content via the **Analysis and Interactive Reporting** section that we have highlighted in the preceding screenshot.

To create a new report, we click on **Analysis**. We are then prompted with options, as shown in the screen below. If we have enabled direct SQL entry for a user, then we will have options to enter Logical or Physical SQL in order to query our data source. Otherwise, we will be prompted to choose from an available **Subject Area**.

Remember that we created an RPD complete with two subject areas in *Chapter 8, Developing a BI Repository*. We can create analyses from within either of these areas. So let's go ahead and choose the **Tennis Matches** subject area.

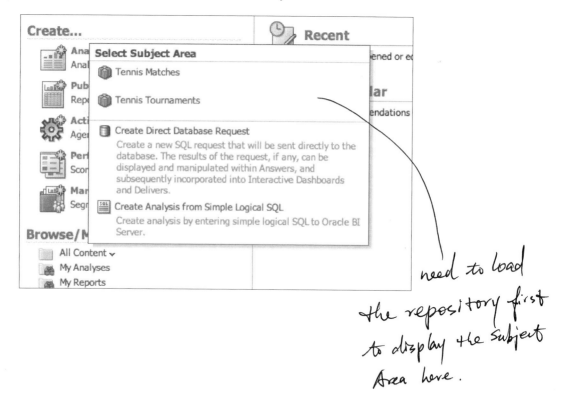

need to load the repository first to display the subject Area here.

Analysis Editor

Once we have chosen our subject area, we are directed to the **Analysis Editor**. It is here that we will be spending the majority of our time while developing in the catalog.

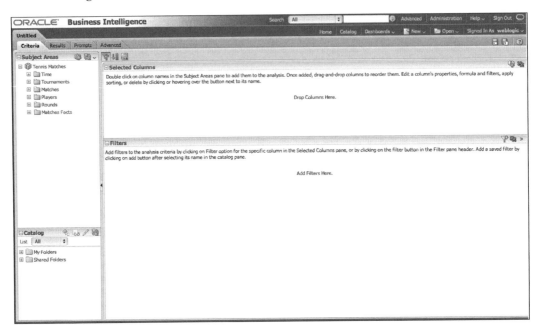

Criteria Tab

The first tab that we see when entering the Analysis Editor is the **Criteria** tab. As you can see in the previous screenshot, the available panes are as follows:

- **Subject Areas**: This is where we can explore and choose from the attributes and measures that we previously set up in the RPD for the Subject Area that we choose when creating a new analysis.

- **Selected Columns**: Once we have chosen objects from the Subject Area, then these will appear in this pane and form the basis of our analysis.

- **Filters**: This is where we can add and amend any filters on the result set produced by our Selected Columns.

- **Catalog**: Here we can access any previously created and already saved items; for example, filters or calculations that we may want to use in our current analysis.

So let's choose a few columns from our subject area. We can do this by double-clicking on a column, or by clicking on and dragging them to the **Selected Columns** pane. In the following screenshot, you can see that we have done this for **Year** and **Month** from the **Time** presentation table, **Nationality** from the **Players**, and **Games Won** from **Matches Facts**. Note that once we have dragged these columns across, that as well as the column name information, we can also see the name of which presentation table that this column has come from. Also the Analysis Editor can differentiate between a fact and an attribute. Note that the **Games Won** fact column is indicated by a yellow slide rule and that a tabular icon indicates the attribute columns.

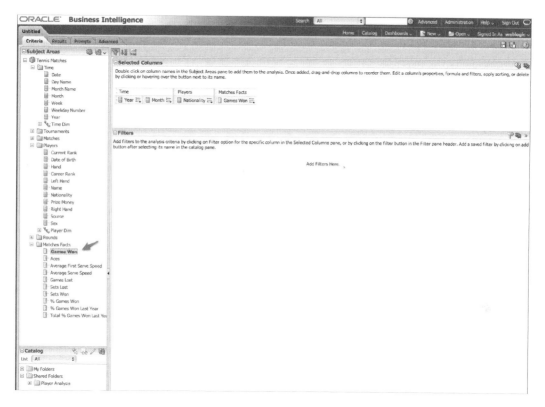

We will cover other options in the **Criteria** tab during this chapter, but for now let's click on the **Results** tab and see if our selected columns bring back any data.

The Results tab

The query has run successfully and returns a dataset. This is initially restricted to the first 25 rows but we can navigate to other rows by using the arrows at the bottom of the table. We initially see the data in a simple Table view that is part of a **Compound Layout** view. In a Compound Layout, we can add multiple views and representations of data, along with descriptive objects. For example, in the screenshot, you can see that there is a **Title** view on top of the table. We can amend this title to whatever we desire and in the end show both views together to an end user.

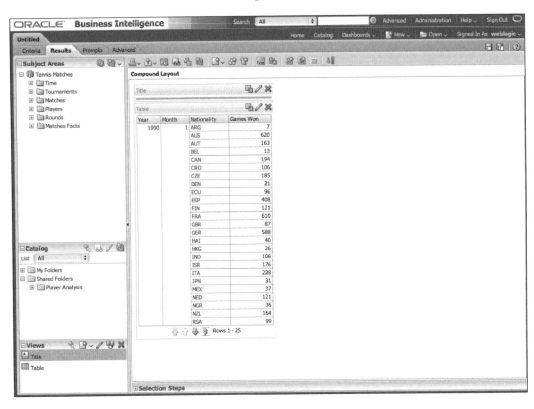

Note, that at this stage we can still add a column to a table view. We want something rather more meaningful for Month, so let's click on the **Month Name** column from the **Time** folder. Also, note that in the **Results** tab we can click on the **+** sign under an attribute column in order to have a quick look at what values are available. Let's look at the result of both of these actions:

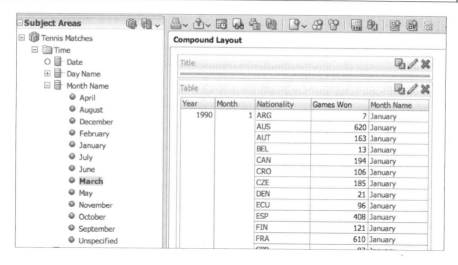

Filters

We now have a result set with many years of data, in a very basic table format. Let's go back and learn how to filter the data and reorganize the columns. We navigate back to the **Criteria** tab. The **Month** column is meaningless for us as it just shows the month number in a calendar. It may have been useful if it signified the Tennis Tour's sporting calendar, for example, 1 representing March as the first month in the sporting calendar instead of showing 1 for January. We can delete that by clicking on the options in the **Selected Columns** pane:

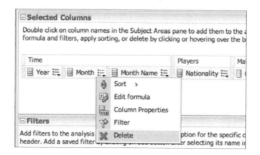

Another of the options you can see in the preceding screenshot is **Filter**. Currently, we have data from 1990 but let's say we only want data from this century. Let's click on **Filter**, on the **Year** column. We then get the **Edit Filter** prompt:

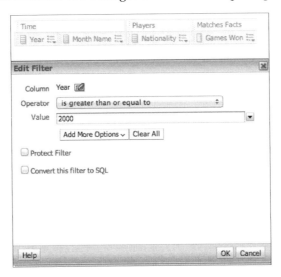

Here, we can stipulate many different operators such as less than, greater then, between, and is null. We want data from the Year 2000, so we choose **is greater than or equal to**, input the appropriate value and click on **OK**. We then see that the filter is added in the **Filters** pane:

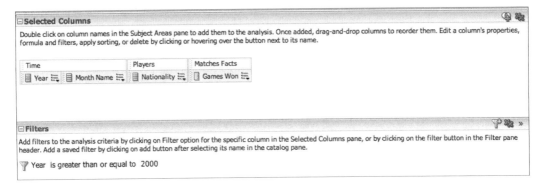

 Note that you do not need to have the column in **Selected Columns** or displaying in an analysis when adding a filter. You can add a filter for a currently non-selected column by using the buttons on the far right of the **Filters** pane.

Let's save this filter, so that other users can utilize it as well. We can do this by clicking on the floppy disk icon in the **Filters** pane (click on the double arrows to access it), and then choosing an appropriate name and location in a shared area.

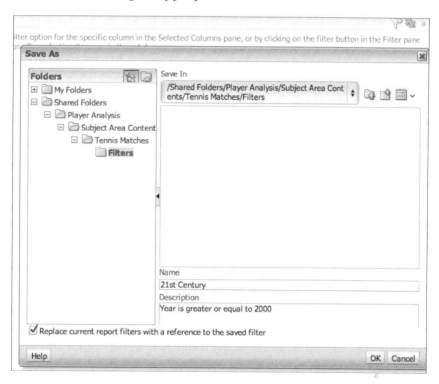

Note that we have kept checked the option at the bottom of the **Save** prompt. This means that in the **Filters** pane, we refer to the filter by the name we have given it rather than the actual content of the filter. This is helpful when saving large groups of filters or nested filters as one object that can be saved and shared with other users. You will see the reference (**21st Century**) when you return to the filters pane. This is also best practice in reports, as if you change a shared filter then all reports that contain that reference will reflect your change. Any report where you have added the contents of the filter, rather than the reference, will need to be manually updated.

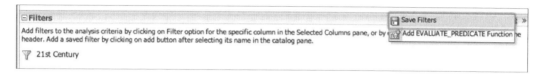

If you click on the **Results** tab now, you will see data only from the Year 2000:

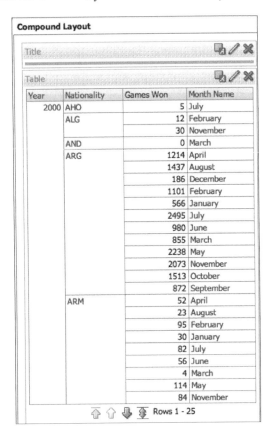

Selection Steps

We can also filter our results after the aggregated set of data has been returned, via **Selection Steps** in the **Results** tab. So let's delete the **21st Century** filter we have just added and then return to the **Results** tab, and open up the **Selection Steps** pane:

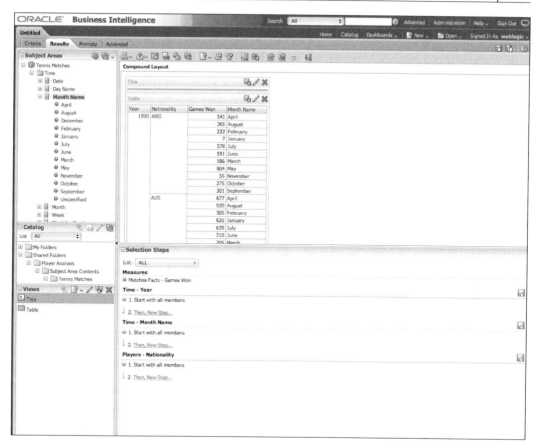

We then click on the pencil icon (edit) for the first step for **Time-Year**:

This will prompt you with a box choosing which data members we wish to include in this analysis.

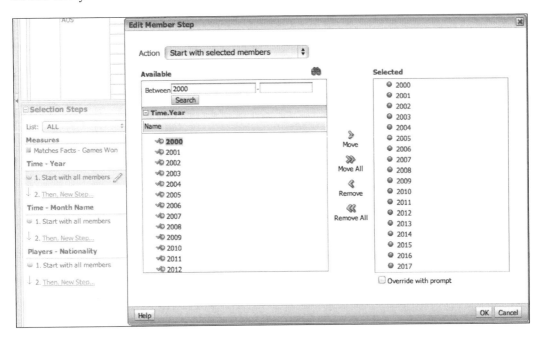

Notice that in the preceding prompt we filtered the **Available** members from 2000 onwards, and then moved all of those across. Once we have clicked on **OK**, notice how the table is once again restricted to data from the year 2000 onwards:

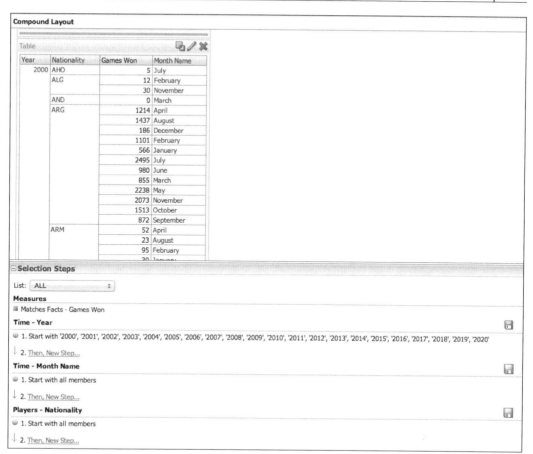

Compound Layout

Year	Nationality	Games Won	Month Name
2000	AHO	5	July
	ALG	12	February
		30	November
	AND	0	March
	ARG	1214	April
		1437	August
		186	December
		1101	February
		566	January
		2495	July
		980	June
		855	March
		2238	May
		2073	November
		1513	October
		872	September
	ARM	52	April
		23	August
		95	February

Selection Steps

List: ALL

Measures

Matches Facts - Games Won

Time - Year

1. Start with '2000', '2001', '2002', '2003', '2004', '2005', '2006', '2007', '2008', '2009', '2010', '2011', '2012', '2013', '2014', '2015', '2016', '2017', '2018', '2019', '2020'

2. Then, New Step...

Time - Month Name

1. Start with all members

2. Then, New Step...

Players - Nationality

1. Start with all members

2. Then, New Step...

There are other options available when using Selection Steps so have a play around and you will see that you can make some quite complex views of our initial dataset.

Filters: Limit data before the aggregated result set. Can be used on measures and attributes.

Selection Steps: Limit data after the aggregated result set. Cannot be used on measures.

The distinction above is important as Selection Steps only affects the data members that are displayed in your analysis, and not the aggregated values themselves. This can be useful if we want multiple views, for example, multiple tables in the same analysis, but want them to show different data members. This would not be possible with a pre-filtered analysis as the dataset has already been restricted.

Saving an Analysis

At this point, let's remember to save our work. We will save the analysis that uses the filter. We do this by clicking on the floppy disk icon in the top-right of the screen and then choosing our desired location to save, as well as naming the analysis. Note that there is a double disk icon next to this that can be used to duplicate your saved report in another name.

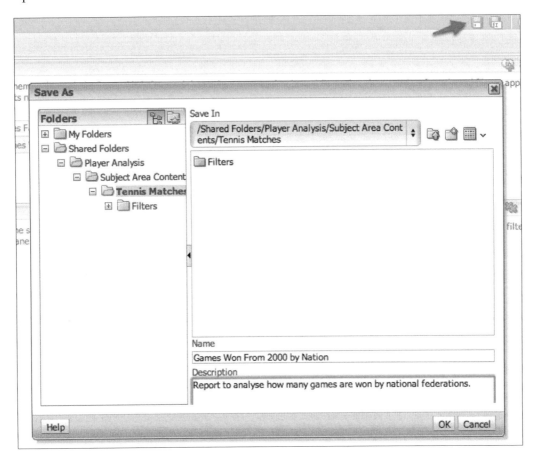

Basic table formatting

The analysis is a bit basic at the moment, so let's amend it so that it is a bit more presentable to an end-user. We can edit the Table view by clicking on the pencil (edit) icon.

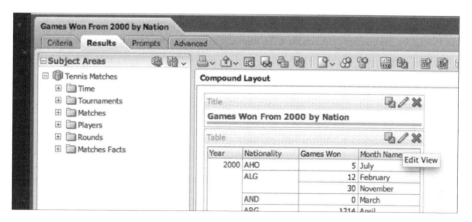

Notice that as we saved the analysis that the Title view already inherits and displays the name that we gave when saving. We can override this if we wish by editing the view.

Anyway, back to editing the table. Once we choose to edit, we will then be directed to an editing mode that you can see in the next screenshot. All of the layout/view editors that you encounter are made up of three sections:

- **Toolbar**: You can change the View types and subtypes. You can also edit view properties, apply formatting, print, and preview.

- **Preview pane**: As you alter options, this pane will automatically reflect your choices.

- **Layout**: You can alter the layout and content of the view, for example, you can exclude columns from a view or rearrange an order.

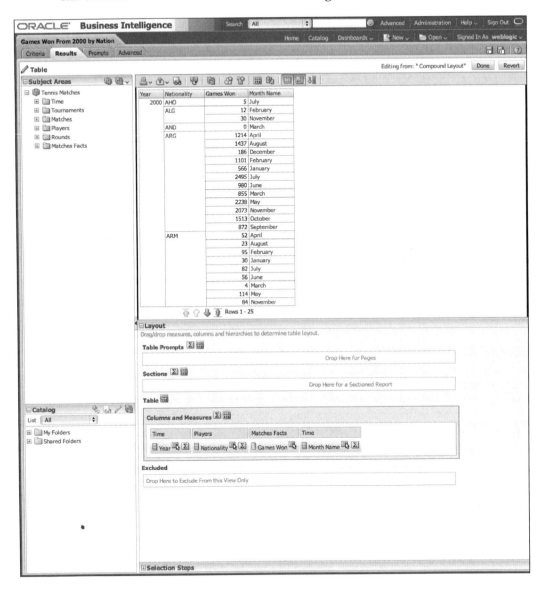

Our user does not want Month Name at the end, and also wants a total for Games Won for each Nationality for each Year. We can reorder columns by dragging and rearranging them in the Columns and Measures pane at the bottom. Each attribute has a sigma $\sum$ icon that can be clicked on in order to create a total.

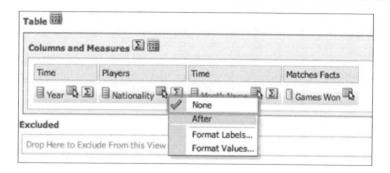

As you can see, currently **None** is chosen for the Nationality total. Let's choose **After** and look at the results:

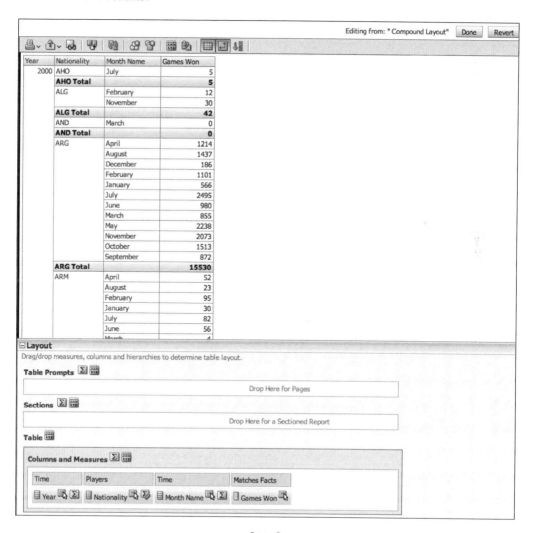

The totals have now been added after each **Nationality** level. We can now click on **Done** to get back to our Compound Layout.

Bins

The user has also decided that they are now more interested in regional figures rather than broken down by nationality. We do not have regions in our warehouse, and at the moment it is a requirement for only this one analysis. Also, there is no prospect of this requirement cropping up again in the future. After discussion with our team, we decide that it is best to handle this at this level rather than in the RPD or warehouse. This will also help us to deliver this requirement far more quickly. To enable this, OBIEE has a **Bins** functionality that allows you to group one or more values and then present them as a new value, rather like a DECODE statement in Oracle. To do this, we go to the **Criteria** tab, and click on the options for the **Nationality** column, and then **Edit Formula**. Note that you can also add sort criteria from the options here.

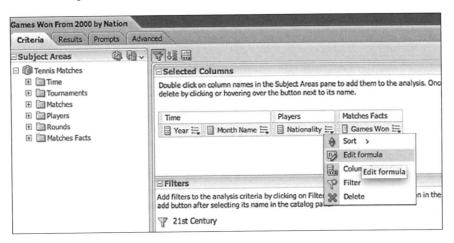

We then navigate to the **Bins** tab and click on **Add Bin**. We are then presented with a prompt similar to the one we previously encountered when choosing a filter.

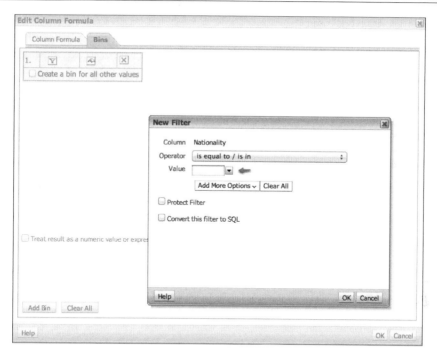

This time, rather than input a value we will get OBIEE to retrieve all current values from our warehouse. We do this by clicking on the drop-down indicated by the red arrow in the preceding screenshot and then click on **More/Search…**.We will then be presented with the **Select Values** screen, which you should recognize by now.

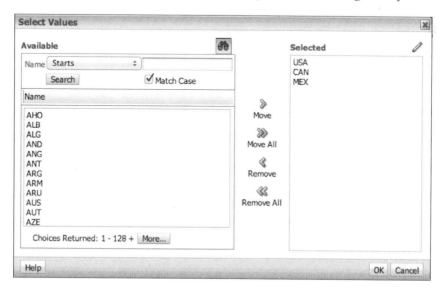

The first sets of values we are interested in are for North America. According to our business requirements, this means Canada, Mexico, and the USA. So we choose those values and click on **OK**, then on **OK** again. At this point, we are prompted to provide a name, in other words how we would want this group of values to be presented in the analysis.

As you can see, we have chosen **North America**. Once we click on **OK**, we can see the full bin statement:

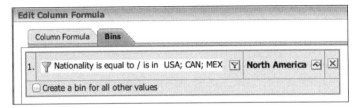

Let's go ahead and create Bins for the other geographical regions. We will also check the **Create a bin for all other values** checkbox and when prompted input *Rest of the World*. We will then end up with something like this:

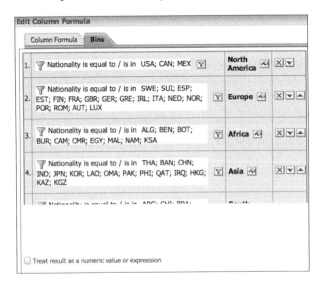

We can comeback and change these groups anytime if our requirements change. Note that we have unchecked the **Treat result as a numeric value or expression** checkbox as our end result is a descriptive string.

The description of this column as Nationality is no longer apt so let us rename it. We will click on the column options and choose **Column Properties**:

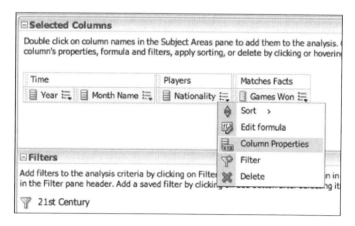

Here, you will find a whole host of formatting options to do with fonts and colors, but we are only currently interested in the **Column Format** tab:

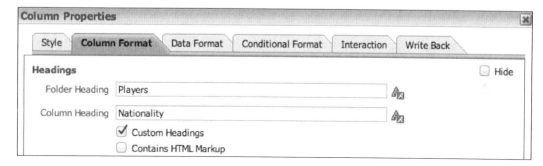

In the preceding screenshot, we will check **Custom Headings** so that we can override the **Column Heading**, and then rename it to **Region**. This will rename the column only in our analysis; so do not worry about affecting other reports.

So let's return to the **Results** tab and have a look at how this has affected our analysis:

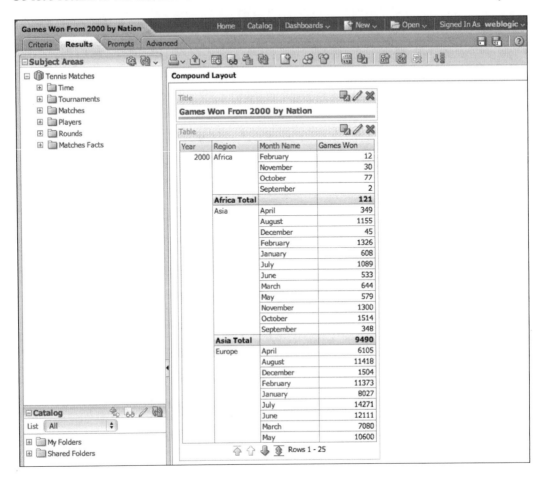

As you can see in the preceding screenshot, the individual Nationality values have been replaced by the Bin values that we have set. The measure value is aggregating at this group level rather than being broken down by nation as previously. Also, the column has been renamed to **Region**.

Pivot Tables

Our user is happy with the result so far, but does not like this flat table view and would like the data presented in a more spreadsheet-like format that takes advantage of the real estate on their screen. We can do this by creating a **Pivot Table**. Let's add one for this analysis in addition to the Table that we have just created. Firstly, we click on the **Add View** icon and choose **Pivot Table**.

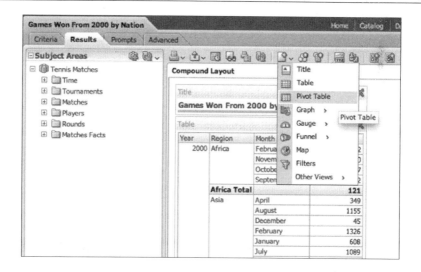

A basic pivot table will then be added to our Compound Layout. Note that all three of our current views appear in the Views pane in the bottom left of the screen, and that we can edit individual views from here at any time regardless of whether they appear in our Compound Layout.

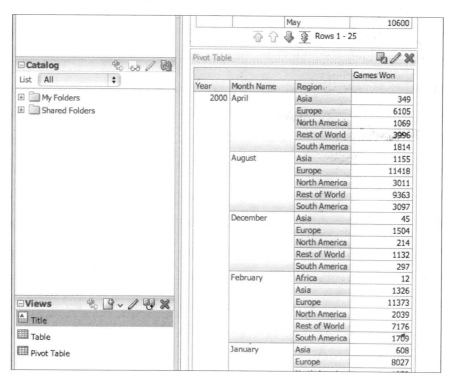

If we now edit the new Pivot Table view, we get to the Layout Editor. As you can see, we have options over whether to place attribute columns as a row or column.

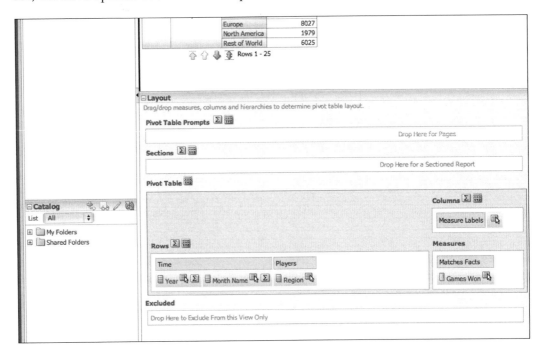

Let's place **Region** in the columns and see what happens. At the same time, let's create a total for the year by clicking on the sigma icon and choosing **Before**.

Year	Month Name	Games Won					
		Africa	Asia	Europe	North America	Rest of World	South America
	2000 Total	**121**	**9490**	**109932**	**25302**	**78032**	**25146**
2000	April		349	6105	1069	3996	1814
	August		1155	11418	3011	9363	3097
	December		45	1504	214	1132	297
	February	12	1326	11373	2039	7176	1709
	January		608	8027	1979	6025	777
	July		1089	14271	3199	9603	4131
	June		533	12111	3322	7715	1768
	March		644	7080	1396	4818	1378
	May		579	10600	2039	9072	3195
	November	30	1300	7212	3472	5490	2780
	October	77	1514	12203	2643	8786	2715
	September	2	348	8028	919	4856	1485
	2001 Total	**188**	**9110**	**111380**	**27175**	**80142**	**35123**
2001	April		598	7539	1536	4168	2626
	August	80	850	14224	3427	9521	4830
	December		278	310	95	482	577
	February	32	998	11765	1888	7908	2155
	January	7	482	9057	2106	6242	2495
	July		866	14158	3899	9485	5598
	June		725	11585	2960	8470	2120
	March		724	7420	1803	4352	1479
	May		514	9835	1872	7910	2645
	November	6	307	4117	2972	3831	2446
	October	18	1998	12566	3503	9484	4214
	September	45	770	8804	1114	8289	3938
	2002 Total	**522**	**8989**	**106805**	**27972**	**74470**	**29535**
2002	April		749	8734	2226	5035	3150

Layout

Drag/drop measures, columns and hierarchies to determine pivot table layout.

Pivot Table Prompts Σ 🔢

Drop Here for Pages

Sections Σ 🔢

Drop Here for a Sectioned Report

Pivot Table 🔢

Columns Σ 🔢

Measure Labels 🔧 Σ

Players 📋 Region 🔧

Measures

Matches Facts

📋 Games Won 🔧

Rows Σ 🔢

Time

📋 Year 🔧 ⤵ 📋 Month Name 🔧

Excluded

Drop Here to Exclude From this View Only

Great! We are now showing the data in a matrix format with our Regions as columns on the y-axis and our Time on the x-axis. We also have total rows for each year/region combination.

Let's leave pivots for now and have a look at a few of the other visualizations that are available. Before we do that though, let's amend the sort order for the Month column. It currently sorts by alphabetical order rather than according to the calendar. We need to go back and add the Month column that has a numeric value and use it to sort the report. However, we do not want those integers showing in our report, so we add the new column and mark it
as **Hidden** via the column options.

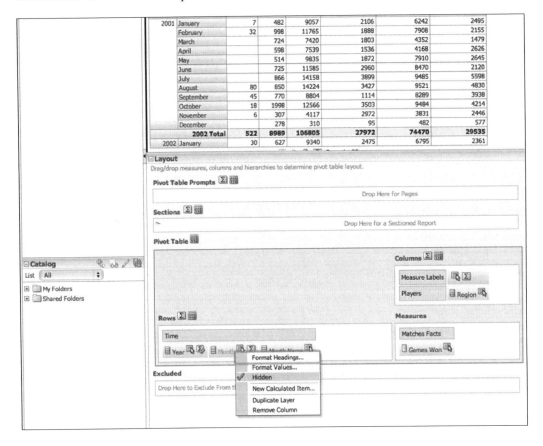

You can see the Months column is now correctly sorted. Remember, that we would not have needed this workaround if we had set the numerical Month as the sort order column for the Month Name in the RPD.

Before we proceed, remember to save your analysis!

Graphs

OBIEE has a vast number of display options. These include all manner of Graphs, Gauges, Funnels, and Maps. We can also add static items, such as the Title you have already seen. This extends to legends and tickers, as well as views that display what filters are currently in place or even the logical SQL that is being produced!

We do not have time to delve exhaustively into all of these but the knowledge imparted in this chapter gives you the tools in which to explore all of these in your own time.

For our example, let's create a simple graph that we will display alongside our Pivot view. Again, there are numerous types of graph; for example, bars, lines, pie charts, Pareto, radar, and so on. Each of these has further options, but our user wants a simple vertical bar chart. Let's add a new view as we did previously. This time we choose an appropriate graphing option.

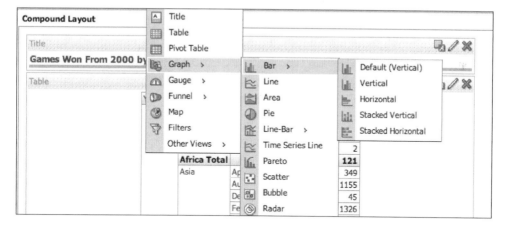

Once we do this, a chart will be added to the bottom of our Compound Layout. However, there are far too many data points to be of any use to our user, so let's edit it and go to the layout editor for **Bar Graphs.**

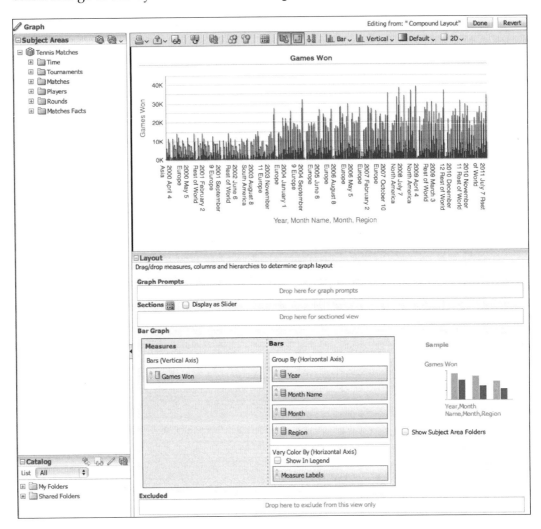

Sectioned views

For the bar chart, our user just wants a summary view of the information at the Year level. The month is too granular a level for our needs, so we can drag the Month Name and Month columns to the **Excluded** section, so that they do not appear on the chart. It would be clearer if we had one chart for each year, so let's produce a sectioned chart by dragging the Year to **Sections**. Let's look at the results:

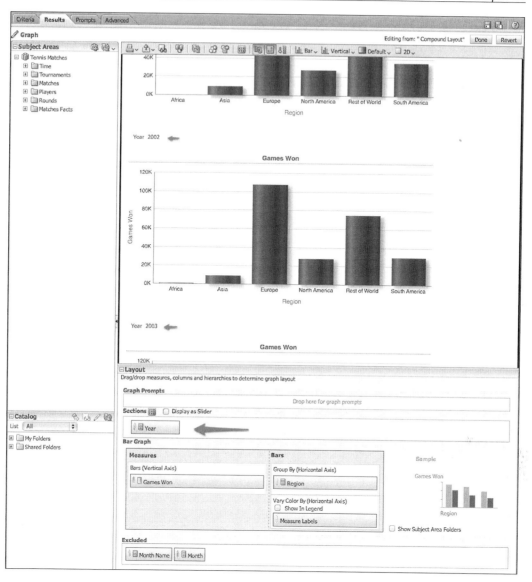

As you can see above, the **Sections** option can produce multiple charts/reports individually filtered by the column that we have set, that is **Year**.

View prompts and section sliders

It is subsequently decided that this will look too unwieldy and will involve too much scrolling for the business. We might implement this for our tabular reports later, but for now, they still want a chart per year and also want to be able to choose which year they are seeing. We have two options:

- **Prompt**
- **Slider**

Firstly, we can drag **Year** from **Sections** to **Graph Prompts**. This will result in the following:

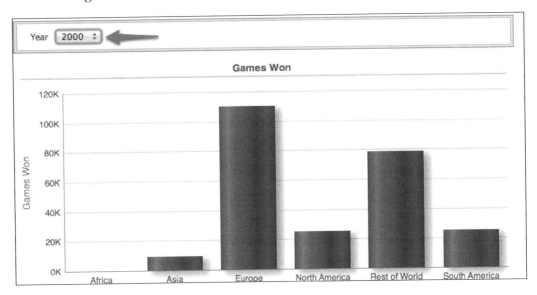

We now have one chart, but the display changes in situ depending on the **Year** chosen via the drop-down menu.

Alternatively, we can keep **Year** in **Sections**, but check the **Display as Slider** checkbox:

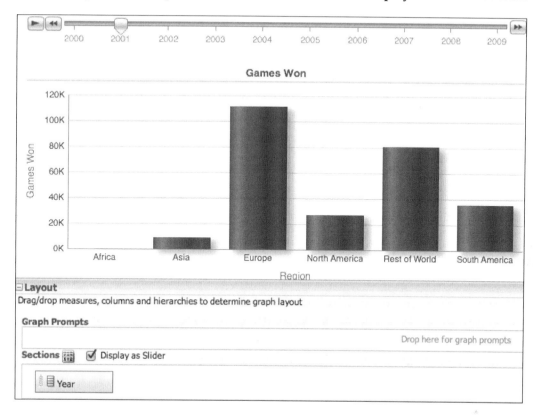

As you can see in the preceding screenshot, we now again have one chart. The **Year** value can be changed via the slider, but we also have the option of clicking the play button by the slider and the chart will transition from one year to the next in an animated format.

For our purposes, it is decided that this is too distracting so we will stick with the first prompted option.

Conditional Formatting

Upon further feedback, it has been requested if that we rename the chart and have individual colors for the bars so that each region stands out. We can do both of these via the properties button. You can see this being accessed from the toolbar:

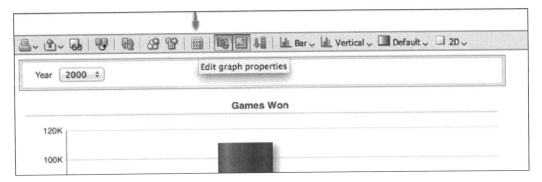

Here, we can access all sorts of formatting options including, for example, setting axis scales, scrolling and zooming controls, and size/text options. For our purposes, we want the **Style** tab and the **Style** and **Conditional Formatting** sections. You can access it through the icon shown in the following screenshot:

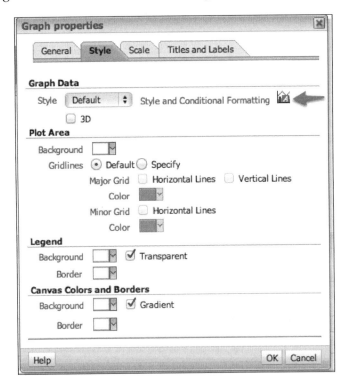

We are now prompted with two tabs. The **Style Formatting** tab allows us to set colors depending on the position of the bar e.g. to set the first to always be yellow and the second to always be red. The **Conditional Formatting** tab allows us to set colors based on values. As you can see below, we have the option of setting colors depending on the measure in the y-axis or the Region in the x-axis. Let's add a condition to Region:

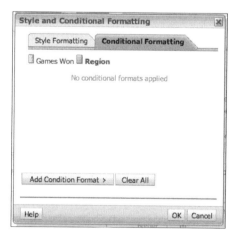

As you can see, we click on **Add Condition Format** and choose the Region column:

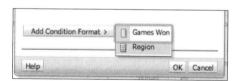

We then choose a condition for that column. In this example, we are choosing **is equal to/is in Europe**.

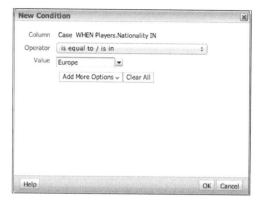

Once we click on **OK**, the condition is set but we need to pick a color. Clicking on the drop-down menu, we choose from the presented palette or input a standard hex value. Hex values are commonly passed down from corporate design standards:

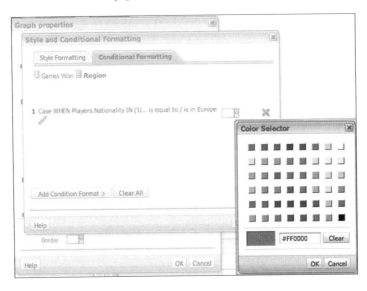

Let's repeat this for all of our Region values, with a different color for each one. We can then proceed to change the **Title** of the chart. For this, we stay in **Graph Properties** but navigate to the **Tiles** and **Labels** tab. We uncheck **Use measure name as graph title** and input our own. In this case, a more appropriate title would be Year Games Won by Region:

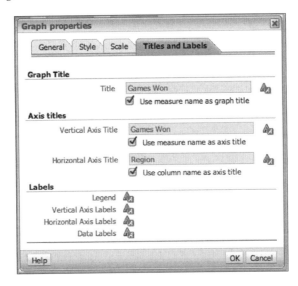

Once done we click on **OK**, however, before we look at the graph, let's change the look of the bars from a **Gradient** filled type to have a flatter **Rectangle** look. We can do this from the layout editor toolbar:

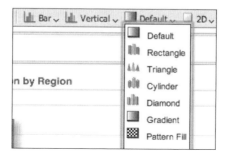

Finally, we are ready to see the impact of our changes. As you can see in the following screenshot, the bars now have separate colors depending on their value and are displayed in a flatter 2D look. The Title has also changed:

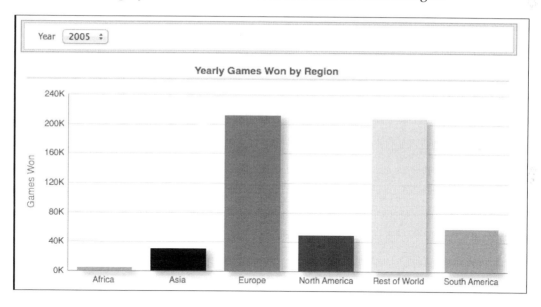

Conditional formatting has a wide set of uses, and can be used in other views. For example, in tables you can access conditional formatting via column properties in the **Criteria** tab. You can conditionally format both measures and attributes, and you can format one column based on the value of another. You can also set icons to replace or be shown in addition to values. For example, a common request is to have a traffic light report. Based on a certain range of values, we would conditionally display a red, amber, or green ball instead of the actual values.

Another common request in financial reports is to show negative values in red. This type of capability appears elsewhere. As you can see in the following screenshot, you can set this in the **Data Format** tab in **Column Properties** under the **Criteria** tab:

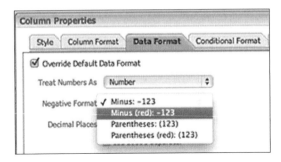

So, we have now created a simple analysis with multiple views. Let's learn how to display this to an end user.

Building Dashboards

We can present multiple objects and analyses to an end-user via a container called a **Dashboard**.

Creating a dashboard

We can create a new dashboard from the **Home** screen in the same place as we created a new analysis:

We will click on the create dashboard link and then give it a name, and optionally, a description. We also stipulate the catalog location that we want to save our dashboard object in. If we leave **Add content now** chosen, then when we click on **OK** we will enter the **Dashboard Builder**.

Dashboard builder

The Dashboard Builder is where we can add, remove, and amend objects that we want on our dashboard:

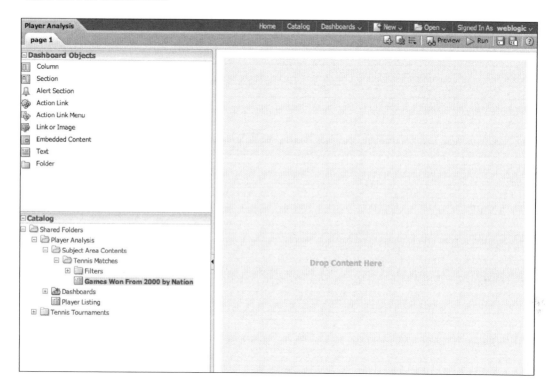

The builder is made up of three panes:

- **Dashboard Objects**: Here, we can add formatting options such as columns and sections to the dashboard. We can also create outgoing links, text, reference catalog folders and embed content (internal and external).

- **Catalog**: We can add analyses that we have created to sections in the dashboard. If we have already created dashboards, then we can add whole parts from these to the new dashboards.

- **Page Layout**: Objects from the previous two panes are added here, and we can see and control how these are shown in our dashboard.

So let's drag the analysis that we previously made from the Catalog into the main Layout pane:

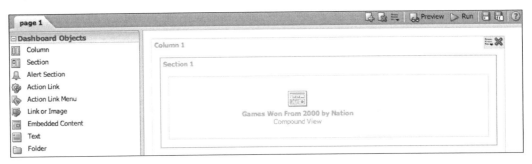

As you can see, we now have a reference to the analysis in the middle of our layout. Note that as our layout was empty, **Column** and **Section** objects were also automatically added as a frame for this reference. Also, note the controls in the top right. We can preview a page that initiates a pop-up, which roughly shows us how the page will look in our dashboard. We can also click on **Run**, which takes us to the actual dashboard. If you choose **Run**, make sure that you have saved your dashboard via the floppy disk icon; otherwise, you will lose your changes. So let's save and go ahead and run the dashboard.

As you can see in the following screenshot, the dashboard shows the Compound Layout of our analysis that currently has a table, pivot table, and graph stacked vertically. This is wasting a lot of space and involves scrolling so we need to make some changes so that our users have a better experience. We can search the catalog to find the analysis, but we can just as easily edit the presented analysis straight from here:

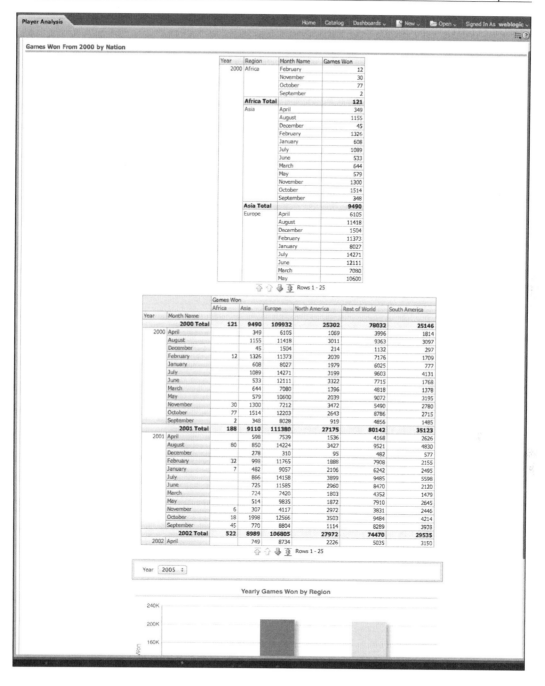

Editing a dashboard

In the top-right of the screen, we have an options icon from where we can choose to edit the dashboard:

We will then be sent back to the dashboard builder below, from there if we hover over the right-hand corner of the section containing our analysis reference, we will see controls for deleting the section and the options icon. Within the options, at the bottom, we can choose to edit the analysis:

This returns us to the Compound Layout of our analysis. Firstly, we delete the table from the compound layout as the customer has decided they do not need it. We do this via the X icon in the top-right of the object. You can see the hover tool text for the delete icon for the pivot table, below. Remember that this does not remove the table from our analysis; it just removes it from the compound view. We can then drag objects around in the compound view by clicking and holding on an object header. So let's drag the graph from the bottom and place next to the pivot. Let's look at the results:

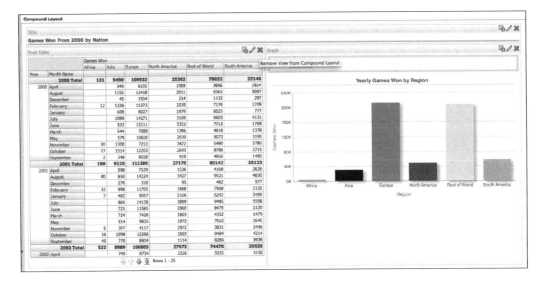

We save our report and we can now return to our dashboard by choosing the **Most Recent** option from the **Dashboards** drop-down menu. We also have the option of navigating to other dashboards if they have been created:

Adding a page

Before we show you what our dashboard looks like now, let's add a second page to it and put that table view in as its content. We click on the icon with the green **+** sign. This adds a page:

We are then prompted to add an appropriate name, and an optional description:

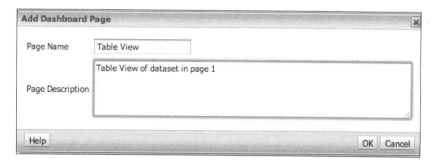

Once we click on **OK**, we can see that our builder now has two tabs; one for each page. You can see the tabs at the uppermost-left in the following screenshot:

Now, when we add an analysis to a dashboard, the default view shown is the Compound Layout. However, we have deleted the table view from ours. So we need to tell the builder to show the table view rather than the Compound one. We do this by clicking on options for the report, then **Show View** and choosing the appropriate option. In our case, this would be **Table 1**:

We can re-order and rename pages from the **Dashboard Properties** option in the toolbar:

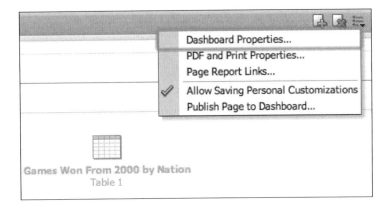

You can see the rename icon. Let's go ahead and rename **Page 1** to something more appropriate. From here, we could also hide pages and re-order them if we wish:

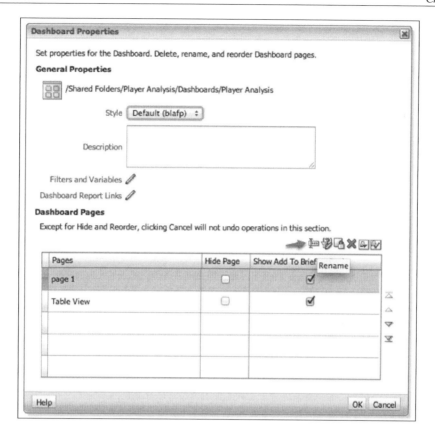

When renaming, note the option in the following screenshot to **Preserve references to old name of this item**. This would be useful if we have created external links to this page in other previously created dashboards. Checking this would ensure that these links do not break:

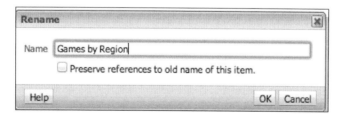

Report Links

Now that we have created our new page, our user has said that they would like to be able to download data from the table view in the second dashboard page. We can do this by choosing **Report Links...** from the options for the analysis reference in dashboard builder:

You then get the **Report Links** options prompt. We choose **Customize** and choose **Export**, **Refresh** (allows the user to refresh the data in the report) and **Print**:

Once we click on **OK** and save the dashboard, let's look at the results. You can see that we have a second tab, which only contains the table view. It also has links at the bottom to support exporting the data; for example, to PDF, Excel, and XML:

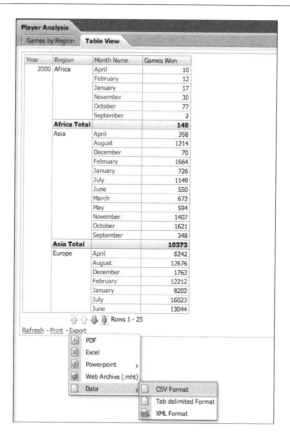

Player Analysis

Games by Region | **Table View**

Year	Region	Month Name	Games Won
2000	Africa	April	10
		February	12
		January	17
		November	30
		October	77
		September	2
	Africa Total		**148**
	Asia	April	358
		August	1214
		December	70
		February	1664
		January	726
		July	1149
		June	550
		March	672
		May	594
		November	1407
		October	1621
		September	348
	Asia Total		**10373**
	Europe	April	6242
		August	12676
		December	1763
		February	12212
		January	8202
		July	16023
		June	13044

Rows 1 - 25

Refresh - Print - Export

- PDF
- Excel
- Powerpoint >
- Web Archive (.mht)
- Data >
  - CSV Format
  - Tab delimited Format
  - XML Format

In our first page, we see the same analysis, but only the Compound Layout that has been changed, so that the two views (pivot and graph) are side by side:

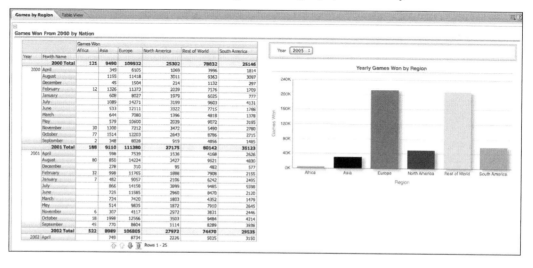

Dashboard Prompt

We show our simple dashboard to the user and they are happy with it for a first iteration. However, they like showing a year at a time for the graph and would like to pick that year themselves. They would also like the same for the pivot table. We could add a view prompt for the table, but the business would prefer to only have one prompt and, hence, one click. We can implement this via a **Dashboard Prompt**.

To do so, we can create the prompt from the **Home** screen, or alternatively from the toolbar:

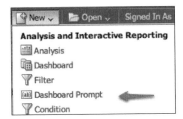

As when creating an analysis, we are prompted to choose a subject area. Our analysis was from **Tennis Matches** so we will, again, have to choose that area:

This leads us to the **Definition** editor for the prompt. You can see the multiple entry lines where we can add multiple prompts. We will be adding just one, based on the **Year** column:

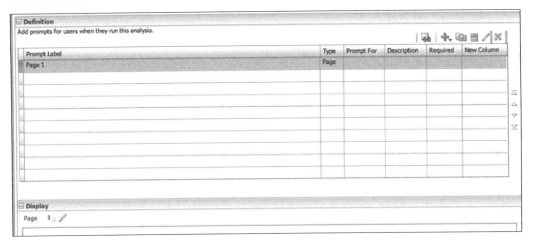

To do so, we click the green + (new) icon and choose **Column Prompt...**.

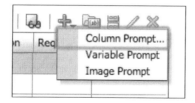

We are then given a choice of columns from our chosen subject area. We are choosing **Year** from the **Time** folder:

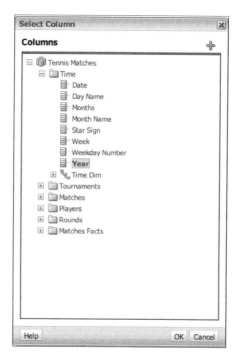

This leads us to the main options for the prompt. We label it and give an optional description for our purposes. We then have a choice of operators and **User Input** types. We want our user to choose from a drop-down so we choose a Choice List and the **is equal to** operator. We also want to limit them to choosing one value, so we uncheck **Enable user to select multiple values**:

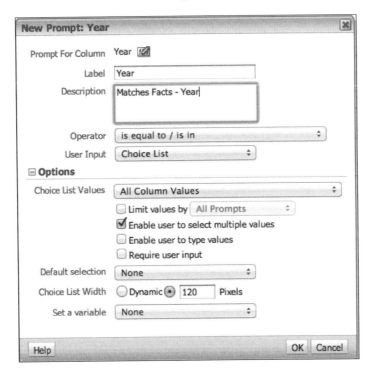

Initially this is fine, but when we preview the prompt, we notice that our Year has values back to 1945 despite there being no data in the facts for those years, and remember that our report needs to be restricted to data from the Year 2000. So, we need to restrict what appears in the drop down so as to save our user the hassle of having to scroll through so many irrelevant values:

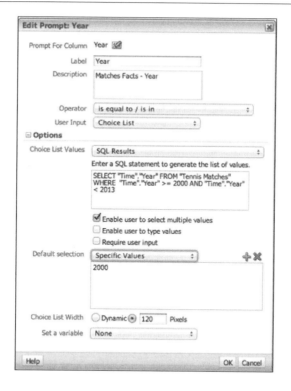

In the values section above, you can see that we have chosen to populate the list using logical SQL. We have also set a default value to the year 2000. Now, it is best to avoid hard coding, especially in that SQL statement, as it makes future maintenance more complex. I could instead create a SQL statement that joins the dimension to the fact table restricting the value set, but if we had a large fact table, this is an additional burden on the server and database. It is issues like this you should be thinking about when straying from simple functionality.

We could have also populated the prompt by actually choosing values from the Year column, by choosing the **Specific Columns** instead of **SQL Results** or **All Values**. For our current purposes, we will go ahead with what we have done.

Once we click on **OK**, we are returned to the editor. If we wish to change the aesthetic options for the prompt, we can click the edit button in the **Display** (preview) pane:

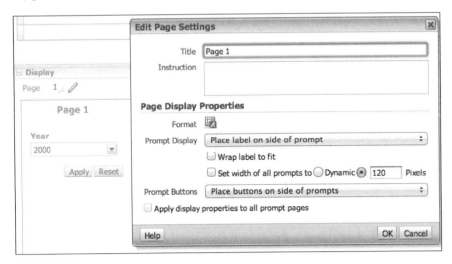

The title looks ungainly so we will make that blank. We will also move the prompt buttons to the side and the label to the left. So, we are done. Let's save that prompt, choosing a shared area. Like we did for filters, it is a good idea to create a separate prompts folder so that our catalog is organized in an easy and transparent manner.

Let's add the prompt to our dashboard:

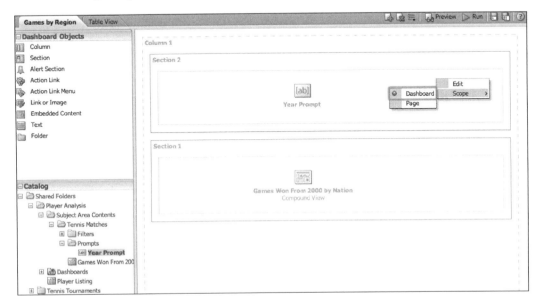

So, as you can see, we have dragged the prompt from the folder in the catalog pane where we saved it into our first dashboard page. Additionally, we have edited the options for the dashboard so that it only affects the page it is on. This is because our user wants to be able to download all data without restriction from the view in the second page. So let's have a look at our amended dashboard:

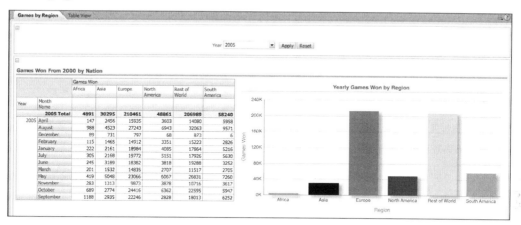

Great! Both views show one year of data that changes as we change the prompt. The prompt only shows values from 2000. You can see above that we have amended the graph by excluding the previously individually view prompted Year from it. The only troubling feature is the Title that says **Games Won from 2000.** This doesn't make sense anymore. It would be nice if we could dynamically change this so that it reflects our prompt choice.

Presentation variable

We can do this by returning to edit the prompt and setting a variable:

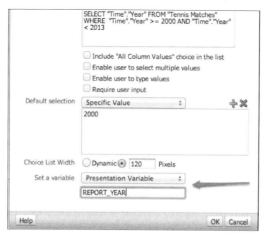

We have set a **Presentation Variable** with the name REPORT_YEAR. A variable of this type is client/browser based. That means it does not reside on the server and is not accessible by others. It will hold the value of our choice for that prompt. We could use it in the **Title** view, but for maintenance, it is better if we have a separate dashboard object. Let's go back to the analysis and delete the **Title** view from the Compound Layout. Then, we can go to our dashboard editor and add a **Text** object:

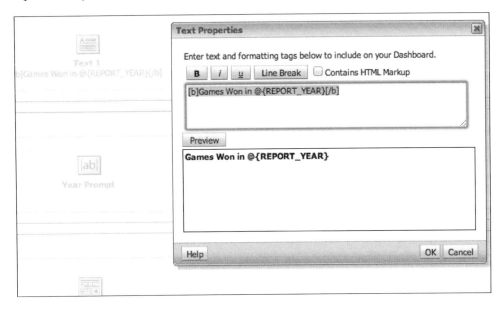

The syntax for referencing a presentation variable is an @ sign with curly brackets; for example, @{REPORT_YEAR}.

 You can also format the variable, or add a default value using the following syntax:

@{variables.variablename}[format]{defaultvalue}

For example, if we had a date variable called REPORT_DATE:

@{variables.REPORT_DATE}[hh:mm:ss]{13:42:00}

We have masked a date value and extracted the hours to seconds, and set a default.

Once done, for formatting purposes let's remove the lines around sections and make sure they are not collapsible. We do this via the section and column options in the dashboard editor:

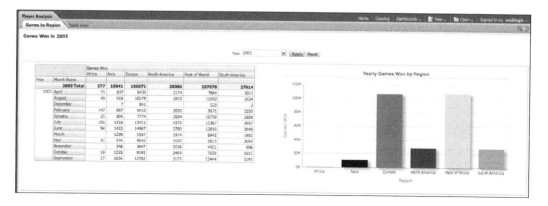

Finally, you can see the title (using a text object) says **Games Won in 2003**, and our chosen prompt is **2003**. The title updates as we change the prompt.

> We can also create a prompt, called the **Variable Prompt**, which exists solely to create a Presentation Variable (it does not filter analyses). This is an option when creating a new prompt and can be chosen instead of a column prompt.

Protected and "is prompted" filters

Before we proceed, let's look at the required filters for a dashboard prompt:

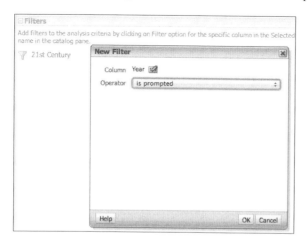

Our dashboard prompt affected our analysis without us amending the filters for that analysis. This is not always the case. The reason we did not have to make any changes is that we already had a filter called **21st century** that used the same column (**Year**) and operator (**is equal to/is in**) as our prompt. If this had not been the case or we had no filters, then we would have needed to add the **is prompted** filter to our analysis. You can see this above. This is a placeholder prompt that says that this analysis is expecting to be passed a filter value and operator based on this column.

 Include "is prompted" on analyses if no default filter for that column exists.

Now, let's say that we wanted an analysis added to our dashboard that filters by the current year. However, we want this report to stay the same despite the choices made in the dashboard prompt. Well, on our filter we can remove the "is prompted" filter and add back a default filter value. We then make sure that this filter has the **Protect Filter** option checked. This option ensures that this filter cannot be overwritten by other values passed to the analysis.

So let's do that. We make a copy of our analysis, remove all filters, and set a new filter to the latest full year. As I said before, for maintenance reasons, it is best not to hard code this so let's use a **Repository Variable** instead.

Repository/Session variable

As you may remember from *Chapter 8*, *Developing a BI Repository*, we had created a couple of custom variables in the RPD via an Initialization Block. We are going to use one of those now as a filter:

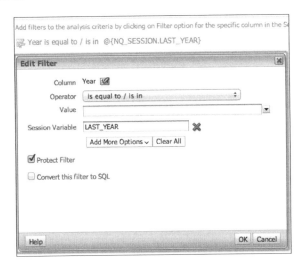

As you can see in the filter, we have chosen to filter on Year, but through **Add More Options** we have added a repository variable that we previously created in the RPD. We have also protected it so that the value cannot be overridden by a prompt. Let's add this new analysis to our first dashboard page and choose a prompt value:

Year 2005

		Games Won					
		Africa	Asia	Europe	North America	Rest of World	South America
Year	Month Name						
	2005 Total	**4891**	**30295**	**210461**	**48861**	**206989**	**58240**
2005	April	147	2456	15935	3603	14080	5958
	August	988	4523	27243	6943	32063	9571
	December	89	731	797	68	873	6
	February	115	1465	14912	3351	15223	2826
	January	222	2161	18984	4085	17864	5216
	July	305	2168	19772	5151	17926	5630
	June	245	3189	18382	3818	19288	3252
	March	201	1532	14835	2707	11517	2705
	May	419	5048	23066	6067	26831	7260
	November	283	1313	9873	3878	10716	3617
	October	689	2774	24416	6362	22595	5947
	September	1188	2935	22246	2828	18013	6252

		Games Won					
		Africa	Asia	Europe	North America	Rest of World	South America
Year	Month Name						
	2011 Total	**1095**	**27612**	**145945**	**31153**	**191134**	**47294**
2011	April	37	3942	16008	2799	19872	7932
	August	100	1918	12280	2758	17632	4538
	February	103	1544	12181	3048	21707	3468
	January	62	3117	17923	3863	24637	6191
	July	23	2506	24364	5805	27572	5124
	June	120	5033	19794	5442	24261	7847
	March	265	2843	18572	2630	21202	3262
	May	385	6709	24823	4808	34251	8932

The original analysis on top is filtered by the year 2005, as per the chosen prompt value. Our new analysis is protected and remains with a 2011 value.

OBIEE has lots of system functions and variables that we can call on. For example, as an alternative to the LAST_YEAR variable that we created ourselves in the RPD, we could use the **Convert this filter to SQL** option and input:

```
Time.year>= year(CURRENT_DATE) - 1
```

This uses the OBIEE system's native CURRENT_DATE call, and the Year function to strip the year from that timestamp.

Some advanced options

We have covered a lot of ground in creating dashboards and analyses from scratch. We now have time to look at some other functionality, some of which is new in 11*g*.

Column Selector

After presenting the dashboard to the business, they are very happy with the development so far. In fact, they want the same analyses/dashboard, but with the 'Sets Won' metric instead of Games Won. We have a variety of ways in which we can satisfy this requirement. We could replicate the dashboards and analyses, but swap out the former metric for the latter. Alternatively, we could introduce Sets Won into our current analyses and create multiple pivot/graph views excluding one or other of the metrics. There is a third option which allows us to switch between the two in our current analysis. This is called the **Column Selector**.

To add one, we do so from the **Other Views | Column Selector** add view option:

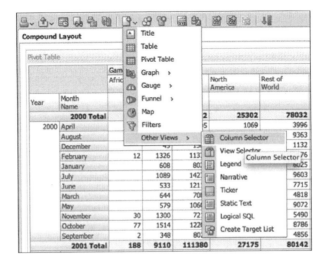

From the compound layout, we edit the selector. We choose the column that we want to have a selector on, and then choose the alternative columns that we want:

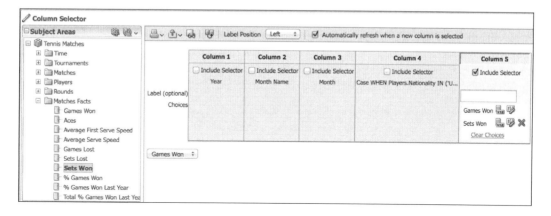

As you can see in the preceding screenshot, we have chosen our Games Won column to have the selector, and selected **Sets Won** from the **Tennis Matches** subject area. You can also see a preview of the drop-down and we can edit the names that will appear in the drop-down if we wish to.

So that's it! Let's position the selector above our pivot table in the compound layout, save and view the dashboard:

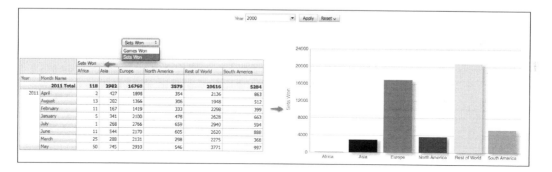

You can see the drop-down and that the **Sets Won** option has been chosen. As the red arrows point out (see the preceding screenshot), both the metric for the pivot and the graph have changed.

If we look at the selected items in the **Criteria** tab, then we can see that this column is now defined as a Column Group, with our original metric as the default:

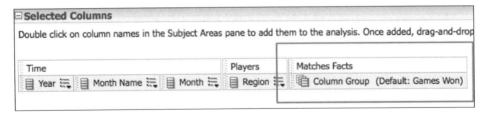

It's as simple as that! Column selectors are a great way to increase the flexibility and choice for your users who do not have access to create/amend reports themselves. It is also ideal in the situation we have described where both metrics come from the same fact table and are, thus, at the same level of granularity. We can, of course, add selectors to both measure and attribute columns.

View Selector

Next, we are asked if we could extend that functionality to have a choice between a graph and a pie chart. As you may have noticed in the add view options, there is also the choice of a **View Selector**.

Before we go ahead and choose to add that, let's add the Pie Chart. This time though, rather than add one to the compound layout, we will just add the Pie chart separately via the **Views** pane:

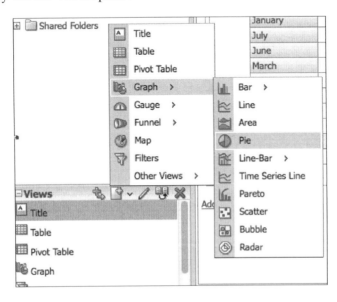

Once we are done creating the new chart, and have changed options as required, we can go ahead and add the view selector to our compound layout in the same way we did for our column selector. Let's go ahead and edit the new selector:

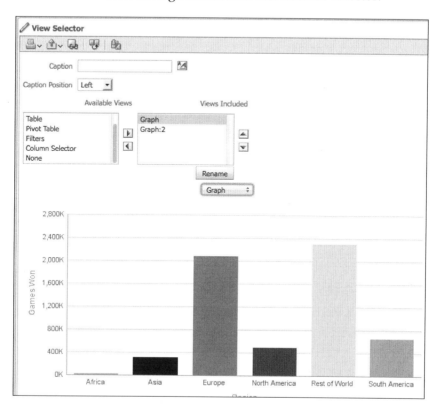

In the **View Selector** editor, we have a selection of views from which we will pick those that we want to appear in our selector. We also have a preview of the drop down and their associated views. We have chosen the two charts. Currently, these are named by the system-generated **Graph** and **Graph:2**. This is intelligible to our users so we can rename the drop down entries to "Bar" and "Pie" for ease of use. Let's do that now by choosing a view and clicking on **Rename**:

We are renaming the second graph so that it is called **Pie** in the drop-down. This will be easily understandable by our users. Let's save and go back to the compound layout:

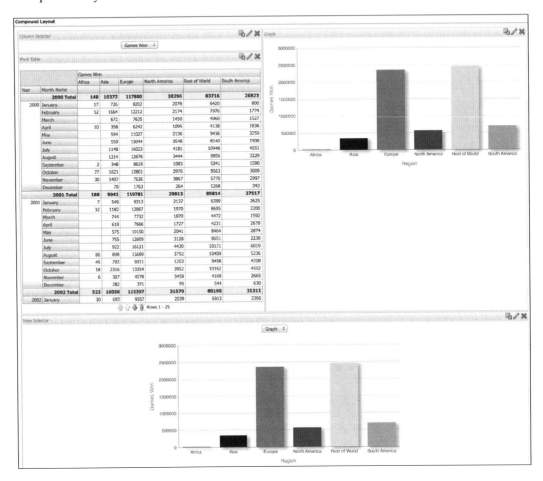

You can see that we now have two of our bar views in the Compound Layout. This is because, unlike the column selector which just adds a drop-down, a view selector comes with a frame for showing its associated views. This is why we did not add the Pie chart to the compound layout and also why we will delete the initial bar chart from the compound layout. Once deleted, we can position the view selector to the right of the pivot, taking the old chart's place. Let's save and view our dashboard:

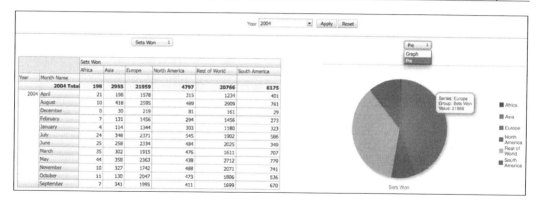

So, as you can see, we now have a selector that changes the view between a Bar and a Pie chart. Again, this is useful functionality that adds richness to a dashboard and saves real estate on a screen.

Master-detail linking

Our analyses already inherit the drilling paths that we set up in our RPD. For example, in our pivot table, the time columns are hyperlinked so that we can drill down to detail. A new and interesting capability in 11*g* is the **Master-Detail** link. Rather than drilling, this enables you to make choices in one view (Master) that changes the display of one or more other views (Child). We can then have parent and detailed child views on the same page, and with some added flexibility. Let's go through a simple demonstration.

For our purposes, we want our bar chart to reflect the Region that we choose in our pivot table. Firstly, we make a change in the **Criteria** tab of our analysis:

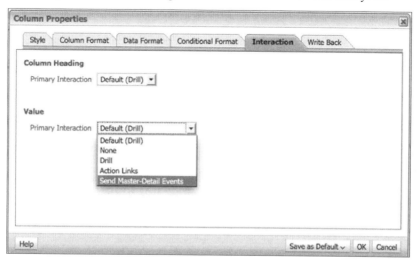

We have gone to column properties for Region and gone to the **Interaction** tab. This tab can be used to turn off our default drilling, or add other types of links. It can also be used to turn on Master-detail events by changing the **Value** of the **Primary Interaction** drop-down:

Now, we have changed the interaction to **Send Master-Detail Events**. This means that OBIEE will look at changes made in this column and broadcast that as a message that other views can receive. We have to give that signal a unique name under **Specify Channel**. This is because we could have multiple columns sending events to multiple views. We will name ours MD1:

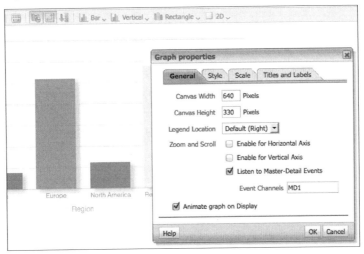

We then tell our child views to expect that signal. We will use the graph as a child. In the graph properties, we have the option to **Listen to Master-Detail Events**. We choose this and input the name of our signal (**Even**t **Channels**). For our demonstration, we will make some changes to the graph:

We add the region slider again, but we have also set strict axis limits, as if we allowed axes to dynamically change depending on the bar value, we would not be able to instantly see the difference in value for a region. Let's save and view our analysis:

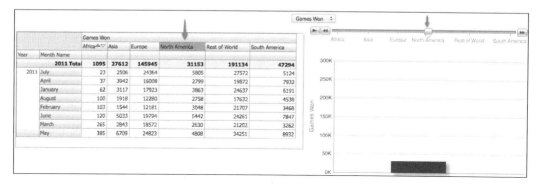

As you can see in the preceding screenshot, we have clicked on the **North America** column. This is now highlighted in blue, and the slider has chosen **North America** and displays the appropriate value (we have chosen 2011 in our prompt this time):

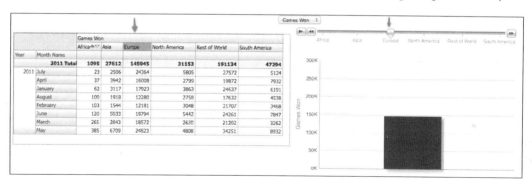

If we click on another column, as we have done with **Europe**, then the slider and graph choose **Europe** and the bar changes appropriately.

This is a very basic example, but can be elaborated on to show radically different views and levels of data.

Hierarchical columns

All of the examples that we have worked through in this chapter have used standard OBIEE columns. These allow drilling behavior that we have set in the RPD via our dimensional hierarchies. For example, in the pivot table we had **Year** and **Month Name** in the analysis:

These columns are part of the time dimension that we set up and they have further child levels. We can drill automatically by clicking on a value. Let's choose **March**:

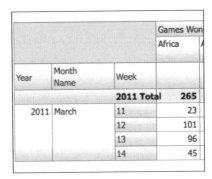

We automatically drill to a lower level of detail as we defined in the RPD. We can turn off this drill, but we did not have to make any changes in the webcat to initially turn this on.

11*g* adds a new type of column: the **Hierarchical column**. If we look at our subject area and specifically at the Time dimension, you can see the normal columns. However, notice at the bottom that there is a new column with an icon that denotes a hierarchy. This column is named exactly as our dimension is in the business model of the RPD and reflects the same levels:

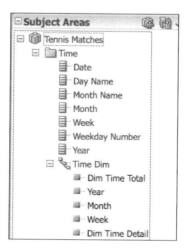

So, let's get rid of our current **Time** columns in the criteria tab and replace them with this new hierarchical one:

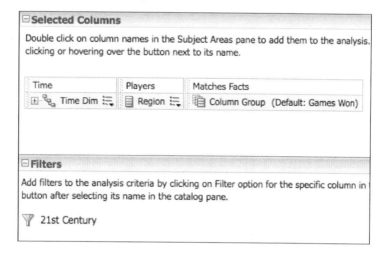

Note the **+** and **–** signs, which we can use to expand or collapse levels. The advantage with this type of column is that we can drill down to detail using our dimensional hierarchies set in the RPD, but we do not have to lose levels of detail:

	Games Won
	Africa
Time Dim△▽	
⊟ Dim Time Total	28391
⊟ 2011	1095
⊞ May	385
⊟ March	265
⊞ 14	45
⊞ 13	96
⊞ 12	101
⊞ 11	23

For example when we drilled down with normal columns, we lost the total for Year. With a hierarchical column, we can still see that figure, as well as the ones with more detail in the same view. In the RPD, you can create hierarchies (and, thus, hierarchical columns) that are:

- **Level Based**: We set strict parent-child relationships within a time dimension.

- **Value Based**: There are no proper levels but there are relationships. For example, an employee hierarchy where people are on the same level but in reality can actually each other; for example, a Director reporting to another Director.

There is a lot more to this area, especially if you want to implement skip or ragged hierarchies, which are too advanced for the purposes of this book in educating beginners. However, if you have advanced requirements like these in your project, then take the time to investigate and explore these bits of functionality.

Security

As yet, we have not discussed any security in this chapter. This is a complicated subject and we could actually write a book in itself on the topic. As a beginner's guide, we will now take a brief look at some of the basic options.

Object security

As you learned in the preceding chapter, you can set permissions for every object in the Presentation Catalog. From folders and filters to analyses and dashboards. Let's look at an example.

Let's say that we only wanted one group of users to see one page of our current dashboard, and another group to see the other page. We can go to dashboard properties from the dashboard editor. We choose one of the pages and click on the padlock icon:

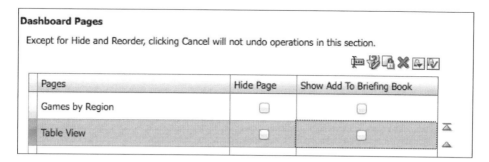

This brings us to the **Permission** screen. We can then click on the green + sign to add a new group and access rights to this page:

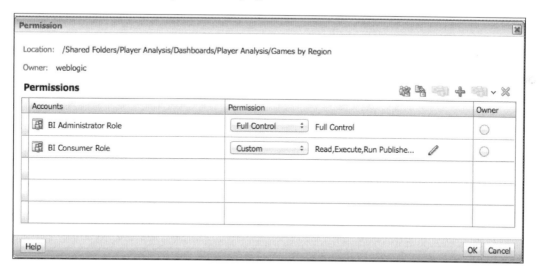

Now we get to the **Add Application Roles...** screen. We can search for roles, groups, or indeed individual users. We will bring in the East USTA Player role that we set up in a previous chapter:

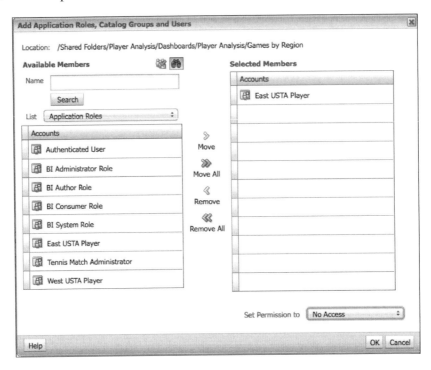

We **Set Permission** for this role to **No Access**, and then click on **OK**. Let's do the same for the **Table View** page in the dashboard, but this time we will block access for the **West USTA Player** role.

We can now see what affect this has on object visibility for users. If you remember from one of our earlier chapters, we had a player **Tommy Racquet** that was set up as part of the West group. Let's log in as him and see what he sees:

So, we can see that he can only sees the first dashboard page tab, and does not have access to the **Table View** tab.

Let's now log in as one of our East group players:

We log in as **Frank Forehand**, and can see that he can only view the second tab and cannot see the dashboard page with our pivots and graphs.

We can do this for most objects in the catalog, and it is quite common to create different dashboards for different groups.

Data security

Another very common requirement is for users to access the same analysis, but having it display different datasets depending on the logged in user's role. This is called **row-level security** and can easily be implemented in OBIEE. However, this requires changes completely outside of the Presentation Catalog.

In our scenario, we will say that there is a requirement for our users to view different regional data. We want to restrict Tommy Racquet to see data for North and South America and the ROW (Rest of the World) regions. We want Frank Forehand to see Europe, Asia and Africa.

Somewhere in our source system we will need to have this login-user relationship captured and brought over to our warehouse. A simple setup is shown in the tables, as modeled in the RPD as follows:

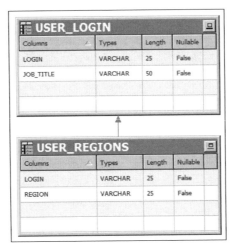

These tables show a 1:M relationship between a user's login and their linked regions. Once we have this data, we can capture the regions for an individual user by creating a **Session** variable. At this point, you may want to refresh your memory and refer back to creating variables in the RPD in *Chapter 8, Developing a BI Repository*. Remember, that a **Session** variable differs from a **Repository** variable in that it is set individually for each user upon their login.

We go back to our RPD and create a new initialization block that returns an individual's regions:

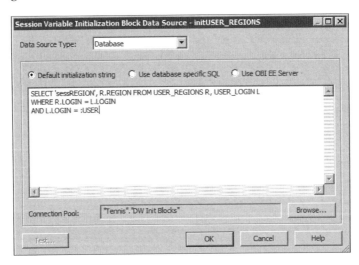

:USER is an OBIEE system set session variable that records the login of a user. We can use this to restrict our query to the data of the logged in user. Also note, that in our select statement we have hardcoded one of the returned values. This **sessRegion** name will be used as our variable name. As we have many regions for one user, this is a common method of instantiating a variable with multiple values. In addition to this we need to set our variable target within the initialization block as having **Row-wise initialization**:

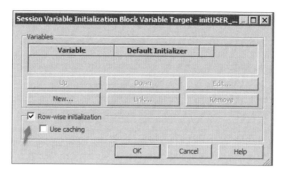

Checking the appropriate box, as shown in the preceding screenshot does this. Note, that in this case we do not need to stipulate any actual variable names as we have already done so in our select statement. Our initialization block will now look something like the following screenshot:

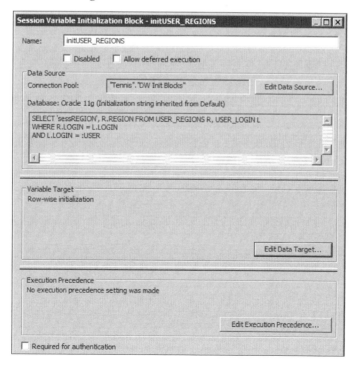

Now that we have setup a variable to return regions for a user, we can use it to automatically filter their queries. We do this by adding the filter to the appropriate **Application Roles** via the **Identity Manager**. This is accessed by navigating to **Manage | Identity**:

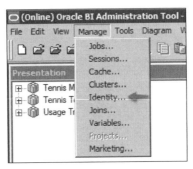

Here we can access **Application Roles** or users that we have set up within OBIEE. By double-clicking on one of the roles that our users are members of, we can set data permissions:

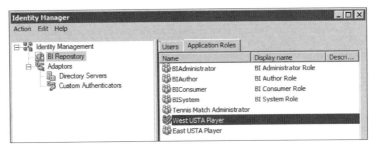

We are concerned with the **Data Filters** tab. Firstly, we will click on the **Name** field to add the object that we want to filter on:

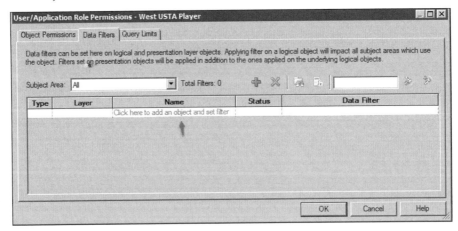

In our case, that would be the **Players** presentation table as this contains our **Region** column that we use in our analyses. For the purposes of this example, we have newly created this column in the RPD rather than having it based on **bins** in the Presentation Catalog, as previously in the chapter:

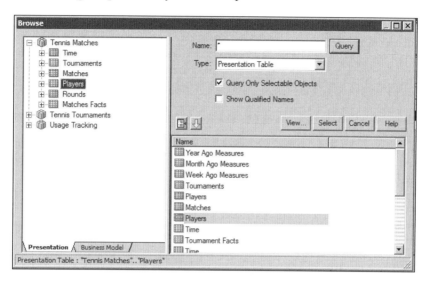

Once we have chosen the object we wish to filter, we can stipulate the actual filter criteria by clicking on the **Data Filter** column. We can use the familiar **Expression Builder** to do this by clicking on the **fx** icon:

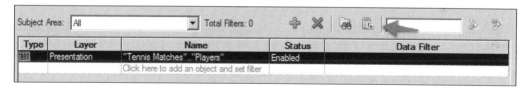

At this point we can reference our previously created variable to filter on our **Region** column:

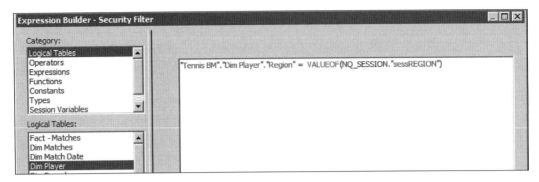

Once this is done, we can click on **OK** for the multiple screens. We will have to repeat this process for all of the Application Roles that we wish to have this filter run on. Once we are happy then we can save our changes. If you made the changes offline then you will, of course, need to add the new RPD to the system.

So, now we can log in to our dashboard as Tommy. We can see that as we have restricted the **Application Role** that he is part of, his analysis has been filtered with his own regions without changes in the **Presentation Catalog**:

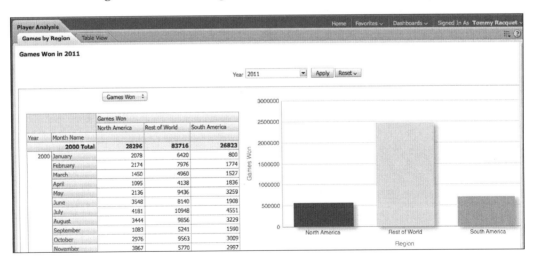

Likewise we can see the same filter in action by logging in as Frank:

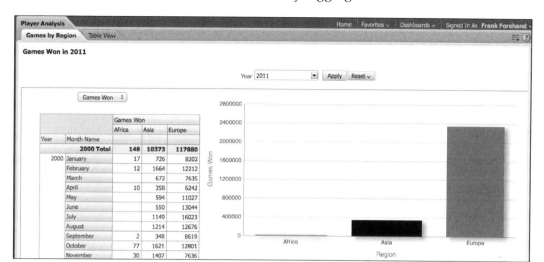

This is an especially useful piece of OBIEE capability. Although it can get far more complicated, especially when you need to filter complex employee hierarchies, the basic methodology does remain the same.

Design – best practices

Hopefully, you are in a project where there is a robust business analysis process that you can influence. However, all too often there are projects where analysts are not familiar with BI and data warehousing concepts. Rather than guide users and help form requirements, they commonly just jot down requirements verbatim and forward them to developers with no real added value. This can be manageable in mature projects with educated users, but sometimes when OBIEE is up-sold, as just another component in an enterprise solution, this can mean that you are asked to develop something in OBIEE that is really not appropriate. For example, a user just wants to keep their Excel sheet and asks for the same in OBIEE! So, as a developer, try to keep the aim of your development and a tool's appropriateness in mind and push back on any egregious demands. Understandably, this can be quite difficult in certain environments without appearing querulous, but unlike a traditional developer, you will need to develop business skills and domain knowledge so that you can empathize with, and better serve, your users.

With all this in mind, let's go over a few practical guidelines that we have found useful through our own experience:

- **Iterate**: Sometimes users will not know what they want until they see it. As long as you have spent a lot of time on data warehouse and RPD development, you can iterate with users in a very rapid manner.

- **Usage Tracking**: Monitor usage statistics and if published items are not being used, despite originally heavy deadline pressure from the business, then seek to find out why.

- **White Space**: Analytical reports should be quickly taken in by end-users, so try not to waste too much real estate and space. This may require you to look into the most common monitor and resolution sizes of your users and altering your dashboards appropriately.

- **Scrolling**: As with white space, whenever possible strive to avoid horizontal scrolling. If a user needs to scroll left and right for one piece of information, they will become increasingly frustrated. Also, try to limit vertical scrolling as much as possible.

- **Animations/decoration**: Avoid these if they have no informational requirement, for example a bar chart that starts empty and animates until completion. Outside a proof of concept or sales pitch they can become quite annoying with day-to-day use.

- **Design standards**: Try to have an in-house set of guidelines for dashboard production e.g. colors, title/legend placement, naming conventions, so that users roughly know what to expect when viewing a new analysis.

- **Insight**: Try to produce high-level analysis with drill downs or navigation to detail if necessary.

Additional research suggestions

You can refer to the following sources for additional information:

- Help files in the catalog frontend
- Oracle documentation: http://www.oracle.com/technetwork/middleware/bi-enterprise-edition/documentation/index.html
- *The Visual Display of Quantitative Information*, *Edward Tufte*
- *Information Dashboard Design: The Effective Visual Communication of Data*, *Stephen Few*

A review – what I should now know!

For self-review and a recap of the chapter, here are a few questions based on important topics covered in this chapter:

- How do I create a new Analysis?
- What is a Compound Layout?
- How do I add multiple views of the same analysis?
- How do I create and amend a Pivot table?
- What types of views and graphs are available?
- How do I create a Dashboard?
- How do I amend object permissions?
- What do I need to think about when designing good dashboards?

Summary

We have covered the basics of Dashboard building in OBIEE. As you have seen, there are a vast array of tools and options available for your project and development. It is easy then, to get to a state where we start including lots of objects just because they are there or to display OBIEE's flexibility. This may be appropriate for a Sales cycle where we are wowing executives with all sorts of colors, animations, and graphics. However, for an implementer and developer, we really need to concentrate on how we can help our business users to take in, and process, data in the most efficient manner. This means homing in on essential needs first, rather than all bells and whistles or flashy displays.

We have also discussed "best practice" for dashboard design. In addition to what we have covered there are some great tool agnostic resources and books out there. If you want to delve further into good dashboard design we would highly recommend books by Edward Tufte for an aesthetic and academic look into presenting data, and those by Stephen Few for a more BI and industry specific viewpoint.

11

Agents and the Action Framework

Up to this point, we have investigated and demonstrated the reporting features of OBIEE 11*g*. All this is targeted at delivering business analysis to our end users by enabling them to cut through the complex datasets and discover new insights about their business. These insights would then be acted upon, away from OBIEE in other systems or via internal business processes.

In 11*g*, Oracle has introduced new functionality with a hope that OBIEE can be more tightly integrated into business processes and the actions that result from producing analytical reports. In previous versions, we had the Delivers portion of OBIEE where you could invoke basic actions, such as the delivery of reports or dashboard alerts. 11*g* has drastically enhanced this capability through the **Action Framework**, where we are now able to initiate a multitude of additional noncore actions. For example, web services, business processes, or other analyses and reports.

The vision going forward for OBIEE is that it will provide a system that can deliver processes as well as analyses. If you attend any talks by Oracle, you may hear them describing OBIEE as a closed-loop system in that they want the platform to be able to move an individual user from a transactional environment to an analytical one, and then onward onto the actual decision making processes in a seamless and continuous manner. During this chapter, we will look at a few examples of the new actions that Oracle has provided in attempting to succeed in this goal.

Agents

As we stated in the introduction, previous versions of OBIEE contained functionality to deliver analyses to a targeted set of end users via a delivery method, such as e-mail. The method of delivery was described as an **iBot**. In 11*g*, this capability has been retained and iBots have been renamed as **agents**. To support this functionality, we need to have the BI Scheduler tables and service running, as we have covered previously. So, let's go through the process of creating an agent.

The example that we will go through involves e-mailing one of our previously created analyses to a user. To do this, initially you have to set up the OBIEE with details of a mail server. To configure this, open Enterprise Manager and go to the **Deployment** tab, Then go to the **Mail** subtab for our application:

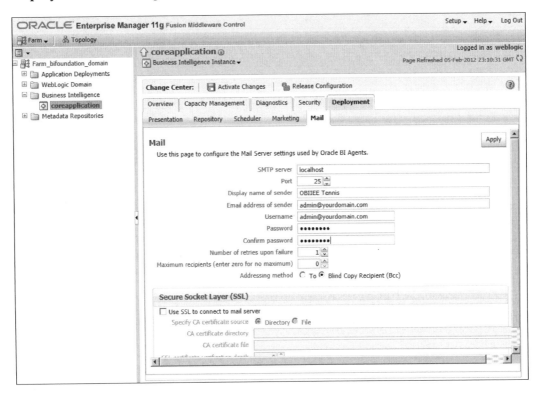

Here you need to fill in the details of an SMTP server in the **SMTP server** field, including the **Username** and **Password** details, and SSL information if required. OBIEE will then use this server while sending out analyses via e-mail. You can also change the display name of the sending party. For our example, we will use **OBIEE Tennis**. Once you have applied these changes, you can then move onto actually creating an agent. You can do so via the **Home** screen.

Note that if you want a simple mail server for testing/prototyping needs, we recommend you to download one such as hMailServer at `http://www.hmailserver.com`. Once you download it, you can create a local mail account such as `admin@localhost`, and if you have MS Outlook or a free mail client such as Mozilla Thunderbird, you can actually do all of your testing locally on a single box.

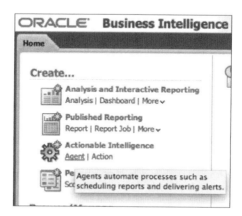

Alternatively, you can find the analysis that you want to send out, in the Presentation Catalog. Click on **Schedule** from the options:

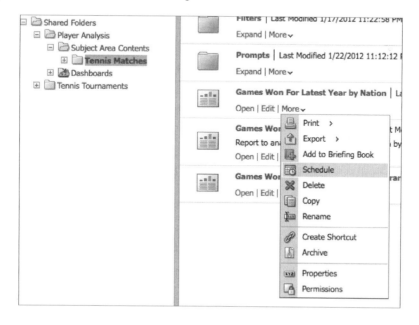

Either method will bring us to the agent definition tabs. We will first encounter the **General** tab:

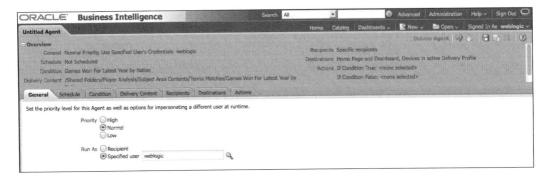

You can set **Priority** for an agent. This relates to the users that are able to define their delivery profile. A **delivery profile** is set individually by users and contains their preferred devices for receiving information and the manner in which it should be received. For example, the users may stipulate that high priority agents are sent to their mobile phones, while normal ones are sent to their e-mail addresses.

More importantly, in this tab, you can decide which user OBIEE will run this agent as. In our example, we have stipulated our admin user. This means that every recipient of this agent will receive the same report. However, if you have a report with some type of data-security, you can set the agent to **Run As** the **Recipient**. This means that the content that is delivered, will be filtered or personalized by that recipient user or group's data visibility. For example, in this agent we will be sending out the report of games won by a region. If we had a set of users with access to only North American data, another set of users with access to European data, and the relevant data-security, we could ensure that users only received the appropriate region's data by using this setting.

The next tab is the **Schedule** tab:

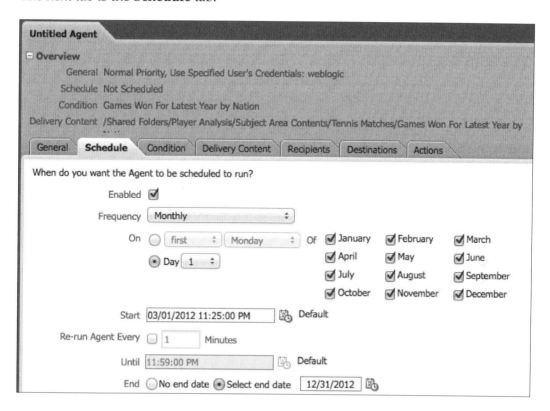

This tab is pretty self-explanatory as well, as it ensures that the agent is turned on (via the **Enabled** checkbox). You can set a schedule for an agent. You can decide whether the agent is run once or recurs, and on which days/times. This is useful, for example, for a sales report that needs to be sent out monthly with updated figures.

Moving onto the **Condition** tab:

This is another tab that adds greatly to the flexibility of an agent. A condition in this context is a check run by the OBIEE, normally in the form of another analysis. In our example, we have run a check on the row count of the analysis used as the condition. In the preceding example, we have used the same analysis that we will be sending out as a condition, as well. Here, we are checking if it is producing any data at all or not by seeing whether it produces a row count over 0. If the analysis has not produced any data, it is not worth sending it out. So, this is why we have added this as a condition. Note that you can save conditions and reuse them in other agents. Also, you can check the current status of a condition by clicking on the **Test** button:

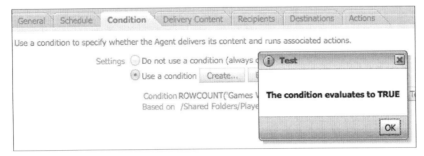

We can see that for our condition, our analysis currently does have a row count over 0, so when we run this agent, the process will complete and send out our data.

This neatly moves us onto the **Delivery Content** tab where you will actually decide what content this agent will send out:

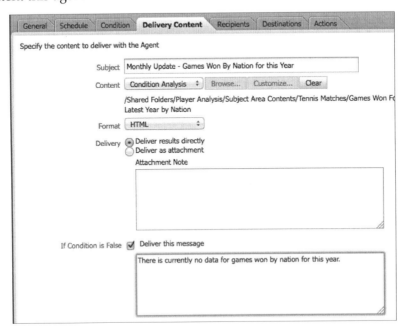

You will see the following fields under the **Delivery Content** tab:

- **Subject**: You can set the subject in this field. The content of this field will be shown in the subject header of our e-mail.

- **Content**: This is where you can stipulate what you are actually sending. If you have created an agent from the **Schedule** option of an analysis, the **Content** field will show that analysis. Otherwise, you can browse the catalog and choose one. Note that your content will get registered as **Condition Analysis**. This is due to the condition that you have set in the **Condition** tab. We demonstrated it in the preceding section.

- **Format**: You can choose the default format of the delivery device or you can override and choose your own, as we have done here in this example—**HTML**. You also have the choice of sending the content out as CSV data, an excel sheet, a PowerPoint slide, PDF, or a plain text.

- **Delivery**: We have chosen the **Deliver results directly** option to deliver the results directly within our e-mail, rather than an attachment.

- **If Condition is False**: If your previous condition proves to be false, your agent will not run. However, your users may think that something has gone wrong. You can send them a message, in this case, to allay these fears and tell them that currently there is no data for this analysis.

The next tab is for detailing the **Recipients**:

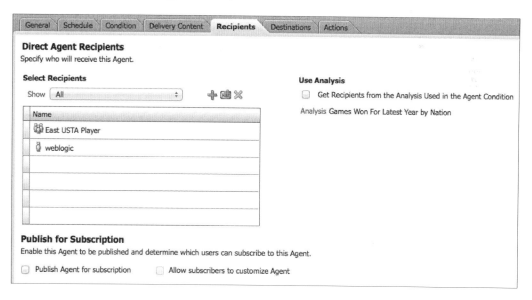

You can choose individual users or **Application Roles** and **Catalog Groups**. We have taken examples of both.

In this tab, you also have the option called **Publish for Subscription**. This means that you can open up the agent and make it visible to individual users for subscriptions. This allows them to pick and choose which agents they want to receive.

Additionally, by clicking on the envelope icon, you can actually type in hardcoded e-mail addresses, as shown in the following screenshot:

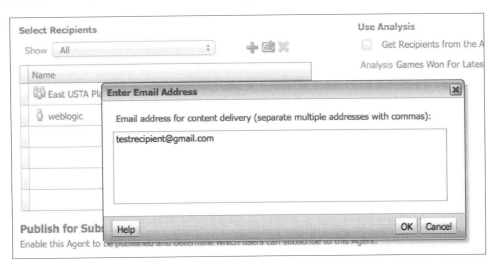

The last major section is the **Destinations** tab:

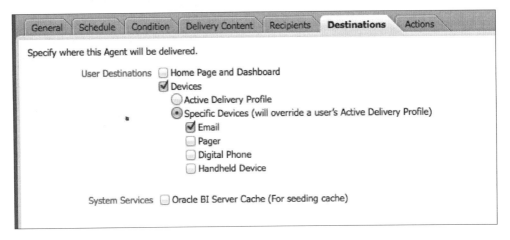

We will cover the topic on using the agents for caching in a later chapter. The main options under this tab deal with the devices. Again, you can allow users to choose their own methods of receiving data through their delivery profile, or you can override and choose a device by yourself. Let's choose **Email** for now.

At this point you are ready to run the agent. Rather than waiting for the schedule to kick in, you can run the agent now by clicking on the agent icon—a robot with a green arrow/play sign:

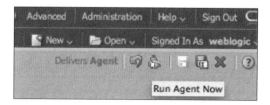

Now, you will get a message saying that the agent is running:

If the agent does not run, for example, due to a mail server issue, you will receive an appropriate message. Otherwise you should receive the **Agent Successful** message, as shown in the following screenshot:

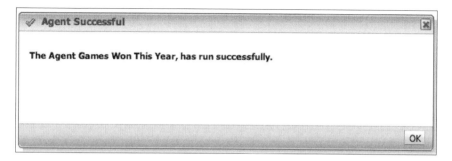

Now let's look at the result. You should get the analysis sent to you in an e-mail (you should check the e-mail associated with your weblogic user):

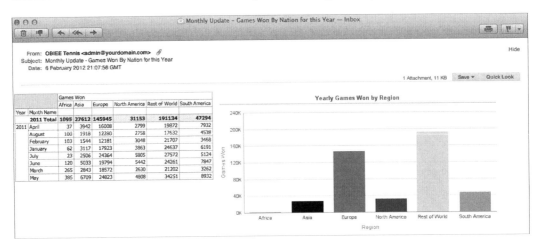

Note that the **From** and **Subject** fields are as we stipulated during our example, and that the analysis is shown in an HTML format within the e-mail, as we requested.

Before we move on, let's see how this would look if we would have sent it to the **Home** screen as an alert:

You can see that we have a new **Alerts** section in our **Home** screen that has a link to the results of the agent, that is the analysis that has just run. You will also have a yellow bell icon in the toolbar on which you can click to see all of your current alerts, as shown in the following screenshot:

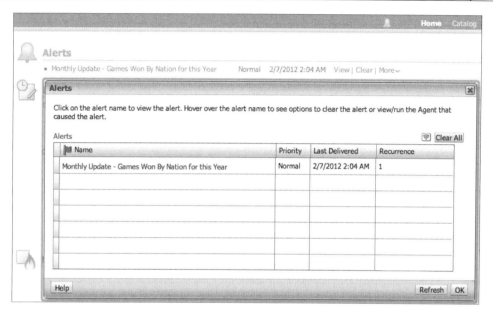

You can send this alert to both the device and the **Home** screen of a user. This can be a useful option for enhancing a user's workflow, especially in conjunction with the conditions that you can add to an agent. For example, you can proactively look for certain conditions in a dataset, for example, a drop in sales for a region, and instantly alert the appropriate user when this happens.

Actions

So, we have covered agents in OBIEE. Now, we can move onto actions, which are a major enhancement in OBIEE 11*g*. These can be actions or processes initiated within OBIEE that navigate to other areas or invoke external systems. With this, you can utilize OBIEE as part of your full business workflow.

We will go through a couple of examples of basic navigation using actions. Then, we will briefly talk about the possibilities that exist in invoking other system functions.

BI navigation

The most basic action is that of navigating from one OBIEE object to another. We have already covered drilling using RPD hierarchies and Master-detail linking in the previous chapter. Both of these types of behavior can be changed for a column heading or value via the **Interaction** option on a column in the **Criteria** tab for an analysis.

So let's do that for our Games by Region analysis. Set up **Action Links**, so that if you click on a Region in that report, you will get navigated to another analysis that has a wider variety of metrics:

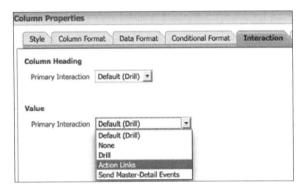

As you can see in the preceding screenshot, you have to override the choice of interaction in the **Value** section by choosing **Action Links**.

Then, you will be presented with a table of **Action Links**, which is currently empty:

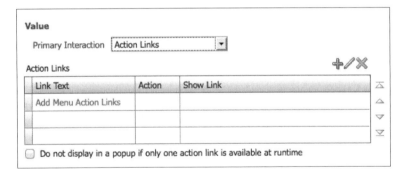

Note that, here you have a table where you can actually add a variety of links if you desire. The end user would have a menu of **Action Links** to choose from, after clicking on a value for Region.

In our example, we are only concerned with adding a navigation action. To add a new one, click on the green plus (+) sign. Then you will see the **New Action Link...** prompt:

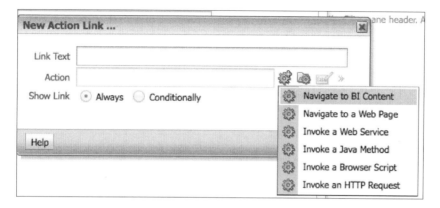

Now, you can enter **Link Text** that the user sees when picking this action. Label your link as **Other Metrics**. You can also add a new action. Choose **Navigate to BI Content**. Then, you will be prompted to choose another analysis from the Presentation Catalog. Choose the **More Metrics...** analysis:

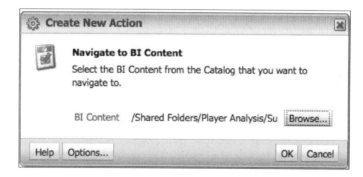

Once you have chosen the analysis to which you want to navigate, you can click on **OK** at the confirmation prompt, as shown in the preceding screenshot.

Going back to our original analysis, click on one of the Region values and see what happens:

		Games Won		
		Africa	Asia	Europe
			Other Metrics	
Year	Month Name			
	2011 Total	**1095**	**27612**	**145**
2011	April	37	3942	16

Clicking on **Africa**, you will see an **Action Links** pop-up menu with one option for our **Other Metrics** link. If you click on it, you will be transported to the **More Metrics** report:

More Metrics For Latest Year by Nation

		Africa					Asia					Eu
		Sets Won	Sets Lost	Games Won	Games Lost	% Games Won	Sets Won	Sets Lost	Games Won	Games Lost	% Games Won	Se W
Year	Month Name											
	2011 Total	**118**	**125**	**1095**	**1120**	**88**	**2922**	**3215**	**27612**	**28528**	**87**	
2011	April	2	9	37	53	67	414	452	3942	4064	88	
	August	13	6	100	70	120	197	250	1918	2064	84	
	February	11	10	103	94	98	162	152	1544	1496	93	
	January	5	13	62	99	59	333	372	3117	3283	86	
	July	1	6	23	39	57	268	284	2506	2521	89	
	June	11	18	120	149	75	539	566	5033	5140	88	
	March	25	37	265	315	77	281	353	2843	3063	85	
	May	50	26	385	301	109	728	786	6709	6897	87	

You can see that this is a very simple process. You can add multiple links in a menu to give the user greater flexibility in navigating to other reports and representations of data.

Web navigation and passing a parameter

We have covered our first basic action link. Now let's cover another type, specifically navigating to a web page. As our starting analysis, let's build a basic report that contains some details and career stats for the world's best players. If our user wants to be able to link to the current statistics for these players from the official tour sites, it would help them if they could quickly do it from the report, rather than having to open a browser, type in a web address, and search for that data:

Now, add a link on the **Name** column. Follow the same process, as discussed in the preceding sections but this time choose the **Navigate to a Web Page** option. This will bring you to a screen where you can define the web address and parameters that you may want to pass:

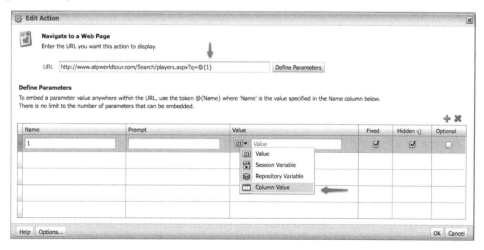

In the preceding screenshot there are a few elements that we need to discuss. First put a **URL** in. We want to be able to pass an individual's name. So set up a parameter for this. Note that you have to add @{1} in the search part of the **URL**. This is the syntax for passing a parameter with 1 being the ID (this can be alphanumeric) that we have set for ourselves.

The **Define Parameters** table is where you should define the IDs (the **Name** column) and **Value** that you are passing. Note that we are passing the actual value of the column but we could pass a fixed value or a variable instead.

You can also prompt the user for a value but we do not need this in our example. So, leave the **Prompt** column empty and mark the prompt as **Fixed** (the value passed cannot be changed) and **Hidden** (the user does not need to see the value passed as we already have it in the column on which they are clicking).

Having chosen that we are passing a column value, choose the actual column (**Players.Name**) that we want to pass:

Conditionality

You may have noticed in our first example that we had the option to conditionally show a link. Our current example is ideal for this. The URL that we have entered as an input is for the men's tour. So, it does not make sense to have this link for the female players. So go ahead and choose to create a condition on the sex of the player:

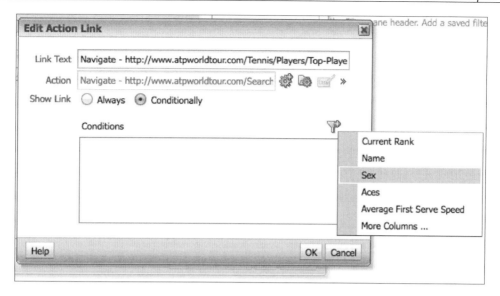

Like a filter, check if a player is male, before showing the link to the user:

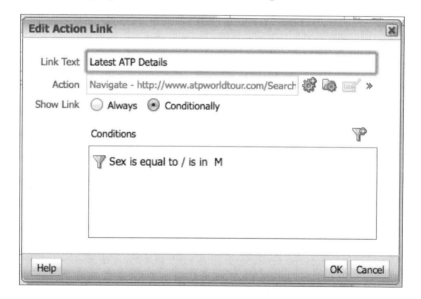

Then click on **OK** and you will be navigated to the **Interaction** tab.

Note that you can also save and store an action in the Presentation Catalog as a separate object, just like a filter or agent. This is useful if you commonly need to use the same action in multiple reports. In the current example, we could save the action and if the website changes its player query URL string, we only have to update this information at one place. This saves our time required to search and amend the information at every place where it might possibly be used.

Refer to the following screenshot:

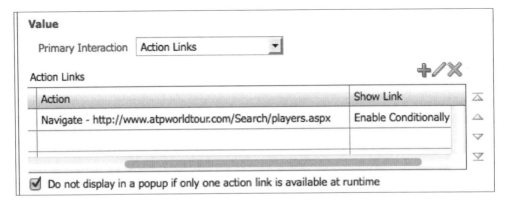

Note that this time we have ticked the **Do not display in a popup if only one action link is available at runtime** option. This is because it is not worth prompting the user with an **Action Links** menu that only has one entry. We want them to have a seamless experience in clicking through. So let's save the menu and see what effect it has on our report:

Top Players

Sex	Name	Current Rank	Aces	Average First Serve Speed
F	Caroline Wozniacki	1	0	0.00
M	Novak Djokovic		1872	26.20
F	Vera Zvonareva	2	0	0.00
M	Rafael Nadal		1358	28.28
F	Kim Clijsters	3	0	0.00
M	Roger Federer		3564	30.05
F	Victoria Azarenka	4	0	0.00
F	Na Li	5	0	0.00
M	Robin Soderling		2145	12.04
F	Petra Kvitova	6	0	0.00
M	David Ferrer		827	10.07
F	Maria Sharapova	7	0	0.00
M	Mardy Fish		1827	6.94
F	Francesca Schiavone	8	0	0.00
M	Gael Monfils		1651	15.69
F	Marion Bartoli	9	0	0.00
M	Tomas Berdych		1942	12.29
F	Samantha Stosur	10	0	0.00
M	Jo-Wilfried Tsonga		1792	16.56
F	Andrea Petkovic	11	0	0.00
M	Nicolas Almagro		1833	4.91
F	Agnieszka Radwanska	12	0	0.00
M	Gilles Simon		1072	5.64
F	Svetlana Kuznetsova	13	0	0.00
M	Richard Gasquet		1413	10.07

⇧ ⇧ ⇩ ⬆ Rows 1 - 25

We have rejigged the report slightly, but note that the conditionality works and only the names of male players are highlighted as links. We can go back and add an appropriate link for the female players later.

Let's test the link by clicking on a player name, for example **Nicolas Almagro**:

Now, you will be navigated to the ATP world tour site. Here, note the URL that our column value for player name has passed as a parameter, as we had set up and envisaged.

Note on invoke actions

In addition to the *navigate* type of action, we can also *invoke* the actions. **Invoke actions** are those which allow you to manipulate functions and processes outside of OBIEE via a variety of methods. You can create actions that invoke the following:

- Web service
- Java method
- Browser script
- http request

These actions can be used to simply bring back the information from an external system into a dashboard for a user, or even to update that external system directly, as a result of an analysis run in OBIEE. For example, you may have noticed that when creating an agent, there is a tab for adding an action. We could create an agent that periodically runs and if it produces a certain result, feeds that into an invoke action to update an external system. We can also create actions that can be invoked directly from a dashboard. The potential for automating your workflows, with your BI system as a central step, has increased greatly with this release.

Invoke actions provide a huge opportunity in which companies can open up OBIEE to core business processes and workflows. This is especially the case with this release of OBIEE, as now there is also the potential to create actions within Oracle's **Service Oriented Architecture (SOA)**. SOA is a set of modular web services that can be combined via a common set of standards. For example, within this architecture you can get your CRM system communicating with both OBIEE and your HR system via common standards based on https calls and XML messaging. This can provide your business with a virtuous loop of gathering data, analyzing it, and then acting upon it.

This is an advanced topic, but if your client is interested in truly incorporating OBIEE into their workflow, you should take some time to look into these options. A first port of call for further information on invoke actions would, of course, be within the Oracle Documentation on the subject. You can currently find that at `http://docs.oracle.com/cd/E21764_01/bi.1111/e10544/actions.htm#autoId4`.

A review – what I should now know!

For self review and a recap of the chapter, here are a few questions based on important topics covered in this chapter:

1. What is an agent?
2. How do we send an analysis by e-mail?
3. How do we send an alert to a dashboard?
4. What is an action?
5. How do we pass a parameter to a web address?
6. What types of actions can we create?

Additional research suggestions

Following are the files that will help you in using the Presentation Catalog:

- **Oracle Documentation**: `http://www.oracle.com/technetwork/middleware/bi-enterprise-edition/documentation/index.html`
- **Oracle SOA Documentation**: `http://www.oracle.com/technetwork/middleware/soasuite/documentation/index.html`

Summary

In this chapter, we introduced you to agents and actions. I hope that you saw the amazing potential for flexibility that they can bring to your system. There are boundless opportunities for automation, increased navigation, and workflow processing.

As we have stressed in other chapters, to add this functionality without confusing your users relies on a very good business analysis and consultative process with your end users. You do not want them to be confused with a plethora of unneeded options, but instead you should seek to have very targeted functionality available to them. Business Intelligence, at its best, is a prompt to action. It should be providing insight that requires you to explore, amend, or seek further possibilities in your business. Without sounding too much like an arm of Oracle's marketing department, we really do feel that with the Action Framework, Oracle has succeeded in putting emphasis and providing great capability on this. So, you should be looking to see how it helps your BI implementation lead into actual process and business changes.

In the next chapter, we will be looking at another method of presenting reports to your end users via an additional tool called BI Publisher.

12
Developing Reports Using BI Publisher

With the 11*g* release, Oracle BI has taken a leap to fully integrate a common Oracle reporting technology that is almost ubiquitously embedded in Oracle Applications — **BI Publisher (BIP)**. Once known as **XML Publisher (XMLP)**, BI Publisher has been associated with analytics, reporting, and business intelligence under the ranks of Oracle for a long time. In the previous versions of Oracle BI, an attempt was made to integrate BI Publisher with the larger enterprise suite of **Oracle BI Enterprise Edition (OBIEE)**. However, they remained more separate than together. In Oracle BI 11*g*, the tools have been merged in a very functional way — thus achieving the goal.

This chapter covers some of the new features of BI Publisher 11*g*, as well as the general functionality of BI Publisher in order to get you up-to-speed on using the tool. Oracle BI Publisher is quite robust and this topic could make up an entire book on its own. As a matter of fact, there is an expansive book on BI Publisher 11*g* — *Oracle BI Publisher 11g: A Practical Guide to Enterprise Reporting, Packt Publishing*. However, the material in this chapter is aimed at providing a crash-course, which should give any reader enough hands-on exercises to get their feet wet and enough food for thought for further research.

Don't miss the installation integration checkpoint!

It is important to know that Oracle BI Publisher 11*g* is provided in the core Oracle BI 11*g* installation disk(disks). During the installation process, you are able to choose to install, or not to install, one or all of the three Oracle BI software suites—Oracle BI Enterprise Edition, Oracle BI Publisher, and Oracle Real-Time Decisions. All suites are selected to be installed by default. Toggling one or more of the options will define the software that gets installed, but it also determines the default integration between these software items. By keeping Oracle BI and Oracle BI Publisher selected, the security integration with Fusion Middleware Security and other integration configurations are set during the installation. You cannot go back at a later time to modify this installation configuration. Any post-install integration would be a manual effort.

With that said, those previously exposed to BI Publisher will appreciate that BI Publisher 11*g* can still be installed as standalone software. That is, it would function correctly and contain all of the features inherent with BI Publisher in the absence of the core OBIEE platform component (Presentation Services, Oracle BI server, and so on) installation. This configuration could be required in some circumstances, such as an organization only purchasing a license for Oracle BI Publisher. This book focuses on the default installation integration option (that is, both Oracle BI Enterprise Edition and Oracle BI Publisher selected during the components installation configuration) and will continue on with that as a prerequisite for all subsequent exercises.

As a quick side note, even when Oracle BI and Oracle BI Publisher are installed on the same server, as per the default installation configuration, BI Publisher continues to leverage its legacy standalone application context root, which can be accessed via the URL, `http://<server_name>:<default_port>/xmlpublisher`.

The default installation configures BI Publisher with the Fusion Middleware Security options. Users can potentially log in to both the `/xmlpublisher` application path and the `/analytics` application path. BI Publisher is still ultimately administered via the BI Publisher Administration page interface, although a link exists on the Oracle BI Presentation Services Administration page, which merely navigates to the BI Publisher Administration page.

Where BI Publisher excels?

The BI Publisher tool has a plethora of integration points. Likewise, it has the ability to connect to many disparate data sources, which makes it a very powerful tool within any organization's enterprise business intelligence toolbox. But the real power comes in two main forms—the ability to manipulate each report at a very granular level by modifying XML and the ability to print crisp, pixel-perfect reports referred to as **highly formatted documents**.

Pixel-perfect reporting entails that Oracle BI Publisher has the ability to allow a report template to be developed in one of the BI Publisher's several template development outlets such as Microsoft Word (Template Builder for Word), Microsoft Excel (Analyzer for Excel), Adobe Reader, or web-based interface, then print a hard copy of the report to render exactly as it looks when developed on the computer. Several organizations leverage BI Publisher to print shipping labels, checks, invoices, W-2 forms, and utility statements. As an example, in the mail you may receive a quarterly mutual funds investment statement complete with page headers, footers, page numbers, and charts, and not even know that potentially you are holding a document created dynamically via Oracle BI Publisher.

What's all this XML talk?

The original name of BI Publisher was XML Publisher. The original name emphasized the basis of the tool—XML. At its debut it was one of the only reporting tools that leveraged the power of the XML open standard to retain its core metadata This is still true, even though the name of the tool has changed. XML is now ubiquitous throughout the web. Just about all major report vendors and web technologies can consume, parse, or otherwise leverage XML to produce dynamic information. A good example of this would be the **Portable Document Format (PDF)** standard, which BI Publisher interacts with completely.

The basic development functionality of BI Publisher is straightforward and provides excellent results. However, the greatest flexibility of developing with BI Publisher comes when knowledge about advanced XML formatting can be leveraged. At its core, BI Publisher details, data sets, templates, and so on, are stored as XML. These XML files can be manipulated manually or via the GUI interface. For basic efforts, manual editing of the XML is most likely not required. But, when attempting clever solutions and advanced customizations, manual editing of the XML is preferred. Ramping up on your XML knowledge is a great idea in general and it is highly recommended when engaging with BI Publisher development.

Yes, BI Publisher is now Published Reporting

Moving Oracle BI Enterprise Edition into the Fusion Middleware stack came with many changes. For BI Publisher this set of changes also came in the form of a name change. In previous versions of Oracle BI an ad-hoc analysis (previously Answers) request was often referred to as a report, but with the embedded integration of BI Publisher into the Oracle BI 11g, a clearer distinction was needed. The guidance is that an ad-hoc analysis request querying against a subject area should be called an **analysis request** and that a report created in BI Publisher should be called a **published report**. Keep in mind that Oracle BI cannot create an ad-hoc analysis request with the same pixel-perfect perfection that a published report from BI Publisher can. So, the distinction in nomenclature is warranted from both a technical and functional perspective.

One more confusing reference, depending on your experience with Oracle analytics tools, is the fact that the act of creating an analysis request, dashboard, dashboard prompt, filter, or condition is referred to as **interactive reporting**. You can see this description — **Analysis and Interactive Reporting** — from the Oracle BI 11g portal **Home** page under the **Create...** section:

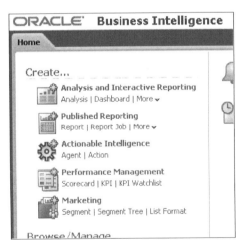

For those familiar with the Oracle Hyperion Enterprise Performance Management products, you will recognize the name interactive reporting as the name of an existing hyperion reporting tool that has been used in financial reporting for a long time.

Ultimately, the gist is that, because of the Oracle BI Publisher 11*g*'s embedded integration with Oracle BI Enterprise Edition and future integrations with Oracle tools, inevitably there is some overlap. The overlap will drive the need to clarify on terms and nomenclature. There is no doubt that nomenclature will become more fine-tuned as the Oracle BI roadmap gradually comes to fruition. For now, it can't be emphasized enough that every organization should ensure that consistent nomenclature and terminology is used, so that confusion is mitigated.

Oracle BI Foundation versus Oracle BI Publisher

When to use Oracle BI instead of Oracle BI Publisher is a common question. The question has become more frequent since the integration of Oracle BI Publisher inside the Oracle BI Enterprise Edition platform. Unfortunately, the answer to the question is itself a question—what are the primary reporting requirements? The reason for the rebuttal question is because of subtle differences in the tools. Oracle BI and Oracle BI Publisher both have strengths and weaknesses. A few proactive follow-up questions might be as follows:

1. Will the reports be delivered externally to clients for formal presentation?
2. Do these reports need to be printed in a certain format consistently?
3. Do reports need to be available in both online and print format?
4. Will the documents need to be sent automatically to a printer or via fax?
5. Will reports get built dynamically or programmatically via code?
6. Can the report developers upload their own data sources?
7. Do watermarks need to be added to reports?

If the answer is yes to any of these questions, that places a check in the column for Oracle BI Publisher. Clearly more questions along these lines should be asked with the purpose of exposing pros and cons of each.

Operational reporting is another scenario that gets brought into the conversation when determining which tool to leverage. Both tools can be used for **Operational Data Store (ODS)** type reporting requirements, but with Oracle BI Publisher's new Interactive Viewer, another check just may go into the column for BI Publisher. OBIEE can also handle this, but with more of a top-down approach and enterprise deployment cycle.

Ultimately, OBIEE contains analysis and interactive reporting tools for building ad-hoc queries, dashboards, and distributed reporting architecture. Oracle BI Publisher reports can be displayed in Oracle BI portal dashboards and can also be distributed via the Oracle BI platform's distributed reporting and delivery architecture, or via its own standalone tools and configuration. With such a powerhouse of flexibility and each having certain capabilities that the other doesn't, it is not surprising that these two tools are now seamlessly integrated into the Oracle BI 11*g* software product suite.

New features and enhancements

As mentioned previously, Oracle BI 11*g* is basically a rebirth of Oracle BI. For Oracle BI Publisher, the same phoenix like traits apply. The tool has a long history. Those who are new to the BI Publisher, or those who have used its functionality up to this point, will benefit from the latest 11*g* edition enhancements. By no means is this a complete list of all the best and newest features of Oracle BI Publisher 11*g*. However, the features discussed in the following sections stand-out as items that we think the masses would want to know about.

Improved Oracle BI 11*g* look and feel

The rewrite that took place on the Oracle BI 11*g* platform also applies to Oracle BI Publisher 11*g*. The clean Web 2.0 interface makes the **user experience (UX)** working with BI Publisher much more intuitive. In addition to the new graphics, layout, and features, the biggest enhancement that relates to the look and feel is the ability to create the pixel-perfect template and reports within the web-based interface. A BI Publisher developer no longer needs to be tied to the platform-dependent BI Publisher plugins for Microsoft Office that was once mandatory for most BI Publisher report development.

Interactive Viewer

One of BI Publisher 11*g*'s most promising features allows a dashboard-like experience using the BI Publisher Enterprise Edition. This gives BI Publisher a similar presence of the Oracle BI Enterprise Edition, but without the overhead and licensing costs. Interactive Viewer allows for dynamic selecting, sorting, and column movement that you would expect to see in any dynamic dashboard reporting. The most interesting part is the ability to provide master-detail data set connectivity within the single report layout. Therefore, clicking on a row of a table could change a related view on the report to show detailed information about that row. Interactive Viewer works best for simple data sets that are related, but provides enough configurations to manage the interactivity between the data sets.

Dynamic upload and source from MS Excel spreadsheets

This may seem like such a simple function, and in time users won't know why the product ever existed without this feature. However, for the longest time the product did not have this ability. The new shift in mechanics allows an end user to upload a Microsoft Excel spreadsheet using the BI Publisher 11*g* interface in order to leverage that physical file as a data source from which reports can then be derived.

Leveraging LDAP user attributes in queries

The ability to create a report based on LDAP user information is somewhat unique to BI Publisher under the Oracle BI platform. The ability to extrapolate specific attributes using this new functionality and pass that information into templates, as with any other data source, is a great new feature. The Oracle BI metadata repository—RPD—had the ability to retrieve data from an LDAP source, but Oracle BI Publisher is a better fit to actually render usable reports leveraging LDAP data.

Sharing a Presentation Catalog with Oracle BI 11*g*

Oracle BI Publisher metadata files and templates are now stored in the same filesystem based on Web Catalog that has been associated with the OBIEE platform for a long time. This is true, even when you install BI Publisher 11*g* in a standalone mode. The Oracle BI Web Catalog continues to exist in the filesystem but now it includes BI Publisher templates, metadata, and other information. This enables propagation of security privileges to be handled centrally. It also allows for the Oracle BI Publisher objects to be searched or exported using the Catalog Manager interface.

Data Model Editor

We haven't covered what a data model is, but we shall do just that, complete the examples, later on in this chapter. A data model basically contains the instructions for retrieving and structuring data that can be leveraged in a BI Publisher report. In the Presentation Catalog, these are ultimately individual physical files comprised of an XML structure. The **Data Model Editor** is a web-based GUI that has an enterprise Web 2.0 look, feel, and response. It removes dependency on a specific operating system or software suite that once ruled previous versions of the tool.

A data model can contain one or more data sets, parameters, list of values, and other objects that are core to the dynamic functionality of BI Publisher.

Leverage view objects – Application Development Framework

In *Chapter 1, Understanding the Oracle BI 11g Architecture*, it was briefly mentioned that several portions of Oracle BI 11g were developed using the Oracle **Application Development Framework (ADF)**. This development tactic allows for a flexible application architecture. Better yet, it adds the potential for seamlessly leveraging other applications, components, and libraries developed by Oracle, or a third-party, which can then be used within any Oracle BI 11g implementation. In the case of this new feature for Oracle BI Publisher, the ability to pull in view objects from an Oracle ADF application is now possible. Oracle ADF is a technology that is maintained and supported mainly by Oracle and has an almost homogeneous relationship with the Oracle JDeveloper IDE.

Report design basics, terminology, and locations

The new integration with BI Publisher and OBIEE can be confusing. Aside from basic terminology, it is also important to note the nuances that exist because of this integration. That is to say, many people assume that basic items such as data sources are one and the same for BI Publisher as they are for Oracle BI, which is false. This section highlights a few basic terms that will be used throughout this chapter when stepping through the development of reports. It will also highlight when to go where for what as it relates to basic management of BI Publisher and the integration with Oracle BI 11g.

Report design components

Several components must be configured before adding a table, dropdown, or otherwise building a report in BI Publisher. Here are the basic items that will comprise most reports that you will develop.

Data model

BI Publisher must define one or more data sources and/or subsets of data—data sets—that can be used in one or more reports. The structure in which these items are defined is referred to as a **data model**. It also provides the structure and relationship between the data sets. The complex data sets and simple data sets, such as a list of values, parameters, and other metadata, which describe how data is provided in a report, are configured here.

A data model usually has the ability to configure one or more data sets, event triggers, flexfields, list of values, parameters, and bursting property options. A BI Publisher data model is not an RPD. It cannot be leveraged as a source for creating ad-hoc analysis requests in Oracle BI Presentation Services.

Layout

In order for the data to be presented as desired in the report, first it must be designed. A layout consists of a template file and a set of properties for rendering the template file. The legacy template design tools such as MS Word and MS Excel still exist. However, with Oracle BI 11*g*, the template design can dynamically take place in the BI Publisher GUI for true Web 2.0 functionality.

Properties

Properties allow you to control design formatting, display, and generation of the report.

Translations

BI Publisher allows for both catalog translation and template translation. Both are achieved via an export, translate, and import process, and leveraging the open standard **XML Localization Interchange File Format** (**XLIFF**) to handle the structuring of this process. The template translation is ultimately a way to translate just the final report presented by metadata. A catalog translation can potentially translate all objects in the BI Publisher catalog. Both translation types can handle multiple locale code translations.

Where to administrate BI Publisher

Security is always a good topic to learn first about a tool. Without it, you generally have no control on the application. As mentioned before, BI Publisher could standalone as its own FMW application. In a standalone BI Publisher deployment, security can be configured using FMW security or several other authentication and authorization types. In either case, the BI Publisher Administration page can be located by accessing the URL, `http://<server_name>:9704/xmlpserver/servlet/admin`. During the default Oracle BI installation configuration, BI Publisher is automatically configured to be embedded within OBIEE. This means that the BI Publisher Administration page can also be accessed by clicking on the **Manage BI Publisher** link in the OBIEE Administration page– `http://<server_name>:9704/analytics/saw.dll?Admin`. Both administration pages require you to log in with user credentials having administration (BI Administrator role) privileges, such as the WebLogic administrator user account.

Default embedded BI Publisher configurations

Based on the default Oracle BI suite installation and configuration, the transparent integration between Oracle BI and BI Publisher is made. This default setting implies several configurations:

- BI Publisher Security is set to Fusion Middleware Security.

- Files such as BI Publisher data sets, templates, and so on, are stored in the Presentation Catalog.

- BI Publisher administration can be accessed from the Oracle BI Administration page and the BI Publisher /xmlpserver application.

- BI Publisher integration with Oracle BI Presentation Services is automatically configured for the default instance of Presentation Services which installed to the same server.

- A BI Publisher JDBC data source pointing to the Oracle BI ODBC port 9703 is created by default, so that BI Publisher can use certain Oracle BI objects as data sources.

Where to build a data model

A data model defines the data sets that we can use to build one or more reports. The data model can be created via the /xmlpserver application URL or the /analytics application URL. The former is primarily used for standalone BI Publisher deployments although you could also use it when the full integration with the Oracle BI 11*g* suite has been deployed on your server.

> For the exercises in this book, you can use the Oracle BI 11*g* analytics portal—http://<server_name>:9704/analytics/—unless otherwise stated.

Where to add a data source connection

Out of the box, data source connections cannot be created in BI Publisher unless you have administration privileges. More importantly, the only place to create a new data source, which may be used globally in BI Publisher, is within the Oracle BI Publisher Administration page. This centralizes data source creation across the application. It also allows an administrator to restrict access to the predefined data sources. As mentioned in the preceding section, the BI Publisher Administration page can be accessed via two options. The following screenshot shows the **Data Sources** control section within the BI Publisher **Administration** page:

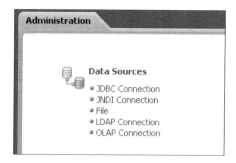

What is a JNDI data source?

Oracle BI 11*g* brings, to the forefront, many advanced configurations that were subdued in the previous releases of the tool. From the myriad of data sources that BI Publisher can reference, one is quietly labeled as a JNDI connection. Most people having the general data warehousing experience know what the other four types of data source connections are. However, JNDI is somehow elusive.

JNDI stands for **Java Naming and Directory Interface**. It is a powerful type of connection that resides on the application server (in this case WebLogic Server) and is especially favorable for using with deployed JEE applications that are related in some way. More importantly it provides a means to connect to a JDBC data source, using a connection pool. Connection pools create certain efficiencies in applications when multiple users are querying the same data source from one or more applications. The JNDI connection must be established on the application server itself and cannot be accomplished from the BI Publisher interface. In this case, you would have to open the WebLogic Server Administration Console and navigate to **Services | Data Sources** to create a new JNDI connection. Once the JNDI connection has been created the JNDI connection name/alias can be entered in the **JNDI Name** field while creating that data source type in BI Publisher.

The third-party tool, MDSearch for Oracle BI (at `http://mdsearch.fyght.com/`) leverages a JNDI data source that gets created in WLS during its installation and configuration in order for the Java web application to communicate with its relational repository. The MDSearch data source, which contains metadata lineage and impact information for Oracle BI 11*g*, can then be retrieved via BI Publisher to create additional reports. The new auditing capability, which ties BI Publisher to Fusion Middleware Auditing functionality, is more tightly integrated with BI Publisher. This auditing feature could also use a JNDI connection to log audit information into a database schema instead of a filesystem log file which is the default.

Let's get publishing

As promised, the rest of this chapter will get you rolling with hands-on exercises for learning BI Publisher. Here, the goal is to step through the critical parts for setting up a BI Publisher 11g environment, creating a report or two, and preparing a report for delivery. Along the way, there will be highlighted things that you should keep an eye out for, research on your own at a later date, or simply understand to make your development cycles easier.

Let's start with administration. Because without that there isn't much else you, or any of your users, will be able to do.

Administration management of BI Publisher

This section gets away from the theory and core explanations that you've read so far in this chapter. You will take a step-by-step journey of a real-world implementation on how to assess the Fusion Middleware Security application roles, create several data sources, and ensure that application roles have access to the desired data sources. All of this effort prepares you for creating an actual BI Publisher—sorry (!)—Published Reporting report.

Accessing the BI Publisher Administration page

Getting to the Administration page is the first step in this process. Start by following the next steps:

1. Log in to the Oracle BI Analytics portal—`http://<server_name>:<default_port>/analytics/`—with the WebLogic administrator user credentials.

2. Click on the **Administration** link in the global header section.

3. In the subsection labeled as **BI Publisher**, click on the **Manage BI Publisher** link.

 The first time you click on this link, the page may not seem to render correctly. Wait for three minutes or so for the contents of the page to render as this may be the first time that the BI Publisher application `/xmlpublisher` has been called.

Verifying application roles

From the BI Publisher Administration page, verify the existing application roles available from FMW Security. Again, FMW Security aims to manage all privileges by application roles as a more streamlined way of organizing users from multiple identity providers. It is also an open standard way of authorization:

1. Click on the **Security Configuration** link under the **Security Center** subsection.

2. Scroll down to the bottom of the page and notice that, as per the default installation configuration, BI Publisher security has been set up to use the Oracle Fusion Middleware security model:

3. Scroll back to the top of the page and click on the **Roles and Permissions** tab:

4. Review the application roles available under this tab. These are the same application roles that were created in *Chapter 5, Understanding the Systems Management Tools*.

Notice that there is one application role, authenticated-user, that doesn't show in this list of roles This application role has special properties within Fusion Middleware Security. Special consideration should be taken before removing this role from the Enterprise Manager Fusion Middleware Control application roles panel. But if your project's security calls for stringent control and you need to remove this role, please note that this will immediately affect the BI Consumer application role and all other principals related to it.

Creating the Tennis data source JDBC connection

As a prerequisite to this chapter you should have already deployed the Tennis database to your relational database management system. This exercise will make reference to the database dump conducted against an Oracle RDBMS. The JDBC connection information should be similar if you are using a MySQL database:

1. Navigate back to the BI Publisher Administration page.

2. Click on **JDBC Connection**.

3. On the **JDBC** tab, click on the **Add Data Source** button.

4. Enter your database connection information in the fields available under the **General** section of the **Add Data Source** page.

5. In the **Data Source Name** field, enter **Tennis DB**:

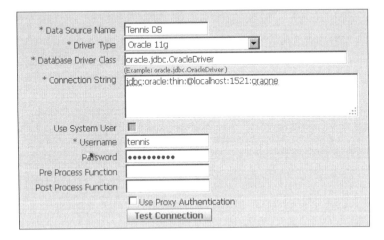

6. Click on the **Test Connection** button to validate that the information entered is accurate and returns a successful test message.

7. Scroll down to the bottom of the page and focus on the **Security** section.

8. Select **BI Author Role** in the **Available Roles** column and use the **Move** button to add this role to the **Allowed Roles** column.

9. Scroll back to the top of the **Add Data Source** page.

10. Click on the **Apply** button located towards the right of the page.

Creating a File (XLS) data source

In order to use any type of file as a data source with BI Publisher, the potential data source filesystem location must be declared as a data source, using the same principle as creating any other connection. The interesting thing about the filesystem data source is that you have to assign a top-level filesystem directory as the source, and not the individual file itself, in the administration page. At a later time, this allows you to either upload the file or leverage a file that exists in the data source directory as a feed for your reports. To keep it simple, let's create a File data source in a readily available path on your server:

1. In the BI Publisher Administration page, click on the **File** link under the **Data Sources** subsection.

2. Click on the **Add Data Source** button.

3. In the **Data Source Name** field, enter `Tennis Files`.

4. In the **Full Path of the Top-level Directory** field, enter `C:/Temp/` or some other folder that is located on the server where you have installed Oracle BI Publisher. On a Linux system, this may be `/home/<user>/`, for example.

 If you are using an MS Windows OS, it may be necessary to enter the directory path using forward slashes and not the standard backslashes. This is usually due to the Java OS agnostic escaping of special characters of which a Nix system is already compliant when it comes to the handling of a directory path syntax.

5. In the **Security** subsection, select **BI Author Role** in the **Available Roles** column and use the **Move** button to add this role to the **Allowed Roles** column.

6. Click on the **Apply** button located towards the right of the page.

Verifying application role data source privileges

After creating several data sources, there is a simple way to verify the data source assignment privileges for each application role:

1. On the BI Publisher Administration page, click on the **Roles and Permissions** link under the **Security Center** subsection.

2. On the **BI Author Role** row, click on the key image under the **Add Data Sources** column.

3. The resulting page **Add Data Sources: BI Author Role** shows all assigned data source privileges from the data sources created so far.

Please note that this is not the same as row-level security. It merely denotes the data sources that users assigned to the BI Author application role are allowed to access.

4. Scroll back to the top of this page and click on the **Cancel** button towards the top-right of the page.

Be aware that the session timeout settings differ in BI Publisher when compared to Oracle BI Foundation Presentation Services. You may be conducting configurations in the BI Publisher Administration page via Oracle BI Presentation Services and notice that some commands don't function properly. This may be due to your BI Publisher session timing out. If so, click on the **Administration** link in the global header again and navigate to **Manage BI Publisher** once more.

Setting up a data model

Now that the data sources have been created, the data model modeling can begin. This is a standard initial process. First, plan and select the data sources. Second, create a data model.

A helpful hint for any administrator is to plan out the initial process as diligently as possible to avoid a maintenance burden.

During the creation of data sources, enter proper descriptions, and keep notes as to why the data sources were created, and so on. Because of the ease of adding data sources without enterprise top-down guidance like the Oracle BI metadata repository RPD, it is easy to have superfluous or nonutilized data sources cluttering the tool. Part of a BI Publisher administrator's duties may be to design a solid security model that restricts the number of users who can build a data model in order to keep the number of data models in the system manageable. On that note, let's get cracking with creating our first simple data model.

> This exercise and the remainder of the development exercises will take place in the Oracle BI Presentation Services portal. Although the BI Publisher environment /xmlpserver application can be used for development, our examples follow the principle that the two environments are fully integrated and the most common entry point to the system will be the OBIEE Presentation Services.

Creating a new Presentation Catalog folder

Like **Object Orient Programming (OOP)** all Oracle BI artifacts should be organized in a way that common artifacts are grouped together and made able to be easily repurposed whenever possible. Oracle BI Publisher 11*g* provides this capability to reuse data models across multiple reports. Let's begin by creating the container folder:

1. Log in to the Oracle BI /analytics portal with the WebLogic administrator user credentials.

2. Click on the **Catalog** link in the global header:

3. On the **Catalog** page, click on the **Shared Folders** folder in the **Folders** pane.

4. Click on the new icon from the menu bar and click on the new **Folder** icon to create a new folder:

5. Name the folder as **Tennis** when the **New Folder** prompt appears.

6. You should now have a folder named **Tennis** under the **Shared Folders** catalog directory. In the next step, we will create a data model and add it to this folder.

Creating a new data model

In this section, you will create a single data model for the tennis reports that we will create soon:

1. Click on the **New** dropdown from the **Global Header** section and select the **Data Model** option under the **Published Reporting** section:

2. On the resulting page, several fields are available to begin entering metadata for the data model.

3. In the **Description** field, enter **Tennis DB Data Model**.

4. In the **Default Data Source** field, change the drop-down field value to **Tennis DB**.

5. Click on the **Save disk** icon in the upper-right corner of the web page. It is located underneath the **Sign Out** link area. The **Save As** dialog box will appear.

6. In the **Name** field, change the **Untitled** value to **DM_Tennis**.

7. Select the **Tennis** folder, which you created in the previous exercise, from the folders in the dialog box on the left-hand side of the page.

8. Click on the **OK** button in the **Save As** dialog box to complete the operation.

Creating a SQL query data set

A data model can hold one or more related or unrelated data sets. Data sets are the means to which the data we wish to populate reports is organized. The first data set to create is one that allows the data in our Tennis database to be joined logically. Even though a relationship may exist at the physical database via a primary key/ foreign key relationship, it must still be logically represented in BI Publisher. This logical representation of the relationships allows the GUI interface to manage and optimize queries, parameterization, and so on. Follow the next steps to create a simple data set for the main report that you will create:

1. Open the **DM_Tennis** data model, created while following the steps mentioned in the preceding section, if not already open.

2. Expand the **Data Model** node in the left pane of the **Data Model Editor** and click on the **Data Sets** option.

3. The main editor window will show that the **Diagram** tab is selected and the **Global Level Functions** layout node is available.

4. Click on the new data set icon and select the **SQL Query** option:

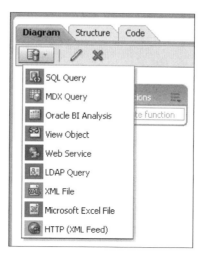

5. In the **Create Data Set – SQL** prompt:
   ° Enter **DS_Tournament_Info** in the **Name** field.
   ° Select the **Tennis DB** option from the **Data Source** drop-down list.

6. Click on the **Query Builder** button in order to select the SQL tables that will comprise the data set.

7. The **Query Builder** window will open and the data source's available objects will be listed on the left pane of the window.

8. Click on the following tables in the left pane of the window to bring them into the main panel of the **Query Builder**:

   ○ **W_TOURNAMENT_F**

   ○ **W_PLAYER_D**

   ○ **W_DATE_D**

   ○ **W_COURT_TYPE_D**

   ○ **W_TOURNAMENT_D**

9. Join the tables with their respective relationships by clicking on the empty box corresponding to the column of each table where a relationship exists.

10. Click on the empty box besides the **W_COURT_TYPE_WID** column of the **W_COURT_TYPE_D** table.

11. Now click on the empty box besides the **COURT_TYPE_WID** column in the **W_TOURNAMENT_F** table.

12. This creates the join between the two tables. The join is indicated by a light blue line:

13. Check the checkbox next to **COURT_TYPE** in the **W_COURT_TYPE_D** table.

14. The join will be successful but the columns that will be retrieved from that table will not be defined. To surface columns in a data set, the checkbox corresponding to the desired column of each table must be checked.

15. Using the same join routine as mentioned in the preceding step, join the following table (column) references below to the respective columns in the **W_TOURNAMENT_F** table.

    ○ **W_TOURNAMENT_D (TOURNAMENT_WID)** to **TOURNAMENT_WID**

    ○ **W_PLAYER_D (PLAYER_WID)** to **PLAYER_WID**

    ○ **W_DATE_D (DATE_WID)** to **START_DATE_WID**

16. To surface the correct column fields that we wish to use in a report, click on the checkbox corresponding to the following table (column) references:

    ○ **W_TOURNAMENT_D (TOURNAMENT_NAME)**

    ○ **W_TOURNAMENT_D (START_DATE)**

    ○ **W_PLAYER_D (NAME)**

    ○ **W_DATE_D (YEAR)**

17. Click on the **Save** button in the **Query Builder** window.

18. This will return you to the **Create Data Set – SQL** window.

    This window will show the joins that have been made during your interaction with the Query Builder. However, the generated syntax is not always the best syntactically. Advanced queries should leverage a predefined SQL statement to save time and ensure accuracy. Create your SQL in a SQL IDE, such as Oracle SQL Developer first, and then copy and paste it into the **SQL Query** field. This is often a best practice. As a shortcut, remove the content from the **SQL Query** field and type or paste in the following more advanced SQL statement:

```
SELECT D.TOURNAMENT_NAME, COUNT(B.NAME) AS PLAYERS, COURT_TYPE,
START_DATE
FROM W_TOURNAMENT_F A
INNER JOIN W_PLAYER_D B ON B.PLAYER_WID = A.PLAYER_WID
INNER JOIN w_date_d C ON C.DATE_WID = A.START_DATE_WID
INNER JOIN w_tournament_d D on D.TOURNAMENT_WID = A.TOURNAMENT_WID
INNER JOIN w_court_type_d E ON E.court_type_WID = A.court_type_wid
WHERE
C.YEAR = 2001
GROUP BY D.TOURNAMENT_NAME, C.CALENDAR_DATE, COURT_TYPE, START_
DATE, END_DATE
ORDER BY TOURNAMENT_NAME
```

19. Click on the **OK** button to close the **Create Data Set – SQL** window.

20. The resulting data set will be displayed in the main editor pane and also in the left pane with the name that we have defined:

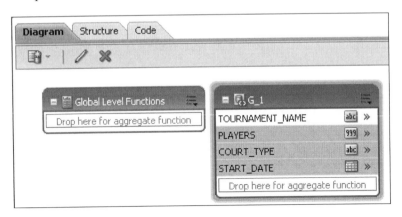

Adjusting data set display names

Each data set has the ability to represent columns with an alias just like in a standard SQL. Using the Query Builder, the names that would ultimately be shown to report developers and report viewers are the physical data source column names. However, they can be changed in the data set, so that these business names are there by default when development starts:

1. Click on the **Structure** tab in the main editor window. The tabs are located directly above the option you selected earlier to create a data set.

2. Make sure the **Table View** option is selected.

3. In the fifth column to the right under the **Business View** header, the **Display Name** column shows the value displayed for this data set column. Click in the field for each of the **DS_Tournament_Info** columns and change the values in the **Display Name** field to the following business name representations:
   - **TOURNAMENT_NAME** to **Tournament Name**
   - **PLAYERS** to **Players**
   - **COURT_TYPE** to **Court Type**
   - **START_DATE** to **Start Date**

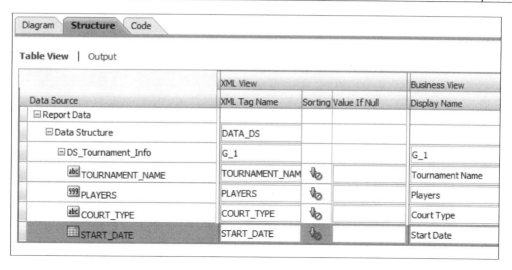

4. Click on the save disk icon to save the data model. The save disk icon is located under the **Sign Out** link in the upper-right corner of the web page.

Creating a parameter

By default a SQL data set is static. That is to say that the current logic you have coded in your SQL statement will not change or be dynamically filtered. Static reports are too rigid to be effective in today's enterprise. So, parameterization or the ability to change a data set by passing a variable to replace a filtered value within the query, creates a dynamic result. One or more parameter variables can be created for a data model. A parameter can be created explicitly just as you created a data set by selecting the option in the left pane and then creating the parameter in the main editor, or it can be done using the Data Set Editor itself. Now we'll conduct an exercise using the latter approach:

1. Return to the **DS_Tournament_Info** data set.
2. Click on the **Diagram** tab in the Data Model Editor.
3. Click on the data set to select it.
4. Click on the pencil icon for editing a data set from the menu under the **Diagram** tab.
5. In the **SQL Query** field, in the SQL statement find the WHERE clause with the following syntax:

```
WHERE
C.YEAR = 2001
```

6. Change the SQL syntax to the following by modifying the value `2001` to `:p_year`:

```
WHERE
C.YEAR = :p_year
```

7. Ensure the syntax is correct (that is a colon before `p_year`) and click on the **OK** button.

8. Notice that after you click on the **OK** button, you are prompted with the following question:

   Do you want to create a bind parameter? :P_YEAR

9. Click on the **OK** button to accept and close the prompt. You'll receive a successful information notification prompt after the parameter gets created. Click on the **OK** button on that prompt also.

10. Save the data model again.

11. On the left-hand side of the Data Model Editor, you will notice that under the **Parameters** option, a new item now exists—**p_year**.

Creating a list of values

A parameter is now in place to dynamically adjust the SQL query result set. A good idea is to provide a drop-down list, or similar, to allow for selecting one or more values to manipulate our new dynamic query. In BI Publisher, this is commonly referred to as a **list of values**. A list of values can be either a hardcoded static list defined once, or it can stem from a data source query. This example uses the former approach. To create a static list of values follow the next instructions:

1. Click on the **List of Values** option on the left-hand side pane of the data model.

2. Click on the green plus icon to add a new list of values.

3. Enter new values in the following column fields:
   - Enter **LOV_YEAR** in the **Name** field.
   - Select **Fixed Data** from the **Type** dropdown.

4. A new sublevel appears after selecting the **Fixed Data** value from the **Type** dropdown.

5. Click on the green plus icon in the sublevel table to create the first record of the static fixed data, which will ultimately become a value in a drop-down list containing years that will get passed into the data set, which we created earlier.

6. Enter the following values for the new record:

    ° Enter **ATP-1999** in the **Label** column field.

    ° Enter **1999** in the **Value** column field.

7. Click on the green plus icon again to confirm the above input and create a new record.

8. Repeat steps 5 and 6 to enter values for years 2000 and 2001 for a total of three records.

9. Click on the **Save** button icon to save the data model:

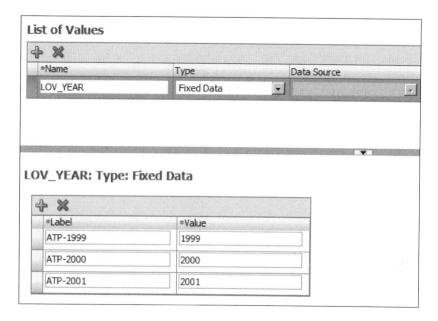

Connecting the parameter to the list of values

1. The parameter p_year is associated with the data set, but now the list of values **LOV_YEAR** needs to be associated to the parameter. This is fairly straightforward and one of the last steps in wrapping up this data model exercise:

2. Click on the parameter **p_year** on the left pane of the Data Model Editor.

3. On the **p_year** row:

    ° Change the **Data Type** column to **Integer**.

    ° Enter **1999** in the **Default Value** column field.

    ° Select **Menu** from the **Parameter Type** dropdown.

4. After selecting the **Menu** as **Parameter Type**, a subsection is revealed in the main editor.

   ° Change the **Display Label** value from the default value to **Year**.

   ° Change the **List of Values** dropdown to **LOV_YEAR**.

5. Deselect the **Multiple Selection** and **Can select all** checkbox options:

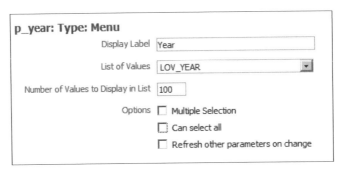

6. Save the data model.

Getting the sample data

Once you are satisfied that the data model is complete for your data requirements (or even during the course of your iterative development), it is always a good idea to look at the data that now stems from your creation. BI Publisher looks at this as sampling your data. This sample data has three purposes. The first allows you to see that your data set has been created correctly and allows you to test your parameterizations and other properties on a small scale. The second allows you to see your data represented in XML format, which is ultimately how BI Publisher data is put together so that it can then leverage open standards for formatting, and so on. The third is that a sample data file will be saved in XML format, so that it can then be used to assist you in creating your reports without having to send repetitive queries back to the underlying data source.

The third point highlights a key distinction from report development with OBIEE's ad-hoc analysis tool versus the production reporting of BI Publisher. With OBIEE's Interactive Reporting, the focus is mostly on the consumption of data. So, even when developing the report, the query attempts to ping the underlying data source each time the analysis request is displayed. BI Publisher has a heavier focus on aesthetics. So, leveraging a sample data file prevents overhead and keeps an emphasis on production report development.

To get at the sample data, follow the next instructions:

1. From the Data Model Editor, click on the XML icon in the upper-right corner of the web page. The icon is to the left of the save icon:

2. The resulting page shows the parameter for **Year** at the top of the page and also provides an option to select the number of rows that should be returned.

3. Change the **Year** dropdown to **ATP-1999**.

4. Change the **Number of rows to return** to **50**.

5. Click on the **Run** button.

6. The results are returned in the XML format and this sample set of data is ready to be saved as our sample data.

7. Click on the small icon menu next to the **Return** button towards the upper-right corner of the web page.

8. Select the **Save As Sample Data** option:

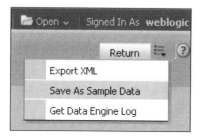

9. Review the Data Model Editor main page that you are now returned to after selecting the option to save the sample data. Click on the data model parent level in the left pane hierarchy, if not taken to this area by default. Under the **Attachment** section, you should see a listing for a **sample.xml** file.

You've successfully created a data model that provides some dynamic functionality. You should now have a good idea of how the baseline data source configurations are put together. Let's wrap up by creating a simple report, using the web-based GUI.

Creating a BI Publisher report using Layout Editor

Just like the Data Model Editor, which handles the configuration of data sources by using a **Dynamic HyperText Markup Language (DHTML)** web-based interface, a complementing report design tool within BI Publisher—**Layout Editor**—also uses DHTML. Prior to the 11*g* release of BI Publisher, users were relegated to using software suite (for example MS Word) plugins in order to create templates to layout reports and ultimately publish those reports for consumption. Now, the same pixel-perfect layout and design efforts can be achieved in full Web 2.0 glory, using the Layout Editor.

 Fortunately for those still enamored with the legacy plugin template approach, backwards compatibility is in place.

Some argue that using the software plugins to develop BI Publisher templates, provides more control than what the Layout Editor currently provides. This is debatable. However, for those moving forward on the 11*g* roadmap, any templates created using the software plugins can be uploaded to the Layout Editor for immediate or later use.

Each time you attempt to create a published report in Oracle BI 11*g*, you will be prompted to select an existing data model, create a new one, or upload a spreadsheet to leverage as the data model. You've created a simple data model in the exercise shown in the preceding section, so that it won't be a problem. After that selection is made, you'll be prompted to select a layout that defines the initial format of your report. You can create a new template, select from a set of very generic starter templates, upload an existing template, or have BI Publisher generate the layout for you based on the structure of the selected data model. You will use the latter option by following the next steps:

1. From the global header, select **New** | **Report** under the **Published Reporting** section of the drop-down list:

2. Select the **Use Existing Data Model** option from the prompt that appears:

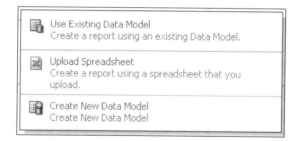

 In version 11.1.1.6+, selecting this option opens a **Create Report** wizard with several steps that facilitate report creation. If you are using an Oracle BI 11*g* version less than 11.1.1.6, no wizard is available and after you select to use an existing data model, you would locate the model and click on the **OK** button to close the prompt. The new **Create Report** wizard is intuitive to the user, allows you to search for artifacts related to your initial report creation and provides guidance that is great for a beginner.

3. Locate the **DM_Tennis** data model file from the **Shared Folders | Tennis** folder.
4. Select the **DM_Tennis** file and click on the **Next** button.
5. Select the **Use Report Editor** option and click on the **Finish** button:

6. In the **Save As** dialog box:
   ° Create a new folder called **Reports** by using the new folder icon option.
   ° Save the file in the **Shared Folders | Tennis | Reports** folder.
   ° Enter **Tennis Tournament Report** in the **Name** field by replacing any existing default text.

7. Click on the **OK** button to close the dialog box.

8. Click on the **Generate** page image under the **Upload** or **Generate Layout** section:

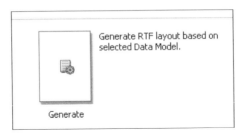

9. The **Auto Generate Layout** prompt will appear.

10. Enter **Players Per Tournament** in the **Template Name** field.

11. Click on the **Generate** button to confirm and initiate the autogenerate layout process.

    The resulting page shows the report's layout inventory page with a single autogenerated layout. Most of what needs to be done next requires that you first save the report.

12. Click on the save icon in the upper-right corner of the web page. You should frequently save reports as you develop to prevent loss of work.

13. Click on the **View Report** icon/link next to the save icon to display the autogenerated report:

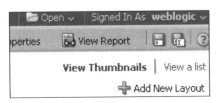

14. The **Players Per Tournament** layout of the **Tennis Tournament Report** is displayed in all of its very basic data grid glory, along with the parameterized **List of Values** dropdown at the top of the page.

15. Change the value in the **Year** dropdown from **ATP-1999** to **ATP-2000** and click on the **Apply** button.

16. Notice that the report changes. You can confirm the change from the **Start Date** column:

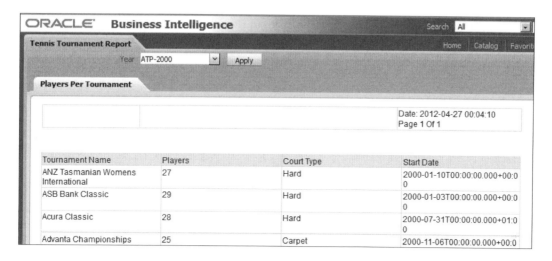

The report is now at a stage where much more in-depth aesthetic design with charts, and so on could ensue. Using the basic functionality and nice autogenerate feature of the Layout Editor, you saw how easy it is to leverage an existing data model to build a quick report. You can see that a published report can contain one or more layouts. Those layouts can stem from templates designed using the Layout Editor or from an uploaded template from one of the software plugins. The standard data format for a template is a **Rich Text Format (RTF)** file noted by the RTF file extension. This Tennis Tournament published report could now be embedded in an Oracle BI dashboard in the /analytics portal for user consumption or for quick export to MS Excel, if one is only after the data.

Auditing and monitoring BI Publisher

The release of Oracle BI Publisher 11*g* brought with it a new capability to retrieve and analyze details about the way users interact with the tool. As a mainly web-based consumption tool for reporting, users are logging in to the system, viewing reports, and spending time analyzing data. It should be clear that there is a need from both a security compliance perspective and a performance improvement perspective to collect information regarding how users are using the tool. Since BI Publisher 11*g* is integrated with Oracle Fusion Middleware, it can now leverage the Fusion Middleware Audit Framework.

This is a profound change to the way spelunking through log files for this information was done in the past. The auditing system information can be dumped to a file's system log or a relational database. Clearly with the relational database as the repository, BI Publisher, or some other reporting tool, can easily consume that data feed and frontend some quality auditing analytics. It is fairly straightforward to set up and configure. This exercise will walk you through how to achieve this ancillary configuration, since the configuration is not set up by default out of the box.

Modifying a few configuration files

This is fairly straightforward. A configuration change needs to be made in two files so that BI Publisher can recognize the change for capturing and writing the audit information. The following steps should take place on the server where BI Publisher and the Oracle BI server are installed:

1. Locate the `xmlp-server-config.xml` file. This file is located down the long directory path of `$BI_HOME\user_projects\domains\bifoundation_domain\config\bipublisher\repository\Admin\Configuration\`.

2. Edit the `xmlp-server-config.xml` file using WordPad or similar.

3. Set the following element value properties to `true` from their default value of `false`:

    ○ `MONITORING_ENABLED`

    ○ `AUDIT_ENABLED`

4. Add the following element and syntax to the `xmlp-server-config.xml` file directly before the closing `</xmlpConfig>` tag:

    `<property name="AUDIT_JPS_INTEGTRATION" value="true" />`

5. The last part of the file should appear as shown in the following screenshot:

```
<property name="SAW_USERNAME" value=""/>
<property name="SAW_URL_SUFFIX" value="analytics/saw.dll"/>
<property name="MONITORING_ENABLED" value="true"/>
<property name="MONITORING_DEFAULT_HISTORY_SIZE" value="30"/>
<property name="AUDIT_ENABLED" value="true"/>
<property name="JSESSION_RESET_DISABLED" value="true"/>
<property name="SECURITY_MODEL" value="ORACLE_AS_JPS"/>
<property name="AUDIT_JPS_INTEGRATION" value="true"/>
</xmlpConfig>
```

6. Save and close the `xmlp-server-config.xml` file.

Connecting to the Audit Framework

The FMW Audit Framework will now need to have reference to how BI Publisher handles the collection of its auditing information. Copying the existing BI Publisher audit events file to the common directory, where auditing information can be read, is done in a few simple steps:

1. Locate the directory path `$BI_HOME\oracle_common\modules\oracle.iau_11.1.1\components\`.

2. Create a new directory called `xmlpserver` in this path using the native OS make a directory command, for example `mkdir xmlpserver`.

3. If on a Nix OS, be sure to set the read/write permissions according to the same folders existing in this directory.

4. Locate the `component_events.xml` file from `$BI_HOME\user_projects\domains\bifoundation_domain\config\bipublisher\repository\Admin\Audit\`.

5. Copy the `component_events.xml` file to the `xmlpserver` directory created in step 2.

Enabling Audit Policy in the Fusion Middleware Control Enterprise Manager

Using the Fusion Middleware Control Enterprise Manager, the last major configuration to set up auditing can be completed:

1. Log in to Fusion Middleware Control Enterprise Manager.
2. On the left-hand side pane, expand **WebLogic Domain**.
3. Right-click on the **bifoundation_domain** option.
4. Select **Security | Audit Policy**.
5. Click on the row for **BI Publisher Server** to select it.
6. Change the **Audit Level** drop-down value to **Medium**.
7. Notice that the **Enable Audit** column will render several green check marks in place of the **BI Publisher Server**.
8. Click on the **Apply** button in the upper-right corner of the page.
9. As you can see from the Information note at the top of this section, all changes made to this page require a server restart to take effect.
10. Restart the WebLogic Server, which will first entail stopping all Oracle BI system components.

After the Oracle BI 11*g* system restarts, the configuration for auditing will now be in place for Oracle BI Publisher. All login, logout, and report access information will be captured and stored into a physical file on the server. This information could also be stored in a database schema that the RCU utility creates specifically for FMW Auditing. To extend the auditing information for storage in a relational database, and not the filesystem, a few additional steps, including running the RCU utility again, (remember you ran the RCU once before during the installation of Oracle BI 11*g* in *Chapter 2, Installing the Metadata Repository*) are required.

Viewing the auditing log file

Confirm that the WebLogic Server has been restarted. Start the Oracle BI system components and confirm that the /analytics application is available. You would normally check it when making the Oracle BI server available. To check if the log file is working properly, follow the next steps:

1. Log in to the /analytics server, for example,
   http://<server_name>:<server_port>/analytics/.

2. Click on the **Catalog** link from the global header.

3. Expand the folders **Shared Folders** | **Tennis** and click on the **Reports** folder.

4. Click on the **Open** link for the **Tennis Tournament Report**.

5. Clicking on this link will open the report within the Oracle BI Analytics application and will trigger the audit log file to be created and begin retaining entries.

6. On the Oracle BI server, locate the audit.log file in $BI_HOME\user_ projects\domains\bifoundation_domain\servers\bi_server1\logs\ auditlogs\xmlpserver\.

7. Open the audit.log file to view the entries.

Viewing the audit.log file, you can see that one or more entries have been made based on your actions against the BI Publisher report. If you change the report display to HTML or PDF, another audit line will be registered in the file. You cannot delete the file while the WebLogic Server is running as it is locked for writing by the **Java Virtual Machine (JVM)** process that is controlling the auditing functionality. The audit log entries are somewhat cryptic but still legible. You can clearly see the name of the user accessing the report, the report display type, timestamps, and so on. The next step which is beyond the scope of this book would be to configure the auditing and monitoring data to be placed into a database instead of the filesystem. A database audit repository would allow you to frontend some of this information and analyze its data with any other data.

BI Publisher nuances

A few common questions have arisen with the new BI Publisher and Oracle BI embedded integration of 11*g*. Though not an exhaustive list, these few items warrant mention here.

Timeout issues

You may have noticed that your session timed out while conducting the exercises in this chapter. If you didn't this time around, you will most likely experience this at some point while developing within Oracle BI Publisher 11*g*. The session timeout is actually not readily configurable for BI Publisher via any GUI as it is with Oracle BI Presentation Services. The timeout for BI Publisher is set to 30 minutes, by default, with a warning around 15 minutes of inactivity. In order to change this, you will need to inflate/decompress the BI Publisher JEE **Enterprise Archive (EAR)** file deployed on the WebLogic Server. Then you will need to access the web.xml file and modify the session-timeout property to a higher value in order to increase the timeout period. From there you can recompile the inflated files back into the EAR file format and redeploy the application to the application server.

Connecting to Oracle BI server data sources

Yes, Oracle BI server can be used as a data source to create a data set in the BI Publisher. A newcomer to the Oracle BI might think that since the Oracle BI server RPD is accessible via Presentation Services and an ODBC connection, then BI Publisher should be able to access the RPD subject areas, just as Oracle BI can. This logic is only partially correct. BI Publisher does not currently have the ability to cherry pick Oracle BI subject area elements as if using the Analysis Ad-Hoc Editor. BI Publisher has two options to reference the Oracle BI server data. The first is to select an saved analysis request developed in the Analysis Ad-Hoc Editor. Typically, this will be an analysis request created specifically for the purpose of being consumed in a BI Publisher report. That report is usually saved in a folder location close to the BI Publisher report that ultimately leverages the said data. The second option is to create an analysis request, select the **Advanced** tab in the Ad-Hoc Editor, and copy the SQL that is generated for that request. That SQL can then be pasted into a BI Publisher data set. The latter option is the best option.

BI Publisher Application Programming Interface (API)

BI Publisher offers third-party or custom integration functionality via a Java API and a set of web services that communicate with the BI Publisher server. These API methods can interface with just about all areas of BI Publisher including user management, translation deployment, managing portions of the catalog, scheduling artifacts for delivery, and more. In many ways, this API is similar to the Oracle BI API, however for day-to-day functionality to advanced functionality of communication with an application, the BI Publisher API seems to be better-rounded. Keep in mind that the BI Publisher API does not communicate with the BI server directly or vice-versa.

BI Publisher Scheduler

The Oracle BI development team hasn't yet flushed out all of the integration points between BI Publisher and the Oracle BI server as of this release. One of those disconnects has to do with the way the Oracle BI Server's scheduler system delivers, distributes, or bursts its artifacts to the masses. Currently the BI Publisher Scheduler, referred to as the **Quartz Scheduler**, and the Oracle BI Server Scheduler, Delivers, are separate tools. Oracle BI Delivers cannot burst BI Publisher reports, although they may reside in the same Presentation Catalog. However, currently the BI Publisher Quartz Scheduler is much more powerful than the Oracle BI Delivers Scheduler and it has a better API. It has delivery destinations that can be configured and a more robust failover system that can take advantage of another open standard application—Apache ActiveMQ.

High availability

Determining failover and highly available architectures for Oracle BI Publisher in standalone mode poses no major challenges when compared to the HA topology and configuration for the Oracle BI Enterprise Edition. Luckily, when Oracle BI Publisher 11*g* is embedded in the Oracle BI Enterprise Edition, the BI Publisher HA architecture follows the core HA topology for the larger Oracle BI Server platform implementation. This makes sense seeing how both applications will be deployed to the same managed application server and, by default, share the same metadata database repository schema created by the RCU.

A review – what I should now know!

For self-review and a recap of the chapter, here are a few questions. There is no answer key. These questions are for your own reflection on this chapter:

1. What is a BI Publisher data model?
2. What is the relationship of layouts/templates to a BI Publisher report?
3. What qualitative information can BI Publisher auditing provide?
4. What does the acronym JNDI stand for? What is the difference between using it and a standard JDBC connection?
5. Describe the main benefit of developing a report in the BI Publisher versus Oracle BI Analysis/Answers.

Additional research suggestions

This chapter looked at the integrated Oracle BI Publisher 11*g* product that comes with the Oracle BI 11*g* Enterprise Edition. Here are a few recommended topics for you to investigate further on your own to continue your learning:

- **Oracle BI Publisher best practices**: http://www.obi11gbook.com/u/9
- **Translation/Localization**: http://www.obi11gbook.com/u/10
- **BI Publisher upgrade**: http://www.obi11gbook.com/u/11
- **BI Publisher API**: http://www.obi11gbook.com/u/12
- **BI Publisher auditing and monitoring to a relational database**:
    - http://www.obi11gbook.com/u/13
    - http://www.obi11gbook.com/u/14

Summary

This chapter provided information about Oracle BI Publisher 11*g*'s new features and several of its nuances. It briefly compared Oracle BI and BI Publisher, and discussed some commonalities. You walked through an exercise that allowed you to interact with the new Data Model Editor and Layout Editor for a first-hand experience. This chapter highlighted terminologies that are used specifically when working with BI Publisher and other terminologies that continue to build your knowledge about Java and the WebLogic Application Server. In the exercises, you continued to use the data source from the Tennis database with which you should now be familiar. Finally, you were able to configure the BI Publisher auditing and monitoring functionality. The auditing configuration currently places metadata into a filesystem location for logging and you saw how that process works and is managed.

The next chapter continues your education on Oracle BI 11*g*'s flexibility by showing you how to customize the look and feel of the application's portal and dashboards.

13
Customizing the Style of Dashboards

Several of the previous chapters have discussed the idea of integrating Oracle BI with other applications and components, such as those derived from the Oracle Application Development Framework. This highlights Oracle BI's externalized data related flexibility, but what about changing the look of the portal or adding a button to a dashboard? What if there is a desire to match the Oracle BI dashboard portal colors to that of the organization, which purchased the software? Is there a way to do this? Better yet, is there a way to do this efficiently? This chapter answers these questions, provides a step-by-step how-to, and provides several other insights for continued development and research.

What's the idea?

Let's first qualify what it means to customize the style of the Oracle BI dashboard. There are several approaches to modify the look, feel, and overall integration associated with the Oracle BI dashboard. This could include anything from adding a custom button or link, appending a third-party widget, changing the logo, or changing the color scheme present in the out-of-the-box Oracle BI product. Now that the definition is out of the way, the question is, what do the customization requirements seek to accomplish? Do the customizations seek to modify form, function, or both?

The most common directive of customizing a dashboard has to do with modifying the color scheme seen in the Oracle BI portal. This is referred to as **Branding**. Branding is actually a marketing term, but it is used ubiquitously for this scenario as it applies to web-based applications. One of the main ideas behind branding the Oracle BI portal is to increase user adoption among the user base.

Internally, users are much more likely to begin using Oracle BI and stay within the tool, if it doesn't seem foreign to their current corporate tools. Think about it this way, if Sally Joe in Finance navigated from her company's Intranet, which clearly displays the company logo, colors, and so on, using a hyperlink on the main page, to an Oracle BI dashboard in order to view a profit and loss report, the segue could potentially appear seamless. That is, Sally Joe would see the requested data in the dashboard and still appear to be within her company Intranet instead of a bland (although kind of good looking) out-of-the-box application that looks like some new tool she has to learn.

This chapter focuses mainly on that branding of Oracle BI 11*g*.

Multiple skins and styles in one environment

Oracle BI can house several customized looks or branding profiles. This is often dynamically set by associating a particular style with a particular user, group, or application role. Let's say Sally Joe in the Finance department logs in to the Oracle BI portal. Sally may be presented with a blue and white color scheme, with the corporate logo showing in the portal, whereas her constituent Erich in the European office, may log in to the Oracle BI portal and be presented with a brown and gold color scheme showing the Deutschland flag as the logo. This dynamic shifting of branding to specific end users can be achieved by relating a specific style to a specific user, group, or application role. It could also be established by setting a default style for all users and having only specified users, groups, and roles associated with a different perspective.

Another nuance is that several aspects of branding can be localized. That is to say that depending on the locale or location from which the end users have associated themselves (usually determined by the browser and language settings of the workstation being used), a different appearance or branding may be applied and rendered during their interaction within the Oracle BI portal. This can be seen ubiquitously in the exercise steps for custom messages in this chapter.

A strategy for something seemingly simple

This could be both a statement and question. Why does an organization need a strategy for customizing their Oracle BI dashboards? Having a plan or well-defined approach to implement or configure anything technology-related, usually saves both time and money. Also, taking best practices into consideration will usually provide a better result and more efficient use of resources with less rework. For the sake of not making this chapter about intangible concepts, the strategy conveyed here simmers down to four concepts:

- Involve the Marketing department
- Don't boil the ocean
- Speed to implementation
- Build a focus group

Involve the Marketing department

In most organizations, the team that governs the company's branding standards, logo specifications, color guidelines, and usages is the Marketing department. This is one of those situations where cross department efforts can garner a big win. Involving the Marketing department in an Oracle BI branding effort may not only contribute to the successful implementation of Oracle BI, but also you could win some friends as well. During the branding process, you will need information that usually stems from the Marketing team, such as logos, hexadecimal color codes (hex codes), and quite possibly some domain knowledge.

 In smaller organizations, the Marketing department and the Web/Application development teams may be one and the same, so adjust accordingly.

Don't boil the ocean

The concept of "Don't boil the ocean" has been used for many corporate initiatives. It ultimately attempts to convey the message of not doing everything at once, but executing a plan in manageable chunks. This is a very important part of the strategy in regards to customizing Oracle BI.

Many organizations believe that a proper customization of the Oracle BI dashboard incorporates not only changing the logo and color scheme, but also manipulating the interface, integrating Oracle BI into some external portal as a portlet, and so on. This often includes dropping in plugins or a variety of other mash-up techniques. This list of customizations can become a near unachievable goal, and it may be seen as ancillary to the core technical implementation, which delivers immediate analytical value. What should take place is a phased approach to achieve the branding end-result envisioned. Getting the basics (usually logo and color scheme changes) of Oracle BI branding out the door first is critical. That is why the first part of the strategy is in understanding that this is okay as long as a full branding implementation follows closely behind.

Speed to implementation

What if hundreds of thousands to millions of dollars were paid for software that no one in the company used? That would be a travesty. Let's ask the question with a bit more reasonable elaboration of statistics in mind. What if millions of dollars were paid for software that targeted a thousand users but only 25 percent of those targeted users actually used the software? And, what if the number of users in the last scenario would increase to 50 percent of targeted users just by branding the software, making it more user-friendly, in-turn increasing usage adoption?

The idea here, is that when planning an Oracle BI implementation, thought should be given to making it user friendly for the end-users. Branding helps to achieve this. It is seen time and time again on the open Internet. Generally people are more likely to use a simple, clean, well-designed interface rather than one that is cluttered, ugly, or unfamiliar looking.

Branding the Oracle BI solution as part of the initial implementation gets the message to the end user base that the organization has adopted the software application as an integral part of the company, not as an afterthought. Branding early on ensures the best potential of capturing the highest number of end users to adopt the Oracle BI solution. Although this requires additional effort to effectively measure logically, the early-on branding approach should be more successful in capturing user adoption than not branding at all, or branding at a later time.

Build a focus group

Before releasing Oracle BI to the mass of end users internally or externally, it is a great idea to use a focus group. As it relates to Oracle BI, a focus group would be a small group of power-users that have the ability to communicate their feedback from using the tool. Whether branding the Oracle BI solution, or not, leveraging the focus group concept is a great idea, but it can really be effective while branding.

Because Oracle BI is a software, let's not confuse leveraging a focus group with beta testing. Beta testing is much more involved in the technical perspective. This chapter's focus is on the frontend component and user experience of Oracle BI. What is sought after here is feedback from a subset of users on how the branding changes made may be perceived by the end user base as a whole. Some subsequent development and focus group testing may iteratively take place, so manage this wisely. A focus group phase of a project should not get out of control or become convoluted. The entire branding process can actually be run in parallel to the rest of the development effort.

General knowledge and tools

At the core the Oracle BI portal, which includes dashboards, the ad-hoc analysis development environment, BI Publisher, and so on, is a web application. As such, it abides by all of the rules and properties of any other web application. It has certain files that render the **HyperText Markup Language** (**HTML**) and it contains **cascading stylesheets** (**CSS**) that tell the HTML how to render and what to look like. One way that Oracle BI differs proprietarily with this standard approach is that it also leverages custom templates to dynamically modify the look and feel at runtime. Custom templates are based on **Extensible Markup Language** (**XML**) files and are a unique concept to Oracle BI. During this chapter, the CSS, HTML, and custom templates will be modified to achieve branding.

As a general skill, most web developers will be versed in CSS, HTML, and XML. It is easy to find a vast amount of information on all of these subjects via a quick web search. There are **Integrated Development Environments** (**IDEs**) that are specific to developing each of these technologies — many lump all three or more into the same IDE as they are so common to web development. For most who are not the web developers, following the exercises in this chapter can be achieved by using any popular and free web development IDE such as NetBeans, JDeveloper, Aptana, or Eclipse. The operating system's default Text Editor is more available and usable. This can be WordPad in Microsoft Windows or VI in *Nix.

This chapter attempts to stay at a high level on CSS, HTML, and XML where possible, but it is highly recommended, if you are involved in an organization's Oracle BI branding to research these topics in more detail as development progresses.

Third-party tools

Although this chapter goes into detail about how to brand an Oracle BI implementation, there are third-party tools, which can ease the pain of this manual configuration available in the market. No matter which angle branding is viewed from, there is no automagic (yes, we've used esoteric term automagic, which parodies automatic) way to modify the default Oracle BI colors, logo, and so on. As such, there are two tools known to the market that provide some level of modular customization and deployment of the configuration files required for branding Oracle BI.

Oracle JDeveloper skinning tool

The skinning tool has only been on the market for a few months at the time of writing and is a derivative of the Oracle JDeveloper application and associated framework. The general purpose for this tool is to easily manage and modify the look and feel of the Oracle **Application Development Framework (ADF)** components. The net result of these manipulations is a physical file, or set of files, that contain the necessary information for an application, developed using ADF to have its branding reconfigured. More information on the Oracle BI Skinning Tool can be found at `http://www.obi11gbook.com/u/15`.

BI Consulting Group Identity product

BI Consulting Group (BICG) has developed a product called **Identity** which provides a user-friendly way to configure the files required for branding Oracle BI. The tool allows a user to input the branding colors, logo, and other artifacts surrounding a branding initiative into the application that produces a branding configuration that needs only be manually interjected into the Oracle BI environment. The product reduces a manual effort from days into hours and provides the ability to document changes and version the configuration files. It also provides the ability to quickly iterate through development modifications without the headache of relocating and readdressing each file one at a time. More information about BICG Identity can be found at `http://www.obi11gbook.com/u/16`.

Hands-on – go time!

The remainder of this chapter provides a systematic guide on implementing what is referred to as basic branding. The goal of the exercise is to take an out-of-the-box Oracle BI portal, and transform the default style to contain the logo and colors of Company XYZ. Each step builds upon the one before it, so following the steps in order will be crucial to the end result. It is recommended to leverage the operating system's default text editor when making changes to base files provided by the Oracle BI platform filesystem.

Overview

The steps in the following section take advantage of the Oracle BI 11*g* skinning and styling customization options. Modifying these options is predominantly manual in nature. The idea of look and feel, as it relates to Oracle BI, translates into skins, styles, and messages. Messages are usually the textual elements that are shown in the Oracle BI portal (Presentation services) and can be anything from the header logo and text, to the name of each link shown above the dashboard tabs. An example of the latter would be changing the sign out link on the portal dashboard to render "get out of here!" instead. Styles and skins relate to both the color scheme, shown in the Oracle BI portal, and the visible nature of Oracle BI analysis views. An example of modifying a style would be to change the background color of a dashboard from the default white color to light grey. An example of skinning would be to modify the bar chart's color scheme from its default to a custom color palette.

In this exercise, we will modify the Oracle BI 11*g* dashboard for a fictional organization, Company XYZ. Their standard company color palette is made up of the following:

- Color #1: LightSteelBlue
- Color #2: Grey
- Color #3: Black

Oracle BI 11*g* assists the customization effort to some degree by providing a sample set of skins, styles, and custom messages from which you can follow as a design template. The template from which this exercise will stem, is the `blafp` template. An alternate template — `fusion` — is also provided. Both templates and folder structures can be found in the directory `<Oracle_Home>/bifoundation/web/app/res/`. The folders that should be used as templates are prefixed with `s_` and `sk_`, which specifies the style and skin folders respectively. As an example, one of the default sets of style and skin folders provided out of the box are `s_blafp` and `sk_blafp`. If you are modifying both the skin and styles, both of these folders will be leveraged.

In addition to styles and skins, custom messages will be used to modify the Oracle BI dashboards. There are hundreds of messages within the Oracle BI 11*g* environment that are dynamically accessed and generated at runtime. The core messages can be located in XML files contained within the following folder at `<Oracle_Home>/bifoundation/web/msgdb/messages`. The following screenshot shows a short list of the XML files that categorize the messages that are contained therein:

```
/bishiphome/Middleware/oracle_BI1/bifoundation/web/msgdb/messages
[oracle@demo messages]$ ls
actionframeworkmessages.xml        deliverstemplates.xml                      mktglist
adminsubsystemtemplates.xml        discovererclientsoaprequestmessages.xml    mktgsegme
adminsystemtemplates.xml           dvtchartformattemplates.xml                mktgsegme
analyzermessages.xml               dvtchartviewtemplates.xml                  privileg
analyzertemplates.xml              editcolumnformatcontrolmessages.xml        promptvi
analyzerviewcontrolmessages.xml    formattemplates.xml                        querysub
answerstemplates.xml               gridviewcontrolmessages.xml                remotesy
calendartemplates.xml              kpitemplates.xml                           reportge
catalogcaptiontemplates.xml        languagenames.xml                          reportin
catalogcontrolmessages.xml         legendtemplates.xml                        reportte
charttemplates.xml                 localenames.xml                            resultvi
commonuitemplates.xml              logoncontrolmessages.xml                   scorecar
controlmessages.xml                manageaccountstemplates.xml                scorecar
criteriatemplates.xml              managejobtemplates.xml                     scorecar
dashboardmessages.xml              markuptemplates.xml                        security
dashboardtemplates.xml             mktgadminuitemplates.xml                   security
deliversmessages.xml               mktgcommontemplates.xml                    segmentc
```

Each XML file acts as a grouping container, as suggested by the name, containing one or more message objects that are referenced by Oracle BI at runtime. These messages can be overridden, and a few will be in this exercise. This dynamic messaging system also allows flexibility for localization (that is, translation into other languages or specific text to other languages). In order to either create custom templates or modify a template to another language, a separate `custom messages` folder and XML file will be established away from the `default message` folder referenced in the preceding section. The message that is desired to be overridden, is usually first assessed from the `default messages` folder location. Attributes about the message are noted and the overriding message is then created in a new arbitrarily named XML file. The XML file is placed in a filesystem folder, `analyticsRes`, under the Oracle BI installation path, which is ultimately a web application that gets deployed to the WebLogic Application Server.

> You should never modify the original default skin, styles, or messages folders and/or files directly. A copy of the base files should be made and then modified.

Let's talk about tools and assumptions

Embarking on this exercise, leverages several basic elements to allow for modification of the styles, skins, and messages within the Oracle BI 11*g* environment. Without meeting these prerequisites, completing the following hands-on exercise will not be possible.

The tool used in this exercise is the default text editor (that is, Vim, Wordpad, Notepad, and so on).

Assumptions in this exercise are as follows:

- Administrator access to Oracle BI 11*g* (that is, WebLogic user)
- Read/write access to Oracle BI 11*g*'s operating system filesystem installation and configuration folders (that is, FMW Home and Oracle Home)

To develop in a more advanced environment, clearly you could leverage one of the IDEs mentioned before. This would allow for things such as formatting of the minified CSS files that are provided by the default style templates, and so on.

Locating existing styles and skins

The first step to design a new look and feel is to assess the default styles and skins. This way you can see what is currently available out of the box and also which default skin or style you wish to leverage as a starting point as you begin the branding process. Before the heads-down effort, let's take a quick look at one of the dashboards that we've created in *Chapter 10, Creating Dashboards and Analysis* to understand how each dashboard could potentially have a different style applied to it:

1. Log in to the Oracle BI 11*g* portal that has been established.
2. From the portal main page, navigate to the dashboard **Player Analysis**.
3. In the upper right-hand corner, click on the **Page Options** icon underneath **Signed In As weblogic**.
4. Select **Edit Dashboard**:

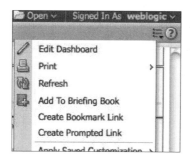

5. From the Dashboard Editor IDE, select the **Tools** menu icon, which is the icon to the left of the **Preview** icon in the menu bar.

6. Select **Dashboard Properties...**:

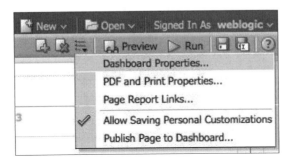

7. The **Dashboard Properties** prompt will appear.

8. A **Style** drop-down is available, which shows an option for each default and custom style available to be leveraged for this specific dashboard being edited.

9. Click on the drop-down to see all available styles.

This quick walk-through will provide insight into the fact that each individual dashboard can be associated with a specific style. Those style options are added dynamically to this list when style template folders are created in the filesystem. You'll learn how to do that in a subsequent section. Conversely, a default style and/or skin for all dashboards can be configured. The latter configuration for setting the default dashboard style will take place during the hands-on exercise. Keep in mind that explicitly setting the dashboard style using the above **Dashboard Properties** editing approach will override the default style and skin configuration.

Developing/designing a new look and feel

In the preceding section we tried to drive the point about branding and how important it is to an implementation. You've finally arrived at the point where you get to do this for yourself by following some step-by-step hands-on exercises.

Getting analyticsRes deployed

Oracle BI 11*g* installs with a default folder, `<Instance_Home>/bifoundation/ OracleBIPresentationServicesComponent/coreapplication_obips1/ analyticsRes`, which is the default location for stashing all custom styles, skins, and custom messages. The folder `analyticsRes` stands for analytics resources. During the Oracle BI installation, this folder is installed by default on the filesystem. Unfortunately, this folder is not automatically deployed as an application on the WebLogic Application Server. Deploying the folder as an application allows Oracle BI Presentation services to acknowledge any files or folders within this directory. This effort must be conducted manually. Deploying the `analyticsRes` folder to the WebLogic Server in order to be leveraged by Oracle BI is the best practice for customizing the Oracle BI portal.

Alternatively, if a developer needed to use another path on a different server or different context root other than `/analyticsRes`, the `instanceconfig.xml` file could be modified using the `CustomerResourceVirtualPath` element in order to have Oracle BI look at a different location for the customization's files. We will discuss the `instanceconfig.xml` file in a subsequent section.

Follow the next steps to deploy the folder `analyticsRes`:

1. Open the WebLogic Server Administration Console and enter `http://<server_name>:7001/console`.

2. On the left panel of the administration interface, click on the **Deployments** link under **Domain Structure | bifoundation_domain**.

3. On the **Deployments** page, the list of deployed java applications and libraries are listed in an alphabetical order. Look quickly to determine if an application named `analyticsRes` is already deployed. If you are following the default installation of Oracle BI 11*g*, there should not be a record for this entry.

 Please note that there will be an existing `analytics` application deployed, but this is not the same as `analyticsRes`.

4. To add `analyticsRes`, the first step in deploying is to lock and edit the WebLogic Server Change Center configuration.

5. On the left panel, click on the **Lock & Edit** button:

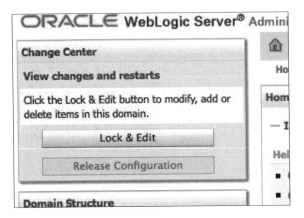

6. Click on the **Install** button on the **Deployments** page.

7. Using the paths and links available, navigate to the **analyticsRes** folder and select the radio button respective to the directory folder from the path `<FMW_Home>/instances/instance1/bifoundation/ OracleBIPresentationServicesComponent/coreapplication_obips1/ analyticsRes`:

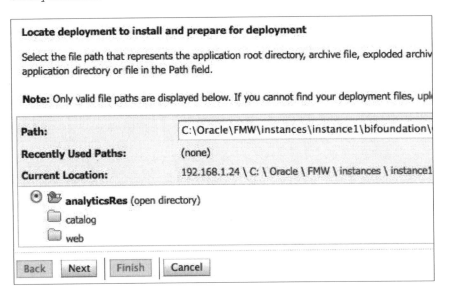

8. Click on **Next**.

9. Select **Install this deployment as an application** and click on **Next**.

10. Check the checkbox next to **bi_cluster** on the **Select deployment targets** step to deploy the `analyticsRes` application to all Oracle BI Managed Server instances across the implementation even if the environment has not yet been scaled-out. This option is bypassed, if the **Simple Installation** option was used to install Oracle BI 11*g* as only the `bi_server1` managed server would not exist.

11. On the **Option Settings** page of the wizard, leave all sections to their defaults except for the **Source accessibility** section. Select the **I will make the deployment accessible** from the following location option.

12. Click on **Finish**.

13. This should return you now to the **Deployments** page. Look at the **State** column for the `analyticsRes` application to note its current status. If the deployment was successful, a message towards the top of the WebLogic Administration Console will describe the current status and any actions that are subsequently required. A message stating that activation of changes is now required should be visible.

14. From the left panel in the **Change Center** section, click on the **Activate Changes** button.

15. After activating changes, check the **State** column of the deployed `analyticsRes` application. It should be in a **Prepared** state. This state tells us that the application is on the server, but it is not ready for any interaction.

16. To set the state of **analyticsRes** to **Active**, check the checkbox to the left of the **analyticsRes** application row. Then, from the **Deployments** options buttons, select **Start | Servicing all requests**:

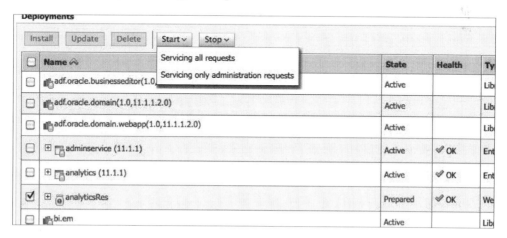

17. A confirmation page for starting the `analyticsRes` application will appear.

18. Click on the **Yes** button to confirm.

19. Refresh or return to the **Deployments** page to confirm that the **analyticsRes** application state has been set to **Active**:

Good artists copy, great artists steal

You could push through hundreds of lines of code to decipher a construct from which to build your own skin, styles, and custom messages, or simply leverage an existing configuration and make modifications to it. The latter is most definitely preferred for customizing the Oracle BI dashboards. In the previous step, you deployed an application path that can be referenced by the Oracle BI portal. Follow the next steps to leverage the out-of-the-box skin and style folders in order to create your own structure, which will be deployed in the application path from the previous exercise:

1. Navigate to `<FMW_Home>/Oracle_BI1/bifoundation/web/app/res`, for example, `C:\Oracle\FMW\Oracle_BI1\bifoundation\web\app\res`.

2. Copy both the **s_blapf** and **sk_blapf** folders to the following location `<FMW_Home>/instances/instance1/bifoundation/OracleBIPresentationServicesComponent/coreapplication_obips1/analyticsRes`, which represents the `analyticsRes` physical filesystem location:

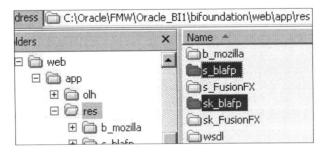

3. Once the two folders are copied to the **analyticsRes** folder, rename the folders to **s_obi11gbook** and **sk_obi11gbook** respectively:

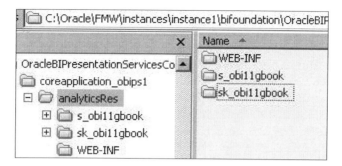

4. While in the `analyticsRes` folder, create a new folder, **customMessages**. From Windows Explorer, navigate to **File | New | Folder**. If you are following along in a *Nix environment, create a new directory using `mkdir customMessages` from a terminal window. The `analyticsRes` directory should have the structure shown in the following screenshot:

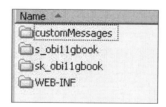

The `WEB-INF` folder is centric to Java web applications and contains the `web.xml` file that may contain extensive metadata about the application in order for it to be deployed on a JEE application server, such as WLS. This folder should remain untouched and within the `analyticsRes` folder, or unexpected results may occur.

In this section, you located the out-of-the-box skin and style template folders and copied them to the `analyticsRes` physical directory on the server. This is the same directory that you located during the WebLogic Server application deployment exercise. You then changed the name of the skin and style folders to reflect the customizations that you are working on in this chapter. Lastly, you created a new folder, `customMessages`, which you will leverage in a subsequent section to store the custom XML message file (files).

Modifying instanceconfig.xml

There is one physical file that manages the core configuration properties of Oracle BI Presentation services' (that is, the Oracle BI portal) look, feel, and functionality. That file is `instanceconfig.xml` and it resides within the `instances` folder structure for each deployed Oracle BI instance. Although a good portion of this file is managed via the GUI of the Enterprise Manager Fusion Middleware Control, several other advanced elements are not. One of these advanced elements relates to setting a custom style or skin as the default. In order to make the newly copied and renamed folders (`s_obi11gbook` and `sk_obi11gbook`), which will contain the style and skin modifications—the defaults—follow the next steps:

1. Navigate to the location, `<FMW_HOME>/instances/instance1/config/ OracleBIPresentationServices/Component/coreapplication_obips1/`.

2. Locate the `instanceconfig.xml` file and make a backup of the file. On Windows, copy the file and then paste it in the same directory. On Linux, execute the `cp` command.

3. Open the `instanceconfig.xml` file for editing by using the default operating system editor. On Windows, WordPad seems to be more consistent with formatting when compared to Notepad. In *Nix, use the Vim editor.

4. Edit the `instanceconfig.xml` file by inserting the following XML syntax underneath the starting `ServerInstance` tag, which is located towards the top of the `instanceconfig.xml` file:

```
<UI>
   <DefaultSkin>obi11gbook</DefaultSkin>
   <DefaultStyle>obi11gbook</DefaultStyle>
</UI>
```

```
<webconfig xmlns="oracle.bi.presentation.services/c
    <ServerInstance>

        <UI>
                <DefaultSkin>obi11gbook</DefaultSkin>
                <DefaultStyle>obi11gbook</DefaultStyle>
        </UI>
```

Notice how the prefixes sk_ and s_ are not required in the XML file. This is because all custom styles and skins folders must be prefixed with sk_ and s_. So, it would be superfluous here.

Note, that while making any advanced modifications to the instanceconfig.xml file, it is best to either place all custom modifications at the top of a section or at the bottom of a section for consistency. Also, notes and comments can be made within the XML file by using the standard XML comment syntax, which starts with the symbols < ! - - and ends with - ->.

5. Save and close the instanceconfig.xml file.

This procedure only needs to be conducted once to declare that a custom skin and style are set as the default skin and style for all dashboards to use. Any future changes to underlying files within the sk_obi11gbook and s_obi11gbook folders will not require any subsequent modifications to the instanceconfig.xml file.

Modifying skins and styles

Now that we have the core customization folders in the analyticsRes directory, it is time to address files within those folders to modify. Again, note that we are not modifying the original folders. We have only copied the originals to the analyticsRes directory and renamed them to be unique for a new customization theme. By modifying one or more files, we will reach our goal of customizing the Oracle BI dashboards to reflect the corporate branding standards of the fictitious organization, Company XYZ. The steps in the next sections will take you through the process.

All file edits, discussed in the following sections, will take place within the custom folders in the /analyticsRes directory. Much of the effort will take place in the form of opening a file, using the find function to locate a specific text, modifying the text and/or its respective values, and saving the file.

Use WordPad in Windows to edit the files—the CSS is minimized, or compressed, to save on extra file size created by white spaces when the Oracle BI development team was developing code. From the **File** menu select **View | Options...**, and then on the **Text** tab, select **Wrap to Window**. Click on the **OK** button to close the prompt.

Changing the banner color

Follow the next steps for changing the banner color:

1. Open the `common.css` file for editing. It should be located at the location `/sk_obi11gbook/b_mozilla_4/common.css`.

2. Find the text `.HeaderContainer` and change value for `background-color` from `#OD4988` to `lightsteelblue`.

3. The resulting modification should appear as follows:

   ```
   .HeaderContainer{background-color:lightsteelblue;font:11px
   Tahoma;}
   ```

4. Save the file.

Changing the global header menu link's color

Follow the next steps for changing the global header menu link's color:

1. Edit the same `common.css` file. It should be located at the location `/sk_obi11gbook/b_mozilla_4/common.css`.

2. Find the text `.HeaderMenubar` and change the value for `color` from `#A9DFF5` to `midnightblue`.

3. The resulting modification should appear as follows:

   ```
   .HeaderMenubar,.HeaderQuickSearchPrompt,.HeaderSearchGo{color:
   midnightblue}
   ```

4. Save the file.

Changing the header separator bar

Follow the next steps for changing the header separator bar:

1. Edit the same `common.css` file. It should be located at the location `/sk_obi11gbook/b_mozilla_4/common.css`.

2. Find the text `.HeaderBarSeparator` and change the value for `border-top` from `1px solid #61A1EF` to `1px dashed magenta`.

3. The resulting modification should appear as follows:

   ```
   .HeaderBarSeparator{font-size:1px;height:1px;margin-
   bottom:2px;text-align:right;border-top:1px dashed magenta;margin-
   left:-5px;}
   ```

4. Save the file.

Changing the header brand name

Follow the next steps for changing the header brand name:

1. Edit the same `common.css` file. It should be located at the location `/sk_obi11gbook/b_mozilla_4/common.css`.

2. Find the text `.HeaderBrandName` and change the value for `color` from `#093E7D` to `black`.

3. The resulting modification should appear as follows:

```
.HeaderBrandName{font-size:14px;font-weight:bold;font-fami
ly:Tahoma;position:absolute;left:130px;top:2px;color:blac
k;font-size:17px;white-space:nowrap;overflow:hidden;text-
overflow:ellipsis;display:inline-block;}
```

4. Save the file.

Changing the Login page background

Follow the next steps for changing the Login page background:

1. Open the `login.css` file for editing. It should be located at the location `/sk_obi11gbook/login/login.css`.

2. Find the text `body` element.

3. Then, change the `background-color` value from `#FFF` to `grey`.

4. Add `background-size:0px;` in the code.

5. The resulting modification should appear as follows:

```
body{background-image:url(background_blue_whitegradient_.
png);background-position:top left;background-
color:grey;background-size:0px;background-repeat:repeat-x;margin-
left:0;margin-top:0;margin-right:0;margin-bottom:0;}
```

6. Save the file.

Restarting Presentation services

At this point, a straightforward and basic set of modifications have been made to files within the custom folders. After restarting the Presentation services component, the adjustments that were made to the `instanceconfig.xml` file, will be recognized. The settings for default skins and styles will send the Presentation services system component to search for the custom folders under the `/analyticsRes` virtual path, and it will then use those folders to help paint the Oracle BI portal.

As previously discussed, there are two methods for restarting the Oracle BI 11*g* Presentation services system component. Preference for using the Fusion Control option is recommended for beginners. All services do not need to be restarted, only the Presentation services system component requires a restart as the only change made thus far to the default Oracle BI system has been to the configuration file that presentation services relies on, instanceconfig.xml.

Restarting Presentation services from the command line

Follow the next steps for restarting Presentation services from the command line:

1. Open a command prompt (Windows) or terminal window (*Nix).

2. Change the directory to <FMW_HOME>/instances/instance1/bin/:

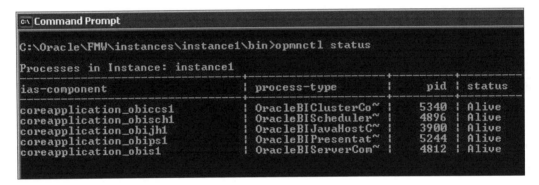

```
C:\Oracle\FMW\instances\instance1\bin>opmnctl status

Processes in Instance: instance1
-----------------------------+--------------------+-------+---------
ias-component                | process-type       |   pid | status
-----------------------------+--------------------+-------+---------
coreapplication_obiccs1       | OracleBIClusterCo~ |  5340 | Alive
coreapplication_obisch1       | OracleBIScheduler~ |  4896 | Alive
coreapplication_obijh1        | OracleBIJavaHostC~ |  3900 | Alive
coreapplication_obips1        | OracleBIPresentat~ |  5244 | Alive
coreapplication_obis1         | OracleBIServerCom~ |  4812 | Alive
```

3. Run the following command:

   opmnctl status

> The status provides a look at all system components managed by the Oracle BI 11*g* instance of the OPMN.
>
> Take note of the Presentation services component, coreapplication_obips1, under the ias-component column. This is the value that must be passed into the opmnctl command to selectively restart the system component.

4. Run the following command:

   opmnctl restartproc ias-component=coreapplication_obips1

5. The result should be a clean return to the command prompt. This should indicate that there are no errors and that the component is restarting in the background:

Restarting Presentation services from Enterprise Manager

Follow the next steps for restarting Presentation services from Enterprise Manager:

1. Navigate a web browser to `http://<server_name>:7001/em`.
2. Log in with the Weblogic administrator credentials as per the installation.
3. From the left panel, expand **Business Intelligence** and click on **coreapplication** to select it.
4. Click on **Capacity Management**.
5. Click on the **Availability** sub-tab.
6. Under the **System Components Availability** table, all status arrows should be green and pointing upwards. Select the **BI Presentation Services** row to highlight the component:

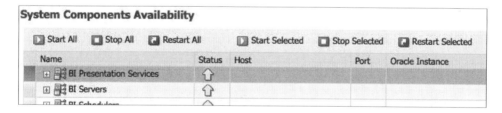

7. Click on the **Restart Selected** button.
8. A confirmation prompt will appear. Click on the **Yes** button to confirm that the restart of the component should commence.

9. The component will begin restarting and upon completion, it will alert you with a prompt stating that the restart has completed:

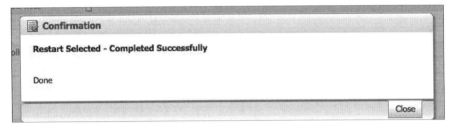

Viewing the results

After Presentation services has been restarted, return to the Oracle BI portal and refresh the web page by holding the *Shift* key and clicking on the **Refresh** button.

Press *Ctrl + F5* on Windows or *Shift + Command + R* on Mac OS.

Note, that if upon clicking on the **Refresh** button, your session is not already terminated, and you are not prompted to re-log in, you may need to restart all system components just to be certain that the portal has been bounced. Restarting the Presentation services system component should end all user sessions and require re-login from the portal. We've seen on several occasions where restarting just a single system component doesn't always work accurately. In which case restart all system components. The login page that is rendered after a successful restart of Presentation services should show the grey background that we have introduced in our custom folders.

Configuring a custom message

Let's look at another way to brand the Oracle BI portal to boldly reflect Company XYZ's ownership of this implementation. This exercise explores creating a custom message folder hierarchy, developing a localization strategy, and modifying the header brand name for the Oracle BI portal.

As mentioned before, custom messages can be language dependent or default to a global message for all languages, if no other language-dependent messages are specified. To create a message for a specific language, a subfolder representing the locale of the desired language, needs to be created underneath the main customMessages folder. An example of this hierarchy would be /customMessages/l_de/ to represent German/Deutsch (DE) or /customMessages/l_en/ to represent English (EN). For the sake of this exercise, we will create two language specific folders underneath the /analyticsRes/customMessages/ folder that we created earlier.

Creating new language specific folders

Follow the next steps for creating new language specific folders:

1. Under the `/analyticsRes/customMessages/` directory, create the following folder structures:

   ○ `l_en/messages/`

   ○ `l_de/messages/`

2. Navigate to the `/analyticsRes/customMessages/l_en/messages/` folder.

3. Create a new file called `companyName.xml` in this directory.

4. Add the following text to the `companyName.xml` file:

```xml
<?xml version="1.0" encoding="utf-8"?>
<WebMessageTables xmlns:sawm="com.siebel.analytics.web/message/
v1">
  <WebMessageTable system="ProductMessages"
  table="ProductNames">
    <WebMessage name="kmsgHeaderBIBrandName">
      <TEXT> Company XYZ </TEXT>
    </WebMessage>
  </WebMessageTable>
</WebMessageTables>
```

5. Save the file.

6. Copy the `companyName.xml` file into the `/l_de/messages/` folder.

7. Open the `/l_de/messages/companyName.xml` file for editing.

8. Modify the text element value from Company XYZ to Firme XYZ.

9. Save the file.

The resulting folder structure should appear similar to the following screenshot:

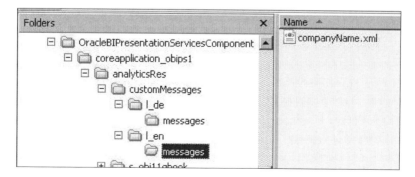

Refreshing metadata files and custom messages

Something that is quite interesting about implementing custom messages is that they do not require Presentation services to restart in order for their instantiation or subsequent modifications to be recognized by the Oracle BI portal. Once a change has been made to a custom message, the refresh of all messages can be triggered from the **Administration** page within the Oracle BI portal. There is no need to logout. To refresh all custom messages in order to see any recent modifications follow the next steps:

1. Log in to the Oracle BI 11*g* portal as the administrator user created as per the installation, that is, weblogic.

2. Click on the **Administration** link from the global header menu.

3. On the **Administration** page under the **Maintenance and Troubleshooting** section, click on **Reload Files and Metadata**.

4. The description underneath the text will change to the following message:

   Reloading, please wait...

5. Then, it will return to normal once the refresh has completed.

6. Navigate to the **Home** page of the Oracle BI portal, then conduct and refresh the browser (*Shift + Refresh*) to see the modification(s). Now, the company name should be visible instead of the default Business Intelligence value.

To see the language localization for the custom message strategy that you designed, follow the next steps:

1. Log out from the Oracle BI portal by clicking on the **Sign Out** link in the upper right-hand corner of the web page.

2. On the login screen under the **Sign In** button, change the language drop-down option from **English** to **Deutsch (for German)**. The header will immediately change from **Company XYZ** to **Firme XYZ**.

Wrap it up!

The finished product should look as shown in the following screenshot:

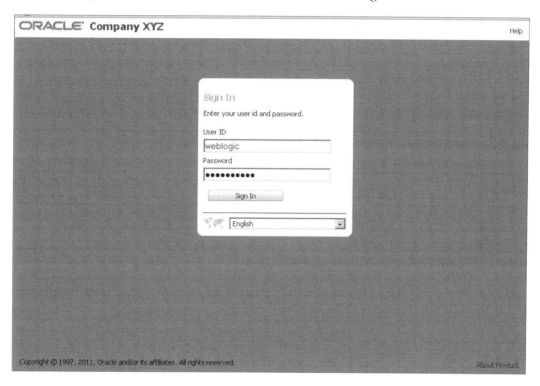

As you can see, the styles and skins have changed just enough so that Company XYZ is branded with its corporate colors and the organization name is brandished in the header of the Oracle BI portal. That is a big step in the right direction for engaging users early on and getting their buy-in for an enterprise business intelligence solution. The techniques you've learned here are the same that you would use to change the logo or to modify other aesthetic areas within the Oracle BI portal.

Advanced learning topics

The above exercises took a very manual look at branding the Oracle BI portal by using the customization functionality inherent within the software. There are a lot of other ancillary tidbits and gotchas that go along with this type of development. As a quick heads-up, here are a few helpful pointers that may assist you in further efforts to brand Oracle BI 11*g*.

Firebug

As a plugin to the most popular open source web browser on the market—Firefox—Firebug has changed the way developers study their CSS website manipulations. Firebug allows a developer to highlight a web page item such as an image, text, table, and so on, and determine what CSS class or classes assist in rendering a specific object. All of this is accomplished in real time.

This tool can be essential in determining which aspects of Oracle BI, an organization may wish to brand over or remove completely from the Oracle BI portal. Some advanced knowledge of CSS is helpful here, but using this plugin is a great way to advance your knowledge of CSS as well.

NetBeans IDE

Having an IDE available to assist with the branding effort can speed up the development time. An IDE, such as NetBeans, has code sensitivity, highlighting, code completion, and several other features that can mitigate mistakes and provide code suggestions. There are several free IDEs on the market. NetBeans is part of the Oracle Corporation's software enterprise and is also free to use and develop in.

Formatting CSS (prettify)

When taking a barebones approach to branding Oracle BI and working with the cascading style sheets, it could be helpful to leverage some free websites available on the web. Several sites provide users with the ability to paste in the CSS code into the web page and have the compressed CSS code, such as that seen in the default Oracle BI skin and style folders, into a more legible format. This format can then be edited in a similar way as done in the preceding exercise, and saved in a more legible format.

NQ_SESSION.SKIN and NQ_SESSION.STYLE session variables

Briefly touched upon earlier in this chapter, each user that logs in to the Oracle BI portal, potentially may be addressed with a custom skin and/or style that is associated with that user's role, department, and so on. In order to configure this, leverage an initialization block within the Oracle BI metadata repository to set the NQ_SESSION.SKIN and/or NQ_SESSION.STYLE variables once the user logs in. The variable(variables) can be set to either the defaults or a custom skin and style based on profile configurations developed by the Oracle BI Administrator.

AnalyticsRes Application Caveat

If any issues are encountered during the process of making customizations and restarting Presentation services, the culprit is usually the `instanceconfig.xml` file or the deployed `/analyticsRes` application. Once the `instanceconfig.xml` file is modified to set the default skin and/or style, Presentation services will always look for this virtual path to be started. If it is not deployed or if it is not running within the application server, Oracle BI Presentation services may fail to start.

A review – what I should now know!

For self-review and a recap of the chapter, here are a few questions based on important topics covered in this chapter. There is no answer key. These questions are for your own reflection on the chapter material:

1. What is the name of the default deployment folder and application where customizations are inserted?
2. In which file can the default skin and style be set?
3. How do you define a custom message within Oracle BI?
4. What is localization?
5. What two methods are available in order to restart Oracle BI Presentation Services?

Summary

In this chapter, you have learned about strategy and technique for branding Oracle Business Intelligence within an organization. You learned about cascading style sheets and other tools that could make branding of Oracle BI 11*g* a lot easier. Engaging in a hands-on exercise, you saw how manual the process of manipulating individual elements within customization files can be. During that exercise, hopefully you paid attention to all of the image files (that is `gif`, `jpg`, and `png`) that were within the style and skin folders. Just about all of these images have the potential to be modified or replaced with custom images to provide an even broader, nearing advanced, level of customization. Image replacement is perfect for modifying the default logo to match that of the organization. Ultimately, there are plenty of take-aways from this chapter, which will allow you to feel confident in speaking about branding Oracle BI 11*g*. In the next chapter, you will walkthrough improving Oracle BI 11*g* performance by managing several key areas of the Oracle BI 11*g* platform.

14
Improving the Performance

So far in this book, you have installed your system, set up your database sources, created dashboards and have monitored the usage. This is not the time to sit back and relax! You have designed your database with the principles in *Chapter 7, Reporting Databases*, and have installed OBIEE on a machine with the suitable levels of CPU, disk speed and RAM, but is your system actually performing well?

In this chapter, we will learn some common techniques to reduce the bottlenecks that can exist in the process of delivering dashboards and reports to the users.

We will look across the whole system, defining poor performance and where required, takes steps to improve the performance.

What is poor performance?

If a dashboard loads in 20 seconds, is that good or bad performance? I tend to answer this question in terms of user expectations and technical capability.

User expectations are what we manage every day on a project and sometimes these are really easy to meet, other times totally impossible! I recently had a client who was switching from a very slow reporting system (which will remain nameless) where a report would take 45 minutes to run. When we replaced the report with a dashboard that took 20 seconds, they were delighted. A similar dashboard, at another recent investment-banking client, was deemed to be far too slow at 20 seconds, as they required information in less than 3 seconds per dashboard page. Because the first client was happy with a 20-second wait, there was no further performance work undertaken, even though I knew that we could get the report down to less than 3 seconds. The banking client demanded better performance so we spent hundreds of man hours reducing the dashboard time down to a one second response. One recent client has 30,000 users. If each user logged in once per week and ran a dashboard that took one minute more than necessary, then they could be wasting 9.5 MAN YEARS per year.

If your client is happy with the response times, but your current system is technically capable of reduced dashboard delivery times then should you spend time delivering these improved times? The simple answer is "yes". As your system grows, with more users and more dashboards, there will certainly be a hit to performance overall. Improving the performance of every dashboard, request, and report will help to increase total capacity and keep your project being funded and expanded. There will probably be a need to prioritize the order in which to improve performance of dashboards, and for this I suggest a combination of client priorities and picking on the slowest ones first.

In practice, this means that the estimated total time to develop a dashboard should always include an element at the end to review performance and make suitable changes.

Where can I improve the performance?

As we have seen in the previous chapters, there are several components in your OBIEE system. Each one of these can be tuned to help improve performance, along with some other factors. The areas to look for the most gains are:

- Hardware
- Database
- BI Server
- Web Server
- Domain Settings
- Network

We will look at each of these to see the techniques that could be employed.

For each of the above areas there are three main ways to improve performance:

- Do less work
- Do the same work, but faster
- Cheat!

Doing less work means making parts of the system work with smaller datasets, such as using aggregate fact tables. Working faster essentially means getting better equipment that can cope with the volumes of data and with the system components. Cheating means getting the results ready before the user needs it.

Hardware

There are no "'silver 'bullets" when it comes to improving performance, but there are some recent developments in hardware that come pretty close. Massive gains can be had in request response times by buying some impressive new hardware.

The first piece of hardware that has been available for a few years is the Oracle **Exadata**® V2 machine. This "Sun Oracle Exadata Storage and Database machine" has transformed the ability of Oracle databases by bringing together several technology advances into the one box. The statistics are impressive:

- 160 CPU Cores + 4 TB RAM for database processing
- 168 CPU Cores dedicated to SQL processing
- Two database servers
- 14 storage servers
- 5.3 TB of Flash cache
- Infiniband switches
- Up to 224 TB space per rack
- Up to eight Racks can be connected

The above stats can transform even the most stubborn client demands into reality. A recent proof of concept that I undertook reduced a dashboard response from 3 minutes to 8 seconds. Another recent client uses an Exadata box and has over 2 terabytes of live data that is regularly used in dashboards. So far, the performance has been so good that no tuning has been required by the end users (although we will still tune for expansion).

At the same time that OBIEE 11gR1.6 was released, Oracle also released the **Exalytics**® machine. Another super-fast machine from the Sun part of Oracle, but this time aimed directly at OBIEE users (Exadata is for any database use). The Exalytics machine contains a huge amount of memory (hundreds of GB) and lots of processing power, along with some in-memory software that will optimize the way the data is extracted for OBIEE to use. Also included in the machine is the OBIEE software itself, thereby reducing the need for another set of application servers. Its impressive stats include:

- 1 terabyte of RAM
- 40 CPU Cores on 10 quad-core chips
- Infiniband networking

- In-memory "Times Ten"® database
- Memory optimized Essbase

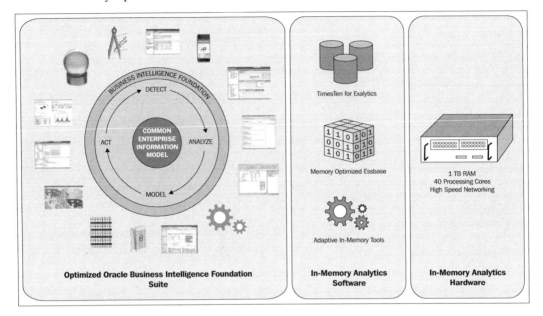

The use of OBIEE on an Exalytics machine enables a special Admin tool feature called **Summary Advisor**. This tool uses the Usage Tracking statistics to provide advice on which summary tables will improve performance, and then help to generate in memory "Times Ten" database tables that are then integrated into the BI Server Repository. These tables are normally aggregated data that will respond quicker than going to your database source. The result is instant response times on dashboards that previously could take minutes and, therefore, will allow for more concurrent users, and more advanced features, such as the new graphical tools and master detail instant reports.

Full Speed Ahead

If you combine the power of the Exadata Storage and Database machine with the clever power of the Exalytics machine, you will have a superb platform to delight the end users. The Exadata Database machine is used for the warehouse and is the source for a large detailed analysis, with the Exalytics machine providing the summary aggregated data and Essbase cubes.

The investment in the machines described above is not insignificant, but the benefit to the end users is huge. Take our large user base example and you can see that even a few seconds can add up to a big reduction in efficiency for an organization. You will also save a large amount of developers' and DBA time, which for external consultancy, or even internal teams, can be relatively expensive.

Database

The database is crucial to the reporting performance and can be improved in two ways.

The first way is with the configuration of the database in terms of the parameters used and the structure of the data files/tablespaces. There are a large number of options, on many types of database and, therefore, too many to go through them in this book (I recommend that you read *Oracle Database 11gR2 Performance Tuning Cookbook* by *Ciro Fiorillo*), but what I can say is that there will certainly be some parameters that will make a big difference. For example, setting STAR_TRANSFORMATION_ENABLED in an Oracle database can make a huge difference when reporting on your Star schema-based data.

Work closely with the database administrators to tune the settings that meet your needs. The settings that normally have a large impact on an Oracle database are those relating to memory and those relating to the storage such as block sizes and tablespace structures.

Testing of the database performance should be done in isolation of OBIEE, by use of a SQL development tool, such as the Oracle SQL Developer, but use the SQL generated by the OBIEE server as a basis for tuning.

The second area for a database to be tuned is with the object structures. Using a smaller set of data, or the smart use of indexes, stats, joins, and views can make a huge difference to speed.

Let's take an example using the Tennis database. We currently have a fact table with 1.2 million records (W_MATCH_F). This table has several dimensions, which is why the table has so many records. The dimensions include:

- Date
- Tournament
- Match
- Player

These dimensions allow us to store a record for each player, for every match. Let's assume we now want to run a report showing the players' statistics for a whole tournament. We can create a table (or a materialized view if you prefer) that aggregates the data at the tournament and player level. Such a table now contains 50 percent less records and, therefore, should be able to respond to queries much faster but does require extra space.

Automatic Query re-write can be a feature of materialized views. When you create a materialized view with this option set, then queries that run in the database will automatically be re-written when they match the data requirements with the materialized view contents. So, in our example a query that summarizes YEAR and PLAYER from the W_MATCH_F table could automatically run against a materialized view called MVW_PLAYER_TOUR_TOTAL.

BI Server

Once you have created a smaller dataset, as shown earlier, you need to use it when it matches the scope of the dimensions in your analysis. There are two ways you could do this:

- Separate Fact Tables
- Aggregate Logical Table Sources

Using a separate fact table for aggregate facts is not a commonly used option. The only time it is suitable is where the aggregate facts are not simple sums (or simple averages).

Aggregate Logical Table Sources is my favorite feature of the OBIEE Server. We can create an aggregate table (or materialized view) and use this directly in the BI Server repository, alongside the detailed fact tables. The BI server then chooses which table

Let's walk through a working example. The steps are:

1. Create an Aggregate Materialized view of the Match Fact, using only Tournament and Player dimensions. Call it MVW_PLAYER_TOURNAMENT_AGG.
2. Import the new object into the physical layer in OBIEE. Remember that it is best practice to create an alias for your physical layer objects. See the chapter on developing the BI Repository for the import metadata steps.

3. Add the new physical table as an additional **Logical Table Source (LTS)** for the Match Logical Table. The following screenshot shows three aggregates that have been added as logical table sources:

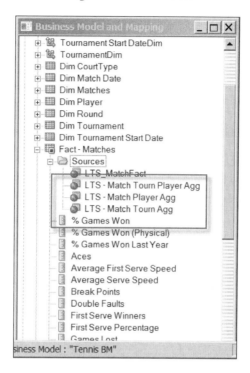

4. Map the fields as appropriate. For example, we have mapped the **Aces** logical column to the aggregate table, as well as the detail table.

5. Set the content level so that the BI server knows how to use the new LTS. The Logical Table Source content level needs to be set to "detail" for the Tournament and Player level, but not set for the other dimensions.

Now we have created a summary set of data and added it to the BI Server repository. The BI server will now use the smaller table to answer requests if it is suitable. In this example if a user ran a request for a tournament and player then the smaller table would be used and not the large detail W_MATCH_F. This will speed up the response times.

The following code listing shows how the aggregate materialized view is used:

```
select sum(T2129.ACES) as c1,
     T2163.TOURNAMENT_NAME as c2
from
w_tournament_d T2163 /* Dim_Tournament */ ,
  MVW_PLAYER_TOURNAMENT_AGG T2129 /* Fact - Match Tourn Player Agg */
where   ( T2129.TOURNAMENT_WID = T2163.TOURNAMENT_WID )
group by T2163.TOURNAMENT_NAME)
```

More performance tips

Follow these tips to improve performance:

- Try to avoid using normal (opaque) views unless they are the only way to introduce hints and an SQL that performs well

- Make sure you leverage the features of the database, and understand what they mean to performance

- Try not to overload the BI server and database with lots of queries by keeping to the general rule of seven or less requests per dashboard page

The use of cache

When a user request is made, the result of the request can be stored in a local file on the BI server. This is called a cached result.

The BI server normally works by sending a query code to a database, file, or Excel, and processing the results it gets. The slow part of the process is usually the waiting for the data source system to get the answer together. Passing the call to the data source, and having the result already, is a great way to cheat the system into being faster. Luckily, it is possible to get the results before the user runs their dashboard, then store these results in a "cache". Cache entries are results that are stored in a file on the BI server machine and the BI server knows when it can use these "pre-prepared" results, instead of going to the database to get the answer. If the same request is made again, by the same user or even a different user, then the result cache is used instead of issuing an SQL against the database.

Cache is not the only answer to all your performance issues. In fact, it should be treated as a last resort and only as a temporary solution, until you get the hardware/database performance that you need. There are limitations as to how much you can store in the cache, in terms of both individual result sets and the total overall size of the cache. There are also issues relating to how you refresh the cache, removing old stale data, and populating new data. Without a pre-populated cache, the first user to run the dashboard will still experience a slower performance.

Setting up the cache

The global cache is shared by all BI Servers participating in your cluster. In addition, each BI Server maintains its own local query cache for regular queries. The global cache needs to be stored in a shared file system.

Shared file's requirements for the global cache are as follows:

- All BI Servers must have read and write access to the global cache directory.
- The global cache parameters are configured in the NQSConfig.INI file for each BI Server node participating in the cluster. The global cache is controlled centrally.
- The BI Servers maintain a query cache, which is a local cache of the query results.

To enable the cache, carry out the following steps in Fusion Middleware Control:

1. Log in to Fusion Middleware Control.
2. Expand the Business Intelligence node in the **Farm_domain_name** window.
3. Click on **coreapplication**.
4. Click on **Capacity Management**, and then click on **Performance**.
5. Click on **Lock and Edit Configuration**.
6. In the **Global Cache** section, specify the shared location for the Oracle BI Server Global Cache and specify **250 MB** for the **Global cache size**. In a Windows environment, the Enterprise Manager Fusion Middleware Control requires that a UNC path be used to define the shared location of the Oracle BI Server Global Cache.
7. Click on **Apply**.
8. Click on **Activate Changes**.

The following screenshot shows the cache enabled, with a maximum of 1051 entries:

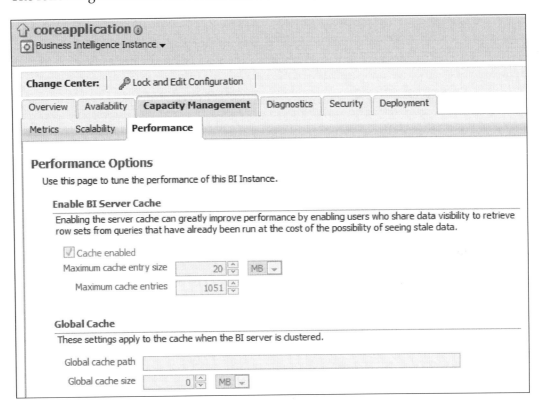

The cache entries that are made will become stale when new data arrives in the warehouse. It is, therefore, possible to set a length of time that a cache entry is still usable. This can be minutes, hours, days, or unlimited. There is also a method called "Event Polling" which is a way to tell the BI Server that one of the tables in the cache has been updated. For more details about event polling, see the Gerard Nico wiki at `http://gerardnico.com/wiki/dat/obiee/event_table` or the Oracle documentation on "Cache Event Processing with an Event Polling Table" at `http://docs.oracle.com/cd/E14571_01/bi.1111/e10541/querycaching.htm#i1005513`.

Also, see the documentation of the shared folders used in OBIEE at: `http://docs.oracle.com/cd/E21764_01/core.1111/e10106/bi.htm#CHDCEDHI`.

Web servers on top

There are configurations available for an OBIEE system, which include the use of a pure Web Server on top of the installed application. The use of a web server layer will enable load balancing and high availability. The web servers will also be able to serve up objects such as images quicker than the Weblogic server can.

Back in *Chapter 4, Installation Options*, we demonstrated how to install the proxy plugin which enables the separate web layer. Go back and give it a try!

Domain setup

The usual suspect when it comes to slow performance is the database, and hopefully you have tuned this as much as possible. If you are expecting very high numbers of users then, in addition to adding web servers (as above), you will need to deploy more application servers. This will spread the load across different machines and will provide high availability cover.

For an enterprise setup, this will mean installing separate machines with a full application installation, including an Admin server and managed servers.

This is outside the scope of this book, but you can find information in the Oracle documentation that explains the steps.

Find the High Availability section of the documentation, currently at:

```
http://docs.oracle.com/cd/E21764_01/core.1111/e10106/bi.htm
```

A review – what I should now know!

For self review and a recap of the chapter, here are a few questions based on the topics covered in this chapter:

1. Where can I improve performance?
2. What is performance data?
3. How do I implement a web server into the OBIEE system?
4. What are the cache settings?

Summary

In this chapter, we introduced the idea of improving overall performance by working on the individual components that make up an OBIEE system. We showed how the new hardware can accelerate the performance to a near real time point, making performance good enough even for the most demanding of customers (including Investment Bankers!).

Monitoring performance is vital to ensure that the system is delivering what the users want in a timely manner, and with 11g R1.1.6 it is now easier, thanks to the storage of the physical SQL. Use this information to tune your system, and keep tuning—never stop tuning.

15
Using the BI Admin Change Management Utilities

We have covered the fundamental techniques of OBIEE development, and through that process we have also covered the fundamental tools that are needed for OBIEE development. Having this knowledge in hand, we can go over some of the other facilities in the Administration tool. These facilities are less utilized, but can aid and smooth the development process.

Previously, we have carried out all of the tutorials and development examples as a lone developer, but in larger projects we may have a group of developers accessing and modifying the same RPD. To this end, the OBIEE Administration tool provides the ability to merge multiple versions of an RPD as well as functionality for groups to manage development on a sole repository (multiuser development).

Problems with multiple developers

As in any IT project, source and version control are points of concern in OBIEE. There are a couple of issues specifically associated with multiple developers working on an RPD.

Unlike other forms of development, all of our metadata is contained in a single file, that is, the RPD. If we are using a form of revision control, such as CVS software, we are restricted to saving a version of the whole RPD file, even if it is possibly containing many projects/business areas. This does not help us if we want to work independently on subsets of the RPD. It also makes it difficult to record what changes individual developers are making and on what objects. All of these increase the difficulty of having developers work on multiple development paths with an aim to consolidate them into one RPD at the end, as would commonly be the case in large projects.

As we cannot use third-party tools for version control, Oracle has provided us with tools for merging separate RPD development paths and recording changes. In previous versions, these tools have been buggy and cumbersome to set up, but there have been improvements in these areas, so it is worth taking a look at the possibilities.

Outside of these inbuilt tools, we can also consider how to manage multiuser developments by ourselves.

Merges

During the initial development, for example, for a proof of concept, it is common to have one developer working on the system with a full release of an RPD from development to production. At that moment, change control is simple as the whole updated RPD is kept with versioning via a third-party tool, such as **Visual SourceSafe (VSS)** or **Subversion (SVN)**.

However, as a project matures in a live environment, you may have minor changes that are made online or quick point releases made directly to production in order to support urgent user requests. In parallel, we would commonly be developing a major DEV to PROD release as a part of the next stage for the project.

This means that you need to merge changes from both the amended PROD RPD and the new DEV release candidate. If the PROD changes are minor, developers may keep a log of changes and manually add them to the DEV RPD. For more involved or for a larger amount of changes, it would be best to utilize a tool that will help to merge the process. As we previously mentioned, the RPD is one encapsulated file, so tools used for programming are not useful. One way around this is to try and utilize the Administration tool's inherent merger facility. Let's take a look at the types of methods of merging processes that are possible.

Three-way merge

A three-way merge is widely seen as the most robust method for the revision control in the IT industry, and it is recommended by Oracle. It is especially important to have a robust process when you are merging repositories with the same base and possibly, conflicting objects. In our example, we will have three RPDs:

- **Current repository**: This is the RPD where we merge our changes. In our example, the latest DEV version.

- **Original**: It is the original and base PROD release from which the other two RPDs are branched off.

- **Modified**: It is the Current PROD version with live changes.

So let's begin. Firstly, open the **Current repository** (in offline mode) and select
File | Merge:

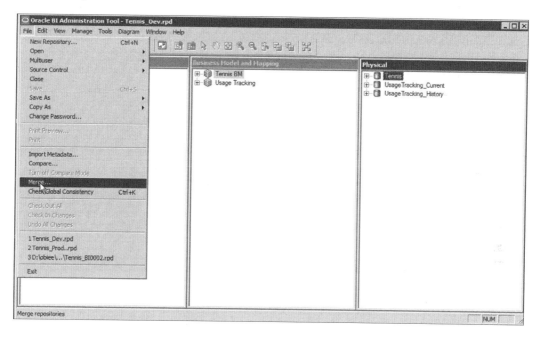

You can see the **Merge Repository Wizard - Select Input Files** screen in the
following screenshot:

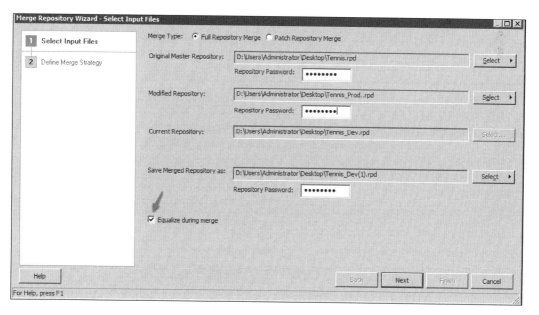

Then, select the **Original** and **Modified** RPDs, and input their passwords as well. Also select the **Full Repository Merge** radio button, at the top of the **Merge Repository Wizard** screen, as we are dealing with whole repositories.

Note, that we have checked the **Equalize during merge** box. This solves a potential issue where the same object in both changed RPDs have different IDs. This can happen if we needed to recreate the object from scratch in one of the RPDs.

Once this has been done, click on **Next**. At this point, you will get the option to check the global consistency of the RPDs that we have referred to. In preparation for this process, we should have already checked this and been happy with the results, so click on **No**:

The merge tool will now check for conflicts between the RPDs. If there are any conflicts, those will be displayed in the **Define Merge Strategy** screen. Here we will be able to choose how to rectify the conflict:

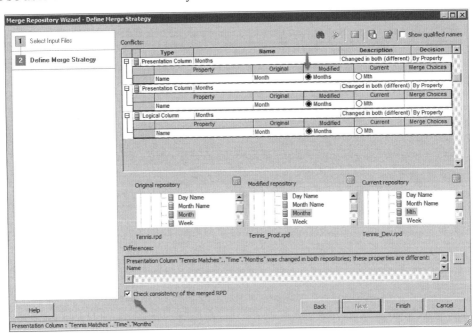

In the preceding screenshot, you can see that we only have three conflicts and they all stem from differing names for the **Months** column in the three RPDS. Via a radio button, we can choose whether to go with the **Modified (Current PROD)** or the **Current (DEV)** version. Let's go with the PROD version, as that is what our users are used to working with.

Once we have resolved all conflicts, check the **Check consistency of the merged RPD** box. This is good practice, as it ensures that the consistency of the newly merged RPD is ascertained straight away.

Note, that if we want a file record of all of the conflict resolution decisions that we have made, we can generate that using the floppy disk icon on the top right of the screen:

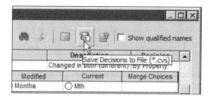

Once you are happy, you can click on **Next** and the merge process takes place. This may take some time depending on how big your RPDs are, and how many merge conflicts need to be resolved:

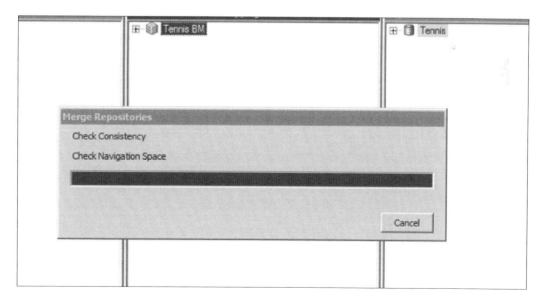

Once the process has finished, we are left with the **Current RPD** file, but with the newly merged changes within it.

 Remember to perform a Regression Test for all of your Current PROD reports with this newly merged RPD. You will also need to test any development reports to ensure that the merge has not affected those pieces of development as well.

Two-way merger

This is commonly carried out when you have two separate RPDs that need to be merged, but they have no common parent. This happens when, for example, you are combining two entirely separate streams of work. An example of this would be the Tennis and Usage Tracking examples that we have discussed in this book. If the two RPDs contain completely different subject areas, business models and data sources, you can easily cut and paste these objects entirely from one RPD to another. However, this is sometimes far from ideal and requires an experienced and knowledgeable developer who has implicit knowledge of both RPD developments.

Best practice is to carry out a two-way merge using the merge tool, as discussed in the preceding section. When you are prompted for an **original RPD**, as we do not have an original trunk parent, you can provide a dummy RPD. This is known as a **parentless three-way merge.**

Multi-User development

Now consider a scenario where you need to merge multiple RPDs, and there is the possibility that your project and RPD can become so large that you will need multiple developers. In small proven teams, access to the RPD for development can easily be maintained through open communication, such as verbal means or even e-mail/messaging in conjunction with a change log where developers record their amendments. However, in larger teams where there is the possibility of development conflicts over shared objects, and the need for more robust version control, we will need to look at other options.

Online development

One option is to have the RPD accessed via a centrally running OBIEE environment. This means that all developers will access the RPD in an online mode via the Administration tool. When working on objects, developers will have to check them in and out on the server itself.

Therefore, from the Administration tool, we can open the online repository by navigating to **File | Open | Online** or by choosing the blue folder icon in the toolbar:

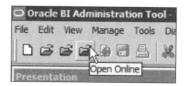

We are then prompted for the online RPD details:

Once we are within the online RPD, we can amend the objects that we want to change. So let us change the name of the logical column **Month**. Double-click on the **Month** logical column. At this point, you will see the **Check Out Objects** screen:

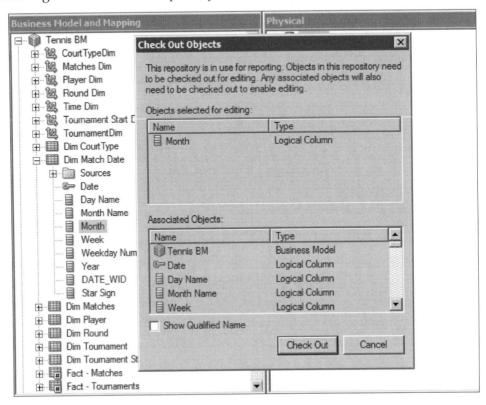

Note, that all associated objects up to the business model level have also been checked out, even when such a simple amendment is made. Once we click on **Check Out**, we are then returned to the RPD. However, note that the icons have changed for the objects that we have checked out. This shows that they are locked for the amendment:

Once we have made our change, we can check in the objects by choosing the check-in icon in the toolbar, as shown in the following screenshot. As a general note, as well as the check out icons, you can see that we are in online mode due to the **Online** title heading of the Administration tool:

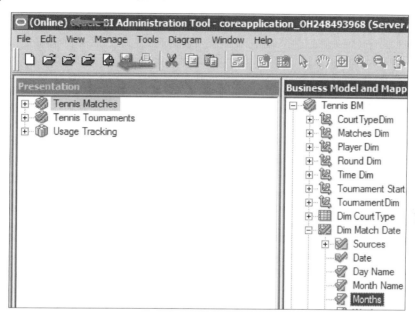

Once you are happy with the settings and have checked in your objects, you will be asked to confirm whether you want to publish the changes on the central server:

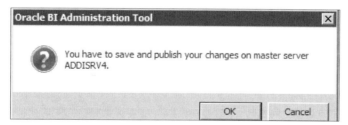

We are also reminded that if we are in a **clustered** environment, we will need to restart these nodes. This is done through the Enterprise Manger:

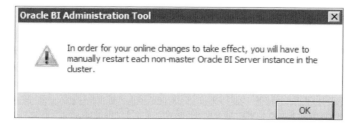

Advantages and disadvantages

There are multiple drawbacks to this method:

- Low-level objects cannot be checked out without checking out their parents. For example, if you want to change a logical column name, the whole logical table gets checked out. If you want to change a logical table, the whole business model is checked and locked for other users.

- There is no recommended limit to the number of developers that should use this process at the same time. This depends on having an adequate server architecture in place. However, in the experience of the authors, not all DEV environments are specified correctly due to budget/resource constraints. In this case, the constant checking in and out, running of consistency checks, and saving online RPDs can result in corruption. This is common when you have large RPDs on low memory machines.

- There is no version control. You cannot check which developer changed which object.

- You still have to manually restart nonmaster nodes in a cluster environment. Bear this in mind if you ever need to a make a change in online mode on a production environment.

- If you have a very large RPD such as in Oracle Business Intelligence Applications, the checking in/out and saving process can take a very long time. This can possibly lead to corruption of the RPD.

The advantages are as follows:

- Developers only need a local Administration tool.

- All other components, for example, BI and web server are shared.

- Testing is done on that shared environment.

- No setup is needed outside of a normal OBIEE install.

- You do not need to deploy the RPD to the server for report/dashboard developers to see the changes.

Multi-User development

Another alternative is to implement the **Multi-User Development Environment (MUDE)**. This enables us to split the RPD into self-contained areas or **Projects**. The master RPD is put in a shared area, then projects are worked on by an individual developer and merged back into the master.

This is slightly more complex and convoluted compared to online development. Rather than accessing one central environment, developers must have their own full development environment. They will need a local BI and web server in order to test changes locally, in addition to a local Administration tool. However, due to the possibility of properly segmenting the RPD, it is arguably safer.

So let's step through an example. Firstly, create the **Project** subsets. Navigate through **Manage | Projects** within our master RPD that has been opened in the Administration tool:

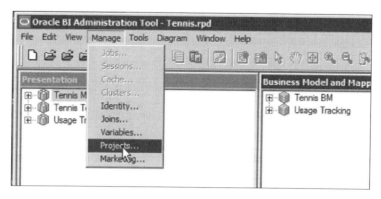

Then, you will enter the **Projects** screen where you can define your subsets. Now, you can choose the objects that our project will contain. You can choose whole business models or subject areas down to tables. You can also choose other objects, such as initialization blocks:

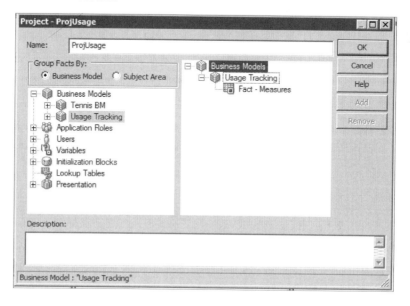

Let's create two projects; one for the main Tennis business model and another for the Usage Tracking model. Once this is done, we can place the master RPD in a shared location of our choosing.

The master RPD has now been set, so we will now access it as one of the developers on the project in their local environment. Firstly, open the local OBIEE Administration tool, without opening an RPD. Now, we want to define where our master RPD is, so that our local Administration tool will know where it can access the master. We do this by navigating to **Tools | Options**:

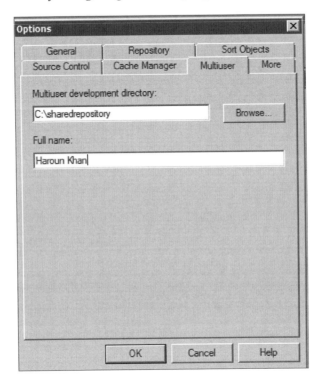

Under the **Multiuser** tab, stipulate the location of the master RPD and your (the developer's) name. This would normally be on a network share that is easily accessible by all users.

The **Full name** field is used for recording change control, as any changes and comments will be recorded with this name attached to them. Once this has been done, we are ready to locally access one of the projects that we have previously set up in the master RPD.

Select **File | Multiuser | Checkout**:

We are then prompted for the RPD password:

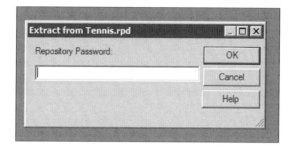

We are then prompted to choose one or more of the projects in the master RPD. Let's go ahead and choose the one that covers the main Tennis business model:

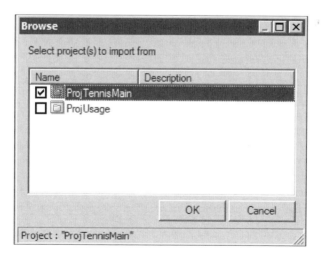

Once we have chosen the project and clicked on **OK**, a subset RPD containing only this project will be copied to our local development machine. Then, we are prompted to name this new subset RPD and save it in our local repository directory:

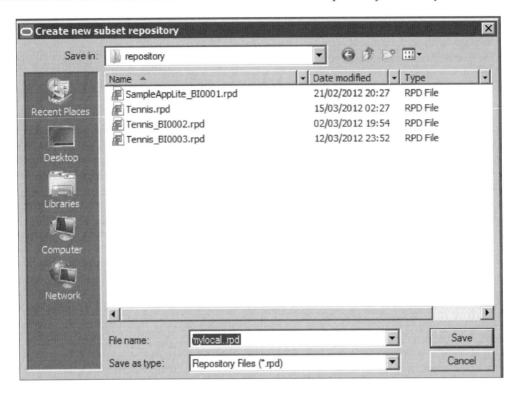

Once this is completed, we are now ready to make changes in our local environment. As a simple example, let's change the logical column **Month** by renaming it to **Months**.

After our changes have been made, and before we merge them with the master, we can compare our subset RPD with the Original. We do this by navigating to **File** | **Compare with Original...**:

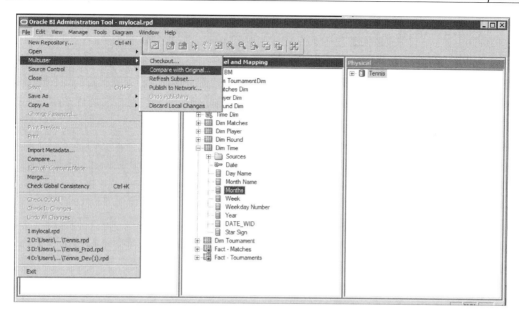

At this point, you will be presented with a screen showing the summary of all the changes that we have made. If you do not recognize a change or a difference, and wish to investigate it further, you can mark an individual change. Let's do that now by choosing the first change and clicking on the **Mark** button:

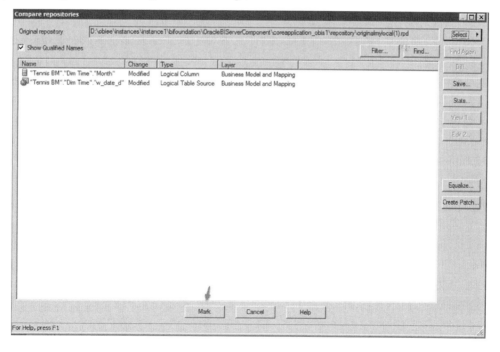

Once you have done this and have returned to the main repository, you can see that the change has been highlighted. Note the subtle icons in the following screenshot that shows our change:

If you are happy with the change, let's go ahead and merge our local changes back with the master. After doing the normal sanity check, such as checking the global consistency, we can merge our local changes with the master by choosing **Multiuser | Publish to Network...**:

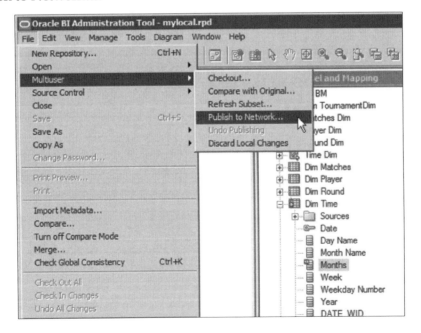

At this point, the master RPD needs to be locked by the system to ensure that no one else is making changes to the RPD at the same time:

The records on the **Lock Information** screen:

- **Login Name**: This field should be filled in with the username that we logged into the RPD.

- **Full Name**: It contains the name that we input when we set up our local Administration tool for multiuser development.

- **Computer Name**: This field should be filled in with your local development environment computer name.

- **Lock Time**: This field contains the time at which the lock and change will be recorded.

- **Comment**: It contains the reason why we are locking the RPD. This will be stored in a history that is accessible by all developers. So, it is worth spending a bit of time to make salient and descriptive comments about the set of changes that have been made.

Once we click on **OK**, the three-way merge process (that we have described at the beginning of this chapter) takes place on your local machine. Once you have stepped through the process, and dealt with any conflicts, the merged master is copied back to the central server.

At anytime, we can access the master to look at the development history. This is done from the **Multiuser** menu, as shown in the following screenshot:

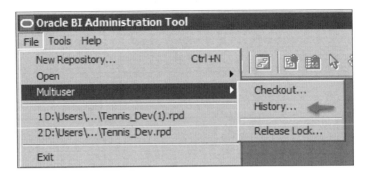

If we do this now, we can see that our change has been recorded in the **History** list. Through the **Action** option on this screen, we can also view or rollback the last set of changes and revert to the previous RPD version:

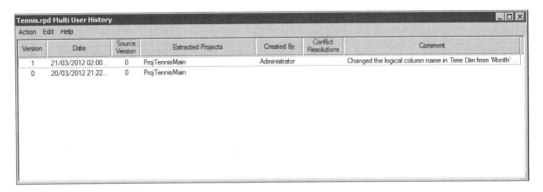

Advantages and disadvantages

Main disadvantages:

- The definition of Projects can be cumbersome and very time consuming to set up correctly.

- Each developer needs his/her own complete development environment including licensing.

- The overhead of the previous two points can make the development process slow.

- Regression and whole system testing needs to be carried out on the whole master RPD after merging is completed. This is in addition to developers unit testing in their own environments.

Main advantages:

- There is version and change control of objects within the RPD.
- The developer who made a change is recorded, and they can make comments.
- Rollback of changes is theoretically possible.

A review – what I should now know!

For self-review and a recap of the chapter, here are a few questions based on important topics covered in this chapter:

1. How do you merge multiple RPDs?
2. What are the options in instituting a multiuser development environment?
3. What are the pros and cons of multiuser online development?
4. How do you set up a local environment ready for MUDE?
5. What is a Project in MUDE?
6. Can you manage change outside of these tools?

Additional research suggestions

- Help files in the Presentation Catalog
- Oracle documentation: `http://www.oracle.com/technetwork/middleware/bi-enterprise-edition/documentation/index.html`

Summary

We have demonstrated methods of merging. We have also highlighted the two main Administration tool assisted ways of conducting multiuser development. Any well-run project must have a well-managed and formal change process in place. Ideally, your project should choose the methods appropriate to the size of both the project and development team, and whether the team is co-located or scattered across multiple sites. Whatever you choose should be documented and adhered to rigidly by developers, so it is well worth consulting them to develop a consensus on what is suitable.

Sharing an online RPD is very simple but lacks the full tracking that is provided by implementation of the full MUDE system. MUDE is great and it provides a non-bypassable system of recording change. However, a MUDE system does require far more overhead in licensing, equipment, and setup time. This is because developers need a full local OBIEE development environment in place, in addition to the central system rather than merely needing a locally installed Administration tool. Also, as we briefly mentioned at the beginning, do not be afraid to use traditional/basic methods such as organizing time-shares on an RPD, creating a change log on a spreadsheet and periodically making RPD backups. Especially when the development team is co-located and experienced, such a simple approach may suffice and has proven to be successful on the majority of projects.

Whatever you choose, ultimately the goal is that changes are made in a systematic and controlled manner so that they are introduced in a way that precludes and ameliorates the risk of faults being introduced. This requires a system that encourages coordination between developers, but at the same time remember we do not want to make the process so onerous that we hinder the rapid development that OBIEE supports!

16
Usage Tracking

Monitoring what your new Oracle BI system is doing and how well it does it, is vital for the long term success of the project. Analysis of the system usage can help to improve performance and user adoption. One of the great features of Oracle BI is that you can use the system, Dashboards and Analysis, to monitor the system itself, which means to say that you can use OBIEE Analysis to tell you how OBIEE is performing for your users.

In this chapter we will learn how to activate the "usage tracking" feature, and create useful reports from it.

There are some examples of a BI Server repository and web catalog containing the usage tracking metadata, and we have included copies for you to download on the supporting book website. This chapter will also demonstrate how you integrate these into your own system.

What is usage tracking?

The idea is simple—save each request that is made to the BI Server in a record, in a table, in a database. In that record of the request, note when and who issued it, and how well it performed. These are the typical attributes that are stored:

- User—who runs the request
- Date and time—the request was started and ended
- What was requested—details of the item that was run
- Time taken—broken down into various parts
- Number rows
- Error codes

System setup

Let's get the system set up to track usage. For our system, which is the standard method, the configuration is in three parts, and they are all linked to each other. The steps are:

1. Setting up the database table.
2. Setting up the BI Server repository.
3. Updating the BI Server's configuration file.

 There is an option to store the usage tracking records in a text file, but as this is not as useful as the database method, it will be more difficult and slower to analyze a text file than a database table.

Setting up the database table

Near the beginning of the book, we ran the RCU. This created a database schema with several tables in, one of which is normally used for the storing of the usage tracking records. The S_NQ_ACCT table has been in use since the nQuire days (hence the NQ in the name) but it has been updated in this release. The change has been to add some columns that are bigger, to cope with large queries. You do not need to use this specific table; you may prefer instead to use another schema elsewhere.

In a standard setup, the records are captured in this table, and the table is also used in the analysis. This is not the most efficient way for either process. The "insert records" process ideally does not want to be slowed down by indexes and column constraints. The analysis process ideally wants indexes, summaries, foreign keys, and so on to speed up the reports. The standard out-of-the-box setup makes a compromise and puts some indexes on the table. I prefer to separate the two processes completely! The benefit is faster insertions of usage tracking records and faster analysis of the results. The downside is that you have to wait until the ETL process has moved your usage tracking data into the analysis tables.

In my preferred setup, we keep the S_NQ_ACCT table in the RCU created schema, and drop any indexes that are created. This is the Capture Table. Then create another table, say W_USAGE_TRACKING, and use this one to report against. This is the Analysis Table. Each night, or more regularly if required, transfer the records from the Capture Table to the Analysis Table. Then make sure that the analysis table is optimized for reporting by ensuring that indexes are on the columns we need to report against and the appropriate STATS are in place. Then create summaries of this table to speed up the reports. These summaries can be materialized views or static tables.

The W_USAGE_TRACKING table is nearly identical to the capture table, except that we add extra fields. One of these fields is DATE_WID. This is so that the table can be linked to our standard W_DATE_D table. We add indexes to the table, on the date_wid field, and on the fields which will be filtered, such as USER_NAME and SAW_DASHBOARD. An additional task could be to create a day-level summary table that calculates performance measures for the day and will be joined to the W_DATE_D table, therefore enabling fast trend analysis.

Depending upon your setup, you may also want to capture user information. I often have a W_USER table in the warehouse anyway and will link this to the analysis table for department or location type reporting.

The changes made from 10g to 11g are:

Add the QUERY_BLOB column

Add the QUERY_KEY column

Rename the RUNAS_USER_NAME column to IMPERSONATOR_USER_NAME.

Additional data

Out of the box Usage Tracking (UT) is not fully configured, nor are the extra data required installed into the Oracle Bi schemas. To add the missing tables and data in an Oracle database, undertake the following steps:

1. Navigate to the SQL_Server_Time folder under F:\Oracle\FMW\instances\ instance1\bifoundation\OracleBIServerComponent\coreapplication_ obis1\sample\usagetracking.

2. Run the following files using SQL Developer or another IDE against the environments BIPLATFORM schema to create the time based tables for UT:
   - Oracle_create_nQ_Calendar.sql
   - Oracle_create_nQ_Clock.sql

3. Run the following SQL scripts to populate the tables created in the previous step.
   - Oracle_nQ_Calendar.sql
   - Oracle_nQ_Clock.sql

4. Run the following script to create a view for the table that leverages users for querying:
   ```
   CREATE OR REPLACE VIEW NQ_LOGIN_GROUP as
   select distinct USER_NAME as LOGIN, USER_NAME as RESP from S_NQ_
   ACCT;
   ```

Setting up the BI Server repository

The record capture process uses a table that is defined in the BI Server repository. This is simply a reference to the S_NQ_ACCT table, with a connection pool that has a write ability.

To create this table, you can either use the import functionality in the BI Administration tool, or you can copy the object from another RPD file (such as the sample one we have provided or that Oracle provides). To use the sample one provided by Oracle, follow these steps:

1. Navigate to this directory on the installation path, F:\Oracle\FMW\ instances\instance1\bifoundation\OracleBIServerComponent\ coreapplication_obis1\sample\usagetracking.

2. Unzip the usagetracking.zip file which contains the UT web catalog.

Copy the Repository objects into your own Repository. You will then have a database, connection pool, and table:

The analysis table can also be added now, although it's not required for the capture stage. Add another database, connection pool, and the analysis table, W_USAGE_TRACKING, plus any related tables such as W_DATE_D. You can use an existing database if you prefer.

Again, this can be an import process or copy from the existing RPD file. I copied from the sample RPD file on the support website.

Now you can create the business model and presentation layer. The result should look similar to the following screenshot:

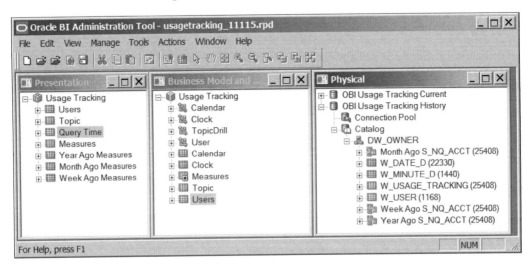

Updating the BI Server's configuration file

In 11.1.1.6 of Oracle BI, the configuration of Usage Tracking is done via Enterprise Manager. Beneath this section is the old legacy approach to configuring Usage Tracking left here for reference:

1. Open Enterprise Manager.

2. Expand the **WebLogic** folder on left navigation and right-click on **bifoundation_domain** to select **System MBean Browser**.

3. Expand **Application Defined MBeans**, and then expand **oracle.biee.admin**.

4. Expand Domain: **bifoundation_domain**.

5. Expand **BIDomain** and select **BIDomain MBean where group=Service**.

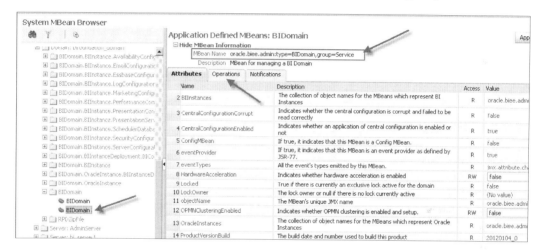

6. Click on the **Operations** tab.

7. Click on the **lock** link and then on the **Invoke** button to lock the domain.

8. Expand **BIDomain.BIInstance.ServerConfiguration**, and then select the **BIDomain.BIInstance.ServerConfiguration MBean**:

9. Set the following values:

Setting	Value
UsageTrackingCentrallyManaged	True
UsageTrackingConnectionPool	"BI Usage Tracking 11g"."Usage Tracking Writer Connection Pool"
UsageTrackingDirectInsert	True
UsageTrackingEnabled	True
UsageTrackingPhysicalTableName	"BI Usage Tracking 11g"."Catalog"."dbo"."S_NQ_ACCT"

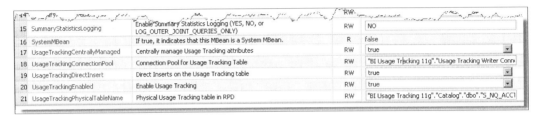

			RW	
15	SummaryStatisticsLogging	Enable Summary Statistics Logging (YES, NO, or LOG_OUTER_JOINT_QUERIES_ONLY)	RW	NO
16	SystemMBean	If true, it indicates that this MBean is a System MBean.	R	false
17	UsageTrackingCentrallyManaged	Centrally manage Usage Tracking attributes	RW	
18	UsageTrackingConnectionPool	Connection Pool for Usage Tracking Table	RW	"BI Usage Tracking 11g"."Usage Tracking Writer Conn
19	UsageTrackingDirectInsert	Direct Inserts on the Usage Tracking table	RW	true
20	UsageTrackingEnabled	Enable Usage Tracking	RW	true
21	UsageTrackingPhysicalTableName	Physical Usage Tracking table in RPD	RW	"BI Usage Tracking 11g"."Catalog"."dbo"."S_NQ_ACCT

10. Click on the **Apply** button to save the changes:

11. Now return to **BIDomain** and select **BIDomain MBean where group=Service** section and click the Operations tab.

12. Click on the **commit** link (the one whose resulting page doesn't not have an area to enter parameters).

13. Click on the **Invoke** button. This confirms the changes you've made and unlocks the domain:

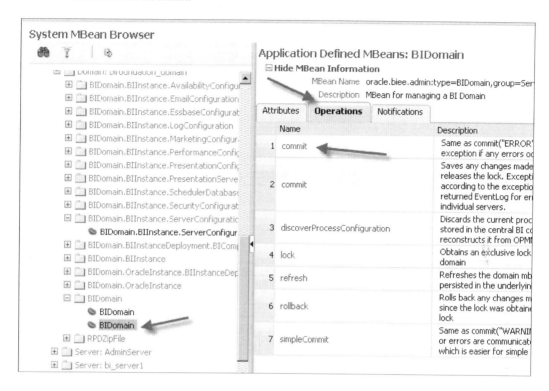

14. Restart System Components.

After the configuration changes have been made, you will need to restart the services.

At this point, every request made to the BI Server will be logged in to the S_NQ_ACCT table. Use an ETL tool, such as the Oracle Data Integrator, to copy the records into the W_USAGE_TRACKING table and refresh any materials views you have created. If you do not have an ETL tool, simple SQL scripts will do the job just as well.

Usage tracking is not related to the LOGGING LEVEL variable that each user has. Logging level relates to the amount of information that is placed into the NQQuery.log file.

Analyzing the usage

Now that we are getting data into the tables and have set up the BI repository to access the data, we can start creating an analysis to see what is going on. Typical analyses that I would create are:

- The top 10 slowest dashboards
- The top 10 slowest analyses
- User activity over time
- Non-users
- Dashboard usage analysis
- Error reports

Oracle have already developed a sample set of reports which may be worth using to start with, but I recommend that you develop your own ones that help to drive better performance and increased usage of your OBIEE system.

Usage measures

Before using some of the measures you need to understand what each one does and, therefore, will understand how they are relevant. The following table describes each field in the main usage tracking table:

Field	Description
TOTAL_TIME_SEC	The time (in seconds) that the Oracle BI Server spent for working on the query, while the client waited for responses to its query requests. This setting is the same as the Response time in the nqquery.log file. Usually, it is the difference between the start time and the end time. The same results are returned from the following function: ROUND((CAST(END_TS as DATE)-CAST(START_TS as DATE))*86400)
COMPILE_TIME_SEC	The time (in seconds) required to compile the query.
ROW_COUNT	The number of rows returned to the querying client.
CUM_DB_TIME_SEC	The total amount of time (in seconds) that the Oracle BI Server waited for backend physical databases on behalf of a logical query.
CUM_NUM_DB_ROW	The total number of rows returned by the backend databases.

Field	Description
NUM_DB_QUERY	The number of queries submitted to backend databases in order to satisfy the logical query request. For successful queries (SuccessFlag = 0), this number will be 1 or greater.
NUM_CACHE_HITS	Indicates the number of times the existing cache was returned.
NUM_CACHE_INSERTED	Indicates the number of times the query generated cache was returned.
QUERY_TEXT	The SQL submitted for the query.
QUERY_BLOB	The data type is ntext when using the SQL Server, and is CLOB when using Oracle, DB2, or Terradata databases. Contains the entire logical SQL statement without any truncation.
QUERY_KEY	An MD5 hash key that is generated by Oracle Business Intelligence from the logical SQL statement.
SUBJECT_AREA_NAME	The name of the business model being accessed.
REPOSITORY_NAME	The name of the repository the query accesses.
IMPERSONATOR_USER_NAME	The user ID of impersonated user. If the request is not run as an impersonated user, the value will be NULL.
USER_NAME	The name of the user who submitted the query, from the USER variable.
PRESENTATION_NAME	The name of the Presentation Catalog in Oracle BI Presentation Services.
QUERY_SRC_CD	The source of the request; for example, Drill or Report.
SAW_DASHBOARD	The path of the dashboard. If the query was not submitted through an Interactive Dashboard, the value will be NULL.
SAW_DASHBOARD_PG	The page's name in the Interactive Dashboard. If the request is not a dashboard request, the value will be NULL.
SAW_SRC_PATH	The path name in the Oracle BI Presentation Catalog for the request.
START_DT	The date the logical query was submitted.
START_HOUR_MIN	The hour and minute the logical query was submitted.
START_TS	The date and time the logical query was submitted.
END_DT	The date the logical query was completed.
END_HOUR_MIN	The hour and minute the logical query was completed.
END_TS	The date and time the logical query finished. The start and end timestamps also reflect the time that the query spent waiting for resources to become available.

Field	Description
ERROR_TEXT	The error message from the backend database. This column is only applicable if SUCCESS_FLG is set to a value other than 0 (zero). Multiple messages will concatenate and will not be parsed by the Oracle BI Server.
CACHE_IND_FLG	The default value is N. Y indicates a cache hit for the query and N indicates a cache miss.
SUCCESS_FLG	This indicates the completion status of the query: 0: The query completed successfully with no errors. 1: The query timed out. 2: The query failed because row limits were exceeded. 3: The query failed due to some other reason.

The following table describes each field in the extra usage tracking table that is used for storing the physical SQL that is sent to the database:

Field	Description
QUERY_TEXT	The first 1024 characters of the SQL query.
QUERY_BLOB	The whole SQL query sent to the database.
TIME_SEC	The time taken to return data from the database.
ROW_COUNT	The number of rows returned from the database.
START_TS	Start time.
START_DT	Start date.
START_HOUR_MIN	The time (in hours and minutes) that the query was sent to the database.
END_TS	The time the results were returned to the BI Server.
END_DT	The date the results were returned to the BI Server.
END_HOUR_MIN	The hours and minutes in the HHMM format that the data returned.

A review – what I should now know!

For self-review and a recap of the chapter, here are a few questions based on the topics covered in this chapter:

1. What is usage tracking?
2. What three areas are configured to get usage tracking working?
3. What is TOTAL_TIME_SEC?
4. Should I use a warehouse table to report against or should I use the RCU table?
5. What types of report should I build to improve usage?

Summary

In this chapter, we showed how to set up the system to "track" the user activity that impacts the BI Server.

Usage tracking is important to help manage the overall health of the OBIEE system. It should be used regularly to identify heavy users and heavy usage times, along with bottlenecks. Use the stats over time to ensure that users are not turning off due to poor performance. User adoption can also be improved by identifying people that are not using the system. It can also be used to check that the cache seeding is effective.

In the next chapter we will look at the BI Administration tool, which will also help in our system management processes.

17
Oracle Essbase and OLAP Integration

Since Oracle acquired Hyperion in 2007, they have steadily increased customer awareness that bringing **Business Intelligence** and **Enterprise Performance Management (EPM)** together provides a much more complete view of how an organization can analyze its business. Hyperion was best known for its core **Online Analytics Processing (OLAP)** tool, **Essbase**. Oracle has successfully rolled Hyperion Essbase into its Application stack. However, Essbase is not the only OLAP tool that Oracle owns. Nor is it the only OLAP engine that Oracle BI can leverage as a data source.

In this chapter, we will look at how OLAP technologies integrate into Oracle BI. After exploring the options, we will focus on Oracle Essbase as the preferred OLAP technology. This chapter will show you how to integrate Oracle Essbase as a data source in Oracle BI and define several best practices for the integration. At the end of the chapter, you should have a well-balanced sense of how Essbase integrates with Oracle BI and the added value that it can bring to an organization.

A bit about OLAP

OLAP technology has been around for many years. It is a technology system in and of itself. Over the years, it has developed its own standards and earned itself a stay in almost every organization's analytical decision support reporting toolbox. The preferred language for querying OLAP data is a technology called **Multidimensional Expressions (MDX)**. Just as a relational database management system (RDBMS) uses SQL (Structured Query Language) to read and write its data, an OLAP structure uses MDX but solely in a read-only capacity.

Competition

There are four major OLAP tools that Oracle BI supports: Oracle Essbase, **Oracle OLAP, SAP BW**, and **Microsoft SQL Server Analytic Services (SSAS)**. There are pros and cons to each. An organization's bias, if any, is usually due to its corporate technology standard. An organization declaring itself as a Microsoft "shop" will usually integrate SSAS if requiring an OLAP technology. However, that does not preclude it from using another OLAP technology. Essbase is usually the exception that finds its way into an organization's OLAP mix, but in many cases it was already the incumbent under its Hyperion moniker.

MOLAP, ROLAP, HOLAP, XOLAP

What would a technology book be without more technology acronyms? Well, here are some more for you to add to your already lengthy list.

We've talked about OLAP technology and in many cases the terminology is misused. When this disruptive technology emerged, there were very few software vendors that understood how valuable it would become to the evolution of structuring data. There were many variations on the same concept. OLAP is a general encompassing term that has an overarching definition for aggregate data storage. **Aggregate Data Storage** means that the data is taken from a lower level or transactional level of granularity such as the date, customer, and store level in a data warehouse and summed to a higher level at some delayed frequency and stored for later retrieval. This process and the OLAP engine allow for complicated data calculations and pre-aggregation of data against varied dimensionality to be achieved. The result provides the ability to quickly query an otherwise large and complex amount of data which is most often required by executive levels of reporting. Compare that to a SQL query against an RDBMS every time a report is needed. The amount of time and processor resources required for an RDBMS to sum, count, or otherwise aggregate, millions of records from the data warehouse to multiple levels of granularity for every combination of data relationship is immense.

Although OLAP is the general term, the OLAP solutions mentioned earlier that are offered by the major software vendors are actually **Multidimensional Online Analytical Processing (MOLAP)** solutions. This was the original terminology of this standard, which is commonly referred to as OLAP. However, due to different business analytics reporting requirements affecting this type of multidimensional system, several variations of MOLAP technology were forged. Requirements such as the need to blend real-time data, combining MOLAP data with its relational data source counterparts, and applying security at different levels helped in bringing on these variations.

Here are short definitions of those variations of OLAP:

- **Relational OLAP (ROLAP)**: This is a system using a multidimensional architecture sourced primarily against one or more relational databases; typically a **Data Warehouse**. The appearance of accessing a multidimensional cube is a derivative created by an **Extract Transform Load (ETL)** process which creates aggregated information. Slicing and dicing is ultimately boiled down to interpreted SQL query syntax, such as using a simple WHERE clause.

- **Hybrid OLAP (HOLAP)**: This is a technology that allows for data stored within separate repositories, such as a multidimensional OLAP system and an RDBMS to be combined at some level of granularity. The goal is to allow for more efficient querying of associated data slices allowing for the query to be optimized by the system that performs best at each respective level. This is usually OLAP for higher summarized levels and the RDBMS for the more detailed levels.

- **eXtended OLAP (XOLAP)**: This is a technology spawned for Essbase that attempts to use the structure of an Essbase multidimensional database metadata outline to control the retrieval of data from a relational data source at runtime. Basically, it is an integration of a relational data source with Essbase, which is primarily used as its own multidimensional OLAP system.

What all of these variations have in common is the concept of dimensions and the ability to aggregate. Dimensions are a way of slicing or gaining perspective against the underlying "fact" data or metrics. Ultimately, the storage repository associated with an OLAP engine is commonly referred to as a **cube** and sometimes a **hypercube**.

Essbase's entrenched past

Hyperion has been a long-time incumbent in most organizations but not under the Information Technology umbrella as some may think. Essbase was originally the champion of the Finance department due to its ability to aggregate financial data, handle calculations, and process complicated allocations with relative ease. It also allowed for ad-hoc analysis of said data via the familiar tool, Microsoft Excel, via a proprietary Hyperion Excel add-in. As a matter of fact, Essbase was born out of the inherent challenges of using spreadsheets for analytics in a standard and scalable way. Essbase is actually an acronym that stands for **E**xtended **S**pread **S**heet data**BASE**. Prior to being acquired by Oracle, Essbase had been developed by software company, Arbor, before it merged with Hyperion Solutions Corporation in 1998. It has been the subject of conversation in many organizations, specifically when it comes to which department would maintain the software – Finance or IT. After its acquisition by Oracle, this conversation arises less because of the repositioning of Essbase into Oracle Fusion Middleware, which is owned by IT.

Unfortunately, with this type of history inside of an organization, building an integration path between Oracle BI and Oracle Essbase can have complications like any other integration. This chapter should give you enough insight and know-how in order to roll out a quick **Proof-of-Concept (POC)** in order to dazzle the business team that usually owns Essbase. Just don't forget that the business users often need a little extra **Tender Loving Care (TLC)** during this process; Essbase is their baby you're playing with.

Oracle Essbase Studio

Oracle Essbase is a server engine. The ability to create the metadata associated with the database cube is usually conducted through the **Essbase Administration Service (EAS)** console. Introduced shortly before Hyperion was purchased by Oracle, a different GUI development interface called **Essbase Studio** was introduced. This separate application allows a user to create an Essbase cube via a GUI IDE. It also is the first of the tools to assist with XOLAP technology development. It can even use Oracle BI as a data source. Using **Oracle Essbase Studio** to build an Essbase cube with Oracle BI as a data source allows an existing enterprise Oracle BI logical model to be translated into an aggregate storage repository. This could potentially create something of a feedback loop, in that the resulting Essbase cube could then be imported into the Oracle BI repository and leveraged as a data source.

More information about Essbase Studio can be found at the **Oracle Technology Network (OTN)** site, `http://www.obi11gbook.com/u/17`.

Oracle BI SampleApp v107+ – VM image

The Oracle BI development team has worked hard at getting its best in class solution to customers. They've produced a composite set of materials and artifacts called the **Sample Application (SampleApp)**, which is comprised of an Oracle BI RPD, Presentation Catalog, supporting sample data, and more. These SampleApp artifacts, downloadable from the OTN in compressed file format, are ready for installation into an existing Oracle BI 11*g* environment for demonstration, education, and testing purposes. More importantly, since the Oracle BI development team has produced the dashboards, models, and so on in the SampleApp, they are sure to highlight the deepest capabilities of Oracle BI.

This team has also developed a ready to deploy sandbox server environment leveraging **Virtual Machine** (VM) technology. This VM image contains an Oracle BI 11*g* server, Essbase Server, Times Ten Server, Oracle DB 11*g* Server, and ancillary software all in one demo environment. It is available for download via the OTN with a registered user account. The download is approximately 25 GB, so prepare in advance for the download time. The VM image is based on **VirtualBox**, which is an Oracle sponsored open source operating system agnostic VM technology. The VM image itself is based on the Linux operating system, **Oracle Enterprise Linux (OEL)**. Download the VM Image from the OTN, http://www.obi11gbook.com/u/18

The SampleApp artifacts (not the Oracle software technologies) are open source. This means that you can leverage the data and models where you see fit, as long as it complies with the open source license or third-party licenses under which it is released.

Getting started – let's get set up

As a pre-requisite to the exercise in this chapter, you must have an Essbase Server from which to operate. If you already have an Essbase Server at your disposal, you are ready to start the exercises. If not, as mentioned above, the Oracle BI **SampleApp** has an Essbase Server ready for you to use and it is perfect for what you will do in the exercise. We are actually using the SampleApp v107 VirtualBox Virtual Machine image in order to create this exercise.

If we had you create an Essbase outline/cube from scratch, it would be several chapters in length; more if we wanted to do it justice. Instead, to save you time, we have provided the necessary Essbase outline (OTL) file, and data files necessary for you. In this way, you can focus on the quick load of the outline into your Essbase Server so that you can get right to the exercises. The set up is fairly straightforward and will be a breeze for anyone already familiar with developing an Essbase cube. Regardless, the steps for how to access the **Essbase Administration Services** (EAS) console, create a base Essbase application and database, and import the exercise files to the file system are explained in the section below.

Prepping the VM image

It doesn't matter if you are using an existing Essbase server that you have access to or the Essbase Server on the SampleApp VirtualBox VM image, there are a few steps required to get going with the exercises. If you are using an existing Essbase Server on your network then you can skip to the section below called Prepping Essbase. Otherwise, complete this section for the SampleApp VM image.

Downloading the VirtualBox application and setting up the SampleApp VM image is already explained in detail from the document that comes with the SampleApp VM download. Follow those instructions found in the PDF, which you may download from the following URL:

`http://www.obi11gbook.com/u/18`

The following instructions assume that you are running the hosted VirtualBox application on a Windows operation system.

Starting the virtual machine image

The machine on which the VirtualBox application is installed is called the **Host** machine. The VM image, in this case the SampleApp VM Image, is referred to as the **Guest**. To start the VirtualBox guest image:

1. Navigate to **Start | Programs | Oracle VM VirtualBox | Oracle VM VirtualBox**.

2. Click on the **SampleApp_<version>** option in the **VirtualBox Manager** and then click on the **Start** button.

3. The VirtualBox guest VM image GUI will then start and should automatically login the user, Oracle. Once the Linux desktop is visible, continue to the next section below. If the Oracle user does not automatically get logged in, the password is `oracle`.

Starting up Essbase

The VM image makes starting up the standalone Essbase Server a breeze. From the Linux desktop:

1. Double-click on the `Startup Scripts` folder on the desktop. A folder list of executable files appears.

2. Double-click on the **4-StartESSB.sh** option to begin the process to start the Essbase Server and the **Analytic Provider Services (APS)** server.

3. Click the **Run Terminal** button that appears in the resulting execution confirmation prompt.

An alternative to the above approach for starting the Essbase server is to open a terminal window and enter `startESSB` followed by pressing the *Enter* key. The `startESSB` command is an alias in the `~/.bashrc` file that acts as a shortcut command to the startup shell script.

The terminal window will open and run. Once the terminal is started, continue to the next step.

Starting up Essbase Administration Services (EAS)

By default, EAS is not started. To start it:

1. Open a Terminal prompt on the Linux desktop via **Applications | Accessories | Terminal**.

2. Change the directory to the EAS directory path using the command:

   `cd/epm/Middleware/user_projects/epmsystem1/bin`

   Alternatively, depending on the SampleApp release:

   `cd/home/oracle/epm/Middleware/user_projects/epmsystem1/bin`

3. Run the Start EAS command: `./startEssbaseAdminServices.sh`. This command will run in the console and complete silently, returning to the command prompt, as shown in the following screenshot. In the next step, you'll prepare the Essbase server to import the database outline and files required for this exercise:

```
[oracle@demo bin]$ ./startEssbaseAdminServices.sh
Starting EssbaseAdminServices.properties
Apache Ant version 1.7.0 compiled on December 13 2006
Buildfile: /epm/Middleware/EPMSystem11R1/common/config/11.1.2.0/resources/instance/start.xml
Finish EssbaseAdminServices.properties
[oracle@demo bin]$
```

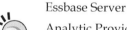

Ultimately, for the communication with Essbase to perform properly the following three Essbase related components must be started:

Essbase Server

Analytic Provider Services

Essbase Administration Services

The scripts `startEssbase.sh`, `startAnalyticProviderServices.sh` and `startEssbaseAdminServices.sh` must be executed in the order listed.

Prepping Essbase

As mentioned previously, we've developed the Essbase outline and ancillary files for you as a jumpstart to this exercise. Your initial job is to load these files onto your Essbase Server. There is really no automated means to import this information so follow the manual steps discussed in the following sections.

Creating the base Essbase application and database

In order to create the base Essbase application and database, carry out the following steps:

1. Open the Essbase Administration Console by navigating to the URL, `http://<server_name>:10080/easconsole/console.html` if using the SampleApp VM. If using an Essbase system on your network, your URL may vary slightly. You can also use the full EAS fat-client application for these steps, if it is available to you. You can download the EAS fat-client from the OTN by selecting the Essbase Clients Release option, `http://www.obi11gbook.com/u/20`, but the EAS thin web client will work fine for this exercise:

> If prompted with a launch screen, click on the **Launch** button.
>
> If prompted with the **Java Web Start Opening easconsole. jnlp** prompt, click on the **OK** button.

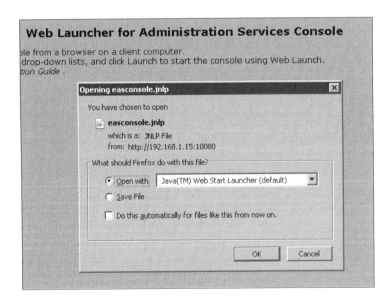

2. Accept any other prompts or warnings and continue.

3. Log in with the Administrator credentials and if you are using the SampleApp VM image, the username is admin and the password is password:

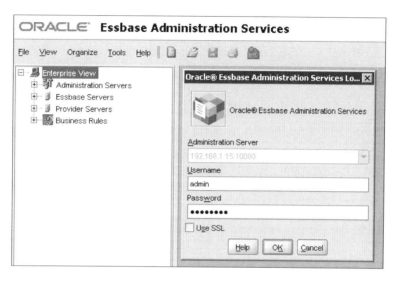

4. Expand the **Essbase Servers** node to ensure the server is started and you are properly connected.

If a TCP/IP error appears and you are unable to access the Essbase Servers list, even though you have started Essbase, APS, and EAS and you are working on the SampleApp VM image, the problem may be due to the VirtualBox Network Adapter settings for the VM image. Change the network settings to a Bridged configuration so that the VM image obtains its own DHCP assigned IP address, restart the VM and start again.

5. Expand the **Essbase Servers** node to show all available applications.

6. Right-click on the **Applications** node.

7. Go to **Create application | Using aggregate storage**:

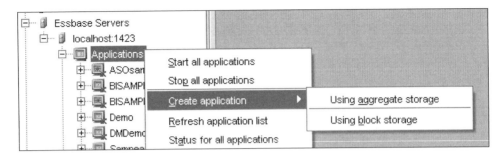

8. In the name prompt, enter OBIBook and accept all of the defaults.

9. The application will be created and should show up under the Essbase Server's Application list hierarchy on the left.

10. Right-click on the Essbase application, **OBIBook**, that you just created and select **Create database...**.

11. Enter OBIBook in the field and click on the **OK** button.

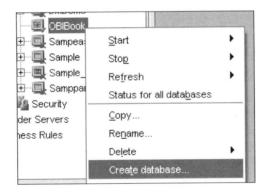

12. Right-click on the **OBIBook** application once again and this time, go to the **Stop | Application** option. Accept the **Confirm Application Stop** prompt.

It is important that the application is stopped because in the next steps you will overwrite the very important .otl (outline) file that holds the dimensional structure and metadata for the Essbase cube.

Migrating the Essbase files

As promised, we have the necessary Essbase files available from the Oracle BI 11*g* Book website or find the link on the Oracle BI 11*g* Book Forum, `http://www.obi11gbook.com/forums/`.

1. Download the Essbase files from the links mentioned above or from Packt's website at `http://packtpub.com`.

2. Copy the `.zip` file to the following location on the Essbase Server, `<EPM_FMW_HOME>/user_projects/epmsystem1/EssbaseServer/essbaseserver1/app/;` for example, `/epm/Middleware/user_projects/epmsystem1/EssbaseServer/essbaseserver1/app/`.

 You clearly need to have access to the physical server on which the Essbase Server resides in order to conduct this copy process. On the VM Image, you can either FTP the files or create a network share to place the files in the path.

3. Notice, that the folders in this directory correspond with the Essbase applications on the Essbase server. OBIBook is the main folder for the application you just created, but a subfolder by the same name exists which represents the database.

4. Unzip the downloaded file using the `unzip` command directly into this location. Several files will be overwritten in the subfolder, OBIBook, as well as some new ones will be added.

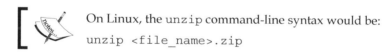 On Linux, the `unzip` command-line syntax would be:
`unzip <file_name>.zip`

5. Accept any overwrite prompts so that the files are moved from the `.zip` file to the OBIBook folder and subfolder correctly.

Validating the Outline

The easiest way to check that the files were correctly copied into the new Essbase Server OBIBook application is to refresh the outline in EAS. Follow these steps:

1. Return to the EAS console.

2. Expand the **Essbase Servers** applications list and locate the **OBIBook** application.

3. Right-click on the **OBIBook** application and select **Start Application**.

4. Click on the **Yes** button to confirm the application start, if prompted.

5. Expand the **OBIBook** application node.

6. Expand the **OBIBook** database node.

7. Right-click on the **Outline** node and select the **View** option.

In the right-hand pane, the outline should render and contain the **OBIBook** outline that has been created for you. It should look like the following screenshot:

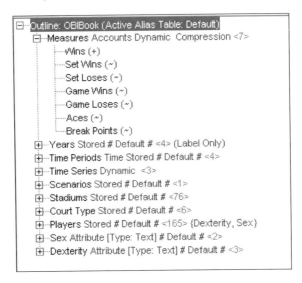

Loading data into the cube

Load the data into the cube by referencing a load rule file and data file that were delivered with the downloaded .zip file you unzipped:

1. Right-click on the **OBIBook** database and select **Load Data....**

2. Click on the **Find Rules File** button at the bottom of the **Data Load** prompt.

3. Select the datatxt.rul file and click the **OK** button.

4. Click the **Find Data File** button at the bottom of the **Data Load** prompt.

5. Select the **Essbase Server** tab.

6. Select the **OBIBook** application level (star icon not database icon) option from the **Look in:** drop-down menu.

7. Select **OBIBook.txt** and then click on the **OK** button.

8. Click on the **OK** button in the Data Load prompt to begin the data load.

9. Click on the **Close** button to close the Data Load process when complete.

The data load will complete with warnings which is an expected behavior. This is because the text file used in the data load and Essbase outline were purposefully developed with inconsistencies for future training on cleaning and maintaining Essbase cubes. Data will still be successfully loaded to the OBIBook cube and you can use an MS Excel add-in or **SmartView** to verify this if you desire. Otherwise, continue on with the exercises below to model the Essbase cube into Oracle BI and create a report to view the Essbase data.

Anything needed to prep the Oracle BI Server?

Out-of-the-box, Oracle BI 11*g* installs with enough information so that it can recognize many metadata sources without the need for an additional driver or API reference configurations. The current Oracle BI version, 11.1.1.6 as of this writing, ships with the Essbase client API libraries, so that no additional configuration is required to connect to and model Essbase data. The Oracle BI server makes reference to any additional drivers and libraries it requires by calling an initialization command file whenever the Administration Tool is launched. Additional library references are required to communicate with separate applications such as Essbase and **Hyperion Financial Management (HFM)**. The two files that assist in the reference of these client libraries are `bi-init.bat` and `opmn.xml`. However, the `opmn.xml` file does not get installed with the Oracle BI client tools only installation; only the full server installation.

The `bi-init.bat` file sets certain environment variable paths once the Administration tool is launched, so that the tool has a sense of where to locate certain libraries and configuration paths specific to the Oracle BI 11*g* client tools. Typically, there is no additional configuration required to this file.

The other configuration file, `opmn.xml`, is available under the Oracle BI 11*g* installation path, `<FMW_HOME>\instances\instance1\config\OPMN\opmn\`. The `opmn.xml` file is the configuration file which sets the locations for the Essbase or HFM client libraries amongst other settings specific to the OPMN. In the latest Oracle BI 11*g* version, the Administration tool is ready to import an Essbase cube as a data source out-of-the-box with no configuration necessary. Additional configuration of the `opmn.xml` file is required for HFM as it is a Microsoft Windows-based software product and the HFM client must be installed separately from the Oracle BI product.

Modeling Essbase into Oracle BI

The techniques that you will learn in this chapter follow best practices and will provide the result of front-ending Essbase data through Oracle BI. After the exercise, you'll get the right direction to further your learning so that eventually you can talk about this high-demand integration like a pro.

A bit of Essbase to Oracle BI knowledge

Importing a multidimensional data source such as Essbase into the Oracle BI RPD requires that Oracle BI is able to represent the multidimensional data, just as it would a relational data source. This provides the potential for federation, or joining, of heterogeneous data sources logically. As a multidimensional source is already well-structured based on the OLAP modeling techniques using facts and dimensions (star schema), the imported metadata about that source get translated cleanly to the Physical layer in the RPD. Extra columns and properties unique to Essbase are immediately available. These include Member Aliases, **User Defined Attributes (UDAs)**, **Member Number Ranking** (memnor—numeric column sorting information instead of the default in Essbase which is alphabetical), and most importantly for hierarchical lineages, information about root, leaf, and parent levels. The hierarchy lineage information may take many extra steps to develop when using a relational source, but it is immediately included with a multidimensional source. When you import the Essbase source in the exercise below and expand a dimension hierarchy in the Physical layer, you will explore some of these columns and properties just described.

Something else to keep in mind is that the Oracle BI repository brings over almost all of the metadata inherent in an Essbase data source. **Substitution variables** (similar to variables in the RPD), at any scope, are imported, converted into **Session variables**, and an **Initialization Block** is created to dynamically cycle changes in those variables to reflect anticipated changes. Essbase generation names are reflected in the Physical layer which is why the best practice is to modify the Essbase outline generation names in advance for consistency. And, although the first Generation of an Essbase dimension is merely the dimension itself, an option exists in the Administration Tool to remove it from the Logical layer when modeling the repository, as it is typically not needed for analysis efforts.

The best practice of creating Essbase generation names can be learned from http://www.obi11gbook.com/u/25.

Hopefully, this section gave you a bit more information into how much effort has gone into ensuring that native Oracle Essbase information is reserved and leveraged as a data source in Oracle BI. Now, let's begin the effort to bring the OBIBook cube into Oracle BI.

Importing Essbase as a data source

Now that the Essbase data source is alive and well on our Essbase server, we will need to open the Oracle BI Administration Tool to import the cube into our repository model.

1. Open the Oracle BI Administration Tool.

2. Open the Repository (Tennis.rpd) file in online mode using **File | Open Online...**.

3. From the **File** menu, select **Import Metadata...**.

4. Select **Essbase** from the **Connection Type** drop-down menu.

5. In the **Essbase Server** field, enter the IP address, or the server name, of the machine where your OBIBook cube is running.

6. Enter the Essbase Server administrator's credentials in the **User Name** and **Password** fields (admin/password).

7. Click on the **Next** button.

8. Expand the server name node under the **Data source view** column.

9. Select the **OBIBook** Essbase cube from the options and click the right-arrow from the center area between the **Data source view** and **Repository View** columns to import the cube.

10. Make sure that the **Import UDAs** checkbox is checked and leave all other default options in place.

11. Click on the **Finish** button.

The Essbase data source now appears in the Physical layer of the RPD. The import creates a Physical Database named after the Essbase Server from where you imported the source, a Physical Catalog named after the Essbase application, **OBIBook**, and a **Cube Table** named after the Essbase application database. Expanding the first level of the **Court Type** dimension, we can see that the Essbase generation naming (**All Courts, Court Types**, and so on) best practice is applied and is pulled from the Essbase server as anticipated:

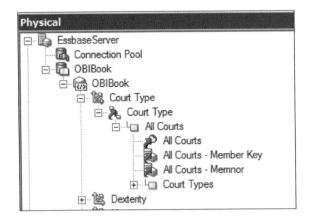

 By default, the dimension-level naming convention given to an Essbase data source imported into the RPD is very generic. To remedy this, in advance of importing the Essbase data source into the RPD, open the Essbase cube outline in EAS and change the name of the Essbase generations to reflect a more canonical form or business name. With this best practice, once the metadata import takes place, the generation names you've modified overwrite the default level names making the metadata identifiable and consistent with the source metadata.

Take a few seconds to review how the Physical layer structure of the OBIBook source looks in the RPD. Look at the measure and dimensions and compare them to the outline in EAS briefly to see that they are basically one-to-one.

A few OLAP adjustments before modeling

The Essbase data source in Oracle BI can be modified at the Physical layer so that its underlying metadata can be correctly interpreted by the Oracle BI Server engine at runtime. Of course, modifications to generation (translated to table column) names can be altered, and more just like any other source elements in the Physical layer. However, there are several other OLAP specific modifications that should be made, or at a minimum, assessed before beginning the full repository modeling process.

These include adjusting the **Hierarchy Type** and **Dimension Type** of the OLAP dimension, flattening a measure dimension's members to individual fact columns, creating columns for **User-Defined Attributes** (UDAs), and creating columns for Alias Table member variations. Let's begin making these modifications in the following sections.

Flattening the Measure dimension

Oracle BI pulls in an Essbase measures (Accounts) dimension as a measure hierarchy with a single measure representing all measures/accounts. In some basic reporting cubes, the number of measures or metrics that are used in the cube should be represented in a columnar structure, rather than in a hierarchy. In Essbase, having a measures dimension for the purpose of a financials-based data source, such as a **General Ledger** (GL) cube, usually means a **Chart of Accounts (COA)**. For example, the GL cube could have a measures hierarchy to identify Margin which would have children elements of Sales and **Cost of Goods Sold (COGS)**. That means Sales - COGS = Margin. Flattening the dimension hierarchy for a Chart of Accounts would not be ideal and would functionally break the desired GL reporting structure. However, for the OBIBook cube you will want to flatten the measures dimension due to the small number of metrics that are used and knowing that no real measure hierarchy exists in the cube design. To flatten the measures dimension, follow these steps:

1. Right-click on the **OBIBook** cube table from the Physical layer and select **Convert measure dimension to flat measures**.

2. As a result, the OBIBook cube table refreshes. Expand the cube table and notice that all of the elements in the measures dimension now appear as columns, as seen in the following screenshot:

You will have noticed that before the measure dimension was flattened, only a single fact measure, **OBIBook – measure**, existed. It was replaced by the other seven measures in this process. Lastly, the **Measures** dimension still exists. However, right-clicking on it no longer shows the option to flatten the dimension. As a best practice, you'll keep the **Measures** dimension intact for the life of the model. It does not get brought into the logical layer after you drag the cube table from the physical layer so there is no harm keeping it right where it is. You'll drag over the physical layer objects to the logical layer very soon.

Getting the UDAs

The UDAs that are assigned to any level of a dimension can be pulled in as separate columns. You can do this for all UDAs across the entire cube, or you can focus on leveraging only the UDAs in one or more dimensions. The OBIBook cube has only one dimension using UDAs - **Players**.

1. Right-click on the **Players** dimension in the Physical layer and go to **Create columns for UDA | Top Country**:

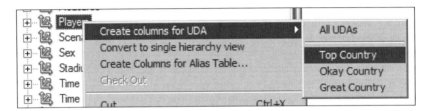

 The option for **All UDAs** exists but here we are trying to highlight a minimalist's approach to getting at the Essbase data.

2. Expand the **Players** dimension and you'll notice how the **Top Country** UDA has become a column at each level in the Players dimension hierarchy.

Dimension and hierarchy types

All Essbase dimensions hierarchies are imported with the default hierarchy type of Unbalanced. An **Unbalanced** hierarchy type is what is referred to as a "ragged" hierarchy where not all levels within an Essbase hierarchy have the same depth. This hierarchy type will work for most dimensions but the other two hierarchy types allowed for Essbase modeling are **Fully Balanced** and **Value**. Fully Balanced refers to a level-based structure where all levels roll-up nicely to their parent levels.

An example would be a time dimension hierarchy of Year, Half-Year, Quarter, and Month. The Value hierarchy type truly refers to a parent-child structured dimension where all members have the same type such as an employee dimension, regardless if its hierarchy is balanced or not. The hierarchy type property helps the Oracle BI Server understand how to define the relationship of members within levels, such as when a user is drilling within a hierarchy in a report.

> A guide to understanding OLAP hierarchies, dimensions, and levels is here:
>
> `http://www.obi11gbook.com/u/21`

Dimension types are used to define the dimension as it was imported from Essbase. The dimension types are **Unknown**, **Time**, **Measure**, **Attribute**, and **Other**. By default, as you'll see by examining the OBIBook dimension hierarchies, Oracle BI correctly aligns Essbase attribute dimensions with the Attribute dimension type, the time dimension with Time dimension type, and so on.

To assess and begin modifying these properties, follow these steps:

1. In the Physical layer, double-click on the **Players** dimension to open the Physical Dimension properties prompt.

2. In the **Hierarchies** tab, select the **Players** hierarchy available from the pick-list, and then click on the pencil icon to edit the hierarchy.

>
> Notice that in the **Physical Hierarchy** prompt that appears, the **Dimension Type** is set to **Other** and that the **Hierarchy Type** is set to **Unbalanced**. This is typical for a standard Essbase dimension.

3. Repeat the same steps as above for the **Sex** and **Time Periods** dimensions. Notice how the **Hierarchy Type** for the Sex and Time Periods dimension are also **Unbalanced** but the Sex dimension's Dimension Type is **Attribute dimension** and the **Time Periods** dimension's Dimension Type is **Time dimension**.

4. Close all the prompts.

This quick look at dimension and hierarchy types should have given you a good idea of how Essbase dimension metadata gets translated into the RPD. No changes were made to the dimension or hierarchy types but now you know where to go in order to ensure that Essbase specific dimension types are being properly construed in Oracle BI.

Getting a quick win

Modeling Essbase has its learning curve complications. However, to get a quick win, such as in a POC, and start seeing data from the Essbase cube right away, it only takes a few steps. Once you complete those steps you'll be able to login to the Oracle BI /analytics application portal and begin pulling data from the Essbase data source via a new Analysis request.

Let's continue with a best practice first. One option that you can set in order to make your model much cleaner is the option to skip the inclusion of Essbase generation 1 levels from showing in the Logical layer. Remember, the first Essbase generation is just the name of the dimension and it is simply redundant in the RPD. To set this option, follow these steps:

1. Select **Tools | Options...** from the file menu bar.

2. Select the **General** tab and check the checkbox for **Skip Gen 1 levels in Essbase drag and drop actions**.

3. Click on the **OK** button to close the **Options** prompt and let's continue on with the quick win.

4. In the Physical layer left-click on the **OBIBook** Essbase cube table icon, representing the Essbase database data source, and drag it onto anywhere in the white space of the Business Model and Mapping layer. This creates a Business Model for the OBIBook Essbase database.

5. Double-click on the **OBIBook** Business Model to open the properties prompt and uncheck the **Disabled** checkbox so that the model is enabled.

6. Expand the OBIBook Business Model in the Logical layer.

7. Inspect how the OBIBook source was translated from the Physical layer to this logical layer.

 Look at the logical fact table, **OBIBook**. It was given the name of the Essbase database by default. You can rename this to **Measures** or **Facts** if desired.

8. Click and drag the **OBIBook** Business Model from the BMM onto anywhere in the white space of the Presentation layer.

9. Save the RPD and check in your changes if prompted. If prompted for a Global Consistency Check, confirm that option as well.

10. Log in to the Oracle BI /analytics application and view this new Subject Area. You may need to click on the **Refresh the Metadata** option in the Administration page of the /analytics application to see the new Subject Area appear in the list of available Subject Areas. Alternatively, you can restart the Presentation Services System Component using Enterprise Fusion Control options.

11. Create a simple query via an Analysis Request using the skills you learned in *Chapter 10, Creating Dashboards and Reports.*

    For example, use the following columns and metrics to create a report that looks like the following screenshot, with **Year**, **Quarter**, **Set Wins**, and **Set Loses** then view the Results tab:

The steps you've covered is often enough to get a Proof-of-Concept (POC) out the door for a department at your organization, such as the Finance Department, so that they can become believers in the power of Oracle BI's technology.

Incremental importing of Essbase metadata

Like any other data source you may leverage in your Oracle BI repository, from time to time you will need to adjust the structure of the underlying data source and have it represented correctly within your RPD. If the metadata of an Essbase data source changes, you can re-import the metadata without much issue. This is referred to as an **Incremental Import**; where after you've conducted an initial metadata import you conduct subsequent imports of the same Essbase source regardless of the intensity of changes to the underlying source system or RPD.

Here are some caveats to keep in mind when requiring an incremental import of your Essbase cube and how it affects your existing Oracle BI model:

- All initial import objects and modifications are retained in the case of an incremental update.

- Removing an element/object from the Essbase cube source (via EAS, for example) does not delete the corresponding item from the Physical layer upon incremental import.

- Renaming an object in the Essbase cube source re-imports the changed object as a new object. It does not modify the existing object in the Physical layer.

- Mainly all objects and new columns (UDAs, Alias Table, and so on) are retained in the Physical layer post incremental import. You must delete the objects in the Physical layer then re-import if wishing to revert, or go with the new source system changes.

- The addition of an Essbase source's dimension or generation within a dimension will require some remodeling effort if the source has already been used to create a Business Model. This effort would be similar to incorporating a new dimension table in a relational model where joins to the logic fact table, and so on must take place.

To re-import metadata for the Essbase cube:

1. Right-click on the **Connection Pool** object of the Essbase Server Physical Database in the Physical layer and select **Import Metadata**:

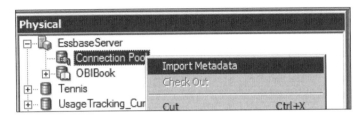

2. Select the Essbase cube from the **Data Source view** column and move it using the center arrow in the same way you imported the data source earlier.

3. A confirmation prompt will appear informing you that "the following cube(s) already exist". Click the **OK** button to proceed:

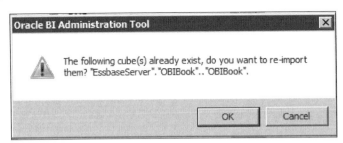

4. Click on the **Finish** button to close the prompt.

That's all it takes to do a basic incremental import. After an incremental import it is always a good idea to look through the Essbase source's dimension hierarchies and other properties to ensure everything you meant to be preserved is indeed so and that the incremental changes did indeed come through. You should always make a backup copy of your RPD before conducting this type of operation.

Federation of data

As discussed in previous chapters, the federation of data sources through Oracle BI is one of the most flexible features of the tool. The ability to take two or more disparate data sources and blend the data in a way that allows for enterprise data interoperability in order to satisfy analytic goals is amazing. Make no mistake about it; Oracle BI is no substitute for an ETL tool but just think of the possibilities for looking at Essbase data and Oracle database data in the same query, from a single reporting system, referencing the same level of granularity. All of that without the need to rework the underlying data source structure of Essbase or the Oracle database—in Oracle BI it just works.

Oracle by Example has a great tutorial on how to federate an Essbase and relational database source in Oracle BI at the following URL:

`http://www.obi11gbook.com/u/19`

Try to combine the OBIBook Essbase cube with the Tennis database.

Oracle BI/EPM roadmap

The integration between Oracle BI 11*g* and the Oracle EPM tools can only get better. In the Oracle BI 10*g* version, an attempt was made to bridge the Oracle BI dashboards with that of the Hyperion Workspace. This was a tricky integration and ultimately not the path Oracle wished to continue on. However, several successful integration points between the two still exist and work very well. One such integration point is that of Hyperion Shared Services security, one of Essbase's security provider options which, when integrated with Oracle BI, allows for existing Essbase cube row-level security to persist for any users accessing Essbase data via Oracle BI.

Workspace integration

Hyperion Workspace is the portal for Hyperion Products that became very popular in System 9 (version 9.x) of the Hyperion tool suite. Introducing Oracle BI users to the Hyperion product suite was a great initial concept, but was not carried over in the first minor releases of Oracle BI 11*g*. The next slated attempt at connecting these two applications will be via Fusion Middleware and is set to be provided in a later version release of Oracle BI 11*g*.

Software license combo

Oracle believes that their **Business Intelligence** and **Enterprise Performance Management** tools are the best in-class offerings on the market. They believe that an organization can get a great amount of business insight by using these two classes of tools in tandem. In an effort to continue that message strategy, Oracle has provided a special licensing package referred to as the Oracle BI Foundation Suite. This combo package of BI tools includes the Oracle BI 11*g* Enterprise Edition license, as well as licenses for Oracle Essbase, Oracle **Essbase Analytics Link (EAL)**, Oracle BI Mobile, and Oracle Scorecard and Strategy Management. Providing this new discounted option of licenses encourages users to partake in the Oracle BI roadmap by giving organizations a chance to leverage the power of the tools Oracle believes will provide an even greater boost in decision making analytics than using OBIEE itself.

A review – what I should now know!

For self-review and a recap of the chapter, here are a few questions. There is no answer key. These questions are for your own reflection on the chapter:

1. Will adding one or members to an existing generation in the Essbase outline affect the re-import of an Essbase data source in the RPD?

2. What is the best practice for readying the Essbase data source into Oracle BI?

3. What are the differences between MOLAP, HOLAP, and ROLAP?

Additional research suggestions

For additional information, refer to the following sources:

- **Essbase Modeling**: http://www.obi11gbook.com/u/21
- **Oracle BI and HFM**: http://www.obi11gbook.com/u/23
- **Financial Management Analytics**: http://www.obi11gbook.com/u/24

Summary

What has been discussed in this chapter answers many of the questions that we get from clients regarding the integration between Oracle BI 11*g* and Essbase. The details discussed in this chapter will provide any organization the means to begin exploring the integration with their Essbase systems. Or, perhaps it will provide enough clarity to commission a new project in order to bring their Essbase environment up-to-date and take advantage of this splendid Fusion Middleware integration. In this chapter you learned about the many OLAP types, how to import an existing Essbase outline to a different Essbase server, and you learned about the Oracle SampleApp Virtual Machine image's Essbase options. Exploring the Oracle BI Administration Tool, you learned how to import an Essbase cube as a data source and how to quickly model it through from the Physical layer to the Presentation layer. Finally, you examined several best practices for the Essbase and Oracle BI 11*g* integration that have slight to major impacts on development and maintenance efforts. We hope you've enjoyed this chapter and this book and look forward to your feedback, questions, and comments on the Oracle BI 11*g* Book forums, `http://www.obi11gbook.com/forums/`.

A
Programs and Definitions

One of the powerful features of OBIEE 11*g* administration is its ability to be controlled by User Interfaces (web browsers and Admin tools), as well as by command line utilities. Many of the manual tasks that you undertake each day can be scripted and, therefore, automated.

The types of tasks that can benefit from the scripting tools include:

- Stress testing
- Database/Repository synchronization
- Repository publication
- Prune unwanted Repository objects
- General Catalog Administration

There are several command line tools, but only a few of them are documented and more importantly, supported by Oracle.

The available tools are shown in the following table:

Command	Used for	Documented
nqcmd	Stress testing	Yes
Biserverxmlgen	Creating XML output of the BI Repository.	Yes
Biserverxmlexec	Executes XML against an existing repository or used to create a new repository. The repositories involved will be offline.	Yes
Biserverxmlcli	Similar to biserverxmlexec, but is used to modify an online repository.	Yes
comparerpd	Used to compare two repositories. This utility is also available on Unix OS.	Yes

Command	Used for	Documented
`patchrpd`	Patch an existing RPD.	Yes
`validaterpd`	Validate an existing RPD. Similar to the check consistency action in the admin tool.	Yes
`prunerpd`	Prune an existing RPD. Removes unwanted objects.	Yes
`Equalizerpds`	Used to equalize objects in two repositories that have the same name, but different upgrade IDs.	Yes
`Sametaexport`	Specialist command to provide information to the Oracle SQL Access advisor.	Yes
`Extractprojects`	Used to extract all the objects within a "Project". Allows for projects to grow without changing your command scripts.	Yes
`AdminTool`	BI Server Repository Administration tasks. Useful for automatically producing the Metadata files used to explore the repository structure from a web browser.	No
`Nqudmlgen`	Generate and implement UDML.	No
`Nqudmlexec` `Nqudmlcli`	Best not to use these commands as they are replaced by biserverxml commands, and were not officially documented anyway.	

Some of the commands above are described in detail below, using real world examples.

Stress testing

The program **nqcmd** is a very useful utility that runs requests against the repository. With nqcmd you can define a selection of logical SQL scripts and run these under various user names. This will mimic the loads of several users logging and running requests or dashboards. Running these scripts can also aid regression testing, which can highlight any errors before moving your code into production.

The process is as follows:

1. Define an Analysis request.
2. Create an ODBC link to your BI Server.
3. Copy the Logical SQL from the Advanced tab into a text file.
4. Run a nqcmd script that connects to the ODBC, calls the SQL file, and outputs the results into another file.

The commonly used syntax of the nqcmd is as follows:

```
nqcmd -d -u -p -s -o
```

Where the switches are:

*   -d: DSN name. DSN names cannot have spaces in.
*   -u: Username.
*   -p: Password (only if required).
*   -s: The file name containing the Logical SQL.
*   -o: The file name that will store the results.

An example command would be:

```
nqcmd –dDev –uAdmin –pPWD –sC:\testing\mylogicalsql.txt –oC:\testing\
results.txt
```

In the preceding example, the file `C:\testing\mylogicalsql.txt` contains a logical SQL script which can be obtained from the **Advanced** tab in the Analysis request interactive reporting area. As you can see in the following screenshot, we've built an analysis and on the Advanced tab, copied the logical SQL, and saved it into a text file:

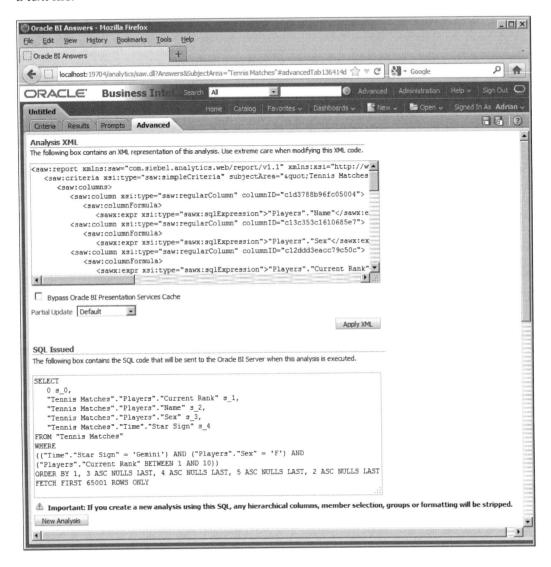

The newly saved text file `C:\testing\mylogicalsql.txt` contains the following entry:

```
SELECT
    0 s_0,
    "Tennis Matches"."Players"."Current Rank" s_1,
    "Tennis Matches"."Players"."Name" s_2,
    "Tennis Matches"."Players"."Sex" s_3,
    "Tennis Matches"."Time"."Star Sign" s_4
FROM "Tennis Matches"
WHERE
(("Time"."Star Sign" = 'Gemini') AND ("Players"."Sex" = 'F') AND
("Players"."Current Rank" BETWEEN 1 AND 10))
ORDER BY 1, 3 ASC NULLS LAST, 4 ASC NULLS LAST, 5 ASC NULLS LAST, 2
ASC NULLS LAST
FETCH FIRST 65001 ROWS ONLY
```

The `nqcmd.exe` file can be found under `OBIEE_HOME\OracleBI1\bifoundation\server`.

> If you are using a client only installation, the file, by default, is installed in the following location:
>
> `Program Files\Oracle Business Intellgince Enterprise Edition Plus Client\oraclebi\orahome\bifoundation\server\bin`

The one mentioned above is the most commonly used syntax; however the full syntax includes all the following switches:

Switches	Description
-a	A flag to enable asynchronous processing.
-d	The data source name.
-D	A delimiter. The default value is a semicolon (;).
-f	A flag to enable to flush the output file for each write.
-H	A flag to enable to open/close a request handle for each query.
-o	The output result file name.
-p	Password.
-s	The SQL input file name.
-u	Username.
-NoFetch	A flag to the disable data fetch with the query execution. Similar to –q except –q will list the columns.

Switches	Description
-NotForwardCursor	A flag to disable the forwardonly cursor.
-q	A flag to turn off the row output. Columns get output into the results file but no data row output is generated.
-utf16	A flag to enable UTF16 instead of ACP.
-v	A flag to display the version. Nothing is run or done, just the version number is returned to the screen.
-z	A flag to enable UTF8 instead of ACP.
-SessionVar	SessionVariableName=SessionVariableValue
-C(n)	# Number of fetched rows by column-wise binding.
-R(n)	# Number of fetched rows by column-wise binding.

It is a good idea to include the NoFetch command when testing for errors and performance against the database only.

It is also possible to run the nqcmd utility in interactive mode.

Open a DOS command window, change the directory to the path, OBIEE_HOME\OracleBI1\bifoundation\server and execute the nqcmd command. You will be given a list of options to run, as you can see from the following screenshot:

```
Administrator: D:\Users\Administrator\AppData\Roaming\Microsoft\Windows\Start Menu\Programs\Oracle Business Intelligence Enterpr... nqcmd

Addidici: >nqcmd

        Oracle BI ODBC Client
        Copyright (c) 1997-2011 Oracle Corporation, All rights reserved

Give data source name: Addi4
Give user name: weblogic
Give password:
        [T]able info
        [C]olumn info
        [D]ata type info
        [F]oreign keys info
        [P]rimary key info
        [K]ey statistics info
        [S]pecial columns info
        [Q]uery statement
Select Option:
```

Selecting T from the options list will return a list of Tables. If you press *T* you will then be given an option to filter the list. The options are:

- Give Catalog Pattern
- Give User Pattern
- Give Table Pattern
- Give Table Type Pattern

The prompts can be left blank or used a % as a wildcard. For example, when prompted for the table pattern, enter %atch% and using the Tennis RPD you developed in this book's exercises we get the Tennis Matches and Matches Facts tables.

Press enter (leave blank) the select option prompt to return back to the DOS prompt.

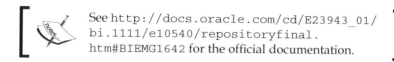

See http://docs.oracle.com/cd/E23943_01/ bi.1111/e10540/repositoryfinal. htm#BIEMG1642 for the official documentation.

XML – a better approach

The OBIEE 11gR1.6 BI Server incorporates an XML API. Objects in the Repository (RPD) file can be represented by XML.

There are three BI Server XML utilities:

- biserverxmlgen: This will generate MDS XML from an RPD
- biserverxmlexec: This executes MDS XML to create or modify an RPD
- biserverxmlcli: This executes the XML against the Oracle BI Server

biserverxmlgen

This utility is useful for creating documentation for all metadata comprising the Oracle BI repository.

The syntax is:

```
biserverxmlgen -R myrpd.rpd -P Admin123 -O c:\myrpd.xml -8
```

Where:

- Myrpd.rpd is the name and location of the repository file from which you want to generate the XML
- password is the repository password. The password argument is optional. If you do not provide a password argument, you are prompted to enter a password when you run the command.
- myrpd.xml is the name and location of the XML output file you want to generate. It is recommended that you use a filename with the .xml extension.
- Specify -8 to use UTF-8 encoding in the generated XML file (ANSI ISO-8859-1 encoding is the default).

The other switches available are:

- -S to create security objects only.

- -Q to create the output without the security objects.

- -M to create MDS XUDML.

- -D to create multiple MDS XUDML files. You must specify which directory to place the files in

- -N to skip the generation of the upgrade IDs.

biserverxmlexec

This utility executes XML on an offline repository to create or modify a repository file. This is useful for applying patches to an existing RPD. You may have some work in one repository that you need in another. Rather than copying an entire RPD you can just add a small patch, by the use of a command line. This can reduce errors and ensure consistency across environments.

The syntax for creating or updating an RPD is:

```
biserverxmlexec -P password -I c:\myrpd.xml -O c:\myrpd.rpd
```

Where:

- password is the repository password. The password argument is optional. If you do not provide a password argument, you are prompted to enter a password when you run the command.

- myrpd.xml is the name and location of the XML file you want to use to create the RPD.

- Myrpd.rpd is the name and location of the repository file that you want to create or update.

To use a directory-based set of separate XML files, you can use the syntax:

```
biserverxmlexec -P password -D c:\my_dir -O c:\myrpd.rpd -C
```

Where:

- password is the repository password. The password argument is optional. If you do not provide a password argument, you are prompted to enter a password when you run the command.

- My_dir is the name and location of the folder where the xml files are held.

- Myrpd.rpd is the name and location of the repository file that you want to create or update.

If you want to combine XML and a repository to create a new repository you can use the following syntax:

```
biserverxmlexec -P password -I c:\myrpd.xml -B c:\base.rpd -O c:\
myrpd.rpd
```

Where:

- `password` is the repository password. The password argument is optional. If you do not provide a password argument, you are prompted to enter a password when you run the command.
- `myrpd.xml` is the name and location of the XML output file you want to use.
- `base.rpd` is the name and location of the repository file that you want to start with.
- `Myrpd.rpd` is the name and location of the repository file that you want to generate.

 The `-P` switch is due to be dropped in future releases.

The full list of switches available is:

- `-P`: Password
- `-I`: Input script File name
- `-I`: Input script File password
- `-B`: Base Repository name (`D:\my_base_rpd.rpd`)
- `-O`: Output Repository name (`D:\my_rpd.rpd`)
- `-D`: Directory where the files are held
- `-M`: Use multiple MDS XUDML files
- `-E`: Do not create the output RPD if a parsing error occurs
- `-C`: Ignore the password check
- `-H`: Get the command help text

biserverxmlcli

Use `biserverxmlcli` to execute the XML against the Oracle BI Server. This utility is very similar to `biserverxmlexec`, but is instead used to modify an online repository.

The process is to use the Administration Tool to make changes to your repository in offline mode, create an XML "patch", and then use this XML patching feature to apply the changes to an online repository, without needing to restart the server or apply the changes manually. A typical example may be to add a new presentation column from an existing logical column.

To use this utility, execute the following at the command prompt:

```
biserverxmlcli -U user_name-P password -R rpd_password-D dsn -I XML_file
```

Where:

- `user_name` is a valid user name. This user must have the manage repository permission (`oracle.bi.server.manageRepositories`).

- `password` is the corresponding user password. If you do not provide a user password you will be prompted for one, and again this switch will be disabled in future releases.

- `rpd_password` is the repository password for the online repository.

- `dsn` is the Oracle BI Server ODBC **Data Source Name (DSN)** to which you want to connect.

- `xml_file` is the name and location of the XML input file you want to execute.

See the Oracle documentation at: `http://docs.oracle.com/cd/E14571_01/bi.1111/e16364/xml_about.htm#BIEIT1341`

Working example using XML

The following steps show how to create a "patch" and implement it on an offline RPD.

1. Open a source metadata repository (for example, `dev.rpd`) in the Administration Tool.

2. Select **File | Copy As...** from the file menu.

3. Save the repository under a new name (for example, `test.rpd`).

4. In the Physical layer, open the connection pools for the relational sources that need to be changed, as well as any variables respective to the target environment for which you plan to migrate the RPD.

5. Update any environment specific variable values in the repository variables, such as the ones for Data Source Name, User Name, and Password to the target environment's values.

6. Select **File | Compare...** from the file menu.

7. Select the original repository file (dev.rpd) to compare to the currently open repository file (test.rpd).

8. Click the **Create Patch...** button and choose a name for the static XML patch file that will reside on the target system for patching when you choose to migrate to that environment in the future (for example, dev_to_test_rpd_patch.xml).

The patch XML file will now be ready to create the correct target RPD by merging the source RPD to the patch XML file which will then get uploaded to the target server using Enterprise Manager.

Create the following script and place it in any environment where a triage of the RPDs will take place before being migrated into the target environments. Save the file as a batch file and modify the variables within the script with the respective values based on the preceding instructions.

```
@ECHO OFF

REM Patch automation script by
REM ArtOfBI.com - Christian S.

SET PATCH_XML=devToTestPatch20120210.xml
SET SOURCE_RPD=myRPD_obi11g_TEST.rpd
SET OUTPUT_RPD=myRPD_obi11g_TEST_ok.rpd
SET BI_HOME=D:/Oracle/FMW/Oracle_BI1/bifoundation/server/bin

echo ..
echo Patch File : %PATCH_XML%
echo Source File : %SOURCE_RPD%
echo OUTPUT File : %OUTPUT_RPD%
echo BI HOME : %BI_HOME%
echo ..

REM The file is being merged by the BIServerXMLExec command line
utility.....

CALL %BI_HOME%/biserverxmlexec -I %PATCH_XML% -B %SOURCE_RPD% -O
%OUTPUT_RPD%
```

For more information on patching the Oracle BI metadata repository, reference the following documentation:

```
http://docs.oracle.com/cd/E14571_01/bi.1111/
e16364/xml_about.htm#CIHIFIHD
```

More repository management

Use the `comparerpd` command line to compare two repositories and create a resultant CSV or XML file that contains the deltas.

The syntax for comparing RPDs is:

```
comparerpd -P rpd2pwd -C C:\new.rpd -W rpd1pwd -G C:\orig.rpd -O c:\
changes.csv
```

Where:

- `-P` is the repository password for the newer repository
- `-C` is the name and location of the newer repository
- `-W` is the repository password for the original repository
- `-G` is the name and location of the original repository
- `-O` is the name and location of a CSV file where you want to store the repository object comparison output

Another option is to generate XML output using:

- `-D` is the name and location of an XML patch file where you want to store the differences between the two repositories.
- `-E` is an optional argument that causes UIDs to be used to compare expression text. If `-E` is not specified, strings are used.
- `-8` specifies UTF-8 encoding.

If the patch contains passwords, such as connection pool passwords, the patch file will then be encrypted using the repository password from the new repository. You might need to supply this patch file password when applying the patch, if it is different from the repository password for the original repository.

Sometimes you can have two RPDs containing the same objects, but they have different internal IDs. When merging, this can lead to the two objects being considered as being different. To get around this problem you can use `equalizerpds`.

Enter `equalizerpds -h` in a command box to get the supported syntax. See the following document for more details, `http://docs.oracle.com/cd/E14571_01/bi.1111/e10540/mngreposfiles.htm#BABFJCCB`

Admin tool

You could use the BI Server Administration tool to create the XML metadata files. This is a straightforward, but manual, task which can be automated. The original method that was in the 10*g* version of OBIEE is still theoretically available and uses the executable `admintool.exe`.

A scenario when you'd use this command line tool would be for automating the creation of the metadata dictionary. The metadata dictionary is an XML based set of files that is leveraged in Oracle BI Presentation Services when a frontend developer is creating an Analysis request. Rendered via XSL stylesheets it provides a frontend developer with insights into elements within the subject areas from which they are developing reports.

- Create a command file called `metaDataExport.txt`:

```
OpenOffline <path to RPD> <RPD Password>
DescribeRepository <path to output file> <encoding>
Exit
```

- Call the command file by using the following command:

```
admintool.exe /command metaDataExport.txt
```

The full list of `admintool.exe` commands are:

 These commands can damage your files if not used properly. The use of `admintool` is undocumented and unsupported. You have been advised!

Command	Description
`OpenOnline DSN [user [password]]`	Opens the online repository. You can't edit properties in online mode.
`Open FileName [user [password]]`	Opens the repository offline.
`New FileName`	Creates a new repository offline.
`Save`	Saves the opened repository.
`SaveAsFileName`	Saves the opened repository under a new name.
`Close`	Closes the opened repository.
`Exit`	Closes AdminTool.
`SetProperty "Variable" "" Initializer ""`	
`SetProperty "Connection Pool" "".""` `"User" ""`	
`SetProperty "Connection Pool" "".""` `"Password" ""`	
`SetProperty "Connection Pool" "".""  "DSN"` `""`	
`MessageBox [message]`	Displays a message box with the text, the default message is "Siebel Analytics Administration Tool".
`ImportRepository {Online|Offline}` `{FileName|DSNname} [user [password]]`	Initiates import from the other repository.
`ImportRepositoryObject {Project|"Present ationCatalog"|User|"SecurityGroup"|Variab le} {Name|*} [True|False [True|False]]`	Imports object(s) from the other repository.
`ImportRepositoryExecute`	Executes the repository import defined by previous calls to `ImportRepository` and `ImportRepositoryExecute`.
`Compare FileName [user [password` `[outputFile]]]`	Compares the current repository with another repository.

Command	Description
`Merge FileName1 FileName2 [DecisionFile] [user1 [password1 [user2 [password2]]]]`	Merges repositories.
`ConsistencyCheck [outputFileName]`	Global consistency check.
`BusinessModelConsistencyCheckbusiness ModelName [outputFileName]`	Consistency check for one business model.
`CreateSubsetNewRepositoryNameMaster RepositoryNamenumberOfProjects project1 [project2 [project3 [...]]] [user [password]]`	Creates and opens multi-user subset repository.
`CheckinSubsetModifiedSubsetRepository NameLockUserFullName [user [password]]`	Checks in ModifiedSubsetRepository into the master repository.
`DescribeRepository Filename UTF-8`	Triggers an export of the RPD metadata to the Filename file in UTF-8 codepage. This is similar to using the Administration Tool utility manually.
`GenerateMetadataDictionaryDestination_ Folder`	Run the Metadata Dictionary export.
`Hide`	Hides the AdminTool.

A review – what I should now know!

For self review and a recap of the chapter, here are a few questions based on the topics covered in this chapter:

1. How do you run a stress test?
2. How do I automatically create Repository metadata XML files?
3. Should I use undocumented commands on a live system?
4. How to I automatically validate an RPD?
5. What tools are available to manage my multiple repositories?

Summary

In this appendix, we introduced the idea of using some Oracle provided utility commands to manage your environment.

These scripts can provide a useful shortcut to some laborious tasks, such as stress testing, but please make sure that what you are using the command for is supported by Oracle. The **WebLogic Scripting Tool (WLST)** is also available and covered in *Chapter 5, Understanding the Systems Management Tools*. Go back and remind yourself what it can do for you.

B

Useful Resources: Join the Oracle BI Movement

Over the last decade, the number of resources focusing on Oracle Business Intelligence has skyrocketed. Oracle's documentation of the software has become increasingly more useful and user-friendly. Blogs all over the globe have popped-up in large numbers (though some better maintained and better written than others). This appendix aims to list a few of the best books, events, groups, and blogs for further reading and further practice. Ideally, the rest is up to you. We can list these resources and point you in the right direction but putting the rubber to the road is a task you must feel the need to accomplish.

This book's resources

A lot of knowledge is contained in the main chapters of the book. But leaving you as the reader high and dry without any further direction for obtaining intellectual ferment is not how we roll. In this appendix, we've listed resources that will allow you to get help about the content and exercises that you've explored already in this book. Also, for any assistance you may need going forward with your Oracle BI related development and integrations, be sure to ping the authors directly via our independent web blogs.

OBI11gBook.com forums

This is the go forward means of community and collaboration for not only this book but for future information and conversation about Oracle BI 11g. This is a community and it is built for people just like you. The idea behind the forum is that it is a means to ask questions about the exercises and content experienced in the book as well as a way to get direct help from us the authors and other practitioners within the Oracle BI community. It is free to join and though there is a specific relationship to the book, it is open to all comments regarding Oracle BI and EPM. Get more information and join http://www.obi11gbook.com/forums/.

Author blogs

As authors, we've contributed a lot to the web via company blogs, personal blogs, Oracle forums, Oracle Technology Network (OTN) articles, and more. However, we find that our personal blogs allow for up-to-date information, best practices, and knowledge on Oracle BI and EPM as well as personal commentary that you just won't get anywhere else. Be sure to add these blogs to your blog roll and the RSS feeds to your RSS aggregator.

- The Art of Business Intelligence (ArtOfBi.com): `http://www.artofbi.com/`
- Addidici: `http://www.addidici.com/blog/`

Other Oracle BI practitioner blogs

We also realize, as authors, that no one man is an island. We have respect for several other bloggers that showcase their Oracle BI skill readily by contributing freely to the Oracle BI community via their own personal blogs. Although, unfortunately these comrades were not directly associated with this book, here is a quick shout out to our other blogging peeps that you should definitely follow for their ongoing skillful contributions.

- John Minkjan: `http://obiee101.blogspot.com/`
- Venkatakrishnan J: `http://oraclebizint.wordpress.com/`
- John Goodwin: `http://john-goodwin.blogspot.com/`
- Gerard Nico: `http://gerardnico.com/wiki/`
- ORACLENERD: `http://oraclenerd.com/`

Oracle development team blogs

We also realize that Oracle, like any large conglomerate, has a lot of red tape to consistently cut through in order to get anything done in an agile manner. That includes product releases, knowledge sharing, or otherwise communicating information. From a knowledge sharing perspective, we would like to highlight a few of the blogs from our friends within the Oracle BI and EPM development teams that consistently go above and beyond. We think you should also give these blogs a good look:

- `http://blogs.oracle.com/xmlpublisher/`
- `http://blogs.oracle.com/pa/`
- `http://oraclebi.blogspot.com/`
- `http://blogs.oracle.com/proactivesupportepm/`

Lastly, we cannot forget the great work that the Oracle BI EMEA Partner Community team is doing on their blog. Clearly, this is for Oracle partners but it deserves a mention here for any of Oracle's global partner practitioners that might be reading this book. Find that blog here:

```
http://blogs.oracle.com/emeapartnerbiepm/
```

Oracle BI user groups

There are several national and global user groups that include a focus on Oracle Business Intelligence and Enterprise Performance Management. Only a few have a more narrowed focus on Oracle BI but since Oracle BI 11*g* is now part of the Fusion Middleware stack all of these users groups are relevant. The users groups provide a membership based community (most have a no fee membership option) with varying privileges. The ones listed here also host yearly conferences which are noted in the subsequent conferences section.

Oracle Development Tools Users' Group (ODTUG)

Headquartered in Wilmington, NC this global user group is the one that we think has the highest focus on Oracle BI and EPM, specifically through its hosting of its yearly KScope conference. It is an independent, non-profit organization, with a strong history from Hyperion and Oracle, and it has done a great job boasting useful member services and community for Java, Fusion Middleware, and other development tools. More details are available at `http://www.odtug.com`.

Oracle Applications Users' Group (OAUG)

Is a global user group with a strong focus on the Oracle E-Business Suite although it represents fairly well all of the products within the Oracle Application stack. It does a very good job of allowing **Special Interest Groups** (**SIGs**) to be associated with OAUG with a more in-depth focus on a specific application suite. The OAUG Hyperion SIG would be an example. More information can be found from its homepage: `http://www.oaug.org/`.

Independent Oracle User Groups (IOUG)

Rounding out the top three North American centric user groups for Oracle BI and EPM is the IOUG which actually has a stronger focus on the Oracle Database than other applications. However, over the years, along with its relationship to the COLLABORATE conference, it is gaining a reputation for proving solid content and best-practices in its SELECT journal publication. As it is gaining ground with the Oracle BI and EPM audience, it is also a great place for up-and-coming authors on BI/EPM topics to submit their original materials with a good chance of getting published. More details are available here: http://www.ioug.org/.

International Oracle Users' Group Community (IOUC)

Representing the worldwide scope of Oracle based user groups is the IOUC. They acknowledge the 870+ independent user groups spread throughout the globe. The IOUC does a great job of connecting members internationally with great resources, conferences, events, and other activities. They are most likely the most visible community for Europe, Middle East and Africa (EMEA), Latin America, and Asia Pacific (APAC) and also are represented at each Oracle Open World conference. Get more information here: http://www.iouc.org/.

Conferences

Attending one of the many Oracle conferences held each year allows the sub-communities such as the Oracle BI practitioners to stay well represented with strong numbers. In addition, the intellectual ferment stemming from conference activities such as training sessions, presentations, keynotes, and social mixers is unmatched compared to just reading a book. Here is a list of our favorite conferences for Oracle BI and EPM. We recommend that you attend at least one conference per year. The top practitioners and evangelists in the Oracle BI and EPM spaces are always in attendance. Learning directly from the pros is the best way to learn.

Oracle Open World (OOW)

Each year tens of thousands of Oracle customers, practitioners, and experts land themselves in San Francisco, California for one of the largest conferences on the globe, Oracle Open World. This is where the Who's Who of Oracle leaders and their biggest customers come to rub elbows, talk about the year's greatest accomplishments, and unveil the next great products coming from Oracle.

Every product that Oracle produces including Oracle BI and EPM are represented during the weeklong conference. At OOW 2011, the Oracle Exalytics appliance was unveiled. Each year representatives from the Oracle BI and EPM development teams are on hand giving great presentations, hands-on workshops, and other demonstrations that can't be seen elsewhere. Our recommendation is that, as a reader of this book and a practitioner of Oracle BI/EPM, you should plan to attend this event at least once in your lifetime. More information on OOW can be found here: http://www.obi11gbook.com/u/29.

COLLABORATE

This is a conference that is the combination of three user groups: IOUG, OAUG, and the Quest International Users' Group (Quest). The weeklong conference is tailored to fit three main areas of Oracle technology: Oracle Fusion, E-Business Suite, and Oracle BI/EPM. Other technologies related to the Oracle Applications stack are represented and COLLABORATE boasts that the OAUG forum is designed for, and by, its members. More information on attending this conference is found here: http://www.obi11gbook.com/u/28.

KScope

Stemming from the main Hyperion User Group conference, Kaleidoscope, which existed prior to Oracle's acquisition of Hyperion in 2007, is the yearly conference KScope. This event seems to have leveraged that existing base of members within the EPM community and earned the respect of many Oracle BI practitioners to become the top event for Oracle BI and EPM outside of OOW. Learn more on this event here: http://www.obi11gbook.com/u/27.

RittmanMead BI Forum

The newest event which is part forum and part conference is now an annual event held in both the United States and the United Kingdom. This is a smaller event with a specific focus on learning advanced topics related to Oracle BI. While other events boast large attendance numbers in the thousands, this event is restricted to a smaller group (less than one hundred) over a three day (five days if counting the Master class) period. The event is scheduled for offset dates to accommodate travelers for either the US or UK locations. Attendees are usually part of the Oracle BI Enterprise Methodology Group (OBIEE EMG). Information about the OBIEE EMG is located at http://groups.google.com/group/obiee-enterprise-methodology/.

More information about the RittmanMead BI Forum event can be found at http://www.obi11gbook.com/u/26.

We don't aim to offend anyone with our possibly narrow sited perspective on conferences. We find that the conferences listed above are the best currently available to the largest audience of Oracle BI and EPM practitioners, each of which garners international acclaim and attendees. If you feel that we have missed a conference, or if you care to share one that you are quite fond of, please be sure to do so on the Oracle BI 11g Book Forum here `http://www.obi11gbook.com/forums/`.

Join the movement

The Oracle BI development team leadership has mentioned on several occasions that they are attempting to develop a strong community around their product. Though they are far from the participation numbers of other established Oracle communities such as the Java community, they are making a concerted effort to garner support. At this point in time, it is important to know that the Oracle BI SampleApp is an open source set of artifacts from which Oracle BI practitioners can learn from and continue to build on. We can all potentially make contributions to the Oracle BI community by enhancing the SampleApp or some other functionality of Oracle BI and sharing that information publically so that others can learn. You can find the most up-to-date information on this community on the Oracle BI 11g Book forum, `http://www.obi11gbook.com/forums/`.

Further reading

Here are a few of the other literature resources that we felt deserved a mention. Either they are books on a closely related topic from our publisher or we have made reference to them within this book.

- Ralph Kimball's book has been extremely important to data warehousing: `http://www.kimballgroup.com/html/books.html`

- Building the Data Warehouse: William "Bill" H. Inmo: `http://www.amazon.com/s/ref=nb_sb_noss?url=search-alias%3Dstripbooks&field-keywords=Bill+Inmon&x=0&y=0`

- Oracle BI Publisher 11*g*: A Practical Guide to Enterprise Reporting: `http://www.packtpub.com/oracle-bi-publisher-11g-practical-guide-for-enterprise-reporting/book`

Summary

Not that this chapter really needs a summary of what was entailed but clearly we've pointed out some very important resources from which you can continue your learning. A parting thought is that we encourage you to help build a strong Oracle BI community. You have the support of the Oracle BI development team in many ways. Your feedback to them is always welcomed. The authors of this book also would like you to join and contribute to the OBI11gBook.com website and forum as much as possible. Consider this a personal invitation. It is free and this is the go forward community for Oracle BI 11*g*. We hope to see you on the forums.

Index

Thank you for buying
Oracle Business Intelligence Enterprise Edition 11*g*: A Hands-On Tutorial

About Packt Publishing

Packt, pronounced 'packed', published its first book "Mastering phpMyAdmin for Effective MySQL Management" in April 2004 and subsequently continued to specialize in publishing highly focused books on specific technologies and solutions.

Our books and publications share the experiences of your fellow IT professionals in adapting and customizing today's systems, applications, and frameworks. Our solution based books give you the knowledge and power to customize the software and technologies you're using to get the job done. Packt books are more specific and less general than the IT books you have seen in the past. Our unique business model allows us to bring you more focused information, giving you more of what you need to know, and less of what you don't.

Packt is a modern, yet unique publishing company, which focuses on producing quality, cutting-edge books for communities of developers, administrators, and newbies alike. For more information, please visit our website: www.packtpub.com.

About Packt Enterprise

In 2010, Packt launched two new brands, Packt Enterprise and Packt Open Source, in order to continue its focus on specialization. This book is part of the Packt Enterprise brand, home to books published on enterprise software – software created by major vendors, including (but not limited to) IBM, Microsoft and Oracle, often for use in other corporations. Its titles will offer information relevant to a range of users of this software, including administrators, developers, architects, and end users.

Writing for Packt

We welcome all inquiries from people who are interested in authoring. Book proposals should be sent to author@packtpub.com. If your book idea is still at an early stage and you would like to discuss it first before writing a formal book proposal, contact us; one of our commissioning editors will get in touch with you.

We're not just looking for published authors; if you have strong technical skills but no writing experience, our experienced editors can help you develop a writing career, or simply get some additional reward for your expertise.

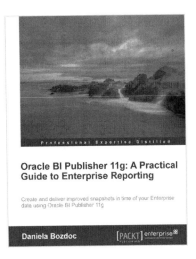

Oracle BI Publisher 11g: A Practical Guide to Enterprise Reporting

Create and deliver improved snapshots in time of your Enterprise data using Oracle BI Publisher 11g

Daniela Bozdoc   [PACKT] enterprise

Oracle BI Publisher 11*g*: A Practical Guide to Enterprise Reporting

ISBN: 978-1-849683-18-0   Paperback: 254 pages

Create and deliver improved snapshots in time of your Enterprise data using Oracle BI Publisher 11g

1. A practical tutorial for improving your Enterprise reporting skills with Oracle BI Publisher 11g

2. Master report migration, template design, and E-Business Suite integration

3. A practical guide brimming with tips about all the new features of the 11g release

Oracle Business Intelligence: The Condensed Guide to Analysis and Reporting

A fast track guide to uncovering the analytical power of Oracle Business Intelligence. Analytic SQL, Oracle Discoverer, Oracle Reports, and Oracle Warehouse Builder

Yuli Vasiliev   [PACKT] enterprise

Oracle Business Intelligence: The Condensed Guide to Analysis and Reporting

ISBN: 978-1-849681-18-6   Paperback: 184 pages

A fast track guide to uncovering the analytical power of Oracle Business Intelligence: Analytic SQL, Oracle Discoverer, Oracle Reports, and Oracle Warehouse Builder

1. Install, configure, and deploy the components included in Oracle Business Intelligence Suite (SE)

2. Gain a comprehensive overview of components and features of the Oracle Business Intelligence package

3. A fast paced, practical book that provides you with quick steps to answer common business questions and help you make informed business decisions

Please check **www.PacktPub.com** for information on our titles

Oracle SOA Suite 11g R1 Developer's Guide

Develop Service-Oriented Architecture Solutions with the Oracle SOA Suite

Foreword by David Shaffer
Vice President, Product Management, Oracle Integration

RUBICON RED
Strategy. Governance. Education.

Antony Reynolds   Matt Wright   [PACKT] enterprise

Oracle SOA Suite 11g R1 Developer's Guide

ISBN: 978-1-849680-18-9   Paperback: 720 pages

Develop Service-Oriented Architecture Solutions with the Oracle SOA Suite

1. A hands-on, best-practice guide to using and applying the Oracle SOA Suite in the delivery of real-world SOA applications

2. Detailed coverage of the Oracle Service Bus, BPEL PM, Rules, Human Workflow, Event Delivery Network, and Business Activity Monitoring

3. Master the best way to use and combine each of these different components in the implementation of a SOA solution

Getting Started with Oracle BPM Suite 11gR1

A Hands-On Tutorial

Learn from the experts – teach yourself Oracle BPM Suite 11g with an accelerated and hands-on learning path brought to you by Oracle BPM Suite Product Management team members

Foreword by Michael Weingartner
Vice President, Product Development, Oracle Corporation

Heidi Buelow   Manoj Das   Manas Deb   [PACKT] enterprise
Prasen Palvankar   Meera Srinivasan

Getting Started with Oracle BPM Suite 11gR1 – A Hands-On Tutorial

ISBN: 978-1-849681-68-1   Paperback: 444 pages

Learn from the experts — teach yourself Oracle BPM Suite 11g with an accelerated and hands-on learning path brought to you by Oracle BPM Suite Product Management team members

1. Offers an accelerated learning path for the much-anticipated Oracle BPM Suite 11g release

2. Set the stage for your BPM learning experience with a discussion into the evolution of BPM, and a comprehensive overview of the Oracle BPM Suite 11g Product Architecture

3. Discover BPMN 2.0 modeling, simulation, and implementation

Please check **www.PacktPub.com** for information on our titles

1073288R00330

Made in the USA
San Bernardino, CA
08 November 2012